Joining a Community of Readers

A Thematic Approach to Reading

Second Edition

Roberta Alexander
San Diego City College

Jan Lombardi
San Diego City College

Longman

New York • San Francisco • Boston
London • Toronto • Sydney • Tokyo • Singapore • Madrid
Mexico City • Munich • Paris • Cape Town • Hong Kong • Montreal

Senior Acquisitions Editor: Steven Rigolosi
Development Editor: Ann Hofstra Grogg
Marketing Manager: Melanie Craig
Supplements Editor: Donna Campion
Project Coordination, Text Design, and
   Electronic Page Makeup: Pre-Press Company, Inc.
Cover Designer/Manager: John Callahan
Cover image by Paul Anderson, courtesy of The Stock Illustration Source
Photo Researcher: Photo Search, Inc.
Manufacturing Buyer: Roy Pickering
Printer and Binder: R.R. Donnelley & Sons, Co.
Cover Printer: Phoenix Color Corp.

For permission to use copyrighted material, grateful acknowledgment is made to the copyright holders on pp. 521–522, which are hereby made part of this copyright page.

Library of Congress Cataloging-in-Publication Data
Alexander, Roberta,
    Joining a community of readers : a thematic approach / Roberta
    Alexander. — 2nd ed.
       p. cm.
    Includes bibliographical references (p.) and index.
    ISBN 0-321-05099-1
    1. College readers. 2. Reading comprehension. I. Title.

PE1122 .A36 2002
808'.0427—dc21

                                                          2001029745

Please visit our website at **http://www.ablongman.com/alexander**

ISBN 0-321-05099-1 (Student edition)
ISBN 0-321-05100-9 (Instructor's annotated edition)
4 5 6 7 8 9 10—DOC—04 03

To
Ethel and Hursel Alexander and Veronica and Francis Ryan

Brief Contents

Detailed Contents

CHAPTER 5   Supporting Details
Popular Culture

CHAPTER 6   **Major and Minor Supporting Details**
Television in Our Society   261

CHAPTER 8   **Complex Patterns of Organization**
The Family in the Community   369

ADDITIONAL READINGS AND EXERCISES   471

To the Instructor

Organized around high-interest, motivational, and contemporary themes relevant to the lives of all students, *Joining a Community of Readers,* Second Edition, provides guided instruction in the reading and learning process and abundant practice in the basic reading and learning skills. As the first-level college reading text in a two-book series, *Joining a Community of Readers* follows the same integrated, holistic approach and thematic organization as its successful companion text, *A Community of Readers.* However, *Joining* focuses more on basic reading skills, such as finding the main idea and identifying supporting details, and provides greater accessibility for students from various language and academic backgrounds.

The first chapter of *Joining a Community of Readers* focuses on strategies for becoming a successful student, including the PRO reading process for becoming an active reader. Each of the following chapters presents a contemporary theme—technology, learning and education, popular culture, families, growing up—and challenges students to employ their reading and related skills, both individually and collaboratively. As students progress through the chapters, they learn, practice, and revisit the reading/learning skills required to succeed in their college courses. Because each unit of the text builds on a single theme, students have the time to develop schema and exchange knowledge on a particular topic.

Special Features

This second edition of *Joining a Community of Readers* offers a number of innovative features to enhance the learning experience:

- **Holistic approach to reading.** Reading skills are presented in the context of real-life issues to help students adapt reading and study strategies to all their academic courses as well as to work situations.
- **Thematic organization.** Each chapter focuses on one theme so that students can work with the ideas long enough to begin to understand and use the material in its complexity. Because the readings and examples used for skills explanations are connected and related to the chapter theme, the skills themselves become more accessible.
- **Abundant examples and practice.** Each skill is introduced with clear explanations and examples. The theme-based content of the practice exercises within the chapters progresses from sentences and paragraphs to longer passages, with exercises tailored to reinforce skills through application to longer readings. The application

of skills, especially vocabulary and finding the main ideas and support, is emphasized throughout the text.

- *NEW!* **High-interest readings from various sources.** In this second edition, we have replaced two-thirds of the readings, drawing new selections from both academic and popular sources, and commissioning essays written specially for this book. A new section of *Additional Readings* contains selections that have been carefully chosen for their accessibility and high interest level. These readings, which come from various sources, should encourage students to find enjoyment in reading.

- *NEW!* **Emphasis on vocabulary skills.** The second edition presents an entirely new chapter on vocabulary skills, and the reinforcement of vocabulary skills is integrated throughout the text.

- **Language Tips.** To provide nonnative speakers of English and other beginning college students with strategies for better understanding their reading materials, this feature provides instructional sections and exercises on language issues such as word forms, complete sentences, and paraphrasing.

- **Organize to Learn.** Learning strategies (including outlining, summarizing, and mapping) are introduced (with ample practice material) throughout the text and highlighted in boxed features labeled "Organize to Learn."

- *NEW!* **Put It Together.** New "Put It Together" summary charts provide chapter reviews to facilitate student learning and retention.

- **Critical thinking skills.** By focusing on one theme at a time, students have the opportunity to understand the topic and its context in more depth. This greater depth allows students to apply critical thinking skills more effectively in class discussions, assigned writings, and collaborative activities. Exercises throughout the text ask students to apply their background knowledge to evaluate issues and make connections among various points of view.

- **Focus on the reading process.** The essential steps to reading—*prereading activities, active reading,* and *postreading tasks*—are built into each chapter. Students apply the new skills learned within the context of the reading process.

- **Collaborative work.** Exercises throughout the text encourage students to collaborate with their peers. Collaborative skills reviews and problem-solving tasks will help students in their academic work as well as in their careers.

- *NEW!* **Mastery tests.** Each chapter concludes with two mastery tests. Each mastery test features a reading selection, along with vocabulary and comprehension questions.

Chapter Organization

Each chapter in *Joining a Community of Readers* is designed to teach specific reading and learning skills within a thematic context. Students encounter the theme, are encouraged to reflect on that theme, and are then prompted to generate responses to the theme. To accomplish this progression, each chapter contains the following features:

- **An opening illustration and quotation** introduce the chapter theme and provide prereading questions that ask students to explore their background knowledge and opinions on the topic.
- **Skills instruction** is carefully interwoven with thematic readings within the chapter. Examples are taken predominantly from content-related material.
- **Chapter Reviews** provide an innovative format for students to collaboratively or individually organize and review the skills of the chapter, postreading extension activities for collaborative group work, and writing assignments that are based on the chapter content.
- *NEW!* **Web site Links.** Each chapter ends with a list of Web sites that offer additional information on the chapter issues and themes. In addition, a book-specific Web site is available at **http://www.ablongman.com/alexander**
- *NEW!* **Mastery Tests.** Two new mastery tests at the end of each chapter give students further opportunities to master the skills learned in each chapter.

The Teaching and Learning Package

Book-Specific Supplements

Joining a Community of Readers comes with a full array of supplements designed to ensure that the course is rewarding for both students and instructors.

The *Annotated Instructor's Edition (AIE)* is an exact replica of the student text, with the answers provided on the write-in lines in the text (0-321-05100-9).

The *Instructor's Manual,* prepared by the authors, offers teaching tips, sample syllabi, transparency masters, and other teaching resources (0-321-05101-7).

The printed *Test Bank* offers a series of skill and reading quizzes for each chapter, formatted for ease of copying and distribution (0-321-05102-5). An *Electronic Test Bank* for reading is also available, offering more than 3,000 questions about all areas of reading, including vocabulary, identifying main ideas and supporting details, identifying patterns of organization, understanding language, applying critical thinking and analytical reasoning, making correct inferences, understanding point of view, interpreting visual aids, and knowing how to approach textbook reading. With this easy-to-use CD-ROM, instructors simply choose questions from the electronic test bank, then print out the completed test for distribution (0-321-08179-X).

For additional quizzes, readings, and Internet-based activities, be sure to visit *Joining a Community of Readers Online* at **http://www.ablongman.com/alexander**. On this Web site you will find a series of PowerPoint Presentations for each chapter in the textbook; they can be downloaded and used for classroom presentations.

The Longman Developmental Reading Package

In addition to the book-specific ancillaries just discussed, Longman offers many other supplements to instructors and students. All of these supplements are available either free or at greatly reduced prices.

For Additional Reading and Reference

The Dictionary Deal   Two dictionaries can be shrinkwrapped with any Longman Reading title at a nominal fee. *The New American Webster Handy College Dictionary* is a paperback reference text with more than 100,000 entries. *Merriam Webster's Collegiate Dictionary*, Tenth Edition, is a hardback reference with a citation file of more than 14.5 million examples of English words drawn from actual use. For more details on ordering a dictionary with this text, please contact your Longman sales representative.

Penguin Quality Paperback Titles   A series of Penguin paperbacks is available at a significant discount when shrinkwrapped with any Longman title. Some titles available are Toni Morrison's *Beloved*, Julia Alvarez's *How the Garcia Girls Lost Their Accents*, Mark Twain's *Huckleberry Finn*, Frederick Douglass's *Narrative of the Life of Frederick Douglass*, Harriet Beecher Stowe's *Uncle Tom's Cabin*, Dr. Martin Luther King, Jr.'s, *Why We Can't Wait*, and plays by Shakespeare, Miller, and Albee. For a complete list of titles or more information, please contact your Longman sales consultant.

The Pocket Reader, First Edition   This inexpensive volume contains 80 brief readings (1–3 pages each) on a variety of themes: the craft of writing, nature, women and men, customs and habits, politics, rights and obligations, and coming of age. Also included is an alternate rhetorical table of contents (0-321-07668-0).

Longman Textbook Reader   This supplement, for use in developmental reading courses, offers five complete chapters from Addison Wesley/

Longman textbooks: computer science, biology, psychology, communications, and business. Each chapter includes additional comprehension quizzes, critical-thinking questions, and group activities. For information on how to bundle the free *Longman Textbook Reader* with *Joining a Community of Readers*, please contact your Longman sales representative.

***Newsweek* Alliance**   Instructors may choose to shrinkwrap a twelve-week subscription to *Newsweek* with any Longman text. The price of the subscription is 57 cents per issue (a total of $6.84 for the subscription). Available with the subscription is a free "Interactive Guide to *Newsweek*"—a workbook for students who are using the text. In addition, *Newsweek* provides a wide variety of instructor supplements free to teachers, including maps, Skill Builders, and weekly quizzes. For further information on the *Newsweek* Alliance, please contact your Longman sales representative.

Florida Adopters: *Thinking Through the Test,* by D.J. Henry   This special workbook, prepared specially for students in Florida, offers ample skill and practice exercises to help students prepare for the Florida State Exit Exam. To shrinkwrap this workbook free with your textbook, please contact your Longman sales representative. Also available: two laminated grids (one for reading, one for writing) that can serve as handy references for students preparing for the Florida State Exit Exam.

Electronic and Online Offerings

Reading Roadtrip Multimedia Reading and Study Skills Software, Version 2.0   This innovative and exciting multimedia reading CD-ROM takes students on a tour of fifteen cities and landmarks throughout the United States. Each of the fifteen modules corresponds to a reading or study skill (for example, finding the main idea, understanding patterns of organization, or thinking critically). Each contains a tour of the location, instructions, a tutorial, exercises, interactive feedback, and mastery tests. To order Reading Road Trip 2.0 with *Joining a Community of Readers*, or for additional information about the Web-based version, speak to your Longman sales representative.

The Longman English Pages Web Site   Both students and instructors can visit our free, content-rich Web site for additional reading selections and writing exercises. From the Longman English pages, visitors can conduct a simulated Web search, learn how to write a resume and cover letter, or try their hand at poetry writing. Stop by and visit us at **http://www.ablongman.com/englishpages**.

The Longman Electronic Newsletter   Twice a month during the spring and fall, instructors who have subscribed receive a free copy of the Longman Developmental English E-Newsletter in their e-mailbox. Written by experienced classroom instructors, the newsletter offers teaching tips, classroom activities, book reviews, and more. To subscribe, visit the Longman Basic Skills Web site at **http://www.ablongman.com/basicskills**, or send an e-mail to **Basic Skills@ablongman.com**.

Teaching Online: Internet Research, Conversation, and Composition, Second Edition   Ideal for instructors who have never surfed the Net, this easy-to-follow guide offers basic definitions, numerous examples, and step-by-step information about finding and using Internet sources. Free to adopters (0-321-01957-1).

***Researching Online,* Fifth Edition**   A perfect companion for a new age, this indispensable supplement helps students navigate the Internet. Adapted from *Teaching Online*, the instructor's Internet guide, *Researching Online* speaks directly to students, giving them detailed, step-by-step instructions for performing electronic searches. Available free when shrinkwrapped with *Joining a Community of Readers*. Contact your Longman sales consultant for information on how to order.

For Instructors

***CLAST Test Package,* Fourth Edition**   These two forty-item objective tests evaluate students' readiness for the CLAST exams. Strategies for teaching CLAST preparedness are included. Free with any Longman English title. Reproducible sheets: 0-321-01950-4. Computerized IBM version: 0-321-01982-2. Computerized Mac version: 0-321-01983-0.

***TASP Test Package,* Third Edition**   These twelve practice pre-tests and post-tests assess the same reading and writing skills covered in the TASP examination. Free with any Longman English title. Reproducible sheets: 0-321-01959-8. Computerized IBM version: 0-321-01985-7. Computerized Mac version: 0-321-01984-9.

ACKNOWLEDGMENTS

We are grateful to our families—Elena, Marley, and Paul, Aasiya, Abdulla, and Hassan; and Laura, Christina, Paul-Vincent, and Chuck—for their patience and help. We would also like to thank all our reading students and our colleagues for their help and positive support, especially Enrique Dávalos, Virginia Guleff, Kelly Mayhew, Jim Miller, and Jill Nakamura.

A special thank you to Steven Rigolosi for his continued support, enthusiasm, and good humor. Thank you to Ann Hofstra Grogg, whose diligence, perseverance, and editorial insights helped us to complete the text so successfully.

Thank you to our reviewers across the country:

Dorothy Fancher, *Alpena Community College*

Amy Wells Girone, *Arizona Western College*

Lesa Hildebrand, *Triton College*

Barbara L. Hughes, *Rio Hondo Community College*

Windy Jefferson-Jackson, *Montgomery College, Takoma Park Campus*

Sarah Jones, *Cypress College*

Charlene Koonin, *Broward Community College*

Lowell Martin, *Meridian Community College*

Donna L. Richardson-Hall, *Mercer County Community College*

Carol G. Shier, *Fullerton College*

Pamela Smith, *Pellissippi State Technical Community College*

Maggie Wade, *Triton College*

Cathy Webb, *Meridian Community College*

Sue Yamin, *Pellissippi State Technical Community College*

Roberta Alexander
Jan Lombardi
San Diego, CA

Features of *Joining a Community of Readers,* Second Edition

Joining a Community of Readers is organized in nine theme-based chapters. Each chapter focuses on the development of certain skills, building on the skills learned in previous chapters.

- **Reading, vocabulary, and learning strategies** are integrated with the themes throughout the text, but reading skills have clear priority. Once a strategy, such as identifying main ideas, is introduced and learned, it is reinforced many times in succeeding chapters.
- **Language Tips** are designed for beginning college students, making them aware of the uses of language, the importance of listening, and the meaning of words.
- **Organize to Learn** describes techniques for mastering the content of reading.
- **Put It Together** consolidates important points as an aid to study and learning.

Reading Skill	Theme	Vocabulary	Learning Strategies	Language Tips	Put It Together
Chapter 1: The Reading Process					
PRO: • **P**repare to read • **R**ead actively • **O**rganize to learn	Becoming a successful student		Setting goals; managing your time; previewing a textbook	Questions and active reading	The PRO reading process
Chapter 2: Working with Words					
	Technology and you	Textbook aids; context clues; word parts; dictionary skills; choosing the right definition	Personal vocabulary plan	Word forms	Vocabulary skills
Chapter 3: Main Ideas					
Topics; stated main ideas; thesis statement	Learning and education		Marking texts	Following directions	Topics and main ideas

Reading Skill	Theme	Vocabulary	Learning Strategies	Language Tips	Put It Together
Chapter 4: Unstated Main Ideas					
Unstated main ideas; writing main-idea sentences	Challenges in education		Working in groups	Writing complete sentences	Unstated main ideas
Chapter 5: Supporting Details					
Recognizing supporting details; separating general from specific details; using supporting details to find unstated main ideas	Popular culture		Outlining	Facts	Supporting details
Chapter 6: Major and Minor Supporting Details					
Major supporting details; minor supporting details	Television in our society		Mapping; writing a summary	Paraphrasing and plagiarizing	Major and minor supporting details
Chapter 7: Patterns of Organization					
Examples; listing; chronological order; mixed patterns of organization; definition; classification	Families in history and around the world	Transitions	Time lines	Coordination	Patterns of organization
Chapter 8: Complex Patterns of Organization					
Comparison and contrast; cause and effect	The family in the community	More transitions	Making a chart	Subordination	Complex patterns of organization
Chapter 9: Inferences, Fact versus Opinion, and Conclusions					
Recognizing inferences; recognizing facts and opinions; drawing conclusions	Growing up	Connotation and denotation	Separating personal opinion from reasonable inferences	Language of imagery	Inferences; fact versus opinion; drawing conclusions

To the Student

Welcome to *Joining a Community of Readers*

You have probably bought this book because you need to strengthen your reading skills and strategies to be ready for the demands of college reading. If you are prepared to take responsibility for your own learning, and if you are prepared to commit yourself to the work involved, you will learn the strategies and skills you will need to become an effective, thoughtful reader. Reading skills are necessary not only to pass this course, but for success in college in general, and, even more importantly, for success in the workplace of the twenty-first century.

Why Is Reading So Important?

Read any newspaper today, talk to any employer or human resource manager, and you will realize that the demands of today's society—not only of college study—require that you always be able to learn new skills and even take on whole new jobs or professions. During your lifetime, you will probably be faced with the need to change jobs or professions three, four, or more times. And even if you are one of the few who stay in one position or who are successful at creating your own business, you will constantly face the need to upgrade your skills. Professionals of any kind must stay up to date in their field. This is true of office professionals, medical professionals, teachers, engineers, auto mechanics, managers, computer programmers, and industrial workers.

Learning cannot stop when you get your degree; learning is a lifelong process. For this reason, the one essential ability to acquire, the one ability that will not become outdated and that can serve you for the rest of your life, is the ability to *know how to learn and grow.* In writing this text we have addressed the basics that will help you become a strong reader and therefore a successful student. The skills you acquire now in school will prepare you for the challenges of lifelong learning for the workplace and equip you to be effective, fulfilled adults and citizens of the modern world.

A recent survey of major businesses and industrial firms (The Secretary's Commission on Achieving Necessary Skills, U.S. Department of Labor, 1993) concluded that the workplace basics to learn in school are

1. *Learning to learn.* This text, *Joining a Community of Readers,* will show you how to become active in your own reading and learning process (Chapter 1). You will learn how you study best and how to put your study time to good use.
2. *Listening and oral communications.* As a college reader, you will learn that reading is reinforced and made more meaningful when

(a) you listen to other people's ideas about a subject and (b) you orally express your ideas to your classmates (all chapters).

3. *Competence in reading and writing.* As you work through this course, your reading competence will constantly improve. You will learn, review, and practice all the basic skills necessary to be a strong reader: the reading process (Chapter 1), vocabulary (Chapter 2), identifying main ideas (Chapters 3 and 4), understanding details (Chapters 5 and 6), identifying patterns of organization (Chapters 7 and 8), recognizing inferences and facts versus opinions (Chapter 9), and organizing what you read so that you can retain information and understanding for tests and future needs (all chapters).

4. *Adaptability based on creative thinking and problem solving.* As a member of your classroom and of a community of readers, you will be involved in bringing what you already know and what you learn through reading and discussion to a variety of issues, and you will practice thinking creatively and problem solving (all chapters), making inferences (Chapter 9), and recognizing facts versus opinions (Chapter 9).

5. *Group effectiveness characterized by interpersonal skills, negotiation skills, and teamwork.* You will learn to work with your classmates, sharing your strengths and learning from each other (all chapters).

6. *Organizational effectiveness and leadership.* You will develop your organizational and leadership skills in the process of working with your classmates toward a common goal.

Are You Ready?

If you are ready to tackle the material of this course, you will be taking a big step toward a successful college career. Can you answer "Yes" to the following key questions?

- Is learning and practicing college reading skills a priority for you at this time?
- Are you willing to make the effort to be *actively* involved in your learning?
- Have you decided that you can and will succeed, one small step at a time?
- Do you have the time to commit to being a student? Remember that as a student, you have a job. The payoff is not only passing grades and a degree, but more importantly, the development of reading and learning skills that you will use for the rest of your life.
- Are you willing to share ideas and to work together with other students to reach your goals?
- Are you willing to learn new reading strategies and to apply them, not

just to pass this class but to any new challenges that come your way?

- Are you willing to open your mind to new ideas and ways of thinking?
- Are you willing to think about ideas and arguments and to form opinions for yourself and with others?

Did you answer "Yes" to all or most of these questions? If so, we will help you reach your goals by assisting you to become a lifelong reader and learner. Welcome to *Joining a Community of Readers!*

Joining a Community of Readers

A Thematic Approach to Reading

Chapter 1

The Reading Process

Becoming a Successful Student

Step by step. I can't see any other way of accomplishing anything.

—*Michael Jordan*

- What are your goals for the next two or three years?

- What steps do you need to take to prepare yourself to accomplish your goals?

- What do you picture yourself doing after graduating or after completing your current educational goals?

Getting Ready to Read

What does it take to be a successful student? One way to answer that question would be, "It takes a combination of skill and attitude." But what do we mean by "skill" and "attitude"? The skills that are probably most important are (1) setting your goals, (2) organizing your time accordingly, and (3) applying the reading process to succeed in your studies. The attitudes that may be most important are (1) recognizing that you have what it takes to be successful, and (2) recognizing that having good relationships with other people can help you meet your goals and enjoy the process.

In this chapter you will read and use information about achieving success in college and in life. As you do, you will improve your organizational and reading skills by learning how to

- set short- and long-range goals
- manage your time effectively
- use PRO, a reading system to help you become a stronger reader in college

READING 1

I Can't Accept Not Trying   Michael Jordan

Michael Jordan, the world-famous basketball star, has clearly been successful in choosing and accomplishing both personal and professional goals. In his book he writes about how he approached the challenges he faced. As you read, think about how his book's title, I Can't Accept Not Trying, *applies to his experiences. Also, think about how his experiences might be similar to yours as you meet the personal and academic challenges of college life.*

1   I always had the ultimate goal of being the best, but I approached everything step by step. That's why I wasn't afraid to go to the University of North Carolina after high school.

2   Everyone told me I shouldn't go because I wouldn't be able to play at that level. They said I should go to the Air Force Academy because then I would have a job when I finished college. Everyone had a different agenda for me. But I had my own.

agenda Plan

3   I had always set short-term goals. As I look back, each one of those steps or successes led to the next one. When I got cut from the varsity team as a sophomore in high school, I learned something. I knew I never wanted to feel that bad again. I never wanted to have that taste in my mouth, that hole in my stomach.

4   So I set a goal of becoming a starter on the varsity. That's what I focused on all summer. When I worked on my game, that's what I thought about. When it happened, I set another goal, a reasonable, manageable goal that I could realistically achieve if I worked hard enough.

visualized
Pictured

5   Each time I visualized where I wanted to be, what kind of player I wanted to become.

6   I guess I approached it with the end in mind. I knew exactly where I wanted to go, and I focused on getting there. As I reached those goals, they built on one another. I gained a little confidence every time I came through.

7   So I had built up the confidence that I could compete at North Carolina. It was all mental for me. I never wrote anything down. I just concentrated on the next step.

8   I think I could have applied that approach to anything I might have chosen to do. It's no different from the person whose ultimate goal is to become a doctor. If that's your goal and you're getting Cs in biology then the first thing you have to do is get Bs in biology and then As. You have to perfect the first step and then move on to chemistry or physics.

9   Take those small steps. Otherwise you're opening yourself up to all kinds of frustration. Where would your confidence come from if the only measure of success was becoming a doctor? If you tried as hard as you could and didn't become a doctor, would that mean your whole life was a failure? Of course not.

10   All those steps are like pieces of a puzzle. They all come together to form a picture.

11   If it's complete, then you've reached your goal. If not, don't get down on yourself.

12   If you've done your best, then you will have had some accomplishments along the way. Not everyone is going to get the entire picture. Not everyone is going to be the greatest salesman or the greatest basketball player. But you can still be considered one of the best, and you can still be considered a success.

13   That's why I've always set short-term goals. Whether it's golf, basketball, business, family life, or even baseball, I set goals—realistic goals—and I focus on them. I ask questions, I read, I listen. I did the same thing in baseball with the Chicago White Sox. I'm not afraid to ask anybody anything if I don't know. Why should I be afraid? I'm trying to get somewhere. Help me, give me direction. Nothing wrong with that.

14   Step by step, I can't see any other way of accomplishing anything.

JORDAN, *I Can't Accept Not Trying*

Exercise 1	

Recall and Discuss

Answer these questions about Reading 1, and prepare to discuss them in class.

1. How did Jordan go about setting realistic goals for himself?

    _____

    _____

2. What do you think Jordan means when he says, "Each time I visualized where I wanted to be . . . ?"

    _____

    _____

3. How do you visualize yourself at the end of this semester? What goals do you plan to accomplish by then?

    _____

    _____

    _____

Setting Goals and Achieving Them

setting goals
Deciding what you want to accomplish

Setting goals is not an easy job. It involves deciding what is important to you and what you want to accomplish. The many decisions you make every day influence your life in both small and large ways. It's important that decisions move you toward, not away from, your goals. To become a successful student, set your goals at the beginning of your college years.

Goals can be broken into different categories based on when and how easily they can be achieved. There is an old Chinese saying, "The longest journey begins with a single step." This certainly is true when we think of our life's goals. When you write your own goals, you need to think about both short- and long-term goals.

short-term
Applying to the day, the week, the month, or the semester

Short-term goals can be accomplished in a limited period of time, such as goals for a day, a week, a month, or a semester. State your goals very specifically, so you can determine whether you achieve them or not. For example, one of your goals for next week might be to complete a complicated biology lab assignment on time and earn a grade of C or better on it. To reach this goal, you can make steps for yourself that are very clear and direct. You can say, (1) I will attend the biology lab; (2) I will make sure I understand the assignment by asking the instructor for clarification; (3) I will spend two hours working on this assignment on Monday, on Tuesday, and on Wednesday; and (4) I will look at my work again before I turn it in to be sure that it is complete. Once you receive your grade, it will be easy to tell whether you achieved your goal and to analyze why you did or did not.

Another fairly short-term goal might be to improve your English skills and to get a B or better in this class. To accomplish this goal, again, you will want to decide on the steps you will take. It's probably not too helpful to decide simply, "I will study harder this semester," because that goal is too vague. It's better to decide something specific like, "I will study at least six hours a week for this class this semester."

long-term Applying to years from now, or even your lifetime

Long-term goals take more time to achieve because they include goals for the distant future. For example, your long-term goal might be to become a research biologist with three children and a house on the beach. In this case, a successful biology lab assignment goal would be one small step toward accomplishing the larger goal. Although our life goals cover all categories—personal, social, economic, and academic—our focus in this chapter is on the goals related to this course and to your future as a student.

Exercise 2

Set Short-Term Goals

Write at least three goals that you plan to achieve this semester, and write the steps that you will take to accomplish those goals. Be specific in your wording so that you can tell at the end of the semester whether you have achieved your goals.

Specific Semester Goals	*Steps to Accomplish Them*
1. *Improve reading skills. Get a B in this class.*	a. *Study and review six hours per week.*
	b. *Attend every class meeting.*
	c. *Be on time for class every day.*
2. _____	a. _____
_____	b. _____
	c. _____
3. _____	a. _____
_____	b. _____
	c. _____

Managing Your Time

One important way to achieve your goals is to be aware of how you spend your time. Being a full-time student is a full-time job. You must learn how to find the time to be a student—to attend classes regularly and to study—as well as to do everything else that you need to do in your life. Once you have found the time for your classes and your study, you must use that time effectively.

time management
A system for using
your time wisely

Time management will help you accomplish everything you want to do in the time you have available. It involves four essential steps:

1. Assess your commitments.
2. Assess your use of time.
3. Get organized.
4. Check your progress.

Assessing Your Commitments

Figure out what your commitments are now and how much time you have for your studies. Decide what is most important for you at this time of your life. You may have to make decisions about what you can and cannot do. To help you assess your comments, fill in the blanks in the following discussion.

Student Responsibilities   If you are to be successful, you will need to plan to spend a certain amount of time on school responsibilities each week. Calculate the amount of time you need to be a student by adding up the number of hours you are in class per week and then adding to that two study hours for every hour in class. For example, if you are taking two three-unit classes (that meet for three hours a week), you need to plan on spending nine hours per week for each class, which means eighteen hours per week for both classes. If you are taking twelve units, you should plan on thirty-six hours of class attendance and study time. Based on this formula, how many hours per week do you need to dedicate to school? _____

Extracurricular Responsibilities   Are you involved in some school activities? Are you a member of an organization? How many hours per week do you spend on these activities? _____

Work Responsibilities   How many hours per week do you work? _____

Family and Community Responsibilities   Are you responsible for other people? Are you married? Do you have children or brothers and sisters to take care of? Do you attend church or do any volunteer work in your community? Estimate how many hours per week you need to spend on these responsibilities: _____

Personal Responsibilities   Remember, you cannot take care of all the people in your life or meet all of your goals if you do not take care of yourself. Be sure to schedule some time for yourself, for socializing (_____), exercising (_____), and relaxation (_____). And don't forget sleeping. You need eight hours of sleep per night (_____). Now total up the hours you wrote down in parentheses to determine the number of hours per week you need to take care of yourself: _____

Miscellaneous Time   Don't forget that you need to set your time allotments realistically. How about little things like shopping, cooking, and doing household chores? Also, transportation to and from the places you have to go takes time. Estimate how many hours per week you need for miscellaneous things: _____

Total Time   Now total up all of your time entries: _____ There are 168 hours in a week. If you are like many students, your total time entries add up to more than 168 hours!

Exercise 3 ## Schedule Your Time

Now let's check the accuracy of your estimates, and get a more graphic picture of where your time goes. Look at the sample Weekly Schedule shown on page 8, and fill in the blank schedule on page 9 with your own information. Be realistic with your time allotments, and do not underestimate the time it takes to do things. Fill in your class hours, your extracurricular hours, your work hours, your family- and community-responsibility hours, your personal hours, and your miscellaneous time requirements. Then mark off the hours that are open for study.

Assessing Your Use of Time

When you totaled your time estimates, was your total less than 168 hours? _____. If not, you will need to make some changes. One way is to analyze how you use your time.

Study Time   Take a careful look at the times you have identified for studying on your Weekly Schedule chart. Have you scheduled time so you can prepare for each class meeting? Have you scheduled time to review regularly, so that you don't have to waste time relearning information? Also, remember that sometimes small amounts of time can pay off in a big way. One such example is reviewing your notes from the last class session and looking over the reading right before you attend a class. Such a review, either the night before or the day of the class—or

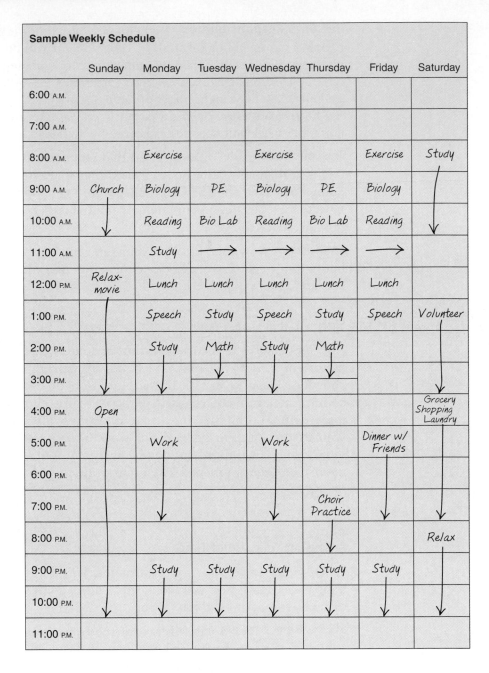

Sample Weekly Schedule							
	Sunday	Monday	Tuesday	Wednesday	Thursday	Friday	Saturday
6:00 A.M.							
7:00 A.M.							
8:00 A.M.		Exercise		Exercise		Exercise	Study
9:00 A.M.	Church	Biology	P.E.	Biology	P.E.	Biology	
10:00 A.M.	↓	Reading	Bio Lab	Reading	Bio Lab	Reading	↓
11:00 A.M.		Study	→	→	→	→	
12:00 P.M.	Relax-movie	Lunch	Lunch	Lunch	Lunch	Lunch	
1:00 P.M.		Speech	Study	Speech	Study	Speech	Volunteer
2:00 P.M.		Study	Math	Study	Math		
3:00 P.M.			↓		↓		↓
4:00 P.M.	Open						Grocery Shopping Laundry
5:00 P.M.		Work		Work		Dinner w/ Friends	
6:00 P.M.							
7:00 P.M.					Choir Practice		
8:00 P.M.					↓		Relax
9:00 P.M.		Study	Study	Study	Study	Study	
10:00 P.M.	↓	↓	↓	↓	↓	↓	↓
11:00 P.M.							

even five minutes before the class begins—will help you be more alert and involved during the class. You will remember where the lesson left off, and if there is a quiz, you will be much more likely to know the answers. If you have some questions about the reading or the lesson, plan to ask the instructor.

My Weekly Schedule	Sunday	Monday	Tuesday	Wednesday	Thursday	Friday	Saturday
6:00 A.M.							
7:00 A.M.							
8:00 A.M.							
9:00 A.M.							
10:00 A.M.							
11:00 A.M.							
12:00 P.M.							
1:00 P.M.							
2:00 P.M.							
3:00 P.M.							
4:00 P.M.							
5:00 P.M.							
6:00 P.M.							
7:00 P.M.							
8:00 P.M.							
9:00 P.M.							
10:00 P.M.							
11:00 P.M.							

Energy Level Look again at the boxes that you highlighted in your chart for hours devoted to your studies. Think about your own habits: are you a morning or a night person? When are your study times scheduled? If you are a morning person and your study hours are blocked off at 3 P.M., you may have designated poor hours to devote to school. You might be more ready to take a nap at this time than to "crack the books." As you look over your chart, adjust your schedule so that you can study during your peak hours. Other chores or responsibilities that may not require the intense focus that studying does—such as shopping, cleaning the house, cooking—can be scheduled for those hours when your ability to think clearly is not at its peak.

Concentration   Once you designate the times of the day when you are full of energy for your studies, consider whether you will be able to concentrate to your fullest during those times. **Concentration**—giving close attention to what you are doing, focusing on your reading—is important. If you are distracted, you will not be able to use your study time well. There are two basic kinds of distractions: environmental and mental.

concentration
Giving close attention to what you are doing, focusing on your reading

Environmental distractions are things that are happening around you that may prevent you from concentrating on your work, such as children playing, a television program in the background, or the telephone ringing. Set up your study time and location when and where you won't have to struggle against environmental distractions. Perhaps there is a quiet room in your house, or maybe you could study in the library.

environmental distractions   Things that are happening around you that may prevent you from concentrating on your work

Mental distractions are all the things you may be thinking about that will prevent you from concentrating on your work, such as the bills you need to pay, the argument you had with your spouse or friend, or your vacation plans. To help yourself overcome these distractions, take care of these problems as best you can before you sit down to study. Sometimes it helps if you put these problems and their possible solutions on a "to do" list so that you know you will not forget to follow up on them. Then you can stop worrying about them and get back to studying.

mental distractions
Things you may be thinking about that prevent you from concentrating on your work

Priorities   As you think about your use of time, also think about what is important at this point in your life. Deciding the order of importance of different goals or parts of your life is called **setting priorities.** For example, if you are a full-time student, doing well in school may be your highest priority. If you are a parent, taking care of your children may take priority and being a good student might have to take second place.

setting priorities
Deciding the order of importance of your goals and activities

Be creative in your thinking. Maybe you will have to reduce or cut out the time that you spend hanging out in the cafeteria or the student union. Maybe you can decrease the number of hours you work, or perhaps you can find an on-campus job that could save you the commuting time. Possibly you should consider dropping a class or reducing the number of other commitments that you have.

| Exercise 4 | ## Plan Your Time |

Write out your plan to focus on what is important to you now and to reduce your commitments to activities or things that are not your current priorities.

1. I will focus on _____

_____

_____

2. I will cut back on _____

_____

_____

3. To give my studies the attention they deserve, I will _____

_____

_____

Organizing Your Time

You need to think about two basic levels of organization in planning the best use of your time. Both are short-term in the sense that they relate to the next few months, but the first is more long-range than the second.

Monthly Calendar   First, establish a calendar for yourself in which you record all your long-range assignments. When your instructors pass out the course syllabi and announce assignments such as the dates of final exams and papers, write down this important information on your calendar. When you make other appointments for yourself, or if you have school activities or community meetings, be sure to write them down on the *same* calendar. Use the sample Semester Calendar on page 12 as a guide.

"To Do" List   Second, at the end or at the beginning of each day, make yourself a "to do" list like the one shown on page 13. Write down your specific jobs for the day and exactly what you plan to do with your time. Be sure to check your monthly calendar so that you don't forget the upcoming big assignments, tests, or appointments. It is very important to check your "to do" list during the day to be sure that you are not forgetting something. At the end of the day, cross or check off the things that you did. Write anything you weren't able to do on the following day's list.

It's a good idea to prioritize your "to do" lists. You might not get around to something, but decide that postponing it is okay. Try to do those things that are most important to you first. For example, if you have an exam in biology, be sure to give yourself the time to review your biology notes, even if it means putting off that trip to the laundromat for a day. (Or maybe you could remember to take your biology book and notes to the laundromat and do both tasks at the same time!)

Semester Calendar Fall

Month September

Sunday	Monday	Tuesday	Wednesday	Thursday	Friday	Saturday
				1	2	3
4 Church	5 Classes begin	6	7	8 Choir	9	10 Volunteer
11 Church	12	13 Campus newspaper	14	15	16	17
18 Church	19	20	21	22 Choir	23	24 Volunteer
25 Church	26	27 Campus newspaper	28	29 Bio Lab Math Test	30 Rdg Test	1 October

Month October

Sunday	Monday	Tuesday	Wednesday	Thursday	Friday	Saturday
2 Church	3	4	5	6 Choir	7	8
9 Church	10	11 Campus newspaper	12	13 Bio report	14 Rdg test	15 Volunteer
16 Church	17	18 Short speech 5 min	19	20 Math test Choir	21	22
23 Church	24	25 Campus newspaper	26	27	28 Bio test	29 Volunteer
30 Church	31					Jogathon Balboa Park

Month November

Sunday	Monday	Tuesday	Wednesday	Thursday	Friday	Saturday
Church picnic		1	2	3	4 Bio test	5
6 Church	7	8 Campus newspaper	9	10 Choir	11	12 Volunteer
13 Church	14	15	16	17 Math Test Choir	18	19 Rdg Test
20 Church Beach party	21	22 Short speech 5 min newspaper	23	24	25	26 Scholarship applic due
27	28	29	30			

Month December

Sunday	Monday	Tuesday	Wednesday	Thursday	Friday	Saturday
				1 Choir	2	3 Mom's birthday
4 Church	5 Campus newspaper	6	7 Speech due (10 min)	8 Math test	9	10 Volunteer
11 Church	12 9:00–1:00 Bio am Final	13 12–2 Math Final	14 10:00–1:00 RDG Final 1–3:00 Speech Final	15 Choir	16	17
18 Church	19 Newspaper party	20	21	22	23	24
25 Church	26	27	28	29	30	31

```
                              To Do List

                                                  Date _____

                                             Priority
                                            (a, b, or c)    Completed
     1. Prepare for tomorrow's biology test      (a)            X
     2. Do the laundry                            (b)            X
     3. Call parents                              (b)            X
     4. Plan Johnny's birthday party              (a)            X
     5. Begin notes for English 101 paper         (a)            X
     6. _____
```

Checking Your Progress

It takes approximately three weeks to establish a new habit. Commit yourself to working on your time management every single day for the next several weeks. Hopefully, you will establish a habit that will serve you well not only throughout school but for the rest of your life.

After you work with your monthly calendar and "to do" lists for a week or so, take some time to make sure they are working for you. Are you able to keep up with all the activities that you schedule? Are you making sure that nothing is falling through the cracks by writing down everything that you need to do in the appropriate places? Are you alert and able to concentrate during the times that you have set aside for your studies? And, most important of all, does your allocation of time correspond to your priorities?

Managing your time means making decisions. Let's begin this decision-making process with a short exercise.

Exercise 5

Make Decisions

List all the "roles" you have right now as an individual. Who are you, as defined by the different roles, responsibilities, or jobs you fill? Each role you list must be a noun, or a name of a role or job in your life. For example, are you a father? An employee of Sears? A tennis player? A television viewer?

1. List below as many roles as you can identify. (You don't have to limit yourself to six.)

   a. _____

   b. _____

   c. _____

   d. _____

   e. _____

   f. _____

2. Next, write these roles again in the order of their *importance* to you. Letter "a" should be the most important role or responsibility in your life, "b" the next most important, and so on.

   a. _____

   b. _____

   c. _____

   d. _____

   e. _____

   f. _____

3. Last, because you're more conscious of how you spend your time now, it should be easy to list the roles you fill in the order of the *amount of time* you spend on each. Letter "a" should be the role in which you spend the most time on the average. Letter "b" should be the role in which you spend the next greatest amount of hours. Caution: answer this with the *actual* way you spend your time, not how you think you should spend it.

   a. _____

   b. _____

   c. _____

   d. _____

   e. _____

   f. _____

4. As you completed this exercise, did you discover any conflicts between where you spend your time and what you think are your most important roles, your priorities, in life? Describe any conflicts in the space provided here. Most of us will notice numerous conflicts when we complete an exercise like this, so don't be surprised by what you discover.

_____

_____

_____

_____

_____

Exercise 6

Make Connections

Write short answers to the following questions based on your answers in Exercise 5.

1. Do you need to make changes in your priorities? Explain.

_____

_____

2. Do you need to make changes in your current use of time? Explain.

_____

_____

3. How possible is it for you to make the changes, if any, that you've indicated in 1 and 2?

_____

_____

Meeting Others, Knowing Yourself

Becoming a successful student involves managing your time in a new way that helps you fulfill the new responsibilities and new challenges you've assumed. One of the major challenges facing you as a new college student is that of entering a new community, an *academic community,* with ease.

Making Friends

The first step you need to take to feel comfortable in your new college environment is to *get to know your fellow students.* The most successful college students are those who know their classmates and who actively build with them a vital and supportive *community of learners.* If you get to know other students in your classes, you can help each other by working together: sharing notes, phoning or e-mailing each other for information if you are absent, and preparing for exams together. Plan on making new friends. Choose people who are also serious about school.

| Exercise 7 |

Introduce Yourself

Think about your answers to the following questions and make some notes on the lines below. When you finish, introduce yourself to your class group by discussing your answers. Be prepared to introduce the members of your group to the whole class.

1. What is your name, and can you give us some ways to remember it? (Does your name have a special meaning? Does it sound like a word that could be used to describe you?)

   _____

   _____

2. Why are you going to college? What is your major? What is your career goal?

   _____

   _____

3. What is one of the special accomplishments you have achieved in your life so far? (Be specific. Select something that you do, or have done, especially well.)

   _____

   _____

Valuing Who You Are

positive self-esteem
Feeling good about yourself

In addition to the ability to make friends, we need to develop the ability to value who we are, to realize that we deserve to have a good life and that we can create that life for ourselves. This recognition of self-worth, or **positive self-esteem,** will help you work your way through college and toward the goals you have set for yourself.

READING 2

Positive Self-Esteem Denis Waitley

In the following reading, Denis Waitley discusses the importance of beliefs of self-worth and then outlines a way to put his advice into practice with ten habits that will help you improve your self-esteem. Before you read the following selection, think about (1) how you felt when you were successful at something and (2) how you felt when and if you doubted your ability to achieve your goals. Why do you think it's important to believe in yourself?

1 *Positive self-esteem* is one of the most important and basic qualities of a winning human being. It is that deep down, inside the self, feeling of your own worth.

2 "You know, I like myself. I really do like myself. Given my parents and my background, I'm glad I'm me. I'd rather be me than anyone else, living at any other time in history."

3 This is the self-talk of a winner . . . and positive self-talk is the key to developing positive self-esteem.

4 Winners have developed strong beliefs of self-worth and self-confidence. They weren't necessarily born with these good feelings, but as with every other habit, they have learned to like themselves through practice. . . .

Building Your Confidence

5 Confidence is built upon the experience of success. When we begin anything new we usually have little confidence because we have not learned from experience that we can succeed. This is true with learning to ride a bicycle, skiing, figure skating, flying a high-performance jet aircraft, and leading people. It is true that success breeds success. Winners focus on past successes and forget past failures. They use errors and mistakes as a way to learning—then they dismiss them from their minds.

6 Yet, what do many of us do? We destroy our self-confidence by remembering past failures and forgetting all about our past successes. We not only remember failures, we etch them in our minds with emotion. We condemn ourselves. Winners know that it doesn't matter how many times they have failed in the past. What matters is their successes, which should be remembered, reinforced, and dwelt upon.

Concentrate on Success

7 To establish true self-esteem, we must concentrate on our successes and look at the failures and negatives in our lives only as corrective feedback to get us on target again. . . . Instead of comparing ourselves to others, we

should view ourselves in terms of our own abilities, interests, and goals. We can begin by making a <u>conscious</u> effort to upgrade our lifestyle and pay more attention to personal appearance and personal habits.

Take Action Today for More Positive Self-Esteem

peers People in the same position (age, grade, rank, status)

1. *Dress and look your best at all times* regardless of the pressure from your friends and peers. Personal grooming and lifestyle appearance provide an instantaneous projection on the surface of how you feel inside about yourself.

2. *Volunteer your own name first* in every telephone call and whenever you meet someone new. By paying value to your own name in communication, you are developing the habit of paying value to yourself as an individual.

3. *Take inventory of your good reasons for self-esteem today.* Write down what your "BAG" is. Blessings—who and what you are thankful for. Accomplishments—what you have done that you're proud of so far. Goals—what your dreams and ambitions are.

4. *Respond with a simple, courteous "thank you"* when anyone pays you a compliment for any reason.

5. *Sit up front in the most prominent rows* when you attend meetings, lectures and conferences. Your purpose for going is to listen, learn and possibly exchange questions and answers with the key speakers.

6. *Walk more erectly and authoritatively in public* with a relaxed but more rapid pace. It has been proven that individuals who walk erectly and briskly usually are confident about themselves and where they are going.

7. *Set your own internal standards* rather than comparing yourself to others. Keep upgrading your own standards in lifestyle, behavior, professional accomplishment, relationships, etc.

affirmative Positive

8. *Use encouraging, affirmative language* when you talk to yourself and to others about yourself. Focus on uplifting and building adjectives and adverbs. Everything you say about yourself is subconsciously being recorded by others and, more importantly, by your own self-image.

modification Change

9. *Keep a self-development plan ongoing at all times.* Sketch it out on paper—the knowledge you'll require, the behavior modification you'll achieve, the changes in your life that will result. Seek out the real winners in life as friends and role models. Misery loves company, but so does success!

10. *SMILE!* In every language, in every culture—it is the light in your window that tells people there's a caring, sharing individual inside and it's the universal code for "I'm O.K.—You're O.K., too!"

WAITLEY, *Psychology of Winning*

Exercise 8

Check Your Understanding

Write brief answers to the following questions about Reading 2.

1. What is positive self-esteem?

   _____

   _____

2. Why do you think positive self-esteem is an important quality for students to possess?

   _____

   _____

3. Why should people focus on successes rather than failures?

   _____

   _____

4. What are the four steps that you think are most important for gaining positive self-esteem?

   a. _____

   b. _____

   c. _____

   d _____

Exercise 9

Make Connections

Write short answers to the following questions based on Reading 2, your experience, and your observations.

1. List your blessings and accomplishments.

   _____

   _____

2. Name the actions from the Waitley list that you already take.

   _____

   _____

3. Name some additional actions you can take to succeed in college.

   _____

   _____

| Exercise 10 | **Make Connections: Collaborative Activity** |

Think about and discuss with classmates the list entitled "Take Action Today for More Positive Self-Esteem" in Reading 2. Then interview each other, asking the following questions and taking time to briefly discuss each other's answers. Fill out the accompanying chart. One example has been done for you.

Interview questions:

- What blessings have you had in your life?
- What are your accomplishments so far?
- What goals do you have?
- What actions from the list "Take Action Today for More Positive Self-Esteem" do you already take?
- What additional actions from the list do you think you should take to help you achieve your goals?

	Student 1 Name _____	Student 2 Name _____	Student 3 Name _____
Blessings	a supportive family		
Accomplishments	graduated high school doing good job raising child as single mother		
Goals	to become a dental assistant		
Actions you already do	dress well (1) say "thank you" to compliments (4) walk erectly (6)	.	
Actions you think you should do to succeed in college	remember BAG (3) sit in front (5) Set own standards (7)		

The Importance of Reading

Reading is a way of communicating with others and of learning about yourself. Through reading you can think about and learn from the ideas of people you have never met, who may live in other countries or have lived in other times. You also learn from your classmates by reading with them and sharing ideas about what you have read. Reading is communication.

Reading also makes it possible for you to understand ideas you've never encountered before, to master skills and concepts you may have thought were beyond your grasp, and to reinforce understandings you have gained in your own life experience. Reading helps you know yourself.

Reading makes an academic community work. By reading better, you become a stronger part of this community.

Becoming an Active Reader: The PRO System

Joining an *academic community* means learning to take charge of your future by setting your goals and managing your time so success is possible. It also means that you will change your learning habits. The word *learning* itself implies "a change in behavior." In college you will discover ways to use all of your learning skills—reading, writing, listening, speaking, computing, and thinking—to become a successful student and to be competent in the career of your choice.

By choosing to enter college, you have joined a community of learners, which includes fellow students, teachers, counselors, librarians, other staff, and administrators. Your learning skills, especially reading and listening, make communication in this community work for you. They will help you to know yourself and others.

The communication involved in reading is easier to understand if you view reading as a *process*. That is, the understandings you acquire by reading don't just happen automatically by looking at a page, or a computer screen, full of print. There are three basic steps that can help you succeed in reading and studying. All good readers follow these steps even though they may not be aware that they are doing so. First they *prepare* to read, then they *read actively*, and then they *organize to learn*. You can remember this process by using the initial letters to form **PRO.**

PRO The process or system you should use to succeed in reading and studying. It stands for *preparing to read, reading actively,* and *organizing what you read.*

1. **P = *Prepare to read***
2. **R = *Read actively***
3. **O = *Organize to learn***

When you've mastered this system, you will be a reading "pro"!

1. Preparing to Read

The first step in the reading process is preparing to read. When you prepare to read, there are various activities that you carry out consciously or unconsciously that help get your brain ready to receive information actively, in a way that makes it easier to understand and think about what you have read, and consequently easier to remember what you have read.

Concentrating

The first consideration in preparing to read is a very practical one. Begin by choosing a time when you won't be disturbed and a place where you can concentrate. By establishing regular times and places to work, you can form a habit of reading effectively. Plan to avoid environmental distractions and mental distractions. For example, choose to play music only if you know it won't detract from your ability to focus on the reading goals you have set for yourself. Studies have shown that some classical music actually helps the mind to focus, but the beat of heavy rock interferes with that ability.

Previewing

preview A quick look at what you are going to read before you read it

Once you have chosen an appropriate atmosphere for reading, you are ready to begin the process itself. The first step is to **preview,** or to look quickly at, what you are going to read before you read it. For studying purposes it's best to preview only a section (no more than three or four pages) at a time. The preview of a short piece should not take more than a couple of minutes. In your preview, look for the "framework" of the reading. The framework is the basic structure, like the skeleton of a house that is being built. In your preview, "read" only the following things:

- titles and subtitles
- introduction
- headings and subheadings
- pictures, charts, tables, and other graphics
- special print: words that appear in **boldface,** *italics,* or are underlined
- summary or conclusion

Exercise 11

Prepare to Read

Now you can practice preparing to read with Reading 3, titled "Self-Actualized People," which begins on page 23. Before you read, preview the entire reading: read the title and headings and the introductory paragraph, the italicized words, and the captions by the figure and the picture. Notice how much information you learn in this quick preview. After your preview, write brief answers to the following questions about Reading 3.

1. What is the reading about? *(See title and first sentence.)*

_____

2. What does *self-actualized* mean? *(See boldfaced terms in the margin.)*

_____

3. List five characteristics of self-actualized people. *(See headings.)*

   1. _____

   2. _____

   3. _____

   4. _____

   5. _____

4. What are the five human needs Maslow identified? *(See Figure 1.1, p. 24)*

   1. _____

   2. _____

   3. _____

   4. _____

   5. _____

READING 3

Self-Actualized People   Paul M. Insel, Walton T. Roth, L. McKay Rollins, and Ray A. Petersen

In this reading from a college health text, Insel and his co-authors explain the characteristics of psychological health and wellness identified by psychologist Abraham Maslow.

1　Psychological health can be defined either negatively as the absence of sickness or positively as the presence of wellness. A positive definition is a more ambitious outlook, one that encourages you to fulfill your own potential. During the 1960s, Abraham Maslow eloquently described an ideal of mental health in his book *Toward a Psychology of Being.* He was convinced that psychologists were too preoccupied with people who had failed in some way. He also disliked the way psychologists tried to reduce human striving to physiological needs or drives.

physiological needs The requirements of the body, i.e., air, water, food, shelter, sleep, and sex.

2　According to Maslow, there is a *hierarchy of needs,* listed here in order of decreasing urgency: physiological needs, safety, being loved, maintaining self-esteem, and self-actualization (Figure 1.1 on page 24). When urgent needs like the need for food are satisfied, less urgent needs take priority. Most of us are well fed and feel reasonably safe, so we are driven by higher motives. Maslow's conclusions were based on his study of a group of visibly successful people who seemed to have lived, or be living, at their fullest.

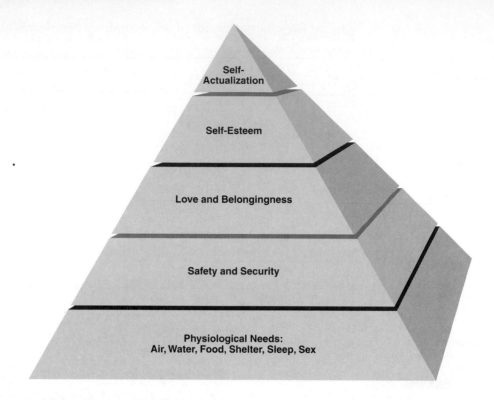

Figure 1.1   Maslow's hierarchy of needs.   *SOURCE:* Adapted from Maslow, A. 1970. *Motivation and Personality,* 2nd ed. New York: Harper & Row.

self-actualized
Describes a person who has achieved the highest level of growth in Maslow's hierarchy

He called these people *self-actualized*; he thought they had fulfilled a good measure of their human potential and suggested that self-actualized people all share certain qualities.

Realism

3   Self-actualized people are able to deal with the world as it is and not demand that it be otherwise. If you are realistic, you know the difference between what is and what you want. You also know what you can change and what you cannot. Unrealistic people often spend a great deal of time and energy trying to force the world and other people into their ideal picture. Realistic people accept evidence that contradicts what they want to believe, and if it is important evidence, they modify their beliefs.

self-concept   The ideas, feelings, and perceptions one has about oneself

Acceptance

self-esteem
Satisfaction and confidence in oneself

4   Psychologically healthy people can largely accept themselves and others. Self-acceptance means having a positive *self-concept* or self-image, or appropriately high *self-esteem.* They have a positive but realistic mental image

of themselves, and positive feelings about who they are, what they are capable of, and what roles they play. People who feel good about themselves are likely to live up to their positive self-image and enjoy successes that in turn reinforce these good feelings. A good self-concept is based on a realistic view of personal worth—it does not mean being egocentric or "stuck on yourself."

Autonomy

autonomy
Independence; the sense of being self-directed

other-directed
Guided in behavior by the values and expectations of others

inner-directed
Guided in behavior by an inner set of rules and values

authenticity
Genuineness

5 Psychologically healthy people are able to direct themselves, acting independently of their social environment. *Autonomy* is more than freedom from physical control by something outside the self. Many people, for example, shrink from expressing their feelings because they fear disapproval and rejection. They respond only to what they feel as outside pressure. Behavior such as this is *other-directed.* In contrast, *inner-directed* people find guidance from within, from their own values and feelings. They are not afraid to be themselves. Psychologically free people act because they choose to, not because they are driven or pressured.

6 Autonomy can give healthy people certain childlike qualities. Very small children have a quality of being "real." They respond in a genuine, spontaneous way to whatever happens. Someone who is genuine has no pretenses. Being genuine means not having to plan words or actions to get approval or make an impression. It means being aware of feelings and being willing to express them—being unselfconsciously oneself. This quality is sometimes called *authenticity*; such people are authentic, the "real thing."

A Capacity for Intimacy

7 Healthy people are capable of physical and emotional intimacy. They can expose their feelings and thoughts to other people. They are open to the pleasure of intimate physical contact and to the risks and satisfactions of being close to others in a caring, sensitive way.

Creativity

8 Psychologically healthy people are creative and have a continuing fresh appreciation for what goes on around them. They are not necessarily great poets, artists, or musicians, but they do live their everyday lives in creative ways: "A first-rate soup is more creative than a second-rate painting." Creative people seem to see more and to be open to new experiences; they don't fear the unknown. And they don't need to minimize uncertainty or avoid it; they actually find it attractive.

9 How did Maslow's group achieve their exemplary psychological health, and (more importantly) how can *we* attain it? Maslow himself did not

answer that question, but we have a few suggestions. Undoubtedly it helps to have been treated with respect, love, and understanding as a child, to have experienced stability and to have achieved a sense of mastery. As adults, since we cannot redo the past, we must concentrate on meeting current psychological challenges in ways that will lead to long-term mental wellness.

INSEL ET AL., *Core Concepts in Health*

| Exercise 12 |

Check Your Understanding

Choose the best answers to the following multiple-choice questions based on Reading 3.

1. "Self-actualized" is best defined as:
   a. the psychological characteristics of the majority of the people.
   b. being happy.
   c. having achieved the highest level of growth and fulfillment.

2. Maslow believed that it was important
   a. to measure people's psychological needs.
   b. to have a positive definition of mental wellness.
   c. to understand the different kinds of mental sickness.

3. According to Maslow,
   a. self-actualized people are seldom satisfied because they are always reaching for higher goals.
   b. people who are self-actualized share certain positive qualities.
   c. most people are too busy meeting their other needs to become self-actualized.

4. According to Maslow, the most urgent needs are
   a. physiological needs.
   b. the need for self-actualization.
   c. the need to maintain self-esteem.

5. Realism is a quality that self-actualized people
   a. have.
   b. don't have.
   c. don't allow to destroy their dreams.

6. Having a good self-concept means all of the following *except*
   a. your successes reinforce your positive self-concept.
   b. you are egocentric and feel superior to others.
   c. you feel good about yourself.

7. "Autonomy" is best described as
   a. independence, being self-directed.
   b. more than freedom from physical control by something outside the self.
   c. the need to respond to outside pressure.

8. Having a capacity for intimacy includes
   a. being open to exposing your feelings and thoughts to other people.
   b. depending on other people for your positive self-concept.
   c. constantly taking risks to please other people in your life.

9. One of the factors that probably helps people become self-actualized is
   a. having been treated with respect, love, and understanding, and having achieved a sense of mastery as a child.
   b. having all of the physiological needs met as a child.
   c. having learned how to take care of oneself without needing to be close to anyone else as a child.

| Exercise 13 |

Make Connections

Write brief answers to the following questions about Reading 3.

1. Who, among the people you know, do you think is a self-actualized person? Why?

   _____

   _____

2. Some people believe that you cannot become "self-actualized" until you are older. Do you agree? Do you know any young people you would consider "self-actualized"?

   _____

   _____

Organize to Learn: Preview a Textbook

As you begin the semester, it's helpful to preview your textbooks. Most college textbooks are divided into a number of parts, or sections. Each of these sections has its own title, and you can expect to find certain information in it. Here is a chart of these divisions, their usual location, and their use to you as a student.

continued

Part of a Book	The Information It Gives	Where to Find It
Title page	Title of the book, name of the author(s), place of publication	The first page of the book
Copyright page	Number of editions, date of publication, ordering information	On the back of the title page
Table of contents	A listing of the book's major topics and subtopics in the order they will be presented, organized in chapters, sections, or units with page numbers	After the copyright page
Preface	Information about the book's purpose, special features, student aids	Before the first chapter
Appendix (appendices)	Additional useful information such as maps, lists (e.g., of presidents), charts, and tables	At the back of the book
Glossary	A dictionary of important terms for the text	At the back of the book, after appendices
Index	Usually an *alphabetical* listing of all important topics, terms, and names found in the text, with page numbers for each	At the back of the book, after appendices and glossary
Bibliography	A listing of sources for additional information on a topic, including books, journals, audiovisual materials, and web sites	At the end of a chapter or in a special section at the end of the book
Answer keys	Answers to exercises so students can check their work	At the back of the book or in an appendix

---

Exercise 14   ## Preview the Parts of a Textbook

Preview this text, *Joining a Community of Readers,* and answer the following questions about it.

1. Who are the authors of this book?

_____

2. When was the second edition of this book published?

_____

3. In which chapters do you learn how to identify main ideas?

_____

4. Where do you find out what you will be working on in each chapter?

_____

5. In which chapter will you be reading about video games?

_____

6. Where will you find instructions on how to write a summary?

_____

7. Where in this book can you find exercises on vocabulary?

_____

8. Which chapter looks most interesting to you?

_____

Using Previous Knowledge

As you prepare to read, think about what you already know about a topic. In your preview you will often recognize information about which you have **previous knowledge**—from your experience and prior learning. For example, in previewing Reading 3, "Self-Actualized People," you should have considered what you already know about self-esteem. If you are reading a chapter in a health text about nutrition, you probably already know many things, like fresh vegetables and fruit are healthy parts of a diet, and french fries and candy are not. Recognizing what you already know will make it easier to understand the new material and to see how it relates to the skills and information you already have. When you preview, always consider how this new material fits in with what you already know.

previous knowledge What you already know about a topic from your experience and prior learning

Asking Questions and Predicting

The last thing you need to do to prepare to read is to ask yourself questions about what you are going to read, questions you think the reading will answer. In this part of the reading process you are **predicting** what you will learn. By predicting, you are preparing to be actively involved as you read.

Use the framework you look at in your preview—titles, headings, boldface print, etc.—to predict what you will learn in the reading. Turn these predictions into questions. Then answer the questions as you read. Answering these **reader's questions** will make sure you are actively engaged when you read.

For example, as you previewed Reading 3, "Self-Actualized People," the first thing you saw was the title. From the title you might form the question, "What are self-actualized people?" From the introduction, you

predict To express what you think will be in the reading

reader's questions Questions you ask to prepare yourself to read

might form the question, "Who is Maslow?" From Figure 1.1, you might form the questions, "What are the parts of Maslow's pyramid? How does it illustrate being self-actualized? What are the main characteristics of self-actualized people? How can people become self-actualized? Why is it important to be self-actualized?"

journalist's questions
Questions that begin with "who," "what," "when," "where," "why," or "how."

Notice how many of these questions begin with *who, what, when, where, why,* or *how.* These are the **journalist's questions.** They are the key questions a reporter needs to answer to write a story. They will help you form your reader's questions, too.

Exercise 15

Ask Reader's Questions

Preview the following excerpt. Read the first sentence or two and the *italicized* words. Then write three reader's questions you predict the excerpt will answer.

1. _____

2. _____

3. _____

Since reading of any sort is an activity, all reading must to some degree be *active.* Completely passive reading is impossible; we cannot read with our eyes immobilized and our minds asleep. Hence, when we contrast active with passive reading, our purpose is, first, to call attention to the fact that reading can be *more* or *less* active, and the second, to point out that the *more active* the reading the *better.* One reader is better than another in proportion as he is capable of a greater range of activity in reading and exerts more effort. He is better if he demands more of himself and of the text before him. (Adler and Van Doren, *How to Read a Book*)

You may have written questions similar to these:

1. *What is active reading?* _____

2. *How can reading be more or less active?* _____

3. *Why is more active reading better?* _____

Among the possible sources for your "reader's questions" are the following:

- **Preview**—When you do your quick preview of a passage, you will find that you might want to formulate questions based on the titles or the words that are highlighted in some way. (In the excerpt in Exercise 15, important words are italicized.)

- **Your experience and previous knowledge**—Think about your own experience and what you already know about the topics to form questions about what you read.
- **Instructor's directions**—Listen carefully. Very often the instructor will make suggestions for reader's questions.
- **Reading introductions**—Many textbooks, including *Joining a Community of Readers,* provide readings from a variety of sources, and usually the authors write an introduction to help you get started thinking about the content of a reading before you begin. This is an excellent place to think about reader's questions.
- **Course objectives**—Keep in mind your purpose in studying for this course. Reread your syllabus from time to time to be sure you're focusing on the right things.
- **Study guides**—Often your instructor or the text itself will provide study guides for the material. Keep these in mind when you form your reader's questions.
- **Questions in the book**—Some textbooks now provide reader's questions or discussion questions at the beginning of a section. They often include questions at the end of a section as well. You can use these questions as your reader's questions.

Whatever the source, raising questions as you prepare to read is an important habit to acquire in mastering the reading process. At first you will need to actually write out reader's questions. Eventually, you will be in the habit of forming such questions in your mind every time you begin to read something new, and you may not need to write them out.

Exercise 16

Preview a Reading

Preview Reading 4, "Some Reflections on Reading" by Daniel R. Walther (on page 32). List the information you noticed in your preview:

Title: _____

From the first paragraph: _____

Heading: _____

Subheadings: 1. _____

　　　　　　　2. _____

　　　　　　　3. _____

　　　　　　　4. _____

Italicized quote in the margin: _____

| Exercise 17 | **Ask Reader's Questions** |

What reader's questions can you ask about the information you recorded in Exercise 16 from your preview of Reading 4? Ask a question for each of the items identified in your preview. The first two have been done for you.

Item from Preview	*Reader's Question*
Title	1. *What are reflections? What are the author's ideas about reading?*
From the first paragraph	2. *What does the author mean by reading process?*
Heading	3. _____
Subheadings	4a. _____
	4b. _____
	4c. _____
	4d. _____
Quotation in a box margin	5. _____

READING 4

Some Reflections on Reading   Daniel R. Walther

The following reading is from Toolkit for College Success, *Walther's widely recognized text written to help students develop the skills and habits they need to be successful in college. While you read, think about the questions that you asked in Exercise 17.*

1   This chapter does not presume to teach you how to read. You already know how to do that. But most students have never approached the process of reading from the perspective of understanding what happens when reading takes place and what practices might be useful to make reading textbook

assignments an easier and more fruitful activity. That's what this chapter is all about.

2   In this theory section, our concern is to develop a better grasp of the process of reading. We can begin by focusing on some new perspectives on the reading process.

Reading Principles

We Become Better Readers by Reading

3   Many people are under the impression that reading improvement comes from learning "tricks" or mastering some mechanical gimmicks that will magically improve reading speed and comprehension. However, most reading professionals agree that we learn to read better simply as a result of reading widely. So much of reading depends on our "prior knowledge"—that information that we carry inside our head when we open the page and begin reading. Many learning theorists maintain that we remember new information only if we relate it to knowledge we already hold. There is no greater guarantee of a person's reading efficiency than extensive experience with words on the printed page. You can make slow but steady progress as a reader simply by reading more extensively to increase your base of knowledge.

extensive A lot

More Than Anything Else, Reading Is a Process of Predicting

4   If you were to pick up a book, turn to the first page, and read the line, "Once upon a time, in a magical land and a magical time . . ." your mind automatically begins to make predictions: "This is a fairy tale or fable of some kind . . . some of the characters will be 'bad' and others will be 'good.' There will probably be a happy ending, and the story will teach a simple little lesson. . . ." and so on. As we actively read, our mind is always racing ahead of where our eyes are on the page, wondering, speculating, predicting, and then eventually either confirming those predictions or correcting those predictions that were not accurate. (In understanding that reading is largely a process of predicting, you are well under way to learning how to improve your comprehension and reading rate in text reading assignments. . . .)

confirming
Agreeing with

Reading Is an Interactive Process, Not a Passive One

5   Many students are under the impression that reading is a "laid-back" activity—that the mind is some sort of sponge that soaks up meaning as the eyes move across the page. Effective readers are mentally involved—questioning, probing, analyzing, disagreeing, doubting, criticizing, or in some other way *reacting* to the words on the page.

interactive
Involving two-way
communication

6   Because textbook reading is an interactive process, we must treat it differently from the reading we do for leisure or entertainment. You may be

able to take a spellbinding novel to your bed, tuck a comfortable pillow under your head, and spend an hour or more reading. You may even have a radio going in the background and still stay focused on your book. Using the same strategy with your chemistry textbook, however, can lead to disaster. You may find that you can read your textbooks much more successfully if you put yourself in a different environment. Go to the library, the kitchen table, or your desk. Read sitting straight up and in a well-lighted area. Choose an environment with a minimum of distractions. You may see a marked improvement in your reading efficiency if you treat reading as the challenging mental activity it is and put yourself in an environment and a posture that will better support it.

> *Reading is a means of thinking with another person's mind: it forces you to stretch your own.*
>
> —Charles Scribner Jr.

Comprehension Improves at a Rate Slightly Above Our Habitual, Comfortable Rate

7   As we fail to do with so many other mental activities, we typically do not work up to our mental potential when we read. More often than not, we lapse into a nice comfortable rate—one that barely keeps the mind busy and that allows us to be distracted by our surroundings or other pressing thoughts unrelated to the task of reading. Many students have been led to believe that they will read better if they just slow down, but that advice is as valid as saying that they will "drive better" if they slow down to forty-five miles per hour on an interstate highway. The slow driver is prone to being distracted by the scenery, may become drowsy from the slower pace, or perhaps will attend to other, more interesting, pursuits, such as adjusting the graphics equalizer on the car stereo system. Driving thus becomes only one of the activities competing for the driver's attention.

8   You will probably do a better job of reading if you press yourself to read 10 percent or so above your typical rate, just enough to require your mind to stay alert and focused. (You are probably capable of reading 30 or 40 percent faster with some effort, but the point is not to make reading a frenzied activity—just a focused one.)

WALTHER, *Toolkit for College Success*

| **Exercise 18** | ## Work with Reader's Questions: Collaborative Activity |

Compare your reader's questions with the questions that other members of class (or your class group) wrote. Of all the questions, pick the ones that you think were the best predictors of what Reading 4 covered. Then answer the reader's questions that your group chose.

| Exercise 19 | Check Your Understanding |

Choose the best answers to the following multiple-choice questions based on Reading 4.

1. Which of the following will help people improve their reading?
   a. learning tricks
   b. mastering mechanical gimmicks
   c. reading a lot

2. What is "prior knowledge"?
   a. information that we carry inside our head
   b. information that has priority
   c. knowledge in general

3. How can more reading make us better readers?
   a. More reading makes us not need to improve our reading skills.
   b. More reading makes reading more interesting.
   c. More reading gives us more experience with words and increases our base of knowledge.

4. Reading is primarily a process of "actively"
   a. predicting.
   b. focusing.
   c. remembering.

5. What is meant when the author says that reading is an "interactive process"?
   a. Information is gained in reading by means of a one-way process.
   b. Reading involves a reaction from the reader.
   c. Readers passively receive information from the writer.

6. You may see a great deal of improvement in your reading efficiency if you
   a. put yourself in an environment where you can be alert.
   b. read while relaxing in bed.
   c. have the radio playing in the background.

7. Reading slowly
   a. helps you understand better.
   b. is likely to allow you to be distracted.
   c. will make you a more active reader.

8. You will probably do a better job of reading if you
   a. read more slowly.
   b. eat while you read.
   c. try to press yourself to read a little faster.

Exercise 20

Check Your Reader's Questions

Write brief answers to the following questions about the process you followed in Reading 4.

1. Did answering your own reader's questions help you answer the questions in Exercise 19? Why or why not?

   _____

   _____

2. How much of the content of the reading did you "predict" with your reader's questions? Which of your questions were answered? Which were not?

   _____

   _____

3. How did your focus on preview items help you understand the framework of the reading?

   _____

   _____

Choosing a Reading Strategy

Once you have previewed and asked reader's questions, you are ready to choose a strategy for reading. This is the final step before actually reading.

purpose Your reason for reading (for fun, to study for a test, to use the information at work)

Purpose   Ask yourself, what is your **purpose** in reading this material? Do you just need a general understanding of the information? You might read the morning newspaper or a magazine article for a general understanding of current events; however, for college course work your purpose is often much more demanding. For example, if you are assigned a chapter in a health text, you may need to be prepared for a quiz on the content at the next class meeting. Or perhaps you are planning to use this information for a job in the future, such as working as a personal trainer in a gym. In both cases, your purpose for reading is much more serious than when you are reading for general understanding, and your reading strategy should reflect this. Plan to devote plenty of time to the reading assignment, and be sure you can concentrate on completing the task.

Difficulty Level   A second consideration in determining your reading strategy is to ask yourself, what is the level of difficulty? Will the material take a lot of time and effort to understand? Plan for more time than you think you will need. How much do you already know about this topic? If the material is familiar to you or looks fairly easy, you can plan to read it faster and a little less carefully. The amount of time it takes you to complete a reading task will vary from assignment to assignment, and it certainly varies from student to student. Schedule your time carefully. Monitor the time it takes to complete assignments. As your reading and study skills improve, your use of time should become more efficient.

2. Reading Actively

Active reading is involved reading. As you've already learned in doing the readings and exercises in this chapter, to succeed as a reader you must be alert and actively involved in every part of the reading process. You must

1. prepare to read.
2. check yourself as you read to be sure you are understanding everything.
3. make connections to what you already know.
4. think about what you know and what new information you are getting from the reading.

As Charles Scribner, Jr., says, "Reading is a means of thinking with another person's mind: it forces you to stretch your own." This openness to new ideas, "stretching your mind," is part of what makes active reading happen.

Making Connections

critical reader A reader who makes connections and who questions whether or not to agree with the reading

connect Put together what you know with what the writer is saying

Reading is a way to receive the ideas of others, to learn what other people want us to learn. But you must also be a **critical reader.** Think about what you read, and **connect** it to what you already know. The new information you are acquiring may or may not fit with information you have learned or experiences you have had in the past. Making connections, using all the information available to you, is part of the process of being a critical reader.

Thinking Critically

As you think about new information in light of what you know, *question* whether you will accept all of what you are reading. In other words, ask yourself if you agree with everything the writer says. Do you agree with part of what she says? Do you think the opposite is true? Do you question her facts? Are some facts missing? Are her points reasonable?

For example, if you are reading an article in which a smoker argues that he smokes because he enjoys it and he doesn't care about the future consequences, you already know what the consequences of smoking are (lung cancer, emphysema, constant cough, etc.). As an active reader, you make connections between what the writer is saying and what you know. You think about what you read and come to your own conclusions about the topic.

LANGUAGE TIP

Questions and Active Reading

Questions are a critical part of the reading process. Good readers, active readers, ask themselves questions as they read, and they answer their questions continuously. Here is a list of types of questions, with examples, to ask yourself during the reading process.

   Preparing-to-read questions:
   - What do I think this passage will be about?
   - What do I already know about this topic?
   - What questions do I hope or expect will be answered?

   Checking-comprehension questions:
   - Do I understand?
   - Were my reader's questions answered?

   Making-connections questions:
   - How does this fit in with what I already know?
   - What do I know that I could add this information to?

   Critical-thinking questions
   - Do I agree with everything I'm reading? If not, what part do I agree with?
   - What part don't I agree with?

Exercise 21

Make Connections

Read the following excerpt about active reading, and answer the questions that follow.

Reading and listening are thought of as *receiving* communication from someone who is actively engaged in *giving* or *sending* it. The mistake here is to suppose that receiving communication is like receiving a blow or a legacy or a judgment from the court. On the contrary, the reader or listener is much more like the catcher in a game of baseball.

   Catching the ball is just as much an activity as pitching or hitting it. The pitcher or batter is the *sender* in the sense that his activity initiates the motion of the ball. The catcher or fielder is the *receiver* in the sense that his activity terminates it. Both are active, though the activities are different. If anything is passive, it is the ball. It is the inert thing that is put in motion or stopped, whereas the players are active, moving to pitch, hit, or catch. . . . The art of catching is the skill of catching every kind of pitch—fast balls and curves, changeups and knucklers. Similarly, the art of reading is the skill of catching every sort of communication as well as possible. (Adler and Van Doren, *How to Read a Book*)

1. Have you ever played catcher on a softball team? Or simply played catch? Explain your experience.

   _____

   _____

2. When you read, do you feel that you are actively receiving the message that the writer is sending? Explain.

   _____

   _____

3. Do you agree with the writer that reading is very much like catching a ball? Why or why not?

   _____

   _____

4. To what other actions do you think active reading could be compared?

   _____

   _____

Exercise 22

Create Questions for Active Reading

Choose one reading from the Additional Readings at the back of the book, pages 471–512. Prepare to read it, and fill in the first set of blanks (Question 1) that follows. Then read it, and fill in the additional blanks for Questions 2–5.

1. Preparing-to-read questions:

   a. _____

   b. _____

   c. _____

2. Checking-comprehension questions:

    a. _____

    b. _____

    c. _____

3. Making-connections questions:

    a. _____

    b. _____

    c. _____

4. Critical-thinking questions:

    a. _____

    b. _____

    c. _____

5. In what way did asking questions improve your understanding and enjoyment of the reading? Did active reading help you? Explain how.

_____

_____

_____

3. Organizing To Learn

After you have completed the first two steps in the PRO reading process—preparing to read and reading actively—you are ready to organize what you've read in order to learn it. Organizing what you've read accomplishes two things:

■ It helps you to understand better what you've read.
■ It helps you to remember what you've read for future tests or job requirements.

There are a number of ways to select and use—that is, to organize—reading material. They include answering questions, marking the text, charting, outlining, mapping, summarizing, and others. (You will learn more about these strategies in later chapters.) Then, recite, or test yourself on what you have learned. Review periodically to make sure you are prepared for the test.

In organizing to learn, consider which ways you learn best. What is your preferred learning style? Do you learn best when you hear information? You might try recording the key points you need to memorize and listening to them. Are you a very social person? Take time to learn and review in study groups. Are you primarily a visual learner? Making a chart, map, or some kind of visual aid may be very useful to you. Does motion help your learning process? Try reviewing math formulas as you jog around the track.

| Exercise 23 | ## Organize to Learn |

How do you learn best? By hearing? By reading? By working with other people? By looking at something? Or by something else? Explain your answer. Then list three concrete ways you can study that will help you learn.

_____

_____

a. _____

b. _____

c. _____

| Exercise 24 | ## Prepare to Read |

Preview Reading 5, "Effective Speaking and Listening," by Curtis O. Byer and Louis Shainberg (on page 42). Then do the following preparing-to-read activities.

1. List three things you notice in your preview that help you to understand the overall ideas of the reading.

   a. _____

   b. _____

   c. _____

2. While you are previewing, consider the level of difficulty of this reading. Is the information familiar to you or unfamiliar?

   _____

   _____

3. Write two reader's questions that you think will be answered in the reading.

   a. _____

   b. _____

Effective Speaking and Listening

Curtis O. Byer and Louis Shainberg

*The following reading from a college health textbook presents some
important pointers for learning how to speak and listen effectively—
important skills for success in college and for life. As you read, think
about which of the suggested activities you are already good at as a
speaker and listener. Which ones do you need to work on? In this
textbook you will notice that every effort has been made to assist
the reader. In addition to using titles, lists, and italics, the authors
even ask questions in the middle of the chapters. Don't skip over
these questions. Use them to test yourself on how well you are
understanding and remembering what you are reading.*

Effective Speaking

1   Do you ever feel that people don't seem to understand what you are saying
or, worse still, just aren't interested in what you have to say? Being an interesting, effective speaker is a characteristic that anyone can develop and one
that contributes greatly to the quality of your relationships.

2   For starters, you need to *have something interesting to say.* This means
having familiarity with a broad range of topics and being sensitive to the interests of the listener.

3   Even though the pressures of school or work may dictate where much
of your attention is directed, you need to reserve time to broaden your interests and expand your awareness of a variety of subjects. If you are highly
knowledgeable about your major field, but have little awareness of other
subjects, there will be relatively few people who find you a stimulating conversational partner.

4   If you find yourself being misunderstood, you may need to *improve
the exactness of your communication.* Vocabulary building may be necessary. Communication is often handicapped by a lack of the precise word
to express a particular idea or feeling. It can be very frustrating to know
what you want to say, but to lack the words that would convey that
thought. Many colleges offer vocabulary-building courses. Books, tapes,
computer programs, and other media are also available to help expand
your vocabulary.

convey To express

5   When communicating with someone from another ethnic group, remember that you may use a word or phrase to convey a particular meaning
but it may only have that meaning to someone with your own background.
Even people from different regions of the United States may interpret the
same phrase differently.

6   In health-related communication, vocabulary is especially important. Many problems arise in communication between health care providers and their clients when the clients are unable to describe symptoms or concerns adequately or the providers speak above or below the ability of the client to comprehend.

Example: "Some people describe any pain between their neck and their crotch as a "stomachache."

terminology
Specialized vocabulary

7   If this book seems to use a lot of terminology, it's because precise communication does require using the proper term. Too often, health-related communication suffers from inadequate vocabulary. One unfortunate result of inadequate vocabulary is that sometimes, not knowing which word to use, we simply fail to communicate at all.

8   To ensure the clarity of your communication, *think through what you intend to say before you say it.* Even though this may cause a slight pause in the flow of the conversation, it reduces the risk of your being misinterpreted. To further reduce this risk, when you have something important to say, repeat it several times, phrasing it in different ways. Of course, don't go overboard with repetition. It can get annoying!

feedback
Response

9   *Be very alert to the verbal and nonverbal feedback* you get from your listener and use this feedback to guide your communication. For example, you may sense the need to speak more slowly or to rephrase your message.

Checkpoint

1. What are four guidelines for effective speaking?
2. Do you feel that you have an adequate vocabulary for most communication situations?
3. What do you usually do when someone seems not to understand what you are saying?

Effective Listening

10 An effective listener is just as actively involved in communication as the speaker. In fact, effective listening requires greater effort and concentration than speaking. Your attention must remain focused on the speaker and not wander. Any momentary inattention can cause you to miss the meaning of what is being said.

11 In any important discussion, it is essential to minimize distractions so that your full attention can be focused on the speaker. Turn off the TV or stereo; close the door; suggest moving to a less distracting location; ask the other person to speak louder. If you can't eliminate distractions, at least make every effort to concentrate on the discussion.

12   Often the speaker's nonverbal communication reveals more than his or her actual words. Be very alert to posture, gestures, facial expressions, eye movements, and the tone and inflection in the speaker's voice.

13   Listeners often misinterpret what they hear. For instance, people sometimes interpret messages as being hostile or critical when they were not intended that way. Major misunderstandings can develop when you fail to ask for clarification of some vague or seemingly hurtful statement. If you have any doubt about the meaning of what you have just been told, immediately ask for clarification.

hostile Angry

14   When someone makes a statement that causes you to feel hurt, angry, or defensive, it is often productive to reveal your feelings, allowing the misunderstanding or conflict to be worked out *at that time.* Otherwise, hostility builds up and will be expressed eventually, often in a nonproductive manner, which can severely damage or even destroy a relationship.

15   In summary, Eugene Raudsepp has identified seven ways to improve your listening abilities.

1. *Take time to listen.* Sometimes people aren't sure just what they need to say or how best to express their message. They think as they speak and may modify their message as they go. Though you may wish they would hurry up and get to the point, effective listening requires you patiently to allow the speaker to finish his or her message, and reassure him or her on that point.

   Example: "Take your time. I'm listening to you. There's no rush."

2. *Don't interrupt.* Even though you think you know what the speaker is leading up to and you are impatient for him or her to make a point, resist the temptation to interrupt and finish sentences. Doing so implies a sense of superiority and may break down communication. Interruptions often confuse the speaker, and there is a possibility that your assumptions may be wrong.

   Example: "I know what you are going to say and I think you're wrong. You think that. . . ."

   If you have the habit of interrupting, as many of us do, Raudsepp suggests breaking that habit by making yourself apologize every time you interrupt. After a few apologies, you'll think twice before interrupting someone.

   Example: "Excuse me for interrupting you. It's a habit I'm trying to break, so let me know whenever I do it."

3. *Teach yourself to concentrate.* One reason we sometimes have trouble concentrating on a speaker is that we can think much faster than a person can speak. We get bored and begin to think about something else. To remain focused on the speaker, keep analyzing what he or she is saying.

4. *Disregard speech mannerisms.* Don't focus on a person's accent, speech impediment, or delivery style; you will lose track of his or her message.

5. *Suspend judgment.* We tend to listen to the ideas we want to hear and to shut out others. We unconsciously do this because ideas that conflict with our own are threatening. But by listening to what others have to say, we can come to understand our own line of reasoning better and may even change our mind.

6. *Listen between the lines.* Much of the important content in the messages we receive is unstated or only indirectly implied. Focusing only on the message actually verbalized leads us to miss most, if not all, of the true message. Be sensitive to what the speaker is feeling and the true message may become evident.

   Example: Lori says, "I've heard that that's a good place to get a sandwich." Lori means, "I'm hungry!"

7. *Listen with your eyes.* Pay attention to the speaker's nonverbal signals. Rarely can the full message be gained from words alone.

   Example: "How are you feeling today?" "I'm fine." "Well, the sad look on your face and the way you're wringing your hands tells me that something is bothering you. Would you like to talk about it?"

Checkpoint

1. List seven suggestions for improving listening abilities.
2. In addition to being rude, what implications does interrupting a speaker carry?

BYER AND SHAINBERG, *Living Well, Health in Your Hands*

Exercise 25   ## Check Your Preparation

Look back to your answers in Exercise 24. Then write brief answers to the following questions. They will help you know how well you prepared to read.

1. Were your reader's questions answered? Write the answers.

   a. _____

   b. _____

2. Was the passage as easy, or as difficult, as you predicted? Explain why.

_____

_____

_____

_____

Exercise 26 ## Check Your Understanding

Choose the best answers to the following multiple-choice questions about Reading 5.

1. Which of the following is *not* a way to become a more effective speaker?
   a. Have something interesting to say.
   b. Think about what you are going to say before you speak.
   c. Ignore the audience's responses so that you aren't distracted.

2. What can you do to improve the exactness of your communication?
   a. Speak in simpler words.
   b. Build your vocabulary.
   c. Ignore technical vocabulary for specialized fields.

3. According to the authors, which requires greater effort and attention?
   a. speaking
   b. listening
   c. both require equal effort and attention

4. What can you do to listen effectively?
   a. Concentrate and listen patiently.
   b. Think about how you are going to respond as you listen.
   c. Interrupt the speaker frequently for clarification.

5. Which of the following is a way to stay focused when you are listening?
   a. Pay special attention to the speaker's mannerisms and style.
   b. Decide from the beginning whether you agree or disagree with his major points.
   c. Keep analyzing what she is saying.

6. What should a listener notice about nonverbal communication?
   a. posture, gestures, facial expressions, eye movements, tone of voice
   b. speaker's clothing and hairstyle
   c. accuracy of expression, correctness of the information

7. What should a listener do if the speaker says something that hurts his or her feelings?
   a. Try to ignore it.
   b. Don't show hostility.
   c. Try to work the conflict out at that time.

8. Why, according to the author, should you "listen with your eyes"?
   a. because the speaker can see how you feel
   b. because you can understand the speaker better if you look at him or her
   c. because it is more polite to keep your eyes on the speaker

| Exercise 27 |

Make Connections: Collaborative Activity

Write brief answers to the following questions about Reading 5. Share your answers with your class group.

1. Do you have any friends you really like to talk to? What kind of listeners are they? List words that describe how they listen to you.

   _____

   _____

   _____

   _____

2. How much time a day do you spend listening? How much time a day do you spend speaking? Compare the two.

   _____

   _____

   _____

   _____

3. What kind of a listener are you? List what you do well as a listener and what you do poorly:

What I Do Well as a Listener	*What I Do Poorly as a Listener*
1. _____	1. _____
_____	_____
2. _____	2. _____
_____	_____

3. _____   3. _____

_____   _____

4. _____   4. _____

_____   _____

5. _____   5. _____

_____   _____

| Exercise 28 | ## Organize to Learn

Use information from Reading 5 to finish filling in the following graphic organizer. A few answers have been filled in for you.

Tips for Effective Speaking

1. *Have something interesting to say.* _____

2. _____

3. _____

4. *Be alert to verbal and nonverbal feedback.* _____

Tips for Effective Listening

1. *Take time to listen.* _____

2. *Don't interrupt.* _____

3. _____

4. _____

5. _____

6. _____

7. _____

Chapter Review

To aid your review of the reading skills in Chapter 1, study the Put It Together chart.

Put It Together: *The PRO Reading Process*	
P = Prepare to Read (see pages 21–37)	Concentrate Preview Use previous knowledge Ask questions Choose a strategy
R = Read Actively (see pages 37–40)	Check on your prereading questions Check your understanding Make connections to what you already know Think critically about the new information
O = Organize What You've Read **(see pages 40–41)**	Answer questions Mark the text Make charts Outline Map Summarize Test yourself

To reinforce your learning before taking the Mastery Tests (beginning on p. 52), complete as many of the following activities as your instructor assigns.

Reviewing Skills

Answer the following skills review questions individually or in a group.

1. In the chart, circle all the steps in the reading process that you already use. Which steps do you need to add to improve your reading process? Explain briefly how you will use the steps of the reading process to complete your reading assignments.

_____

_____

_____

_____

2. Are there some additional steps you might follow at all points of the process? Explain.

_____

_____

_____

_____

_____

_____

_____

Writing

Choose one of the following topics to write about. Your instructor will tell you how much to write, and how to organize your writing.

1. Using the goals you have identified in Exercise 2, on page 5, write a paragraph or a short essay explaining your goals and how, step by step, you plan to accomplish them.

2. Describe yourself ten years from now. What goals have you accomplished? Explain in a paragraph or short essay what steps you took to achieve your goals.

Collaborating

Share with your class group your goals for this semester. Discuss in a group what steps each of you can take to achieve your goals. How can you support each other in meeting your goals for this class?

Extending Your Thinking

1. Choose a textbook from any of your other college courses and preview it. Identify the various features of the book. Does it have any unique parts? What parts, as a student, will you find most helpful in this text?

_____

_____

2. List some of the campus resources available to you, such as the library, tutorial center, counseling office, etc. Investigate two of them and report back to the class. Include in your report the following:

Hours of operation: _____

Location: _____

Services offered: _____

Visiting the Web

The following Web sites provide more information on study skills, time management, and setting goals.

1. *Study Skills Resources*

http://studyweb.chemek.cc.or.us/
Chemeketa Community College in Salem, Oregon, maintains a Web site that provides information on how to prepare and set goals and a large variety of study skills. It provides links to other Web sites with similar information.

2. *Counseling and Development Center*

http://www.yorku.ca/cdc/lsp/lsphome.html
York University in Toronto, Canada, developed this Web site for student use. It has a section that summarizes time management principles and other information for student success. It has a list of links to other schools such as Time Management Techniques from the University of North Carolina at Chapel Hill, Learning Skills Tips from the University of California at Berkeley, and the Learning Skills Center at the University of Texas at Austin.

3. *Management Assistance Program for Nonprofits*

http://www.mapnp.org/library/prsn_dev/set_goal.htm
This Web site from St. Paul, Minnesota, was designed for nonprofit institutions. It has tips on topics such as setting personal goals. It has a long list of related library links on topics such as remembering, time management, learning styles, and student skills. It also links to on-line discussion groups.

Reading Road Trip has sections on time management, concentration, and memorization.

Name _____ Date _____

Preparing to Read "Latinas: Journeys of Achievement and Vision"

Write short answers to the following questions.

1. Who were your role models as a young child?

   _____

   _____

2. Are you aware of people who faced challenges similar to yours in life and have succeeded? Who are they, and what did they do?

   _____

   _____

3. From your preview of the reading, ask two reader's questions that you think will be answered.

   a. _____

   b. _____

Latinas: Journeys of Achievement and Vision
Nicholasa Mohr

Nicholasa Mohr grew up in the barrio, in Spanish Harlem, where she struggled to find role models to foster her self-esteem and pride in her Latino heritage. She writes about her own life as a "female and Puerto Rican in New York City," and goes on to praise the many "talented Latinas" whose stories are available today to inspire us. Mohr is now herself an award-winning writer and artist; she has published a number of outstanding works for children and adults, including Nilda, El Bronx Remembered, In Nueva York, *and* Rituals of Survival: A Woman's Portfolio.

Searching for Role Models

1　There were no positive role models for me—out there in the dominant society—when I was growing up. When I looked and searched for successful Latinas to emulate, my efforts were futile. As a Puerto Rican and a female of color, my legacy was one of either a negative image or was invisible. . . .

emulate Model after, imitate

2　Yet I knew even at an early age that this typecasting was not the truth: Where were the valiant women I knew? Where were my mother, my aunts, and all the courageous females who had been forced to leave Puerto Rico out of necessity, arriving in the United States by themselves for the most part, bringing children to a cold and <u>hostile</u> environment? They had come ill-equipped, with limited education and few survival skills, and no knowledge of English. But they all were determined to give their children a better life—a future. This is where I came from and it was these women who became my heroes.

Omitted
(words take out)

3   Many . . . Latinas . . . are the daughters of these <u>undaunted</u> women, descendants of strong females who passed on the survival techniques they learned and <u>bestowed</u> upon us the strength and determination that pressed the next generation to continue to succeed. . . .

Defying Stereotypes

surmount
Overcome

exclude   Leave out

4   [Latina] women have <u>excelled</u>—in the disciplines of science, law, government, education, social activism, visual arts, music, fashion, literature, sports, media, and entertainment. Their backgrounds vary: some have come from privileged families while many have had to surmount modest beginnings and sometimes, extreme poverty. But these talented individuals share a common bond. They have triumphed over society's bias to exclude them by succeeding brilliantly in their professions and thus, have defied the stereotypes.

Women of Achievement

One person

5   Carmen Zapata, actress, producer, and community activist, born in New York City to a Mexican father and an Argentine mother, first used the name Marge Cameron in a singing and comedy act she created. "At one time it was not 'in' to be Hispanic. I had a hard time getting club owners to hire me unless I shook my fanny and played the <u>maracas</u>." Eventually her film roles caused the producers to claim that Marge Cameron did not look 'All-American.' Zapata began using her real name. However, she was then stereotyped in roles of either a maid or a mother. Despite a successful career that earned her money, Zapata decided to delve further into her Latino roots. Today she is the president and managing producer of the Bilingual Foundation of the Arts, a successful, Los Angeles-based theatrical organization, which she co-founded. She states that the Foundation's goal is to "have everyone learn about, share and become part of our literature and tradition."

6   Astronaut Ellen Ochoa, born in California and of Mexican descent, understands her success may encourage young girls to achieve their goals because she is similar to them.

7   Antonia Novello, born in Puerto Rico, was both the first woman and first Hispanic to hold the position of Surgeon General of the United States. Novello claims she is for the people who deserve help, "I think that as a woman, as a Hispanic, as a member of a minority . . . I bring a lot of sensitivity to the job." . . .

8   In 1992 three Latinas were elected to the U.S. Congress: Lucille Roybal-Allard, Democrat, is the first woman of Mexican-American ancestry; Ileana Ros-Lehtinen, Republican, is the first Cuban-born woman; and Nydia Margarita Velazquez, Democrat, is the first Puerto Rican woman. Velazquez is dedicated to showing that Hispanic women can serve proudly in the political arena, fighting the notion that, "we are the ones who go out and collect signatures but when it comes to the final process, we were not good enough to run for office."

9   Rosie Perez, actress, dancer, and choreographer, was born in Brooklyn and grew up watching her Puerto Rican parents dance *salsa* on the weekends and holidays. Singer Linda Ronstadt reveals that "when we were little, we spoke Spanish at home, but the schools pounded it out of us pretty early." Ronstadt celebrated her paternal Mexican heritage with a successful album of *mariachi* songs that her father used to sing.

10   Nely Galán, television anchor and producer, born in Cuba, came here when she was an infant. As a popular television personality, Galán is determined to help shape the future of television produced for the U.S.-born Hispanics and warns that, "You damage a whole group of people because they're not seen anywhere, and that reflects badly on their self-esteem."

11   Pat Mora, poet and educator, born in El Paso, Texas, is well aware of the influence she has on minority youths and minority issues, "I write to try to correct these images of worth." Mora states her pride in being a Hispanic writer.

MOHR, *Latinas: Journeys of Achievement and Vision*

Write brief answers to the following questions about the reading.

4. Did you think about experiences with role models in your life as you read Mohr's essay? Did doing so help you read and think about her story? Explain.

    Yes, I have one of my role model, that is my mom because she is good in a lot of thing that I learn from her.

5. Were your reader's questions answered? Explain.

    Yes, because everybody have a different kind of difficulty, and people will try hard to make it better like Mohr.

Name _____ Date _____

Choose the best answers to the following multiple-choice questions.

6. When Mohr was growing up, she felt "the dominant society"
   a. included just a few Latinas she could choose as a model.
   b. presented no positive role models for her to follow.
   c. valued females of color positively.

7. In paragraph 2, the words "this typecasting" refers to
   a. her mother and aunts.
   b. the negative image society held about Puerto Rican and other women of color.
   c. successful Latinas for all young women to emulate.

8. The author chose her mother, aunts, and other women immigrants from Puerto Rico as her role models because
   a. they had been forced to leave Puerto Rico out of necessity.
   b. they came to America with limited education and skills.
   c. they were determined to give their children a better future.

9. According to Mohr, the daughters of Latina immigrants have succeeded because
   a. these brave women passed their strength and determination on to their daughters.
   b. society changed its stereotypes of women.
   c. some of them came from privileged families with a rich background.

10. Mohr writes that many Latina women "have defied the stereotypes" (par. 4). By this she means
    a. they have done what was expected of them.
    b. they have become good mothers and wives.
    c. they have accomplished things that they were not expected to accomplish as Latinas.

11. Carmen Zapata used the name Marge Cameron during part of her career because
    a. it was not "in" to be Hispanic.
    b. she was not proud of her background.
    c. she could have access to more roles as a mother or a maid.

12. Mohr features Latina success models for all of the following occupations *except:*
    a. astronaut.
    b. nurse.
    c. choreographer.

13. This Latina U.S. Congresswoman is dedicated to showing everyone that Hispanic women can serve proudly in politics:
    a. Rosie Perez
    b. Antonia Novello.
    c. Nydia Margarita Velazquez.

14. The first woman and first Hispanic to hold the position of Surgeon General thinks
    a. she is the person with the best education for the job.
    b. she is the person who speaks Spanish the best who applied for the job.
    c. she is more sensitive to more people because of her background.

15. Rosie Perez, Linda Ronstadt, Nely Galán, and Pat Mora are all mentioned because
    a. they are Latinas who are proud of their heritage.
    b. they are Latinas who have been successful as entertainers or writers.
    c. they are famous throughout the United States and the world.

16. Overall, we can conclude that Mohr feels that Hispanic women in our society
    a. are now treated equally.
    b. have made progress, but still must struggle for recognition and equal opportunity.
    c. are still at the same status as when she was growing up.

Write short answers to the following questions based on your reading, your experiences, and your observations.

17. What are some of the disciplines mentioned that Latinas have excelled in?

    learning law, government, science, social, art and music, fashion.

18. Name some Latina women you can think of who have been very successful and who are not mentioned in this reading.

    Carmen Zapata + Astronaut Ellen Ochoa.

19. What do you think were some of the personal characteristics that helped the women mentioned to achieve their goals?

   Lucille Roybal-Allard, Ileana Ros-Lehtinen & Nydia Margarita Valazquez.

20. Who are the role models that you might follow in achieving your goals? Briefly explain why you chose these people.

   Latina because the congress is a most power to help country run therefore I would like to be Latina model.

Name _____ Date _____

Preparing to Read "Learning to Read"

Preview this reading, and answer the following.

1. Write two reader's questions that you think will be answered.

_____

_____

Learning to Read   Malcolm X

Malcolm X was born Malcolm Little in Omaha, Nebraska. As an adult, he changed his name to Malcolm X because Little was the name his family had gotten from the slave master. When he was a young boy, his father died in an "accident," but his family believed he was murdered by white racists. When he was twenty, Malcolm was arrested for burglary and sentenced to ten years in prison. While in prison he began to learn about the Nation of Islam, a Black Muslim organization led by Elijah Muhammad. In this passage from his autobiography, he explains his struggle to become an educated person while he was in prison.

[handwritten: Excerpt part of an autobiography (Summary.)]

1   It was because of my letters that I happened to stumble upon starting to acquire some kind of a homemade education.

2   I became increasingly frustrated at not being able to express what I wanted to convey in letters that I wrote, especially those to Mr. Elijah Muhammad. In the street, I had been the most articulate hustler out there—I had commanded attention when I said something. But now, trying to write simple English, I not only wasn't articulate, I wasn't even functional. How would I sound writing in slang, the way I would *say* it, something such as, "Look, daddy, let me pull your coat about a cat, Elijah Muhammad—"

3   Many who today hear me somewhere in person, or on television, or those who read something I've said, will think I went to school far beyond the eighth grade. This impression is due entirely to my prison studies.

4   It had really begun back in the Charlestown Prison, when Bimbi first made me feel envy of his stock of knowledge. Bimbi had always taken charge of any conversation he was in, and I had tried to emulate him. But every book I picked up had few sentences which didn't contain anywhere from one to nearly all of the words that might as well have been in Chinese. When I just skipped those words, of course, I really ended up with little idea of what the book said. So I had come to the Norfolk Prison Colony still going through only book-reading motions. Pretty soon, I would have quit even these motions, unless I had received the motivation that I did.

emulate Act like him

5   I saw that the best thing I could do was get hold of a dictionary—to study, to learn some words. I was lucky enough to reason also that I should try to improve my penmanship. It was sad. I couldn't even write in a straight line. It was both ideas together that moved me to request a dictionary along with some tablets and pencils from the Norfolk Prison Colony school.

6   I spent two days just riffling uncertainly through the dictionary's pages. I'd never realized so many words existed! I didn't know *which* words I needed to learn. Finally, just to start some kind of action, I began copying.

7   In my slow, painstaking, ragged handwriting, I copied into my tablet everything printed on that first page, down to the punctuation marks.

8   I believe it took me a day. Then, aloud, I read back, to myself, everything I'd written on the tablet. Over and over, aloud, to myself, I read my own handwriting.

9   I woke up the next morning thinking about those words—immensely proud to realize that not only had I written so much at one time, but I'd written words that I never knew were in the world. Moreover, with a little effort, I also could remember what many of these words meant. I reviewed the words whose meanings I didn't remember. Funny thing, from the dictionary first page right now, that "aardvark" springs to my mind. The dictionary had a picture of it, a long-tailed, long-eared, burrowing African mammal, which lives off termites caught by sticking out its tongue as an anteater does for ants.

10   I was so fascinated that I went on—I copied the dictionary's next page. And the same experience came when I studied that. With every succeeding page, I also learned of people and places and events from history. Actually the dictionary is like a miniature encyclopedia. Finally the dictionary's A section had filled a whole tablet—and I went on into the B's. That was the way I started copying what eventually became the entire dictionary. It went a lot faster after so much practice helped me to pick up handwriting speed. Between what I wrote in my tablet, and writing letters, during the rest of my time in prison I would guess I wrote a million words.

11   I suppose it was inevitable that as my word-base broadened, I could for the first time pick up a book and read and now begin to understand what the book was saying. Anyone who has read a great deal can imagine the new world that opened. Let me tell you something: From then until I left that prison, in every free moment I had, if I was not reading in the library, I was reading on my bunk. You couldn't have gotten me out of books with a wedge. Between Mr. Muhammad's teachings, my correspondence, my visitors—usually Ella and Reginald—and my reading of books, months passed without my even thinking about being imprisoned. In fact, up to then, I never had been so truly free in my life.

12   The Norfolk Prison Colony's library was in the school building. A variety of classes was taught there by instructors who came from such places as

Harvard and Boston universities. The weekly debates between inmate teams were also held in the school building. You would be astonished to know how worked up convict debaters and audiences would get over subjects like "Should Babies Be Fed Milk?"

13   Available on the prison library's shelves were books on just about every general subject. Much of the big private collection that Parkhurst had willed to the prison was still in crates and boxes in the back of the library—thousands of old books. Some of them looked ancient: covers faded, old-time parchment-looking binding. Parkhurst, I've mentioned, seemed to have been principally interested in history and religion. He had the money and the special interest to have a lot of books that you wouldn't have in general circulation. Any college library would have been lucky to get that collection.

14   As you can imagine, especially in a prison where there was heavy emphasis on rehabilitation, an inmate was smiled upon if he demonstrated an unusually intense interest in books. There was a sizable number of well-read inmates, especially the popular debaters. Some were said by many to be practically walking encyclopedias. They were almost celebrities. No university would ask any student to devour literature as I did when this new world opened to me, of being able to read and *understand.*

15   I read more in my room than in the library itself. An inmate who was known to read a lot could check out more than the permitted maximum number of books. I preferred reading in the total isolation of my own room.

16   When I had progressed to really serious reading, every night at about ten P.M. I would be outraged with the "lights out." It always seemed to catch me right in the middle of something engrossing.

17   Fortunately, right outside my door was a corridor light that cast a glow into my room. The glow was enough to read by, once my eyes adjusted to it. So when "lights out" came, I would sit on the floor where I could continue reading in that glow.

18   At one-hour intervals the night guards paced past every room. Each time I heard the approaching footsteps, I jumped into bed and feigned sleep. And as soon as the guard passed, I got back out of bed onto the floor area of that light-glow, where I would read for another fifty-eight minutes—until the guard approached again. That went on until three or four every morning. Three or four hours of sleep a night was enough for me. Often in the years in the streets I had slept less than that.

MALCOLM X WITH HALEY, *The Autobiography of Malcolm X*

Choose the best answers to the following multiple-choice questions based on the Mastery Test reading.

2. Malcolm decided that he needed to learn how to write better because
   a. he was frustrated at not being able to express what he wanted to say in his letters.
   b. he was bored in prison.
   c. he always knew that a good education was important for success.

3. Malcolm was unsure of his writing ability, but he was not unsure of his ability to
   a. read.
   b. recite.
   c. speak.

4. When Malcolm wrote, "Bimbi had always taken charge of any conversation he was in, and I had tried to *emulate* him" (par. 4), he meant that he tried to
   a. ignore Bimbi.
   b. copy Bimbi.
   c. intimidate Bimbi.

5. Malcolm said that for him the books "might as well have been in Chinese" (par. 4) because
   a. he could read Chinese.
   b. Chinese is difficult to learn, but he thought it might be worth it.
   c. he couldn't understand the books, so they might as well have been in a foreign language.

6. Why did Malcolm decide to start copying down the words from the dictionary?
   a. He recognized there wasn't anything else to do in prison.
   b. He wanted to improve his vocabulary and penmanship.
   c. He wanted to prove to the guards that he was a model prisoner.

7. Malcolm mentions "aardvark" (par. 9) because
   a. It was an important African animal.
   b. It was a difficult word for him to learn.
   c. It is one of the words on the very first page of the dictionary.

8. Malcolm realized that reading became easier for him when
   a. he could understand more words.
   b. he was reading on his bunk.
   c. he read more slowly.

9. In saying he had "never been so truly free" in his life before, Malcolm means
   a. his mind was freed to think more broadly and he was able to express himself better because of what he learned from books.
   b. the guards gave him extra privileges.
   c. he became a "jailhouse lawyer."

10. What did Malcolm do to be able to read until late at night?
   a. He bought a small lamp for himself.
   b. He smuggled in candles.
   c. He read by the light from the corridor.

11. What did the prison authorities think about prisoners who read a lot?
   a. They were suspicious of them.
   b. They approved of them.
   c. They ridiculed them.

12. Many men begin to read and to exercise a lot when they become incarcerated. Why do you think this is so?
   a. They decide to pursue an athletic career.
   b. They hope to impress the guards.
   c. They have a lot of time on their hands.

13. Malcolm X used a lot of his time to
   a. study the dictionary.
   b. exercise all day.
   c. talk to other prisoners.

14. Malcolm says that the dictionary is like a miniature encyclopedia because it contains
   a. the definitions of words.
   b. rules on grammar and punctuation.
   c. information about people, places, and events from history.

15. Malcolm assumed that the reader would be surprised to learn that the prison debate teams would get worked up over subjects like "Should Babies Be Fed Milk" because
   a. people don't think prisoners are intelligent.
   b. people don't think prisoners would be interested in talking about subjects such as babies.
   c. people don't think prisoners are on debate teams.

16. The prison library had a lot of books in part because of
   a. the large amount of funds the prison had to spend on the library.
   b. the donation of the Parkhurst collection of books to the library.
   c. the prisoners buying the books themselves.

17. Malcolm sincerely
    a. appreciated the quality of the prison library.
    b. hoped to go to college when he got out of prison.
    c. desired to become a minister someday.

18. Malcolm wrote that during the night he *feigned sleep* when the
    guards walked by (par. 18). *Feigned sleep* probably means he
    a. fell asleep.
    b. woke up.
    c. pretended to be sleeping.

Write short answers to the following questions based on your reading,
your experience, and your observations.

19. Do you think that it would be a good idea for you to study the whole
    dictionary to improve your vocabulary? Why or why not?

    _____

    _____

    _____

20. What are some other ways that you might go about learning new
    vocabulary?

    _____

    _____

    _____

Chapter 2

Working with Words

Technology and You

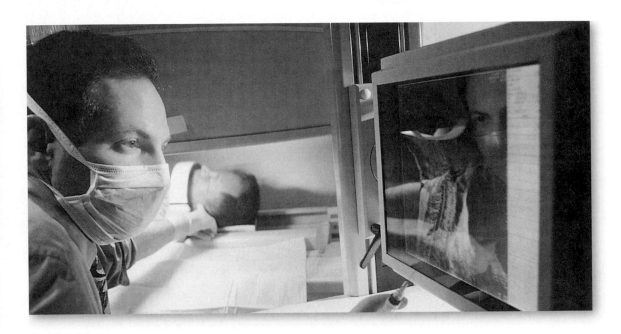

Maybe technology gives us too many things, some of which are not always desirable, but without science and technology we would have very few things at all.
—John Langone

- What is the machine in the picture? What does it do?
- Why do you think the young man in the picture is there?
- How do you think technology will affect our lives in the years ahead?

etting Ready to Read

Technology will change the way you live in the future. Computer gurus tell us the changes, especially in communication, will be revolutionary. Multimedia computer and phone systems will soon make voice and video communication possible instantly anywhere on earth. How will these changes affect human relations? How about entertainment? Business? And education? Will human understanding increase? Will you be ready to participate in the dialogue of an ever-shrinking world community?

In this chapter you will read and think about new developments in technology and how they are affecting your life. As you do this, you will increase your reading and communication skills by learning how to improve your vocabulary through

- textbook aids
- context clues
- word parts
- dictionary skills
- personal vocabulary systems

READING 1

The Challenge of Technology

The following reading comments on the many technological advances that are changing our life now and will continue to do so in the future. In fact, technological change is occurring more rapidly and on a larger scale than ever before. As you read, consider how you will respond to the challenges of technology.

1   Technology is affecting every area of our lives—wherever new knowledge is coming to light. After all, technology *is* the practical application of knowledge, and knowledge is increasing at an unprecedented rate. We will be unlikely to escape its influence in any corner of the globe.

2   The average American home in the year 2000 already had a hundred pieces of equipment to save labor, make our lives easier and more comfortable, and entertain us. We eat fresh food grown and harvested at great distances and air-freighted to our neighborhood grocery store. Travel is quicker, easier, and more common. Physicians diagnose our illnesses and treat them using more and more advanced technology. No job of the twenty-first century will be untouched by the explosion of new information and its resulting technology. Many people will be employed in jobs where technology itself is the main focus. They will create and manage Web sites, maintain e-mail service, and communicate with markets around the globe.

3   In the future, more education will be accessed through "distance learning." The teacher and fellow students may be in another state, or even another country, but the questions and answers will be relayed in only a few seconds.

4   Perhaps no other field will be affected as greatly by technology as communications. Bill Gates wrote in 1996, "The revolution in communications is just beginning." Universal e-mail and a computer on every desk, and in every home, will not be a dream but reality. In 2000, writer John Gage, in an article for the Library of Congress on the future of the Internet, predicted that the economic costs will be minimal. "Tomorrow, with complete computer systems on a single chip, debates about cost will be over. The devices will cost nothing. With the advent of high-bandwidth wireless connectivity, linking them together will cost pennies." He points out that the debate will no longer focus on how and when technology will "create a worldwide conversation," but how these changes will affect the life we live. He wonders "what forms of language will evolve" and, even more dramatically, "what being human will mean" in this new, interconnected universe.

Exercise 1 | ## Recall and Discuss

Answer these questions about Reading 1, and prepare to discuss them in class.

1. What does *technology* mean?

2. How do you think changing technology will affect your life in the future?

3. What do you think are the advantages of the explosion of knowledge and rapid technological change?

4. What do you think are the disadvantages of the explosion of knowledge and rapid technological change?

Working with Words

Computers have introduced hundreds of new words into English. Words that are familiar to you now, such as "download," "software," and "e-mail," simply did not exist thirty years ago. To keep up with developments in technology, you have to keep up with the language of technology, and new words are emerging every day.

Every field of study has its own specialized language; therefore, as a student, you will encounter many new words in your college courses. In fact, anyone who reads a lot will come across new words all the time. Each new word you learn to recognize and use expands your ability to understand others and express yourself. In this chapter, you will learn some of the most basic ways of building your vocabulary and of dealing with unfamiliar words.

Reading and Vocabulary

Probably the one activity that will most improve your vocabulary is reading, whether you are reading a printed book or a computer screen. The more you read, the more words you will learn. It's as simple as that. The more words you know, the easier it is for you to read, and the more you will enjoy reading for its own sake. So, maybe instead of watching a rerun of a television program, try to set aside about half an hour a day to read for fun. Pick anything that you enjoy reading—sports magazines, women's magazines, mystery novels, the newspaper. It doesn't matter what you read at first, as long as you get into the habit. Then, gradually try to push yourself to read material that is a little more challenging and that expands the type of reading you do. Still, you want to enjoy this reading, so pick things that interest you. You will find that developing the lifelong habit of reading a lot will help you continue to build your general vocabulary. And having a large vocabulary helps you in many ways: in school, at work, and whenever you want to communicate. A strong vocabulary is a powerful tool that you can put to work for you.

Textbook Vocabulary Aids

Most college courses have a **specialized vocabulary,** and you need to learn that new, unique vocabulary in order to succeed in the course. When you take a course in math, sociology, psychology, biology, business, computer science, or others, your instructor may explain new terms the first time that they are introduced. In class lectures, if your instructor thinks that a word is important enough to write on the board, you should write it down, make sure you understand it, highlight it in your notes, and study it.

specialized vocabulary Terms unique to a particular field of study

Your textbook will also provide many valuable aids to help you understand the new terms and essential concepts.

Some of the most common **textbook aids** for learning specialized vocabulary are

textbook aids All of the features that textbooks provide to assist students in understanding new vocabulary

- the use of **boldface** or *italics* to emphasize the word when it first appears
- definitions in the margins of the reading itself
- "key words and concepts" sections at the end of the chapter
- vocabulary questions in the chapter reviews
- **glossaries** at the end of the chapter or at the end of the book

glossary A dictionary of important words, frequently found in the back of college textbooks

When you practiced previewing textbooks in Chapter 1, you were introduced to many of the vocabulary aids textbooks provide.

When you encounter a term in your reading that is crucial for understanding a chapter or a reading assignment, be sure to look first at the textbook itself for the author's definition or explanation. Do not go to a separate dictionary until you have checked all the sources in the textbook. The author's definitions will be more precise and appropriate for the specialized field you are studying.

Exercise 2

Use Textbook Vocabulary Aids

Examine two textbooks that you are using this semester. One can be this text, *Joining a Community of Readers*. Write the name of the text on the left, and then list the kinds of vocabulary aids the book has on the right.

Textbook Title   *Vocabulary Aids*

1. _____ _____

        _____

        _____

2. _____ _____

        _____

        _____

Context Clues

context The sentence or paragraph in which a word occurs

Not every book you read in college will have vocabulary aids. Most books, in fact, do not offer this kind of help. One important skill you need to develop is figuring out the meaning of words you do not know from the *context* in which they appear. **Context** is the surrounding words and phrases. It may include the entire sentence or even a paragraph or

[handwritten: Read + do exercise go - 76]

more. Often you can make a very good guess about what a word means by understanding the surrounding words.

For practice in understanding the clues context gives you, read the following sentences, which have some words that you don't know but you will probably understand from the context.

[handwritten: The important pmt of the Context Ex.] Last night, my wife and I went to a *baccalunga* to buy some *wylieny* for my car. It was running rather *prohamply* yesterday, and I saw a *seminque* that I thought would help.

Of course, the italicized words in the above passage are not really words, but they could be. From the context, you know that *baccalunga* is probably a store, *wylieny* is something for the car, and *prohamply* describes how the car was running. *Seminque* appears to be something else that would make a car run better. Why were you able to understand something about these "words"? Because you understood the meaning of the rest of the sentence and paragraph. You understood the *context* in which the words appeared. Although you do not know precisely what each word means, you have an idea of what it refers to. *[handwritten: mean exactly]*

Four kinds of context clues can help you in understanding a word:

- definition or synonym clues
- example clues
- comparison and contrast clues
- general information clues

Definition Clues

definition Answers the question "What is it?"

Sometimes the context gives you the actual **definition** of a word. A definition answers the question "What is it?" Look at the following excerpt on "technology."

Technology is the science that creates practical applications, or solutions, from scientific knowledge. These applications are used in many areas; you have probably heard of educational technology, industrial technology, and computer technology, to name a few.

In this excerpt, the context tells you directly what *technology* is. It is first identified as a science, and then the rest of the sentence describes the particular type of science it is. The second sentence gives examples of fields that use the science of technology to solve problems.

When a new term is defined directly, the definition is usually given close to where the word is introduced. As in the technology example, the meaning often follows the word itself, which may be boldfaced or italicized for emphasis. The definition may also appear

- after the words *is, means, called, refers to*
- between commas

- in parentheses
- between dashes

A definition may also use synonyms to help explain the meaning. A **synonym** is a word that has the same or very similar meaning as the new word. For example, notice how a synonym for *query* in the following sentence is introduced by the word *or*:

> A computer *query*, or search, on a popular topic may produce hundreds of links.

The word *search* is a synonym for *query* in this sentence. This one-word synonym helps you to understand what a query is.

synonym A word that has the same or similar meaning

Exercise 3

Use Definition Clues

Read the following sentences, and write in the definition or synonym for the italicized word or words, using the meanings provided in the sentences themselves.

1. The term *Internet* was then adopted as a shorthand for "internet-worked communication." (Lehnert, *Internet 101*)

   Internet ___The computer technology.___

   _____

2. With the use of new manufacturing technologies, clothes of the future may be created from *camouflage* fabrics, which can actually change color and pattern to match their background.

   camouflage _____

   _____

3. A *computer virus* is a piece of code someone inserts into an otherwise legitimate computer program for the purpose of causing mischief. (Lehnert, *Internet 101*)

   computer virus _____

   _____

4. A search for information on the Internet is called a query, and the document you receive in response is called a *hit*. Sometimes one query can produce a thousand or more hits.

   hit _____

   _____

5. With new agricultural technology, experts are trying to grow plants without soil; instead, they are using *hydroponics* (a method that grows plants in enriched water).

hydroponics _____

_____

Example Clues

transitions Words or phrases that link ideas and/or identify relationships

Sometimes you can figure out the meaning of a word because you understand the examples provided in the context. Examples are often introduced with **transitions** like *for example, for instance, such as,* and *including.* (STOP: Read that last sentence again. Notice how you've just added the word *transition* to your vocabulary. Transitions are words that link ideas and identify relationships. You know what a transition is because you recognize examples of transitions and understand how they work.)

Read the following sentence, and see if you can understand the meaning of *multimedia* from the examples. Notice that the transition *such as* signals that examples are coming:

The Web consists of hypertext mixed with *multimedia* elements such as graphical images, sound clips, and video clips. (Lehnert, *Light on the Internet*)

In this sentence, the examples are *graphical images, sound clips,* and *video clips.* Taken together, they allow you to understand that *multimedia* means communication in several different ways, through elements that can be seen and heard.

Exercise 4

Use Example Clues

Read the following sentences, and write in the definition or synonym for the italicized word or words, using the clues provided by examples. Then write the transition that signaled the use of an example.

1. E-mail is a *versatile* medium; it allows you to do many different things, such as explain a work assignment, send a note to a friend in another country, or share a recipe with a family member.

versatile _____

transition: _____

2. If you insert your own returns in your e-mail, the recipients may see *raggy text;* they may, for instance, see "text that wraps around

to the next line and then abruptly halts after an inch or two, only to continue on the next line when it wraps around again, and then halts, and so on" (Lehnert, *Light on the Internet*).

raggy text _____

transition: _____

3. Because we have electricity, homes now are filled with technological *accouterments* people once considered luxuries. Such things include furnaces, fans, air conditioners, refrigerators, stoves, lightbulbs, washing machines, and various digital items; few of us would function well without them (Langone, *How Things Work*).

accouterments _____

transition: _____

4. Personalized computer files, such as *signature files*, save people from the tedium of typing the same thing repeatedly in their e-mail.

signature files _____

transition: _____

5. The *graphic component* of the new book on how technology works is impressive; for example, there are more than 300 full-color photographs, technical drawings, and diagrams.

graphic component _____

transition: _____

Compare and Contrast Clues

compare Show how items are alike or similar

contrast Show how items are different

Sometimes you can figure out the meaning of a word by understanding what it is similar to, or what it is different from. An author may **compare** two terms by explaining how they are alike or similar. The following words and transitions signal that a comparison is being used: *alike, similarly, in comparison, as . . . as,* and *same.*

An author may also **contrast** two words by explaining how they are different from or even the opposite of each other. Following are some words and transitions that indicate a contrast is being used: *but, on the other hand, in contrast to, however, although,* and *unlike.*

Read the following excerpt about e-mail.

When new mail arrives it is stored in your *inbox*. The inbox is very much like a mailbox, in which new mail waits for you to retrieve it. (Lehnert, *Light on the Internet*)

Here you know what an *inbox* is, because it is compared to the mail-box in which you receive your regular mail. The words *very much like* signal the comparison.

Exercise 5

Use Comparison and Contrast Clues

Read the following sentences, and write in the definition or synonym for the italicized word or words using the clues provided by comparisons and contrasts. Check whether the meaning is clear from comparison or contrast. Then write the transition that signaled the use of a comparison or contrast.

1. Although many jewelry-making techniques are now done *mechanically*, some of the work must still be done by hand.

   mechanically _____

   _____ Comparison   _____ Contrast

   transition: _____

2. Many people don't object to the *cloning* of pigs, but they draw the line at making copies of people.

   cloning _____

   _____ Comparison   _____ Contrast

   transition: _____

3. An Internet connection with a lot of *bandwidth* is one that allows you to move a lot of files around as fast as possible. . . . Bandwidth is like a pipeline: the bigger the pipe, the faster the throughput. (Lehnert, *Light on the Internet*)

   bandwidth _____

   _____

   _____ Comparison   _____ Contrast

   transition: _____

4. In fact, *browsing* [the Web] is a lot like daydreaming: You simply go where your interests lead you. (Lehnert, *Light on the Internet*)

   browsing _____

   _____

   _____ Comparison   _____ Contrast

   transition: _____

5. You can browse Web pages *casually* for entertainment, or you can browse with a serious goal in mind. (Lehnert, *Light on the Internet*)

casually _____

_____ Comparison   _____ Contrast

transition: _____

General Information Clues

Sometimes you can understand an unfamiliar word because you understand, in general, the rest of the information in the surrounding sentence or group of sentences. It was from this type of context clue that you were able to understand the example using the "words" *baccalunga* and *seminque* on page 69. The contexts for the words that follow are a little more complicated, but you will probably be successful in figuring out the meanings of the italicized words because you will understand the context. Often, in the context of technology, explanations of what something does are clues that help you understand the meaning of the new term.

Consider the term *universal* in the following excerpt:

Like conventional telephone and postal service, E-mail will never fulfill its social and commercial promise until it is *universal*. The more people it can reach, the greater its value to all. The already visible danger is that E-mail will become the preserve of the affluent and educated classes, bypassing large segments of the population—much as paper mail and telephones once bypassed rural America. (Frankel, "Universal E-Mail")

In this excerpt the author begins, and ends, his explanation with a contrast between e-mail and telephone and postal service. We understand that the latter two are universal but that e-mail is not. The following sentences use many terms to suggest what *universal* means. Conventional telephone and postal service is available to "more people," "to all." In contrast, other words explain that e-mail is the "preserve of affluent and educated classes," and it is "bypassing" other people. Adding up these various general information clues, the reader understands that *universal* must mean "for everyone."

| Exercise 6 | **Understand Words in Context** |

Read the following excerpt from *Time* magazine about the increase of women on the Internet and guess the meaning of the italicized words by using context clues. Write your definition on the line. Then, in the multiple-choice question, pick the clue—*definition, example, comparison and contrast,* or *general information*—that helped you determine the meaning. Be sure that your definition fits the context.

Since 1999 the number of teen girls online has more than doubled, to 4.4 million. And for the first time in the U.S., more women are *logging on* (1), or signing on, to the computer than men. While the percentage of teen girls is increasing the fastest, women 55 and older are a close second. What's the *lure* (2)? Many attractive websites entice girl and women *surfers* (3) to the net. Teenage girls chat on sites like teen.com and cosmogirl.com, while working moms save time shopping at sites like babygear.com and walgreens.com. Older women frequent health and family *sites* (4), such as merck.medco.com and familyhistory.com. . . .

A retired teacher, Nancy Close, 70, first went online six months ago at her daughter's urging. Now the Columbus, Ohio, widow spends three hours a day auctioning paper dolls on eBay, researching health facts for her Chihuahua and sending e-mail. Why didn't she make the leap sooner? "It was *intimidating* (5)," she says because, at first, it seemed so difficult. "But now I'm trying to get all my senior friends online." (Adapted from Hamilton, "Meet the New Surfer Girls")

---

1. *logging on* _____
   Which clue helped you identify the meaning?
   a. definition
   b. comparison and contrast
   c. general information

2. *lure* _____
   Which clue helped you identify the meaning?
   a. definition
   b. comparison and contrast
   c. general information

3. *surfers* _____
   Which clue helped you identify the meaning?
   a. definition
   b. general information
   c. example

4. *sites* _____
   Which clue helped you identify the meaning?
   a. definition
   b. example
   c. comparison and contrast

5. *intimidating* _____ _____

Which clue helped you identify the meaning?

a. definition

b. general information

c. comparison and contrast

E-Mail Netiquette   Wendy G. Lehnert

The following reading is from an introductory textbook on the essentials of the Internet and the World Wide Web. The author, Dr. Wendy G. Lehnert, is a professor of computer science at the University of Massachusetts at Amherst. Here she explains the rules of etiquette for e-mail users. As you read, notice new terms and unfamiliar words; watch for context clues to help you.

etiquette Rules for polite behavior

1   Practicing good e-mail etiquette, or *Netiquette,* is all about respect. Good Netiquette shows respect for people you don't know and whom you may never get to know all that well in spite of longstanding, online conversations. It is especially important because the Internet encourages interactive communication between strangers on a truly grand scale. It is a scale that people never experience in other public forums in which the reality of physical distance limits their reach and binds them to familiar communities.

2   Whenever you send e-mail, remember a few Netiquette guidelines:

- Keep your messages short and to the point.
- Watch your grammar and spelling.
- Be careful with humor. Avoid sarcasm.
- Use uppercase words very sparingly. UPPERCASE TEXT YELLS.
- Never leave your Subject header blank.
- Include your e-mail address in the message body (e.g., in your sig file).

3   If you are new to e-mail, you have not yet experienced its mixed blessings. Some people deal with 100 or more e-mail messages every day. They are understandably annoyed by any message that wastes their time, especially if the person writing the message doesn't use good Netiquette.

vocal intonations Tone of voice

recipient Person who receives the e-mail

temper Control

4   Online conversations are not the same as face-to-face conversations or even telephone conversations. When you talk online, there are no body language cues or vocal intonations to help the recipient interpret your message. If you are inexperienced with online dialogs, you may not realize how important and useful all of this "unspoken" communication is. For example, a lot of well-intentioned humor falls flat on the Internet. Or worse, it may be completely misinterpreted and end up making someone feel hurt or angry. If you're in the habit of speaking sarcastically, temper that tendency

until you have a good feel for how your words are coming across to people. What you intend is not always what others perceive.

5   Some people use a whole vocabulary of *emoticons* to express themselves—combinations of characters that represent emotions. For example, the most commonly seen emoticon is the *smilee,* shown as :-). A smilee may seem unnecessarily cutesy and perhaps a little annoying :-(if you aren't used to it, but smilees are actually useful :-o. A smilee explicitly tells the reader when something is being said in jest or when something shouldn't be taken seriously <grin>. Messages with smilees are written by people who are trying to make sure that no one misunderstands :-{ the spirit of their words. I don't think I have ever seen someone take offense >:-(at a statement punctuated by a smilee. It's the equivalent of a smile and a wink ;-) or a friendly laugh accompanied by a pat on the back. It works well among people who don't know each other all that well :-}. In general, emoticons allow people to insert some personality {□:-) into their writing without fear =:-o of being misinterpreted.

6   If you do find yourself in an emotional exchange, it's usually a good idea to cool down before you respond. Angry e-mail messages are called *flames,* and people who write them are flaming. Flaming is not polite, and if you ever get flamed, you may feel hurt or downright abused. The Internet seems to encourage some people to indulge their pent-up rage by subjecting innocent bystanders to verbal abuse. Two people trading flames are engaged in a flame war. This behavior seems to be peculiar to the Internet; it probably wouldn't take place in a face-to-face interaction. Flames can be strangely contagious. It seems that heat has a way of generating more heat unless someone is willing to cool off and break the cycle. If a message makes you angry, wait 24 hours before responding. That's usually enough time for the heat to dissipate. You may or may not have misinterpreted what was written (it may or may not have been intended the way you read it), but a flame war usually isn't worth the elevated blood pressure. Sometimes the best reply is no reply.

7   If you value your relationship with someone, be especially careful about emotionally charged e-mail. If you're communicating with someone you work with, do your best to avoid online misunderstandings or unintentional slights. People can read all sorts of things into e-mail. For example, "Gee, that reply was awfully short; I must not matter very much to her." Or, "How come it took so long for him to answer me? Doesn't he know how important this is?" It's easy to damage a relationship with careless e-mail exchanges. Worse yet, you may not even realize that damage has been done. If you care about good working relationships, you can't be too careful with your online communications. If you're angry or upset about something, deal with it face-to-face. E-mail is not a suitable medium for everything.

LEHNERT, *Light on the Internet*

verbal abuse
Unfair verbal attack

Use Context Clues

For the following italicized words, write the definitions on the lines provided. Then write the context clue or clues you used to find the meaning: *definition and synonym, example, comparison and contrast, general information*.

1. Practicing good e-mail etiquette, or *Netiquette,* is all about respect. (par. 1)

   Netiquette _____

   clues: _____

2. Some people use a whole vocabulary of *emoticons* to express themselves—combinations of characters that represent emotions. For example, the most commonly seen emoticon is the smilee, shown as :-). (par. 5)

   emoticons _____

   clues: _____

3. Angry e-mail messages are called *flames*, and people who write them are flaming. (par. 6)

   flames _____

   clues: _____

4. If a message makes you angry, wait 24 hours before responding. That's usually enough time for the heat to *dissipate.* (par. 6)

   dissipate _____

   clues: _____

5. If you're angry or upset about something, deal with it face-to-face. E-mail is not a suitable *medium* for everything. (par. 7)

   medium _____

   clues: _____

Check Your Understanding

Check the best answers to the following multiple-choice questions about Reading 2.

1. Which of the following is the most important point the author is making about Netiquette?

a. E-mail etiquette is all about mutual respect for people you may never meet face-to-face.
b. Emoticons are the answer to any problems you may encounter in Web relationships.
c. Never leave your subject header blank when you send an e-mail message.

2. Which of the following statements about grammar is most consistent with the rules of Netiquette?
a. One of the great things about e-mail is that you don't need to worry about spelling and grammar.
b. Watch your spelling and grammar in e-mail.
c. Correct spelling and grammar is the top priority in e-mail etiquette.

3. Since online conversations are not the same as face-to-face conversations,
a. you can write things that you would never say to someone in person.
b. people usually misinterpret what you write.
c. it is sometimes difficult to tell how your message will be received by other people.

4. If you receive a flame, the author suggests
a. you wait at least 24 hours to respond.
b. you immediately flame the writer in response with all uppercase words.
c. you assume that the flamer didn't mean it and ignore the message.

5. Probably the best way to avoid online misunderstandings is to
a. check your grammar and spelling twice before you send anything out.
b. recognize that e-mail is not the best way to communicate about emotionally charged issues.
c. only e-mail people you work with regularly.

| Exercise 9 |

Make Connections

Write short answers to the following questions based on Reading 2, your experience, and your observations. Then, to extend this exercise, discuss your answers with your class group. Working together, prepare a report for your class as a whole or a written summary for your instructor.

1. Do you use e-mail? What kinds of messages do you think it's best for?

_____

_____

_____

2. Which of the Netiquette guidelines the author provides do you think are most important? Explain why.

_____

_____

_____

_____

Word Parts

One way to multiply the number of words in your vocabulary rather quickly is to become aware of how words in English are made. Often two words are simply put together to create a new word. Consider the word *weekend*. If you know what a *week* is and what *end* means, you have an excellent chance of understanding *weekend*. Many new terms related to computer technology are created in the same way. Think about *download* and *online*. If you recognize the meaning of the parts of these words, you know what these new terms mean, too.

word parts Words or elements of words joined together to make new words.

root Core part of a word to which prefixes and suffixes are added

prefix An addition at the beginning of a word which changes its meaning

suffix Ending of a word, often indicating the part of speech

Word parts are the words or elements of words joined together to make new words. Not all of these words can stand on their own, however. The core part of a word, which can often stand on its own, is called the **root.** Elements of words that are added before the root are called **prefixes;** these often change the word's meaning. Elements of words that are added after the root are called **suffixes;** these often indicate the word's part of speech, or function in a sentence. Consider the word *imagine*. If we add the suffix "able" to the root word, we have *imaginable,* a new word that means "able to be imagined." Then, if we add the prefix "un" to this new word we have yet another new word—*unimaginable*—a word which means "not able to be imagined."

Remember:

- Roots can be at the beginning, middle, or end of a word.
- Prefixes appear at the beginning of the word and change its meaning.
- Suffixes appear at the end of a word and indicate its function in a sentence.

Knowing the meaning of many common word parts can greatly increase your vocabulary. For example, if you know that *media* is a root that means "ways of conveying or expressing," you can understand many words relating to media. For example, *multimedia* begins with the common prefix "multi," which means "many," so a multimedia presentation is one that uses many different media, or ways, to communicate its message.

Roots

The root is the core part of the word. It usually provides the basic meaning of a word. Roots may occur at the beginning, middle, or end of a word, and may be combined with prefixes and suffixes to form a different word. Following is a list of some important roots along with their meanings and an example of each in a word. As you go through this list, add another example for each root in the space provided. If you can't think of another example, use the dictionary to find one.

Root	Meaning	Example	Your Examples
aqua, aqui	water	aquarium	_____
auto	self	automatic	_____
bio	life	biology	_____
cept	receive	reception	_____
chron	time	chronology	_____
cogi	think, know	recognize	_____
duct	lead	aqueduct	_____
gamy	marriage	polygamy	_____
logy	study	sociology	_____
mini	small	minimum	_____
patr, patri	father	patriarch	_____
port	carry	transport	_____
vers	turn	versatile	_____
vid, vis	see	vision	_____
vit, vivi	life	vitality	_____

Prefixes

Following is a list of common prefixes along with their meanings and an example of each in a word. The prefixes in the first group identify a number. Those in the next group mean "no" or "not." Those in the third group identify a time. Those in the fourth group identify a place or position. As you go through each list, add your own examples in the spaces provided. If you can't think of other examples, use the dictionary.

Number A prefix indicating number can completely change the meaning of a word. For example, a *tri*angle is a three-sided figure; a *quad*rilateral has four sides, and a *penta*gon has five sides. Similarly, a *bi*llion dollars ($1,000,000,000) is a lot of money, but a *tri*llion ($1,000,000,000,000) is more, and a *quad*rillion ($1,000,000,000,000,000) is much more money.

Prefix	Meaning	Example	Your Examples
mono	one	monogamy	_____
uni	one	uniform	_____
bi	two	bigamy	_____
tri	three	tricycle	_____
quad	four	quadruplet	_____
multi	many	multitalented	_____
poly	many	polygamy	_____
semi	half, part	semiconscious	_____
dec	ten	decimal	_____
cent	hundred	centimeter	_____

Negative Negative prefixes can reverse the meaning of a word. For example, if you add *il* to *legal*, you change something lawful to unlawful or *illegal*. Notice that several other prefixes mean *not* as well.

Prefix	Meaning	Example	Your Examples
anti	against	antiabortion	_____
dys	ill, difficult	dysfunctional	_____
il	not	illegible	_____
im	not	immature	_____
in	not	inaccurate	_____
ir	not	irresponsible	_____
un	not	unmarked	_____

Time Some prefixes indicate the time that something occurs. For example, the prefix *pre* means before, so we know that *pre*game activities happen before the game. However, we expect *post*game activities to take place after the game.

Prefix	Meaning	Example	Your Examples
ante	before	anteroom	_____
post	after, behind	postpartum	_____
pre	before	prebirth	_____
proto	first	prototype	_____
re	again	return	_____

Place or Position   Other prefixes show position or location. For example, *appear* means to arrive. When we add the prefix *dis*, we get the word *disappear*, which means to go away. Notice how each of the following prefixes affects location.

Prefix	Meaning	Example	Your Examples
circum	around	circumcise	_____
co	with, together	cooperate	_____
com, con	with, together	communicate	_____
dis	apart, away	disappear	_____
en	in, into	entrap	_____
ex	out of, from	exhale	_____
inter	between, among	international	_____
para	beside, related to	parachute	_____
sub	under, below	submarine	_____
tele	far off, distant	telephoto	_____
trans	across	translate	_____

| Exercise 10 |

Build Your Vocabulary Using Prefixes: Collaborative Activity

In your class group, compare your examples of words with prefixes. Then make a class master list. If the list is less than 100 words, brainstorm additional prefixes and words with prefixes until you have 100. Use the dictionary to help you. Each group can share its list with the class to make a master list of 200–300 words. Discuss which of the words would be most important to learn, then make a master list to photocopy so each person in the class has a personal list for vocabulary building.

Exercise 11   ## Use Roots and Prefixes

Read the following excerpt from an article about biometrics and the new technology of voice security. Then use the lists of prefixes and roots, as well as context, to explain the meaning of the italicized words. Identify the prefix or root that helped you and its meaning. The first one has been done for you.

Biometrics (1) is a science that makes use of an individual's *unique* (2) identifiers, easily reading them by *automated* (3) processes. The clues to individual identity that biometrics uses include fingerprinting, analyzing hand shape, eye scans, signature *verification* (4), and facial and voice recognition. Voice identification uses *multiple* (5) speakers, a set of speakers who have provided samples of their speech. In the cellular phone industry, using voice security can make a stolen or fraudulently obtained unit *inoperable* (6) and dramatically reduce fraud. (Adapted from "Voice Security," *PC Tips*)

---

1. *biometrics* <u>Science that measures some aspects of human life for purposes</u>

   <u>of identification</u>

   prefix or root: <u>"bio" - life and "metric" - measure</u>

2. *unique* _____

   prefix or root: _____

3. *automated* _____

   prefix or root: _____

4. *verification* _____

   prefix or root: _____

5. *multiple* _____

   prefix or root: _____

6. *inoperable* _____

   prefix or root: _____

LANGUAGE TIP

Word Forms

Becoming familiar with various word forms can increase your comprehension of what you read, and it can also improve your spelling. *Word forms* are the shapes and spellings that English words assume as they change functions in a sentence. These functions include nouns, verbs, adjectives, and adverbs.

- *Noun:* name of a person, place, or thing—for example, *woman, city, communication*
- *Verb:* a word that shows action (*go, buy*) or a state of being (*be, is, are*). Verbs often have a "to" in front of them—for example, *to go, to buy, to be, to change*
- *Adjective:* a word that describes a noun—for example, *beautiful* picture, *sad* face
- *Adverb*: a word that describes a verb or an adjective—for example, plays *carelessly,* is *very* careless

Notice how the meaning and form of the word *success* change in each of the following sentences.

1. The new computer game was a big *success. (noun)*
2. The computer game was the most *successful* new product this year. (*adjective*—it describes the game)
3. Mari *successfully* loaded the game on her home computer. (*adverb*—it describes how well she loaded the game)
4. She *succeeded* in mastering all the levels of the game. (*verb*, in the past tense)

As you see, the word *success* has a noun form as well as verb, adverb, and adjective forms. Many words go through spelling changes like this as they change function. Recognizing these changes allows you to understand a word that at first looks unfamiliar. If you know the meaning of the *root* word, you'll have no trouble understanding its forms.

Exercise 12 ## Use Word Forms

In the accompanying chart, list the other forms of the word that is given. The first one has been done for you. Use your dictionary if you need help. Not all words have every form.

Noun	Verb	Adjective	Adverb
1. explosion	explode	explosive	explosively
2.			creatively
3.	trick		
4.	inform		

Noun	Verb	Adjective	Adverb
5. _____		supportive	_____
6. _____			cautiously
7. sympathy _____			
8. _____		correct	
9. imagination _____			
10. _____			radiantly

Suffixes

suffix Ending of a word, often indicating the function or part of speech

part of speech Classification of a word according to its function in a sentence, such as noun, verb, adjective, adverb

Suffixes are the endings of many words. They frequently tell us what **part of speech** the word is, that is, whether it is a noun, adjective, or adverb. Parts of speech tell you what function a word has within a sentence. Dictionaries also identify the parts of speech for a word and its various forms.

Look carefully at the following list of common suffixes. As you go through the list, write your own examples in the spaces provided. If you can't think of other examples, browse through the dictionary to find some.

Nouns   Nouns are the names of persons, places, things, ideas, or qualities. Following are some noun suffixes.

Suffix	Meaning	Example	Your Examples
-or, -er, -ist, -ee, -ian	a person	communicator, teacher, futurist, referee, physician	_____ _____ _____
-acy, -archy	an act, form of government	democracy oligarchy	_____ _____ _____
-ence, -ance, -ation, -tion, -sion, -ment	an act, a state, a condition	attendance, communication, restriction, tension, resentment	_____ _____ _____
-ism	a belief, form of government	socialism	_____ _____ _____
-ship, -hood, -ness	having to do with, referring to	relationship, neighborhood, friendliness	_____ _____ _____

Adjectives Adjectives modify (add to, describe in more detail) the meaning of nouns and pronouns. Following are some adjective suffixes.

Suffix	Meaning	Example	Your Examples
-able, -ible, -al, -ic	having a characteristic, related to	reliable, responsible, practical, toxic	_____ _____
-ing, -ive, -ous		insulting, communicative, serious	_____
-ful		plentiful	_____ _____

Adverbs Adverbs explain how or when an action occurs. Following are some applications of the adverb suffix, "ly."

Suffix	Meaning	Example	Your Examples
-ly	describes *how* something is done (sometimes they are added to the endings of adjectives)	efficiently, responsibly, insultingly, communicatively	_show how_ _____ _____

Exercise 13

Use Suffixes (Part 1)

Add suffixes to each of the following words to change its function.

	Noun	Adjective	Adverb
1. help			
2. play			
3. tolerate			
4. mess			
5. tempt			

Exercise 14

Use Suffixes (Part 2)

Read the following excerpt from an article about distance education. Circle the words with suffixes that you recognize. Then list five of these words in the space provided, and identify their part of speech.

With online courses, schools can draw students from just about anywhere. That's *especially* appealing to what *educators* call "*nontraditional*" students, who may be trying to fit in school with *responsibilities* at work and home. This group is one of the fastest-growing in the education world, and it's a main reason that the number of distance-learning programs in colleges and universities has *skyrocketed* in the last few years. More than 1.5 million students signed up for courses. (Krantrowitz, "Finding a Niche in e-ducation")

Word	Part of Speech
1. _____	_____
2. _____	_____
3. _____	_____
4. _____	_____
5. _____	_____

READING 3

House of the Future

The following reading describes how technology will transform the homes of the future. Computers will play a major part in this transformation. As you read, watch for the meaning of words in context and the use of word parts.

1 According to science writer Arthur C. Clarke, "Any sufficiently advanced technology is indistinguishable from magic." Technology will indeed bring its "magical" touch to our homes of the future. In the 21st century people may even have the opportunity to live for a while on space stations like Alpha, a new three-room apartment orbiting 230 miles above us. Even though the Alpha is out in space, sophisticated computers keep the astronauts in communication with coworkers, friends and family on earth. They also continuously track Alpha's location. If you'd like to know when the Alpha is passing over the area where you live, there are several Web sites to help you, including ⟨spaceflight.nasa.gov/realdata/sightings/index.html⟩

orbiting Circling

2 Living on a space station is exciting and challenging. Since there is no gravity, residents float around, and all surfaces—ceilings, floor, and walls— are easily usable. Regular activities such as eating, working, and using the bathroom are, however, much more complicated and time-consuming than here on earth.

3   The same computers that are making life possible on space stations are beginning to also transform our home environments here on earth. Since astronauts lose muscle mass and bone density very rapidly in space, because there is no gravity, computerized measurements are regularly transmitted to medical personnel on earth. Similar systems are being developed here. For example, Japan is experimenting with a toilet that can monitor weight, fat levels, and sugar in urine and transfer that information daily to the appropriate physician.

4   To help older people live independently longer, technologists are also proposing monitoring devices in the home that remind people to take their medicine. These built-in cameras and microphones can also serve as a safety feature; they can alert a resident, for example, if he left a burner on in the kitchen. Some technologies being tested would monitor activity levels and let family members know if a grandparent is not as active as usual.

energy-efficient
Save energy

5   Much of the "magic" in new and remodeled homes will depend on wiring. The majority of builders in the United States now offer network wiring as an option. This kind of wiring makes automated systems such as security, intercom, entertainment, and energy-efficient systems possible. Whole-house automation will control your lights, your heating and air-conditioning, as well as the closing of drapes, just to name a few activities. A single button may replace many traditional light switches. In addition, more electrical power in the future will be generated at home from fuel cells, solar power, or geothermal heat pumps.

touchpad
Computer screen operated by touch

6   Appliances of the near future will be networked, and many will be monitored from a single touchpad computer. Your alarm clock, coffee pot, and heating system may all operate in concert. Refrigerators linked to the Internet will keep track of what is inside, check for the ingredients needed for a recipe, prepare a grocery list, and place an order with an online grocer. "Smart" aprons will, with a touch, preheat the oven.

robotic Machine that automatically completes task

7   Remote controls will make it possible to do your laundry when you're not even home. If you are sensitive to dust, you will be able to have your robotic vacuum cleaner pick up the dirt while you are asleep or at work. New self-cleaning surfaces will also make our lives easier.

innovations New products

8   Multimedia entertainment and communication will be available everywhere in the house of the future. Satellite, cable, or Internet digital TV and radio will be networked through as many rooms as desired. Innovations appear on the market every month. E-TV, the world's first TV with Internet and e-mail access built in, is scheduled to be available in 2001. Videoconferencing, which allows you to speak face-to-face with relatives who live far away, will also become more feasible.

9   Fortunately, as technological knowledge grows, these new products will also become less expensive and more available to all of us. What now seems "magical" will be considered normal in the homes of the future.

| Exercise 15 | ## Work with Words |

Read the following sentences from Reading 3. Based on the context and word part clues, write a brief definition of the italicized words.

1. According to science writer Arthur C. Clarke, "Any sufficiently advanced technology is *indistinguishable* from magic." (par. 1)

   indistinguishable _____

2. The same computers that are making life possible on space stations are beginning to also *transform* our home environments here on earth. (par. 3)

   transform _____

3. Since astronauts lose muscle mass and bone density very rapidly in space, because there is no gravity, computerized measurements are regularly *transmitted* to medical personnel on earth. (par. 3)

   transmitted _____

4. To help older people live *independently* longer, technologists are also proposing *monitoring* devices in the home that remind people to take their medicine. (par. 4)

   independently _____

   monitoring _____

5. This kind of wiring makes *automated* systems such as security, intercom, entertainment, and energy-efficient systems possible. (par. 5)

   automated _____

6. *Remote* controls will make it possible to do your laundry when you're not even home. (par. 7)

   remote _____

7. *Multimedia* entertainment and communication will be available everywhere in the house of the future. (par. 8)

   Multimedia _____

8. Satellite, cable, or Internet digital TV and radio will be *networked* through as many rooms as desired. (par. 8)

   networked _____

Exercise 16	## Check Your Understanding

Choose the best answers to the following multiple-choice questions about Reading 3.

1. Astronauts who live on space station Alpha
   a. have no way to communicate with their family and friends.
   b. can use surfaces on all sides as living spaces.
   c. each have a three room apartment of their own.

2. Computer programs developed to monitor astronauts' health in space
   a. are unlikely to have similar applications on earth.
   b. make their measurements very rapidly.
   c. are models for home health monitoring devices on earth.

3. All of the following are ways technology can help older people to live independently longer *except:*
   a. insure a regular income
   b. remind them to take their medicine
   c. alert them to safety issues

4. What makes whole-house automation possible?
   a. controlling lights, heating, and air-conditioning
   b. a single button
   c. network wiring

5. Which of the following will likely *not* be possible in the automated house of the future?
   a. watch videos in every room
   b. have a computer read your textbooks for you
   c. have the refrigerator order your groceries online

6. According to the author, innovative technology will be
   a. expected in most homes of the future.
   b. too expensive for all but the very wealthy.
   c. impossible unless homes generate their own electrical power.

Exercise 17	## Make Connections

1. Which technological innovations would you most like to have in your home in the future? Why?

   _____

   _____

   _____

2. How do you think the automated house of the future will affect the way people live? Explain your answer.

_____

_____

_____

_____

_____

Dictionary Skills

The ultimate resource for understanding new words is the dictionary. When you read for college classes, it's important to have a dictionary handy. But do not look up a new word in the dictionary as soon as you see it. Doing so will distract you from your reading. If you look up five words on a page (which is really not all that many), by the time you get to the end of the page you will not remember what you have read.

Instead of going straight to the dictionary, put a *small check in pencil* by the word. When you finish the page or the section of the text, go back to it. Maybe you have already been able to figure it out from context or word parts. If not, look for it in the textbook aids. If you don't find it there, then go to the dictionary.

The dictionary is the last resort. Before you look up new words in the dictionary, ask yourself these questions:

- Do I need to know the exact meaning of the word to understand the reading?
- Is the word important? Will it be necessary to remember that word because it is key to understanding the subject?
- Have I tried to figure out the meaning of the word from the context but am still unsure about the meaning?

If you answered "yes" to these questions, then go to the dictionary.

Parts of a Dictionary Entry

If you decide to go to the dictionary, you will want to be aware of the different kinds of information a dictionary entry provides. For example, if, in a recent computer magazine about new technology in music, you read, "Online radio allows free access to a dizzying array of programming," you might want to check the meaning of the word *array* in the dictionary.

You would find an entry something like this:

pronunciation

part of speech

definition

ar·ray (ə-rā′) *tr.v.* ar·rayed, ar·ray·ing, ar·rays. **1.** To set out for display or use; place in an orderly arrangement: *arrayed the whole regiment on the parade ground.* **2.** To dress in finery; adorn. —ar·ray *n.* **1.** An orderly, often imposing arrangement: *an array of royal jewels.* **2.** An impressively large number, as of persons or objects: *an array of heavily armed troops; an array of spare parts.*

other forms of
the word

examples of use

(American Heritage Dictionary)

Notice that the dictionary entry gives you a great deal of specific information. There are many different dictionaries, and there are now some on CD-ROM, like the one we used here. These also have an audio portion to help you with the pronunciation of the word. With some variations, most dictionaries list the following information.

- *Pronunciation* (in parentheses after the word). A phonetic key at the beginning of the dictionary, or sometimes at the bottom of every page, will help you decipher how to pronounce the word.
- *Part of speech* (after each form given for the word). The dictionary has, usually in the beginning, a list of abbreviations that includes those for the parts of speech. The entry for *array* has the abbreviation *tr.v.*, which means transitive verb. Transitive verbs are verbs that have to have an object, such as the verb "hit" in the sentence, "The man hit the ball." "Hit" is the transitive verb and "ball" is the object. An intransitive verb does not have to have an object, such as "zoomed" in the sentence "The plane zoomed overhead." "Zoomed" is the verb and "overhead" is the adverb. (The abbreviation *n.* means noun, *v.* means verb, *intr. v.* means intransitive verb, *adv.* means adverb, and *adj.* means adjective.) *Arrayed, arraying*, and *arrays* are other spellings of the verb *array* used to express tense. After the entry for *array* as a verb, there is another entry for the same word as a noun, and in this case, the abbreviation *n.* follows the word. In the sentence from Reading 3, *array* was used as a noun.
- *Definition(s)*—usually numbered. Often there is more than one meaning for a word. The dictionary shows this by listing additional definitions using both letters and numbers. Notice that *array* has two definitions as a verb and two definitions as a noun listed here.
- *Other forms of the word*. The word *array* has two forms—noun and verb. Some words, as we have seen, have adjective and adverb forms as well.
- *Examples of how the word is used*. Phrases in italics show how the word is used. Some dictionaries give a quotation in which the word has been used by a famous author.

■ *Other information.* Some dictionary entries also give *synonyms* (see the example of *dizzy* in Exercise 18); *idioms,* or special uses (see the example of *bit* under the heading of "Choosing the Right Definition"); slang or informal usages (see the examples of *bit* and *pit* under the same heading); and the origins of words (see the third definition in the example of *bit*).

Exercise 18 ## Use a Dictionary

The sentence we examined on page 92—"Online radio allows free access to a dizzying array of programming"—has other words we might look up in the dictionary. Examine the dictionary entry below for *dizzying,* and answer the questions that follow. (Notice that *dizzying* is not the main entry because it is just one of the forms of the word *dizzy*.)

diz·zy (dĭz′ē) *adj.* diz·zi·er, diz·zi·est. **1.** Having a whirling sensation and a tendency to fall. See Synonyms at **giddy. 2.** Bewildered or confused. **3.a.** Producing or tending to produce giddiness: *a dizzy height.* **b.** Caused by giddiness; reeling. **4.** Characterized by impulsive haste; very rapid: *"The American language had begun its dizzy onward march before the Revolution"* (H.L. Mencken). **5.** *Slang.* Scatterbrained or silly. —diz·zy *tr.v.* diz·zied, diz·zy·ing, diz·zies. **1.** To make dizzy. **2.** To confuse or bewilder. —diz′zi·ly *adv.* —diz′zi·ness *n.* —diz′zy·ing·ly *adv.*

(American Heritage Dictionary)

1. What are the adjective forms of *dizzy*?

   _____

2. How many noun forms of *dizzy* are in this dictionary entry? Name them (it).

   _____

3. Which of the definitions best fits the meaning of *dizzying* in the context of the sentence on page 92?

   _____

4. Although the word *dizzying* is used as an adjective in the sentence, what word form is it listed under in this dictionary entry?

   _____

Choosing the Right Definition

As you've now seen from entries for *array* and *dizzy*, dictionary entries can present several different definitions of a single word. You must choose the correct definition for the word you want to understand.

For example, if you read this sentence, "Computer memory is measured in bits," you might want a more exact definition of *bit*. If you decide to look it up in the dictionary, you will find four separate dictionary entries for *bit*, the first of which looks like this:

> **bit**[1] (bĭt) *n.* **1.** A small portion, degree, or amount: *a bit of lint; a bit of luck.* **2.** A brief amount of time; a moment: *Wait a bit.* **3.a.** A short scene or episode in a theatrical performance. **b.** A bit part. **4.** An entertainment routine given regularly by a performer; an act. **5.** *Informal.* **a.** A particular kind of action, situation, or behavior: *got tired of the macho bit.* **b.** A matter being considered: *What's this bit about inflation?* **6.** *Informal.* An amount equal to 1/8 of a dollar: *two bits.* **idioms. a bit.** To a small degree; somewhat: *a bit warm.* **bit by bit.** Little by little; gradually.

None of these six definitions has anything to do with computers, so none of them fits the context that you need. The third entry for bit is more appropriate:

> **bit**[3] (bĭt) *n. Computer Science.* **1.** A single character of a language having just two characters, as either of the binary digits 0 or 1. **2.** A unit of information equivalent to the choice of either of two equally likely alternatives. **3.** A unit of information storage capacity, as of memory. [Blend of b(inary) and (dig)it.]

Now you have the appropriate definition for the context of your sentence. However, if you were to get the definition from a computer text, it would probably give more information than the dictionary definition above. For example, Wendy G. Lehnert, in her *Internet 101* text, defines a *bit* this way:

> The smallest unit of computer memory is a *bit*. A bit is basically an on/off switch and is usually described as a 1 or a 0. (Lehnert, *Internet 101*)

Exercise 19

Use a Dictionary

Read the following excerpt from an article on a Web game from *Computer Graphics World,* paying close attention to the *italicized* words. Then find the correct definition for each italicized word using the dictionary definitions that follow. Write the definition and the part of speech (noun, verb, adjective, adverb) on the lines provided. Some of these words will be familiar to you, but your job here is to find them in a dictionary entry and choose the correct definition for this context.

Have you ever wondered what it's like to get behind the wheel of an Indy car, *zoom* around the *track* at the Indianapolis 500, and get the wave of the checkered flag? Now, racing fans can trade in their backseat-driver title and compete against the actual performances of Buddy Lazier and other Indy Racing League (IRL) champions in a new on-line racing game.

Developed by AniVision of Huntsville, Alabama, the Net Race Live game places Internet players in the driver's seat of a *virtual* Indy car, which is inserted into data captured from actual Indy events. Within 20 minutes of an Indy race's completion, all the track data from the event—including each *pit* stop, caution flag, and crash—is *streamed* to the company's Web site (www.netrace-live.com) where a player can participate in a re-created *simulation* of the event. (Moltenbrey, "Real-Time Racing")

Definition	*Part of Speech*
1. *pit* _____	_____
_____	
2. *simulation* _____	_____
_____	
3. *streamed* _____	_____
_____	
4. *track* _____	_____
_____	
5. *virtual* _____	_____
_____	
6. *zoom* _____	_____
_____	

pit[1] (pĭt) *n.* **1.** A natural or artificial hole or cavity in the ground. **2.a.** An excavation for the removal of mineral deposits; a mine. **b.** The shaft of a mine.

3. A concealed hole in the ground used as a trap; a pitfall. **4.a.** Hell. **b.** A miserable or depressing place or situation. **c. pits.** *Slang.* The worst. Used with *the: "New York politics are the pits"* (Washington Star). **5.** A small indentation in a surface: *pits in a windshield.* **6.a.** A natural hollow or depression in the body or an organ. **b.** A small indented scar left in the skin by smallpox or other eruptive disease; a pockmark. **7.a.** The section of an exchange where trading in a specific commodity is carried on. **b.** The gambling area of a casino. **8.** A sunken area in a garage floor from which mechanics may work on cars. **b. —pit** *v.* **pit·ted, pit·ting, pits.** —*tr.* **1.** To mark with cavities, depressions, or scars: *a surface pitted with craters.* **2.** To set in direct opposition or competition: *a war that pitted brother against brother.*

(American Heritage Dictionary)

sim·u·la·tion (sĭm′yə-lā′shən) *n.* **1.** The act or process of simulating. **2.** An imitation; a sham. **3.** Assumption of a false appearance. **4.a.** Imitation or representation, as of a potential situation or in experimental testing. **b.** Representation of the operation or features of one process or system through the use of another: *computer simulation of an in-flight emergency.*

(American Heritage Dictionary)

stream (strēm) *n.* **1.a.** A flow of water in a channel or bed, as a brook, rivulet, or small river. **b.** A steady current in such a flow of water. **2.** A steady current of a fluid. **3.** A steady flow or succession: *a stream of insults.* See Synonyms at **flow. 4.** A trend, course, or drift, as of opinion, thought, or history. **5.** A beam or ray of light. **—stream** *v.* **streamed, stream·ing, streams.** —*intr.* **1.** To flow in or as if in a stream. **2.** To pour forth or give off a stream; flow: *My eyes were streaming with tears.* **3.** To come or go in large numbers; pour: *Traffic was streaming by. Fan mail streamed in.* **4.** To extend, wave, or float outward: *The banner streamed in the breeze.* **5.a.** To leave a continuous trail of light. **b.** To give forth a continuous stream of light rays or beams; shine. —*tr.* To emit, discharge, or exude (a body fluid, for example).

(American Heritage Dictionary)

track (trăk) *n.* **1.a.** A mark or succession of marks left by something that has passed. See Synonyms at **trace 1. b.** A path, route, or course indicated by such marks: *an old wagon track through the mountains.* **2.** A path along which something moves; a course: *following the track of an airplane on radar.* **3.a.** A course of action; a method of proceeding: *on the right track for solving the puzzle.* **b.** An intended or proper course: *putting a stalled project back on track.* **4.** A succession of ideas; a train of thought. **5.** Awareness of something occurring or passing: *keeping track of the score; lost all track of time.* **6.** *Sports.* **a.** A course laid out for running or racing. **b.** Athletic competition on such a course; track events. **c.** Track and field. **7.** A rail or set of parallel rails upon which railroad cars or other vehicles run. **8.** A metal groove or ridge that holds, guides, and reduces friction for a moving device or apparatus. **9.** Any of several courses of study to which students are assigned according to ability, achievement, or needs: *academic, vocational, and general tracks.* **10.a.** A distinct path, as along a length of film or magnetic tape, on which sound or other information is recorded. **b.** A distinct selection from a sound recording, such as a phonograph record or compact disk, usually containing an individual work or part of a larger work: *the title track of an album.* **c.** One of the separate sound recordings that are combined so as to be heard simultaneously, as in stereophonic sound reproduction: *mixed the vocal track and instrumental track.* —**track** *v.* **tracked, track·ing, tracks idiom. in (one's) tracks.** Exactly where one is standing: *stopped him right in his tracks.* —**track′a·ble** *adj.* —**track′er** *n.*

(American Heritage Dictionary)

vir·tu·al (vûr′chōō-əl) *adj.* **1.** Existing or resulting in essence or effect though not in actual fact, form, or name: *the virtual extinction of the buffalo.* **2.** Existing in the mind, especially as a product of the imagination. Used in literary criticism of text —**vir′tu·al′i·ty** (-ăl′ĭ-tē) *n.* **virtual reality** *n.* an artificial environment which is experienced through sensory stimuli (as sights and sounds) provided by a computer and in which one's actions partially determine what happens in the environment.

(Merriam Webster's Deluxe Dictionary)

zoom (zōōm) *v.* **zoomed, zoom·ing, zooms.** —*intr.* **1.a.** To make a continuous low-pitched buzzing or humming sound. **b.** To move while making such a sound. **2.** To climb suddenly and sharply. Used of an airplane. **3.** To move about rapidly; swoop. **4.a.** To move a camera lens rapidly toward or away from a subject. **b.** To simulate such a movement, as by means of a zoom lens. —*tr.* **1.** To cause to zoom. —**zoom** *n.* The act or sound of zooming.

(American Heritage Dictionary)

Organize to Learn: Your Personal Vocabulary Plan

Having a good vocabulary is one of the most important factors in becoming a strong reader. Probably the best way to improve your vocabulary is to develop your own system, or vocabulary plan. This system should include general vocabulary as well as the specialized vocabulary you need for your college courses and career plans.

continued

To develop your personal vocabulary, start by listing words you need to learn. Choose them carefully. They should be words that you have encountered more than once, that are important and useful, and that are fairly common in the English language generally or in your field of study specifically.

Enter each word in a notebook, in separate computer documents, or on a 3 by 5 card. Be sure to keep your notebook, documents, or cards in a place where it will be easy for you to check them periodically for a quick review. Using textbook vocabulary aids or a college-level dictionary, write the appropriate definition and part of speech for each word. Next, copy the sentence in which you first saw the word used, followed by a sentence of your own in which you use it. Finally, write the other forms of the word listed in the glossary or dictionary and the part of speech of each.

If you use 3 by 5 cards, they might look like this:

Word: SIMULATION

Appropriate definition: Imitation or representation, as of a potential situation or in experimental testing.

Sentence from reading: "Within 20 minutes of an Indy race's completion, all the track data from the event - including each pit stop, caution flag, and crash - is streamed to the company's Web site, where a player can participate in a re-created <u>simulation</u> of the event."

My sentence using the word: I wonder if playing with the basketball game <u>simulation</u> at Children's Museum will help my brother's game.

Other forms of the word:
   Simulate, simulated, and simulating - verbs
   Simulator - noun
   Simulated and simulative - adjectives

| Exercise 20 |

Start Your Personal Vocabulary System

Select five words that you would like to learn from the readings in this chapter or from any other college reading you're currently doing. Record and practice using them in a notebook, in a computer document, or on 3 by 5 cards. When you have used your new words successfully a number of times, they will have become permanent parts of your personal vocabulary.

RU Ready to Dump Your Glasses?

Christine Gordon

In the following reading, Christine Gordon reports on an exciting new form of eye surgery that has already allowed many people to quit wearing glasses and contact lenses and is becoming more widely available and less expensive all the time. She explains, however, that some risk exists, and the results are not all good for everyone. As you read, consider the uses of new technology and the possible questions of safety. Also watch for new words you may want to add to your vocabulary.

1   Maybe you don't mind the dents your glasses have carved into the sides of your nose. Maybe you actually enjoy cleaning your contact lenses. But if you're anything like the 160 million other people in the U.S. who wear contact lenses or glasses, then you've probably occasionally wondered what your life would be like with perfect vision. Oh, what a beautiful prospect! No more foggy spectacles on winter days. No more fishing for dropped contacts in the bathroom sink. No more misplaced glasses when you're rushing off to work.

2   You could turn those dreams into reality—in less than 15 minutes. Just settle onto the surgical couch at an ophthalmologist's office and let an incredibly precise excimer laser reshape your eyes, or more accurately your corneas. Then get up and experience a bright new world. At least that's what doctors—and, more important, their ecstatic patients—are saying about LASIK. That's short for laser-assisted in situ keratomileusis, which could well become the most popular elective surgery among baby boomers since they all had their tonsils removed in the 1950s.

3   Chances are you already know people who have had their eyes—in that newest of buzz verbs—lasered. Nearly 500,000 Americans are expected to undergo the procedure in 1999—almost double the number in 1998. For 7 out of 10 it worked spectacularly: it corrected their vision to a very normal 20/20. Most of the rest still saw well enough to drive without corrective lenses. By 2010, some surgeons predict, LASIK will have advanced so far that 90% of patients will see better than 20/20. That's impressive for surgery you couldn't get in the U.S. until just four years ago.

4   Most patients aren't just happy with the results; they're positively gleeful. "Everything is so clear," says Yvonne Chapman, a registered nurse in Los Angeles who had her corneas reshaped six months ago. "I still go into the bathroom before bed every night to wash my hands and take my contacts out because I think I have them in." Never mind that LASIK costs upwards of $2,500 an eye and isn't covered by most insurance companies. We're talking about seeing your toes in the shower!

5   Still feeling unsure? Then drive over to the Fair Oaks Mall in Fairfax, Va., outside Washington, and watch through a plate glass window as surgeons

at the Visual Freedom Center perform the operation Mondays through Saturdays. Talk to the patients as they walk out the door. They will tell you how excited they are to be finally throwing away their glasses.

6   Now for the reality check. "LASIK is a surgical procedure with all the **attendant** Related attendant risks of any surgical procedure," says Dr. Mark Mannis, a professor of ophthalmology at the University of California at Davis, who has performed the operation on a weekly basis for the past four years. "It is highly successful in the vast majority of well-chosen cases, but"—and here you have to pay close attention—"each of those words I said is very important." The best candidates, he emphasizes, are those adults whose sight is only moderately distorted, whose vision is stable and who have no other eye problem. Even so, complications occur that can't always be corrected.

7   It's also important to realize that 20/20 vision isn't synonymous with perfect eyesight. The standard eye chart measures vision under conditions in which contrast is high. But there are other factors, like how well you see in dim light or discriminate among various shades of gray, that help determine the overall quality of your vision and that can be adversely affected by LASIK.

8   Just ask Steven Assennata of East Brunswick, N.J. "If I had understood there was a chance I would be worse off, I might have changed my mind," he says. LASIK corrected his eyesight to 20/20 all right, at least in one eye, but left him seeing double and ruined his night vision so that he can no longer drive in the dark. The worst part, he says, is knowing he didn't need the surgery. Although his contacts were becoming a nuisance before the operation, he could have seen fine through admittedly thick glasses. Assennata's doctor says he was made aware of the risks.

9   There are no reliable statistics on people like Assennata who suffer serious post-LASIK complications. Estimates range from less than 1% of patients of corneal specialists to as high as 5% of patients of less experienced ophthalmologists. An additional 10% to 15% of patients must undergo a second LASIK procedure to get their correction right. These repeat procedures are considered "enhancements" rather than complications, but they **enhancements** Improvements do require another round of cutting and lasering. And in the absence of a long track record for the procedure, no one can guarantee that other problems won't crop up in 10, 20 or even 30 years.

10   LASIK is, after all, a young technology. Nearly all the excimer lasers used so far were actually approved by the Food and Drug Administration for a different type of eye surgery. (Doctors are allowed to adapt certain existing technologies to new uses.) The first excimer laser specifically designed for LASIK wasn't approved by the FDA until July 1998. Two more types of excimers are expected to pass muster by the end of this year.

11   In the past two years there have been some dramatic improvements in LASIK technology. And that, no doubt, helps explain why so many eye surgeons have chosen to undergo the procedure themselves.

GORDON, "RU Ready to Dump Your Glasses?"

| Exercise 21 | **Work with Words** |

Read the following sentences from Reading 4 and write a brief definition of the italicized word or words using your knowledge of context clues and word parts. If necessary, use the dictionary.

1. Just settle onto the surgical couch at an ophthalmologist's office and let an *incredibly* precise excimer laser reshape your eyes, or more accurately your corneas. (par. 2)

    incredibly _____

2. That's short for laser-assisted in situ keratomileusis, which could well become the most popular *elective* surgery among baby boomers since they all had their tonsils removed in the 1950s. (par. 2)

    elective _____

3. Chances are you already know people who have had their eyes—in the newest of buzz verbs—*lasered*. (par. 3)

    lasered _____

4. It's also important to realize that 20/20 vision isn't *synonymous with* perfect eyesight.

    synonymous with _____

5. There are no reliable statistics on people like Assennata who suffer serious *post-LASIK* complications. (par. 9)

    post-LASIK _____

6. And in the absence of a long *track record* for the procedure, no one can guarantee that other problems won't crop up in 10, 20 or even 30 years. LASIK is, after all, a young technology. (pars. 9 and 10)

    track record _____

| Exercise 22 | **Use a Dictionary** |

The following words all appear in Reading 4. Using a dictionary, choose the appropriate meaning of each word, and write it on the line. Also, write the part of speech for each word.

1. Just settle on the surgical couch at an *ophthalmologist's* office and let an incredibly precise excimer laser reshape your eyes, or more accurately your *corneas*. (par. 2)

    ophthalmologist _____

    part of speech: _____

cornea _____

part of speech: _____

2. But there are other factors, like how well you see in dim light or *discriminate* among various shades of gray, that help determine the overall quality of your vision and that can be *adversely* affected by LASIK. (par. 7)

discriminate _____

part of speech: _____

adversely _____

part of speech: _____

3. These repeat procedures are considered *"enhancements"* rather than complications, but they do require another round of cutting and lasering. (par. 9)

enhancements _____

part of speech: _____

Exercise 23

Check Your Understanding

Choose the best answers to the following multiple-choice questions about Reading 4.

1. People who wear glasses are excited about the new excimer laser surgery because
   a. it can change cornea color.
   b. it can reshape their eyes so they don't have to wear glasses.
   c. it can prevent cataracts.

2. How does the reading characterize the risk of laser eye surgery?
   a. There is none.
   b. There is so little that no one should be afraid to have the surgery done.
   c. There is definitely some risk involved that has to be taken into consideration.

3. Probably people in the future will
   a. be more likely to undergo laser surgery to correct their vision.
   b. be less likely to undergo laser surgery to correct their vision.
   c. rely on cornea transplants instead of laser surgery.

4. The main consideration when you evaluate eyesight is
   a. whether you have 20/20 vision.
   b. whether your eyes function correctly in a number of ways.
   c. whether you have double vision.

5. According to the author, reliable statistics on post-Lasik complications are
   a. currently available as an aid to decision making.
   b. not really available yet.
   c. unnecessary because we have the testimony of many satisfied patients.

| Exercise 24 |

Make Connections: Collaborative Activity

Write short answers to the following questions based on Reading 4, your experience, and your observations. Then, to extend this exercise, discuss your answers with your class group. Working together, prepare a report for your class as a whole or a written summary for your instructor.

1. Supposing your eyesight needed correction, would you consider having laser surgery now? Why or why not?

   _____

   _____

   _____

   _____

2. What new technologies in medicine and health have become available in your lifetime? Which ones have you or people you know used? With what results? What *disadvantages* could medical technology have?

   _____

   _____

   _____

   _____

Chapter Review

To aid your review of the reading skills in Chapter 2, study the Put It Together chart.

Put It Together: *Vocabulary Skills*

Clues to help you understand the meaning of a word

Context (see pages 68–74)	The sentence or paragraph in which a word appears
Definition (see pages 69–70)	Answers the question, "What is it?"
Synonym (see page 70)	A word that has the same or similar meaning
Transitions (see page 71)	Words or phrases that link ideas and/or identify relationships
Compare (see pages 72–73)	To show how items are alike or similar
Contrast (see pages 72–73)	To show how items are different

Word Parts to help you figure out the meaning of a word

Root (see page 81)	Core part of a word to which prefixes and suffixes are added
Prefix (see pages 81–83)	An addition at the beginning of a word that changes the word's meaning
Suffix (see pages 86–87)	Ending of a word that often indicates the part of speech

To reinforce your thinking before taking the Mastery Tests, complete as many of the following activities as your instructor assigns.

Reviewing Skills

Collect 20 technology-related terms from this chapter, from magazines, or other textbooks. Then, on a separate piece of paper, write a definition for each and state where you got the information—textbook aid, context, word parts, or the dictionary.

Collaborating

Work together in a group to answer the following questions:

1. What kinds of technological aids to communication do you now use?

2. How has this technology already been improved since you first started using it?

3. How has this technology changed your way of doing things? How has it changed your way of life?

Enter your group's answers in the following chart.

Technological Devices for Communication	*Improvements*	*Life Style Changes*
1.		
2.		
3.		
4.		

Writing

Use your imagination, the information you read in this chapter, and the information your group accumulated in the collaborative activity to write a description of the communication patterns and technology that you think will be in place 10 or 20 years from now. Feel free to dream about what you see as ideal, or, on the other hand, to warn about the communication disasters you see looming in the future.

Extending Your Thinking

How advanced is your academic community in utilizing technology to enhance communication? Devise a simple survey and conduct it at your college. What communications technology does your institution use? Is the technology used by a select few or do all students and faculty members have access to it and the skills to use it? What are the college's plans for the future?

Visiting the Web

The following Web sites provide more information on technology, science, and using the Internet.

1. *Learn the Internet*

http://www.lehnert.awl.com
This Web site encourages students to learn the Internet by using it; includes platform-specific information for Windows, Macintosh, and UNIX and detailed checklists for specific browsers and e-mail packages.

2. *Inventions*

www.mit.edu/invent
This is MIT's Web site for inventors. It provides entertainment with its catalog of inventions, contests for inventors, and related Web sites for online innovation information.

3. *The Mad Scientist Network*

www.madsci.org
This Web site provides answers about science from 800 researchers in the Mad Scientist Network. It includes experiments to try at home.

Name _____ Date _____

Why Memory Changes and How

[Adapted from] Sandra Blakeslee

This reading explores the ways that our memories are formed in our brains, and how recent scientific research has discovered much about how memory works. As you read, consider what the advantages and/or or disadvantages might be of being able to change people's memories. Use your vocabulary skills from Chapter 2 to help you understand unfamiliar words in the reading.

1 Have you ever thought about how you remember something that has happened to you? Or why two people who witness the same event will, years later, have different memories of what happened? Now scientists may have found a biological reason for why our memories of an event often change over the years.

2 It seems that every time an old memory is pulled into our consciousness—or remembered—our brain takes it apart, updates it, and then makes new proteins in the process of putting the memory back into long-term storage. The fact that new proteins are made means that the memory has been transformed permanently to reflect each person's life experiences—not just the memory itself. The idea that the production of new proteins can somehow change the memory itself is based on research on fear in animals. Many experts predict, however, that it may also hold true for other kinds of memories in humans. They also say the discovery could lead to ways of altering or erasing people's memories.

3 The research on the animals was done at the Center for Neural Science at New York University, and it was described in the August 17, 2000 issue of *Nature*. According to Dr. Daniel Schacter, a Harvard psychology professor and memory expert, "This is the first good neurobiological explanation of the way memories are updated. It's a mistake to think that once you record a memory, it is forever fixed." Does this mean that we might be able to change people's memories one day? Perhaps.

Good News: We Might Be Able to Erase Traumatic Memories

4 Dr. Elizabeth Loftus, a psychologist who studies memory at the University of Washington in Seattle, said: "We're on the brink of being able to figure out how you might accomplish something like memory engineering." According to her, we might be able to erase traumatic memories in people who are plagued by them. We might also be able to better understand how false memories are implanted into people's minds by suggestion.

5   It has been known for over 100 years that newly formed memories are unstable at first, according to neurobiologist Dr. Yadin Dudai from the Weizmann Institute of Science in Israel. A bump on the head, an electric shock, or certain drugs can disrupt the process that gradually turns short-term memories into long-term memories. This happens because of the production of new connections and protein synthesis in memory circuits.

6   Scientists Dr. Karim Nader and Dr. Glenn Shafe from New York University have carried out new experiments on memory recall in ways that show with much greater precision how cellular mechanisms work. In their experiments, they played a tone and at the same time delivered an electric shock to the feet of caged rats. Later, when the rats heard just the tone, they froze. This process is called "fear conditioning." The rats learned to be afraid of the tone because they learned to associate it with the electric shock. Researchers know exactly how and where this fear memory is hardwired into the rat's amygdala, a part of the brain that processes emotions. But when the rat's amygdala was injected with a drug that blocks protein synthesis shortly after fear conditioning, the rat did not acquire long-term memory of the fear. If, however, the drug was injected six or more hours later, the memory was not blocked. For six hours or so, memory is what scientists call labile—open, or sensitive, to some kind of manipulation. After this time, the brain has already made new proteins to consolidate and store the memory. After this period, the memory is firmly in place.

Memories Can Change

7   Dr. Nader wanted to take his research even further. He wanted to understand what happens to a memory when you remember it. And he wanted to find out if it became "labile" (changeable) again. So he proposed a new experiment: Animals would be trained to associate a tone with receiving an electric shock. Researchers would wait a day or more after the animals have been shocked so that the fear memory has time to consolidate, or become more permanent. Then they would present the animal with the tone (which will make them remember their fear) and a drug that blocks protein synthesis. They were surprised by the results. Instead of freezing from fear at the tone, the rats scarcely reacted. The drug that blocked protein synthesis somehow allowed the rats to forget their experience with the tone. It meant that memories became labile and open to revision every time they are recalled. And new proteins have to be made before the memories are put back into storage.

8   Dr. Nader's research is only a first step in exploring the biology of how the brain consolidates and manipulates memories. It is not known if much older and more established memories are open to editing, or if this mechanism is restricted to fear memories alone. Why would memory have evolved in this way? Why are memories changeable? We would think that memories

have to be reliable to guide our behavior, but they also have to be open to new information.

9   In the long run, these findings may be used clinically to erase traumatic memories. When a patient recalls an event, he or she could be given a drug or other agent to disrupt the memory from being reconsolidated. Of course, if we can change a memory, incorrect as well as correct information can be woven into the fabric of a memory. A person would have no way of knowing what is true or not true.

Adapted from BLAKESLEE,
"Experts Learn More on Why Memory Changes and How"

Use the context clues and word-part clues to chose the best definitions of the italicized words in the following sentences from the reading.

1. It seems that every time an old memory is pulled into our consciousness—that is, remembered—our brain takes it apart, *updates* it, and then makes new proteins in the process of putting the memory back into long-term storage. (par. 2)

    updates
    a. brings it up to date
    b. dates it
    c. replaces the date on it

2. We're on the *brink* of being able to figure out how you might accomplish something like memory engineering. (par. 4)

    brink
    a. aftermath
    b. edge
    c. distant future

3. We're on the brink of being able to figure out how you might accomplish something like *memory engineering*. (par. 4)

    memory engineering
    a. engineering by memory
    b. managing or constructing memory
    c. designing skillfully from memory

4. We might also be able to better understand how false memories are *implanted* into people's minds by suggestion. (par. 4)

    implanted
    a. not planted
    b. put into
    c. taken out

5. It has been known for over 100 years that newly formed memories are *unstable* at first, according to neurobiologist Dr. Yadin Dudai. (par. 5)

   unstable
   a. not reliable
   b. not able
   c. not stable

6. It has been known for over 100 years that newly formed memories are unstable at first, according to *neurobiologist* Dr. Yadin Dudai. (par. 5)

   neurobiologist
   a. a person who forms new memories
   b. a person who studies the biology of neurons
   c. a person who is unstable

7. Researchers know exactly how and where this fear memory is hard-wired into the rat's *amygdala*, a part of the brain that processes emotions. (par. 6)

   amygdala
   a. fear memory
   b. the brain
   c. a part of the brain that processes emotions

8. For six hours or so, memory is what scientists call *labile*—open, or sensitive, to some kind of manipulation. (par. 6)

   labile
   a. open to manipulation or change
   b. open or sensitive
   c. scientists' memory

9. Researchers would wait a day or more after the animals have been shocked so that the fear memory has time to *consolidate,* or become more permanent. (par. 7)

   consolidate
   a. form with a solid fear
   b. become more permanent
   c. research cause of shock

Choose the best definition (from the *American Heritage Dictionary*) for the italicized words in the following sentences.

10. They also say the discovery could lead to ways of *altering* or erasing people's memories. (par. 2)

Name _____ Date _____

al·ter (ôl′tər) *v.* **al·tered, al·ter·ing, al·ters.** —*tr.* **1.** To change or make different; modify: *altered my will.* **2.** To adjust (a garment) for a better fit. **3.** To castrate or spay (an animal, such as a cat or a dog). —*intr.* To change or become
different. [Middle English *alteren,* from Old French *alterer,* from Medieval
Latin *alterāre,* from Latin *alter,* other. See **al-**¹ below.]

a. to change or make different
b. to adjust (a garment) for a better fit
c. to castrate or spay (an animal such as a cat or a dog)

11. According to her, we might be able to erase *traumatic* memories in
    people who are plagued by them. (par. 4)

    trau·ma (trou′mə, trô′-) *n., pl.* **trau·mas** or **trau·ma·ta** (-mə-tə). **1.** *Medicine.*
    A serious injury or shock to the body, as from violence or an accident. **2.** *Psy-*
    chiatry. An emotional wound or shock that creates substantial, lasting damage to
    the psychological development of a person, often leading to neurosis. —*attribu-*
    tive. Often used to modify another noun: *a trauma center; a trauma team.*
    [Greek. See **terə-**¹ below.] —**trau·mat′ic** (-măt′ĭk) *adj.*—**trau·mat′i·cal·ly** *adv.*

    a. a serious injury or shock to the body
    b. having to do with an emotional wound or shock that creates sub-
       stantial, lasting damage to the psychological development of a
       person

12. A bump on the head, an electric shock, or certain drugs can disrupt
    the process that gradually turns *short-term* memories into long-term
    memories. (par. 5)

    short-term (shôrt′tûrm′) *adj.* **1.** Involving or lasting a relatively brief time.
    2.a. Payable or reaching maturity within a relatively brief time, such as a
    year: *a short-term loan.* **b.** Acquired over a relatively brief time: *short-term*
    capital gains.

    a. acquired over a relatively brief time
    b. payable or reaching maturity within a relatively brief time
    c. involving or lasting a relatively brief time

13. This happens because of the production of new connections and
    protein *synthesis* in memory circuits. (par. 5)

    syn·the·sis (sĭn′thĭ-sĭs) *n., pl.* **syn·the·ses** (-sēz′). **1.a.** The combining of sepa-
    rate elements or substances to form a coherent whole. **b.** The complex whole
    so formed. **2.** *Chemistry.* Formation of a compound from simpler compounds
    or elements. **3.** *Philosophy.* **a.** Reasoning from the general to the particular;
    logical deduction. **b.** The combination of thesis and antithesis in the Hegelian
    dialectical process whereby a new and higher level of truth is produced.
    [Latin, collection, from Greek *sunthesis,* from *suntithenai,* to put together:
    sun-, syn- + *tithenai,* to put; see **dhē-** in Appendix.] —**syn′the·sist** *n.*

a. reasoning from the general to the particular
b. the combining of separate elements or substances to form a coherent whole
c. formation of a compound from simpler compounds or elements

Choose the best answers to the following multiple-choice questions about the reading.

14. When the brain remembers something, it
    a. updates it and makes new proteins.
    b. puts it back into short-term storage.
    c. keeps the memory unchanged.

15. According to Dr. Daniel Schacter, it is a mistake to think that memories are
    a. updated.
    b. forever fixed.
    c. changeable.

16. People have known for over a hundred years that newly formed memories are
    a. usually inaccurate.
    b. unstable at first.
    c. able to be disrupted with certain chemical substances.

17. When the rats took a drug that blocks protein synthesis,
    a. they did not react with fear when they heard the tone that they had learned to associate with receiving an electric shock.
    b. they reacted as the scientists expected.
    c. it helped them to remember their experiences with the tone and the electric shocks.

18. Now scientists believe that in the future it may be possible to
    a. train rats to pass memories on to offspring.
    b. make drugs that are even more effective in blocking protein synthesis.
    c. erase traumatic memories

Write short answers to the following questions based on your reading, your observations, and your experience.

19. In what situations do you think that it might be good to change people's memories? What example is given in the reading?

    _____

    _____

Name _____ Date _____

_____

_____

20. When do you think that it might be bad to change people's memories? Give examples.

_____

_____

_____

_____

Name _____ Date _____

The Virtual Surgeon

[Adapted from] Daniel Sorid and Samuel K. Moore

This reading reports on the use of virtual reality to train the surgeons of the future. Like pilots, doctors will be able to practice tasks on computer-based simulators before they encounter real patients in surgery. As you read, notice the numerous new words, and apply the word skills you learned in Chapter 2 to help you understand them.

virtual reality simulator A computer that creates an appearance of reality

cadaver A dead body

1 Virtual reality (VR) games might be coming out of the arcades and into the medical schools. Advocates of modernizing medical practice look forward to the day when surgeons can perfect their skills on virtual reality simulators and medical students can train on virtual cadavers that would be so realistic that they would be nearly indistinguishable from a real person.

2 This new technology comes at a critical time. A recent report released by the Institute of Medicine in Washington, DC, estimates that medical errors may cause 100,000 patient deaths each year in the United States alone. Proponents of virtual reality believe that the incorporation of the technology into medical training will bring this grim statistic down.

Virtual Surgery Practice

3 Already there are a few success stories for the use of medical VR. Some medical schools have begun using VR "games" to test students' surgical aptitude, and one of the most popular surgical trainers is the MIST VR system (MIST is short for minimally invasive surgery training). About 70 schools, including Harvard University, Pennsylvania State University, and Emory University, now use it to teach laparoscopic surgery.

4 Over the last decade, the growing use of laparoscopy has radically reduced the pain and cost of some types of surgery, and it has reduced the recovery time for patients as well. In a real-life laparoscopic operation, the surgeon inserts a tiny camera through a small incision in the patient's body. In this way the surgeon can see the patient's internal organs on a video monitor. Then surgical instruments are inserted and manipulated through several more tiny holes. But the technique requires tremendous dexterity.

5 MIST doesn't look much like this surgical setup. The color monitor displays simple geometric shapes, not the simulated body parts. But the device hooked to the computer has the handles of the actual tools that surgeons use for laparoscopy on the gallbladder or ovaries. So, while it doesn't simulate exactly what a surgeon would see during the operation, it does train students to develop their *psychomotor* skills to become surgeons. The student grasps the tools and then runs through simple drills to improve his or her eye-hand coordination. There are six basic tasks, ranging from pick-

psychomotor Connecting processes in the brain with movement

Name _____ Date _____

ing up a virtual ball and putting it in a box to holding the ball with one hand and cutting three objects from it with the other hand. The computer assesses not only whether students can perform the tasks, but also how efficiently they move, how long they take, and whether they make any serious errors, like cutting a "healthy" part of the virtual ball. Unlike a human assessor, the computer measures performance exactly.

The Virtual Emergency Room

6   One of the largest collections of medical simulators in the world has been assembled at the U.S. military's medical school in Bethesda, Maryland. Most of the simulators are used to teach skills needed by field or emergency room surgeons. The center now owns or is developing virtual tools for doing things like removing blood from around the heart (pericardiocentesis) and diagnosing internal bleeding in the abdomen (peritoneal lavage). Typically these procedures are taught on cadavers or on live pigs or goats. The center also has simulators for treating limb trauma, sewing blood vessels together, catheter insertion, and bronchoscopy.

7   In the center's "emergency room," the simulators surround a synthetic patient, a mannequin that has been programmed to react in physiologically correct ways, as if it were a living person. The mannequin can inhale air and exhale carbon dioxide, and its pulse can be made to fluctuate or fade. In a typical training scenario, the instructor programs the mannequin to bleed internally. Students make their diagnosis by observing the mannequin's reactions; then, using the VR simulators, they can perform the correct treatment. The long-term goal of the center is to have trauma training be entirely virtual so that they won't have to use cadavers or animals anymore. Instead, they would use computer-based simulators.

8   These VR trainers can be adjusted to the user, to pinpoint areas of weakness, and they can be used at any time, without the need for supervision. What's more, they prepare the student psychologically for surgical tasks, because complications can be simulated in a safe manner. They can also give objective scores of a student's ability. Indeed, studies show that computer-based training simulations are at least as good as standard training methods. Eventually, it is hoped, medical students and practicing physicians will be able to walk into the computer laboratory of their local hospital and practice a certain kind of surgery or test their dexterity with surgical tools.

The Limitations

9   We're good at simulating simple things, like poking needles into chests and drawing fluids out," said Alan Liu, a VR expert for the U.S. military in Bethesda, Md. "We're less successful with elaborate procedures, like making incisions and going after tumors. And as for complete end-to-end simulation—

prepping a patient, opening up, doing a transplant or repairing an organ, and closing up again—nobody has done anything like that in its entirety."

10   Physicians rely a great deal on their sense of touch for everything from routine diagnosis to complex, life-saving surgical procedures. So *haptics,* or the ability to simulate touch, goes a long way toward making VR simulators more lifelike. Current technology allows for the simulation of touch and sound (such as a patient expressing discomfort), as well as for the lifelike images; however, the cost of this greater realism—the sense of touch—can be prohibitive. It is because of this cost that haptics has not yet become part of the training available to future surgeons.

11   While the potential is great for virtual reality surgery training, and while there are a few excellent examples of where it has been implemented, unfortunately, medical training practice has not yet changed much. Sleep-deprived medical students still learn by working on whatever cases happen to be wheeled through the door. Patients still undergo extraordinarily painful surgery, requiring weeks of recovery in bed. Surgeons still train using crude, age-old methods, like peeling grapes or operating on dead human bodies or anesthetized animals. Today, only 1 percent of medical students in the United States receive any type of virtual reality training. And virtual reality is more likely to be found in the hospital arcade room than in the operating room. The potentials are there for the new technology, but we have a long way to go before we can use them to the fullest.

Adapted from SORID AND MOORE, "Virtual Surgeon"

Read the following sentences from or about the reading. Choose the best definition for the italicized words. Use context clues and definitions from the *American Heritage Dictionary* to assist you.

1. *Advocates* of modernizing medical practice look forward to the day when surgeons can perfect their skills on virtual reality simulators. (par. 1)

   advocate

   ad·vo·cate (ăd′və-kāt′) *tr.v.* ad·vo·cat·ed, ad·vo·cat·ing, ad·vo·cates. 1. To speak, plead, or argue in favor of. See Synonyms at support. —ad·vo·cate (-kĭt, -kāt′) *n.* 1. One that argues for a cause; a supporter or defender: *an advocate of civil rights.* 2. One that pleads in another's behalf; an intercessor: *advocates for abused children and spouses.* 3. A lawyer.

   a. a lawyer
   b. a supporter
   c. to speak in favor of

2. *Virtual reality* (VR) games might be coming out of the arcades and into the medical schools. (par. 1)

virtual

vir·tu·al (vûr′chōo-əl) *adj.* **1.** Existing or resulting in essence or effect though not in actual fact, form, or name: *the virtual extinction of the buffalo.* **2.** Existing in the mind, especially as a product of the imagination. Used in literary criticism of text.

a. existing in effect, though not in fact
b. a product of the imagination

3. The *incorporation* of technology will reduce the number of errors that lead to patient deaths. (par. 2)

incorporation

in·cor·po·rate (ĭn-kôr′pə-rāt′) *v.* **in·cor·po·rat·ed, in·cor·po·rat·ing, in·cor·po·rates.** —*tr.* **1.** To unite (one thing) with something else already in existence: *incorporated the letter into her diary.* **2.** To admit as a member to a corporation or similar organization. **3.** To cause to merge or combine together into a united whole. **4.** To cause to form into a legal corporation: *incorporate a business.* **5.** To give substance or material form to; embody. —*intr.* **1.** To become united or combined into an organized body. **2.** To become or form a legal corporation: *San Antonio incorporated as a city in 1837.* —**in·cor·po·rate** (-pər-ĭt) *adj.* **1.** Combined into one united body; merged. **2.** Formed into a legal corporation. [Middle English *incorporaten,* from Late Latin *incorporāre,* incorporāt-, to form into a body: Latin *in-,* in; see IN-[2] + Latin *corpus,* corpor-, body; see CORPUS.] —**in·cor′po·ra·ble** (-pər-ə-bəl) *adj.* —**in·cor′po·ra′tion** *n.* —**in·cor′po·ra′tive** *adj.* —**in·cor′po·ra′tor** *n.*

a. formation of a legal corporation
b. admission as a member
c. combination to form a whole

4. *Sleep-deprived* medical students still learn by working on whatever cases happen to be wheeled through the door. (par. 11)

sleep-deprived

de·prived (dĭ-prīvd′) *adj.* **1.** Marked by deprivation, especially of economic or social necessities. **2.** Lacking in advantage, opportunity, or experience: *"Preschool is designed to give children from educationally deprived households an early boost"* (Jeff Brody).

de·prive (dĭ-prīv′) *tr.v.* **de·prived, de·priv·ing, de·prives.** **1.** To take something away from: *The court ruling deprived us of any share in the inheritance.* **2.** To keep from possessing or enjoying; deny: *They were deprived of a normal childhood by the war.* **3.** To remove from office. [Middle English *depriven,* from Old French *depriver,* from Medieval Latin *dēprīvāre:* Latin *dē-,* de- +

Latin *prīvāre*, to rob (from *prīvus*, alone, without; see **per**[1] below).] —
de·priv′a·ble *adj.*

a. marked by economic or social deprivation which affects sleep

b. lacking in advantages to sleep

c. lacking enough sleep

Based on context clues and word-part clues, choose the best definitions of the italicized words in the following sentences from or about the reading.

5. Some medical schools have begun using VR "games" to test students' surgical *aptitude*, and one of the most popular surgical trainers is the MIST VR system (MIST is short for minimally invasive surgery training). (par. 3)

   aptitude

   a. ability

   b. preferences

   b. enjoyment

6. In a real-life *laparoscopic operation*, the surgeon inserts a tiny camera through a small incision in the patient's body. In this way the surgeon can see the patient's internal organs on a video monitor. Then, surgical instruments are inserted and manipulated through several more tiny holes. (par. 4)

   laparoscopic operation

   a. surgery using the operating room and modern medical equipment

   b. the use of a medical camera

   c. surgery that relies on cameras and instruments that reduce the extent of cutting

7. The computer *assesses* not only whether students can perform the tasks, but also how efficiently they move, how long they take, and whether they make any serious errors, like cutting a "healthy" part of the virtual ball. (par. 5)

   assesses

   a. criticizes

   b. measures

   c. restricts

8. The center now owns or is developing virtual tools for doing things like removing blood from around the heart (*pericardiocentesis*) and diagnosing internal bleeding in the abdomen (peritoneal lavage). (par. 6)

pericardiocentesis
a. diagnosing internal bleeding
b. internal bleeding
c. removing blood around the heart

9. We're good at simulating simple things, like poking needles into chests and drawing fluids out, but we're less successful with *elaborate* procedures, like making incisions and going after tumors. (par. 9)

   elaborate
   a. complicated
   b. simple
   c. disappointing

10. And as for complete *end-to-end* simulation—prepping a patient, opening up, doing a transplant or repairing an organ, and closing up again—nobody has done anything like that in its entirety.

    end-to-end
    a. from the final step
    b. prepping a patient
    c. from the beginning to the end

Use context clues and word-part clues to write the definitions of the italicized words in the following sentences from or about the reading.

11. Virtual cadavers can be so realistic that they would be nearly *indistinguishable* from a real person.

    indistinguishable _____

12. One of the most popular surgical trainers is the *MIST* VR system (MIST is short for minimally invasive surgery training).

    MIST _____

13. In the center's "emergency room," the simulators surround a *synthetic* patient, a mannequin that has been programmed to react in physiologically correct ways, as if it were a living person. (par. 7)

    synthetic _____

Choose the best answers to the following multiple-choice questions about the reading.

14. The author seems to support the idea that
    a. doctors are exceptionally well prepared for surgery today.
    b. doctors' training could be improved by the use of virtual reality.
    c. virtual reality should have no place in the training of doctors today.

15. Using simulators in medicine
    a. would help avoid errors.
    b. would be very different from the way airline pilots use them.
    c. would be less accurate than using cadavers.

16. The practice of medicine in the United States now has an estimated
    a. 10,000 fatal accidents a year.
    b. 100,000 fatal accidents a year.
    c. 1,000,000 fatal accidents a year.

17. Current technology allows for
    a. only graphic images.
    b. simulations based on touch, called *haptics*, only.
    c. the simulation of touch and sound as well as some lifelike images.

18. Medical students
    a. all benefit greatly from the availability of virtual reality training.
    b. still learn under the same conditions of many years ago.
    c. need not have the conditions of their training improved. It is thorough enough as it is.

Write short answers to the following questions based on your reading, your observations, and your experience.

19. Have you had the opportunity to experience virtual reality in entertainment or at work? If so, what was your response to this experience? If not, would you like to? Explain your answer.

    _____

    _____

    _____

    _____

20. What part do you think virtual reality could play in the career of your choice? How helpful do you think it could be? Explain your answer.

    _____

    _____

    _____

    _____

Chapter 3

Main Ideas

Learning and Education

Only the educated are free.

—*Epictetus*

- What do you think Epictetus, the Greek philosopher, meant when he said this 2000 years ago?
- Do you agree with the quotation? Why or why not?
- Who is in the photo?

Getting Ready to Read

What is learning? Above all, it is acquiring new knowledge and skills. Students come to college, or any school, to learn, to be educated. You and many generations of students before you have come to schools to learn all that you can to improve your life—to make more money, to learn skills for a career, to make friends, to broaden your thinking, and to enrich your understanding of the world around you. But how do you actually learn all that you want and need to know? How can you continue a lifetime of learning for the ever-changing world of the future?

In this chapter you will read and think about learning—about how and why we learn, about our educational system, and about the role expectations play in learning. As you do, you will improve your reading skills by learning how to

- identify topics
- identify main ideas
- identify thesis statements

READING 1

Building a Better Brain   Daniel Golden

The following reading is from a Life magazine report on how to increase the power of our brains, the physical storehouse of all we know and learn. Recent research suggests that we can control the remarkable power of the brain more easily than we ever expected and that its strength stays with us "well into old age." What do you think are the secrets for making your brain work to its best potential? As you read, think about yourself and people you know. Do you or your acquaintances do some of the things that Golden lists? Do you do different kinds of things, or do you stick with activities that are easy for you?

1 Evidence is accumulating that the brain works a lot like a muscle—the harder you use it, the more it grows. Although scientists had long believed the brain's circuitry was hard-wired by adolescence and inflexible in adulthood, its newly discovered ability to change and adapt is apparently with us well into old age. Best of all, this research has opened up an exciting world of possibilities for treating strokes and head injuries—and warding off Alzheimer's disease.

How to Make Your Dendrites Grow and Grow

2 What can the average person do to strengthen his or her mind? "The important thing is to be actively involved in areas unfamiliar to you," says Arnold

dendritic growth
Growth of nerve cells (dendrites) in the brain

Scheibel, head of UCLA's Brain Research Institute. "Anything that's intellectually challenging can probably serve as a kind of stimulus for dendritic growth, which means it adds to the computational reserves in your brain."

3 So pick something that's diverting and, most important, unfamiliar. A computer programmer might try sculpture; a ballerina might try marine navigation. Here are some other stimulating suggestions from brain researchers:

- Do puzzles. "I can't stand crosswords," says neuroscientist Antonio Damasio of the University of Iowa, "but they're a good idea." Psychologist Sherry Willis of Pennsylvania State University says, "People who do jigsaw puzzles show greater spatial ability, which you use when you look at a map."

- Try a musical instrument. "As soon as you decide to take up the violin, your brain has a whole new group of muscle-control problems to solve. But that's nothing compared with what the brain has to do before the violinist can begin to read notes on a page and correlate them with his or her fingers to create tones. This is a remarkable, high-level type of activity," says Scheibel.

- Fix something. Learn to reline your car's brakes or repair a shaver, suggests Zaven Khachaturian, a brain expert at the National Institute of Aging. "My basement is full of electronic gadgets, waiting to be repaired. The solution is not the important thing. It's the challenge."

- Try the arts. If your verbal skills are good, buy a set of watercolors and take a course. If your drawing skills are good, start a journal or write poetry.

- Dance. "We keep seeing a relationship between physical activity and cognitive maintenance," says Harvard brain researcher Marilyn Albert. "We suspect that moderately strenuous exercise leads to the development of small blood vessels. Blood carries oxygen, and oxygen nourishes the brain." But be sure the activity is new and requires thinking. Square dancing, ballet or tap is preferable to twisting the night away.

cognitive Having to do with understanding and thinking

- Date provocative people. Better yet, marry one of them. Willis suggests that the most pleasant and rewarding way to increase your dendrites is to "meet and interact with intelligent, interesting people." Try tournament bridge, chess, even sailboat racing.

4 And remember, researchers agree that it's never too late. Says Scheibel: "All of life should be a learning experience, not just for the trivial reasons but because by continuing the learning process, we are challenging our brain and therefore building brain circuitry. Literally. This is the way the brain operates."

GOLDEN, "Building a Better Brain"

| Exercise 1 | **Recall and Discuss** |

Answer these questions about Reading 1, and prepare to discuss them in class.

1. What does the statement "the brain works a lot like a muscle" mean?

   _____

   _____

2. What do brain researchers suggest we do to make our brains grow?

   _____

   _____

   _____

3. Why do you think there is a picture of Albert Einstein playing the violin at the beginning of the chapter? How does it tie into what we know about our brains?

   _____

   _____

   _____

4. Which of the activities suggested in this reading do you already do? Which would you like to start doing to keep your mind growing?

   _____

   _____

5. Are there any other activities that you think could be added to the list to strengthen our minds? What are they?

   _____

   _____

What Is a Reading About?

The goal of reading is to understand the information the author is trying to communicate to us. Recognizing the topics and the main ideas of a reading are important skills that assist us in understanding everything that we read.

Topics

topic A key word or phrase that describes the focus of the article and is often repeated throughout the reading

If you understand what you read, you should always be able to answer one basic question about the material: *What is this reading about?* When you answer this question, you are identifying the **topic** of the reading. You should be able to name the topic in just a few words.

For example, if you were asked to identify the *topic* of Reading 1, you might say it was *the human brain.* A more specific answer might be *how to strengthen your brain.* The topic is a key word or phrase that describes the focus of the article and is often repeated throughout the reading. For example, you probably noticed that the word *brain* and phrases such as *strengthening the brain* appeared several times in the reading.

Main Ideas

main idea What the reading says about the topic

In addition to recognizing the topic of a reading, you need to be able to answer another question: *What did the reading say about the topic?* When you answer this question, you are identifying the **main idea** of the reading. The main idea should be stated as a *complete sentence.*

main idea sentence A broad, or general, statement of the main point of the reading

For example, if someone asked you for the main idea of Reading 1, you might say it was the first sentence: *Evidence is accumulating that the brain works a lot like a muscle—the harder you use it, the more it grows.* Or, to state it in your own words, *Scientists now believe that you can strengthen your brain by exercising it.* The **main idea sentence** is a broad, or general, statement of the main point of the reading. When you write a main idea sentence in your own words, do not try to include all the important supporting details. For example, for Reading 1, you would not list any of the six specific suggestions that the author gave for ways to improve the mind.

The Difference between Topics and Main Ideas

To understand the difference between topics and main ideas, it's helpful to first see how they work in paragraphs. Remember, the topic is what the paragraph is about, and it can be named in a few words. The main idea is the overall point the author is making about the topic, and it should be stated as a complete sentence. See if you can tell the difference between the topic and the main idea in the following paragraph from Reading 1.

Dance. "We keep seeing a relationship between physical activity and cognitive maintenance," says Harvard brain researcher Marilyn Albert. "We suspect that moderately strenuous exercise leads to the development of small blood vessels. Blood carries oxygen, and oxygen nourishes the brain." But be sure the activity is new and requires thinking. Square dancing, ballet or tap is preferable to twisting the night away. (Golden, "Building a Better Brain")

What is the topic in the preceding passage? The topic is *the effect of exercise on the brain,* a very brief answer to the question "What is the paragraph about?" Note that the terms *physical activity*, *exercise,* and *activity* are all used in this short paragraph and that dancing is the example of a good physical activity.

What is the main idea of the passage? The main idea statement, *We keep seeing a relationship between physical activity and cognitive maintenance,* answers the question, "What is the author saying about the topic 'dance'?" Notice that the main idea sentence tells us how physical activities seem to benefit the brain.

| Exercise 2 | ## Identify Topics and Main Ideas

Read the following paragraphs from Reading 1, and in the spaces provided, write "T" for the topic and "MI" for the main idea.

1. Try a musical instrument. "As soon as you decide to take up the violin, your brain has a whole new group of muscle-control problems to solve. But that's nothing compared with what the brain has to do before the violinist can begin to read notes on a page and correlate them with his or her fingers to create tones. This is a remarkable, high-level type of activity," says Scheibel. (Golden, "Building a Better Brain")

     _____ a. The effects of playing musical instruments

     _____ b. Creating tones

     _____ c. Playing a musical instrument is a good activity for your brain.

2. Date provocative people. Better yet, marry one of them. Willis suggests that the most pleasant and rewarding way to increase your dendrites is to "meet and interact with intelligent, interesting people." Try tournament bridge, chess, even sailboat racing. (Golden, "Building a Better Brain")

     _____ a. Tournament bridge

     _____ b. Dating interesting, provocative people is a great way to improve your brain.

     _____ c. Dating interesting people and your brain

3. Fix something. Learn to reline your car's brakes or repair a shaver, suggests Zaven Khachaturian, a brain expert at the National Institute of Aging. "My basement is full of electronic gadgets, waiting to be repaired. The solution is not the important thing. It's the challenge." (Golden, "Building a Better Brain")

_____ a. Fixing things

_____ b. Zaven Khachaturian

_____ c. Fixing things is a good challenge for the brain.

Stated Main Ideas

stated main idea
The main idea as found directly stated in the reading itself

Main ideas are often stated in a single sentence. A **stated main idea** is in the reading itself. When writers make a clear main idea statement, they may put it in different parts of a paragraph.

Main Ideas at the Beginning

The main idea of a paragraph is often stated at the beginning, in the first or second sentence. Putting main ideas at the beginning makes it easier for readers to understand them—readers know right away what to expect from the paragraph, and they have a framework for what's to come. Textbook writers often state their topic and main idea at the beginning of a paragraph or longer passage and then go on to explain the main idea in more detail. Read the following two examples of paragraphs that have a stated main idea at the beginning.

There is widespread concern over the condition of education in this country today. Over one-fourth of students drop out of school before graduation. Some 13 percent of the nation's 17-year-olds are functionally illiterate. Achievement tests given to students in 13 industrialized countries show American students rank 11th in chemistry, 9th in physics (for students who have taken two years of physics), and last in biology. Average Japanese 12th graders have a better command of mathematics than the top 5 percent of their American counterparts generally do. (Mings, *Study of Economics*)

What is the topic of this paragraph? *American education or the condition of American education*

What is the main idea? *There is widespread concern over the condition of education today.*

The rest of the sentences in the paragraph explain in detail why we should be concerned: high school dropouts, illiteracy, and low achievement scores in sciences and math.

The following paragraph develops the main idea by explaining it again in other words. Read it and see if you can identify the topic and the main idea.

Your biggest thinking problem, and mine, and everybody's, is that our thinking becomes rigid. We respond to new situations and new problems with the same old ideas. Our thinking falls into a well-worn pattern—a rut. We tend to think in clichés.

What is the topic of this paragraph? *thinking or problems with thinking* What is the main idea of this paragraph? *Your biggest thinking problem, and mine, and everybody's, is that our thinking becomes rigid.*

After the statement of the main idea that rigid thinking is a problem, the idea is repeated three different ways in the rest of the sentences in the paragraph: "same old ideas," "a rut," and we "think in clichés."

Main Ideas in the Middle

Sometimes writers place the main idea statement closer to the middle of a paragraph. For an example, read the following paragraph:

Luisa Hernandez is like a lot of other college students. Every morning she searches for a decent parking place at her local community college. She commutes to school, holds down a full-time job, and is raising her two daughters while trying to study. She is only one example of a current trend in American education: More students who are attending college have adult responsibilities than ever before, and their concerns are somewhat different from the 18-year-old typical college freshman of earlier decades. Very often these older students aren't as interested in sports or extracurricular activities that most campuses offer. They are more concerned with having classes available to them both day and night, and with achieving their goal of getting from school to a good job as quickly as possible. In addition, since these students are usually not receiving aid from their parents, the cost of their education is an even more important factor for them.

What is the topic? *college students*

What is the main idea? The main idea is stated in the middle: *More students who are attending college have adult responsibilities than ever before, and their concerns are somewhat different from the 18-year-old typical college freshman of earlier decades.*

The rest of the paragraph goes on to explain in examples how their concerns are different: less interest in sports and extracurricular activities and more concern with flexible class schedules, getting a good job quickly, and the cost of their education.

Main Ideas at the End

Sometimes writers wait until the end of a paragraph to state their main idea. Often they do this when they are trying to argue a point, because you, as reader, may be more likely to be convinced if you hear the facts first and then hear the conclusions or suggestions. For example, read the following paragraph.

When it comes to homework, Japanese children study an average of 16 hours a week in junior high school and 19 hours a week in high school. U.S. students, in contrast, spend 3 hours a week on homework in junior high and 4 hours a week in high school. Taking into account the relative numbers of school days per year, some simple math brings us to the conclusion that U.S. high school students spend less than half the time studying in a year, whether in or out of school, than their Japanese peers!

What is the topic? *homework or hours spent on homework*

What is the main idea? The main idea is stated at the end: *U.S. high school students spend less than half the time studying in a year, whether in or out of school, than their Japanese peers.* In this case the writer gives her readers the facts and then leads them to the conclusion, or main idea.

| Exercise 3 | ## Identify Topics and Stated Main Ideas |

Read each of the following paragraphs, and circle the letter of the topic and the stated main idea for each. The first one has been done for you.

1. Another major . . . function of schooling is to offer custodial care of children—providing a place to put them and having someone to watch them. Schools keep children off the streets, presumably out of trouble. The importance of this function has increased, as there have been many more two-career and single-parent households. Schools have traditionally been effective in performing their custodial role. In the

past many schools were run under strict discipline, with teachers diligently enforcing rules and regulations and students obeying without question. But since the middle of this century a growing number of schools fit the description of "blackboard jungle," where violence and drugs are rampant. Nevertheless, an orderly routine still prevails in most schools. (Thio, *Sociology*)

What is the topic?
a. Two-career families
b. Violence and drugs
(c.) Custodial care of children in schools

What is the stated main idea?
a. Another major . . . function of schooling is to offer custodial care of children—providing a place to put them and having someone to watch them.
b. In the past many schools were run under strict discipline, with teachers diligently enforcing rules and regulations.
c. But since the middle of this century a growing number of schools fit the description of blackboard jungle, where violence and drugs are rampant.

2. Learning how to think is a two-step process. First you have to understand how your mind works, its strong points and its limitations. Then you need concrete and immediate advice and exercises that will help you improve your thinking skills. Without the basic understanding, the concrete steps are of limited value. You may find how to do something, but you don't know why, and therefore it will be hard for you to apply the techniques in a variety of situations. But the theory without the practical applications is equally limited. Thinking does not flow from the mere accumulation of facts; it's a skill that takes practice. (Cohen, *Re: Thinking*)

What is the topic?
a. Accumulating facts
b. Strong points and limitations
c. Learning how to think

What is the stated main idea?
a. First you have to understand how your mind works, its strong points and its limitations.
b. Learning how to think is a two-step process.
c. Then you need concrete and immediate advice and exercises that will help you improve your thinking skills.

3. Students are also expected to compete with other students in school. They are taught that they must do better than others to receive atten-

tion, good grades, and privileges. Those who do not compete, who pursue the activities they enjoy, may fail, be separated from their peer group, and be labeled as slow, hyperactive, disabled, or otherwise deviant. (Eshleman, Cashion, and Basirico, *Sociology*)

What is the topic?
a. Students and competition
b. Separation from the peer group
c. Deviant behavior in schools

What is the stated main idea?
a. Those who do not compete well are slow thinkers.
b. Students are also expected to compete with other students in school.
c. It is difficult to compete for attention, good grades, and privileges.

4. I am suggesting that we must reach for a higher standard to prepare kids to think for themselves and to think globally. And we must do this at a time when many parents and educators are seeking to lower standards because they have lost faith in our schools and our children. The key does not lie in setting up minimum standards or moderate standards or even stringently high standards. Instead, the key obviously lies in setting up proper incentives, where the principals and the teachers are told the higher the performance of your students, the higher your own rewards will be. Thus, they are always striving to meet a higher, not a minimum standard. And then, when they attain the standard, they will want to strive to achieve still higher goals. (Harris, "2001")

What is the topic?
a. Global thinking
b. Parents and educators
c. Incentives and higher standards

What is the stated main idea?
a. And we must do this at a time when many parents and educators are seeking to lower standards because they have lost faith in our schools and our children.
b. The key does not lie in setting up minimum standards or moderate standards or even stringently high standards.
c. Instead, the key obviously lies in setting up proper incentives, where the principals and the teachers are told the higher the performance of your students, the higher your own rewards will be.

5. The dropout rate in American high schools is still more than 25 percent, even though the relationship between education and future earnings is widely publicized. Industries predict a lack of well-prepared workers for

technical jobs in the future. American students perform poorly in math and science achievement tests compared to students in other industrialized nations. All of these factors—the dropout rate, lack of well-prepared workers, poor performance in math and science—cause many people to be concerned about education and the strength of the American economy in the years to come.

What is the topic?
a. Concerns about American education
b. High school dropouts
c. Technical knowledge

What is the stated main idea?
a. The dropout rate in American high schools is still more than 25 percent, even though the relationship between education and future earnings is widely publicized.
b. Industries predict a lack of well-prepared workers for technical jobs in the future.
c. All of these factors—the dropout rate, lack of well-prepared workers, poor performance in math and science—cause many people to be concerned about education and the strength of the American economy in the years to come.

6. There is a saying in the American culture that "you are never too old to learn." Increasingly, one sees older and younger people studying together in American institutions of higher learning. Women are encouraged to gain new skills to be able to enter the job market after their children are grown. Other people change careers, which often requires additional education. Institutions are attempting to meet the diverse needs and goals of these students. (Levine and Adelman, *Beyond Language*)

What is the topic?
a. Sayings in American culture
b. Diverse ages among college students
c. Women and the job market

What is the stated main idea?
a. There is a saying in the American culture that "you are never too old to learn."
b. Increasingly, one sees older and younger people studying together in American institutions of higher learning.
c. Women are encouraged to gain new skills to be able to enter the job market after their children are grown.

Organize to Learn: Mark Main Ideas

In Chapter 1 you learned that effective readers *organize* (<u>O</u> in the PRO system) what they have learned after they read. One popular way students do this is simply to *mark* the important points in the text itself. Now that you know how to identify stated main ideas, you can begin to mark them in the material you read. There are different ways to mark texts; many students use a highlighter, but you may also choose to underline with a pen or pencil. Be careful not to mark too much, because then everything will look important when you come back to review.

Begin by highlighting or underlining the main idea. The act of marking will reinforce the main points you have learned, and the marked text will make it easier for you to review key points when you study for tests. In Chapters 5 and 6 you will learn how to select important supporting details to mark as well.

Read the following paragraph. Notice that the stated main idea has been underlined for you.

> <u>International students and immigrants attending schools in the United States can experience multiple "culture shocks."</u> Students from abroad, accustomed to their countries' educational expectations, must adapt to new classroom norms in a foreign educational institution. In some countries, students must humbly obey their teachers' directions and remain absolutely silent during a class. Yet in other cultures, students are allowed to criticize or even contradict their teachers. In one country, a prayer in the classroom may be acceptable, while in another it may be forbidden. Cultural differences as well as the experience of being a newcomer account for some of the adjustment problems that non-native-born students experience. At the same time, a diverse student population on campuses helps some Americans appreciate that there are different habits, customs, and attitudes, and that the "American way" is not the only way. (Levine and Adelman, *Beyond Language*)

The topic of this paragraph is the culture shock that students face when they attend school in another country. The paragraph provides a number of examples of the kind of differences international and immigrant students encounter. The main idea is best stated in the first sentence, which provides an overview of what the paragraph will cover.

Exercise 4

Mark Stated Main Ideas and Identify Topics

Read each of the following paragraphs, and underline the stated main idea. Then write the topic in your own words. The first one has been done for you.

1. <u>The American education system is based on the idea that as many people as possible should have access to as much education as possible.</u>

This fact alone distinguishes the U.S. system from most others, since in most others the objective is as much to screen people out as it is to keep them in. The U.S. system has no standardized examinations whose results systematically prevent students from going on to higher levels of study, as the British and many other systems do. Through secondary and sometimes in post-secondary institutions as well, the American system tries to accommodate students even if their academic aspirations and aptitudes are not high, even if they are physically (and in some cases mentally) handicapped, and even if their native language is not English. (Althen, *American Ways*)

topic: *the basis of the American education system*

2. Before the 1960s education in Portugal had long been largely reserved for the rich and, as a consequence, illiteracy was widespread. Since then schools have been made accessible to large masses of children triggering an explosion in enrollment. But school financing remains low. Today, schools are overcrowded, money for books and equipment is scarce, and there is a shortage of teachers. As a result, the levels of student achievement [in Portugal] are among the lowest in Europe. (Thio, *Sociology*)

topic: _____

3. Resistance to change is the tendency to reject new ways of seeing or doing without examining them fairly. It has been the recurrent reaction to creativity throughout the ages. Galileo came close to losing his life when he suggested the sun, not the earth, was the center of the solar system. The inventors of the plow, the umbrella, the automobile, and the airplane were scoffed at, as were the individuals who first advocated using anesthetics during surgery, performing autopsies to determine the cause of death, and extending voting rights to women. Even the ending of child labor, which we now regard as eminently reasonable, was initially scorned: critics called it a Bolshevik attempt to nationalize children. (Ruggiero, *Art of Thinking*)

topic: _____

4. Bilingual and bicultural education at its best does a number of very positive things for our children and for our society. It teaches the children to be proud of themselves and of who they are. It teaches them to be proud of speaking two languages, and that there are advantages to being able to speak two languages. At the same time, these programs must teach children to be completely prepared to succeed in an English-speaking environment. They must not only be able to speak English well, they must be able to read, write, and learn in English as they advance through their years of education. Our society benefits because we

need citizens who can speak more than one language as we enter the global economy of the twenty-first century. Our children benefit because they will be prepared to be contributing citizens of this country.

topic: _____

5. In Japan, the average class size is 37 while ours is 24. One reason the Japanese can teach 37 students and attain a higher level of performance than here is because there is more respect for the school and the teacher in Japan than is true in this country. There is both societal and parental support for schooling in Japan, and neither the home nor the school would be willing to tolerate or accommodate the disruptions and disciplinary problems that disproportionately occupy the time and attention of our teachers and hinder the average student's opportunity to learn. (Gardner, "If We Stand, They Will Deliver")

topic: _____

6. The expectations we have of our students is also a crucial factor. What message have we been giving our students over the years as their grades have risen and their performance has fallen? As with our children, we do our students no favor by expecting less of them than they are able to give. If we expect much of them, they will give us much in return. If we stand, they will deliver. If we expect little of them they will have contempt both for what we are asking them to do and, in the end, for us. (Gardner, "If We Stand, They Will Deliver")

topic: _____

7. The history of American education after about 1870 reflects the impact of social and economic change. Although Horace Mann, Henry Barnard, and others had laid the foundations for state-supported school systems, most of these systems became compulsory only after the Civil War, when the growth of cities provided the concentration of population and financial resources necessary for economical mass education. In the 1860s about half the children in the country were getting some formal education, but this did not mean that half the children were attending school at any one time. Sessions were short, especially in rural areas, and many teachers were poorly trained. President Calvin Coolidge noted in his autobiography that the one-room school he attended in rural Vermont in the 1880s was open only in slack seasons when the twenty-odd students were not needed in the fields. "Few, if any, of my teachers reached the standard now required," he wrote, adding that his own younger sister had obtained a teaching certificate and actually taught a class when she was only 12. (Garraty, *American Nation*)

topic: _____

8. Aside from the differences in the quality of the schools, achievement is also affected by the expectations the teachers have for their students. There is considerable evidence that if teachers expect less from . . . students both in terms of academic achievement and behavior, for some students those expectations become a self-fulfilling prophecy. Robert Rosenthal and Lenore Jacobson performed an interesting experiment to demonstrate this. Experimenters gave a standard IQ test to pupils in 18 classrooms in a neighborhood elementary school. However, teachers were told that the instrument was the "Harvard Test of Inflected Acquisition" (which does not exist). Next, the experimenters arbitrarily selected 20 percent of the students' names and told their teachers that the test showed that these students would make remarkable progress in the coming year. When the students were retested eight months later, those who had been singled out as intellectual bloomers showed a significantly greater increase in IQ than the others. As you might expect, these findings created quite a controversy when they were first published, and many similar studies have since been made. Most of them supported Rosenthal and Jacobson's findings, but some did not, and it is not yet clear under exactly what conditions teachers' expectations are most likely to become a self-fulfilling prophecy. (Coleman and Cressey, *Social Problems*)

topic: _____

Thesis Statements

Now that you've practiced identifying main ideas in short passages, you're ready to tackle longer passages. Short essays are generally organized around a single main idea. You'll usually find that main idea stated close to the beginning of the essay, but it could be at the end. The main idea of an essay is also called the **thesis statement.**

thesis statement
The main idea of an essay

Sections of textbooks, too, are often built around a single concept. Each paragraph may not have a separate main idea, but together the paragraphs present a main idea, or thesis statement, often given at the beginning but sometimes the middle, or even the end, of the section.

Exercise 5 | ### Identify Main Ideas

Read the following excerpts about student learning. Notice how in each excerpt the separate paragraphs are unified by an overall main idea. Write the topic and main idea or thesis statement for each. The first one has been done for you.

1. Student participation in the classroom is not only accepted but also expected in most subjects. Some instructors and professors base part of

the student's grade on oral participation. Courses are often organized around classroom discussions, student questions, and informal lectures, although large classes can involve formal lectures during which the student has a passive role.

In a small percentage of the more informal classes, students may even decide the topics for study and choose appropriate books and articles. In some courses (mainly graduate seminars), the teacher has only a managerial role and the students do the actual teaching through discussions and presentations. It is common for instructors to guide students to take the initiative and to be responsible for their learning. Especially students pursuing advanced degrees are expected to be actively involved in their own education. They must be ready to critique theories, formulate models, and interact with the professor. Students who do not ask questions and do not bring up their own ideas may appear to be uninterested in the course.

A professor's teaching style is another factor that determines the degree and type of student participation. Some instructors and professors prefer to guide the class without dominating it. Many encourage students to question and challenge their ideas. Students who contradict teachers must be prepared to defend their positions. In general, confident and experienced instructors do not object to students who disagree with them.

dominating
Controlling

contradict Disagree with, openly deny

Instruction in science and mathematics is usually more traditional, with teachers presenting formal lectures and students taking notes. However, the educational trends that have influenced the teaching of the humanities and social sciences have also affected mathematics and the "hard sciences." Students may be asked to solve problems in groups or to design projects. Classes that are considered applied rather than theoretical stress such "hands-on" involvement. (Levine and Adelman, *Beyond Language*)

What is the topic?

Student participation, or student participation in the classroom

What is the main idea, or thesis statement?

Student participation in the college classroom is not only accepted but also

expected in most subjects.

2. For quite a while now educators have simply assumed that all you had to do was go to school, and if you absorbed a lot of information, somehow you would automatically learn to think. That assumption has turned out to be quite wrong, and the problems spawned by that false assumption are now being felt.

In New York City, for example, there was great concern over a decline in reading test scores. The decline was considered a scandal and became a political issue, so a massive effort was made to improve reading scores. And the effort paid off, for test scores did improve. But while reading scores were going up, the ability to reason—to think—was going down. Learning to read and learning to think are not the same thing.

A recent Rockefeller Foundation report recommends that training in thinking be among the basic skills taught by all schools. The report recognizes the fact that thinking is a skill that can be learned. It is not something that grows inevitably out of the accumulation of facts. And anyone can learn to be a better thinker. (Cohen, *Re: Thinking*)

What is the topic?

_____

What is the main idea, or thesis statement?

_____

_____

3. In classrooms across the country, there are children who come to school each morning after spending the night in barracks-type shelters. All too often, instead of spending their evenings doing homework, they've had to keep a watchful eye on drug abusers, street criminals, or former mental patients living alongside them. Frequently separated from other family members, wearing clothing that may make them targets of ridicule, and denied a decent breakfast—thanks to shelter policies that rigidly schedule meals without regard to school opening times—these youngsters may be too busy keeping body and soul together to learn the lessons, the sports, and the social skills that we are trying to teach.

According to the Children's Defense Fund, these youngsters are among the estimated 50,000 to 500,000 homeless children, many of whom are of school age. . . .

The increasing number of homeless children means schools will have to become more responsive to their special needs. This will mean rethinking certain bureaucratic rules—for example, homeless children often have been denied admission to school because their parents were unable to produce the coin of the realm: the necessary birth certificates, guardianship papers, and immunization records. School attendance may also be foreclosed by lack of money for transportation to a school no longer nearby, for school supplies, and for adequate clothing. Schools may also have to get involved in providing or coordinating such special services as health care, counseling services, and before- and after-school care, and special tutoring programs—services that benefit the non-homeless as well. (Chenoweth and Free, "Homeless Children Come to School")

What is the topic?

_____

What is the main idea, or thesis statement? (It is not at the beginning.)

_____

_____

Broaden Your Perspective   Vincent Ryan Ruggiero

The following reading is taken from a college critical thinking textbook. In it, the author explains why it is important for you to be able to understand the world and yourself in many different ways. He explains that you should not be limited by others' expectations of you. As you read, think about the expectations that people have had of you and how they have affected your performance in school.

1   Do you know the story of the six blind men and the elephant? Able to rely only on their sense of touch, they reached out and touched an elephant to learn about it. One touched its side and decided that an elephant was like a wall. The second touched its trunk and decided—a snake. The third, its tail—a rope; the fourth, its ear—a fan; the fifth, its leg—a tree; the last, its tusk—a spear. Now each had a clear picture of the elephant in mind. But because all the pictures were based on a limited perspective, all were wrong.[1]

2   All too often we are like the six blind men in our *perspective* on the world. We see narrowly, and our thinking suffers as a result. The first and perhaps saddest way we are victimized by narrow perspectives is in our view of our own potential. Most of us never come to know ourselves fully. We see only what we are and never realize the larger part of us: *what we have the capacity to be.* We never appreciate just how much of what we are is the result of accident.

3   Our development, for example, and our degree of success are strongly influenced by the way others regard us. In one experiment, researchers administered an intelligence test to an entire elementary school. The researchers told the faculty that the test would identify students who were ready to undergo a "learning spurt." Actually, the test did no such thing: The testers merely selected some students at random and identified them as the ones whose learning would enjoy a spurt. Teachers were subsequently observed using the same materials and methods for these students as for others. Nevertheless, at the end of the year, when the researchers again

at random Without order or reason

tested the student body, they found that the students that had been singled out had gained twice as many IQ points as the other students.

4   What was responsible for this gain? Obviously the teachers had formed favorable attitudes toward these students and unconsciously transmitted their attitudes to the students. The students' self-images, in turn, were ultimately changed.[2]

5   If that experiment seems surprising, the following one, similar in its design, will seem astounding. Laboratory assistants were assigned the task of teaching rats to run a maze. They were told the rats were in two groups, fast learners and slow learners. Actually, all the rats were identical. After the test period, the rats that had been designated fast learners were found to have learned the maze better than the other rats. Like the schoolteachers, the lab assistants had formed preconceived notions about the rats, and those notions had not only affected the degree of patience and the amount of attention and encouragement the assistants displayed with the rats but also actually influenced the rats' performance.[3]

6   Studies show that confused, defeatist, helpless reactions are not inborn in us. They are *learned*. In one study people were given problems they were told could be solved but which in fact could not be. As their efforts to solve the problems failed, the subjects experienced increasing frustration, until they finally accepted their helplessness and gave up. The real point of the study, though, came later. When the same people were given solvable problems, they continued to act helpless and to give up without really trying.[4]

7   What do these studies suggest about everyday life? That parents who are inconsistent in their demands and unpredictable in their reactions, teachers who focus on the negative rather than the positive, and coaches and activity leaders who ignore actual performance or contribution can rob us of our confidence, lead us into the habit of failure, and blind us to our real potential.

8   One of the distinguishing marks of many successful people is their refusal to define themselves by other people's assessments. Winston Churchill was branded a slow learner. Martha Graham was told that she did not have the right kind of body to become a dancer. Thomas Edison was urged to quit school because he was considered hopelessly stupid. Later, on his first job, working for the railroad, he set a train on fire with one of his experiments and was dismissed. And Albert Einstein's early record was even worse. Here are some of the details:

- He was not only an unimpressive student; he was told flatly by one teacher, "You will never amount to anything."
- At age 15 he was asked to leave school.
- When he took his first entrance exam to Zurich Polytechnic School, he failed it and was required to spend a year in a Swiss high school before he could be admitted.

- At Zurich he did mediocre work and was so unimpressive to his professors that he was rejected as a postgraduate assistant and denied a recommendation for employment.
- He eventually obtained a job as tutor at a boarding school but was soon fired.
- He submitted a thesis on thermodynamics for a doctoral degree at Zurich. The thesis was rejected.

9   "Wait," you may be saying, "Churchill, Graham, Edison, and Einstein were very special people. The question is whether the average person can overcome negative assessments." The answer is yes. To cite just one example, a teacher noticed that when students saw themselves as stupid in a particular subject, they unconsciously conformed to that image. They believed they were stupid, so they behaved stupidly. He set about to change their self-image. And when that change occurred, they no longer behaved stupidly.[5]

10   The lesson here is not that legitimate criticism or advice should be ignored, nor that one can achieve competency in any field merely by belief. It is that you should not sell yourself short; your potential is undoubtedly much greater than you have ever realized. So when you catch yourself saying, "I'll never be able to do this" or "I don't have the talent to do that," remember that the past does not dictate the future. What people call talent is often nothing more than knowing the knack. And *that* can be learned.

Notes

1. John Godfrey Saxe, quoted in Don Fabun, *Communication: The Transfer of Meaning* (Encino, Calif.: Glencoe, 1968), p. 13.

2. D. Wallechinsky and I. Wallace, *The People's Almanac*, vol. 1 (New York: Doubleday, 1975), p. 1089.

3. Ibid.

4. D.S. Hiroto, "Locus of Control and Learned Helplessness," *Journal of Experimental Psychology* 102 (1974): 187–93. See also C. Diener and C. Dweck, "An Analysis of Learned Helplessness," *Journal of Personality and Social Psychology* 39 (1980):5.

5. Maxwell Maltz, *Psycho-Cybernetics* (New York: Pocket Books, 1969), pp. 49ff.

RUGGIERO, *Art of Thinking*

Exercise 6

Work with Words

Use context clues, word-part clues, and if necessary the dictionary to choose the best definition of the italicized words in the following sentences from Reading 2.

1. The first and perhaps saddest way we are victimized by narrow per-spectives is in our view of our own *potential*. Most of us never come to know ourselves fully. We see only what we are and never realize the larger part of us: what we have the capacity to be. (par. 2)

   potential
   a. problems
   b. possibilities
   c. resolution

2. Obviously the teachers had formed favorable attitudes toward these students and unconsciously *transmitted* their attitudes to the stu-dents. The students' self-images, in turn, were ultimately changed. (par. 4)

   transmitted
   a. changed
   b. communicated
   c. revised

3. If that experiment seems surprising, the following one, similar in its design, will seem *astounding*. (par. 5)

   astounding
   a. extremely surprising
   b. mildly surprising
   c. disappointing

4. Studies show that confused, *defeatist*, helpless reactions are not in-born in us. (par. 6)

   defeatist
   a. the opposite of helpless
   b. the opposite of confused
   c. the opposite of confident

5. So when you catch yourself saying, "I'll never be able to do this" or "I don't have the talent to do that," remember that the past does not *dictate* the future. (par. 10)

   dictate
   a. rule with an iron hand
   b. write what someone says
   c. determine, or decide

| Exercise 7 | **Identify Main Ideas and Thesis Statements**

Choose the best answers for the following multiple-choice questions about Reading 2.

1. Which of the following statements do you think best identifies the main idea, or thesis statement, of this entire passage?
   a. Do you know the story of the six blind men and the elephant?
   b. You should not sell yourself short; your potential is undoubtedly much greater than you have ever realized.
   c. Churchill, Graham, Edison, and Einstein were very special people.

2. Which of the following statements is the main idea of paragraph 3?
   a. The testers merely selected some students at random and identified them as the ones whose learning would enjoy a spurt.
   b. Our development . . . and our degree of success are strongly influenced by the way others regard us.
   c. In one experiment, researchers administered an intelligence test to an entire elementary school.

3. Which of the following statements is the main idea of paragraph 8?
   a. One of the distinguishing marks of many successful people is their refusal to define themselves by other people's assessments.
   b. Winston Churchill was branded a slow learner.
   c. Albert Einstein's early record suggested he would never achieve any kind of success.

| Exercise 8 |

Check Your Understanding

Write brief answers to the following questions about Reading 2.

1. Why does the author begin the selection with the story of the six blind men and the elephant? What is the point that he wants the story to make? (pars. 1 and 2)

   _____

   _____

   _____

   _____

   _____

2. What happened when researchers at an elementary school identified some students as "spurters"? (par. 3)

   _____

   _____

   _____

3. What does the author think was the reason for the students' gains in the elementary school experiment? (par. 4)

_____

_____

_____

4. Who are four people who refused to "define themselves by other people's assessments"? (par. 8)

_____

_____

| Exercise 9 |

Make Connections: Collaborative Activity

Write short answers to the following questions based on Reading 2, your experience, and your observations. Then, to extend this exercise, discuss your answers with your class group. Working together, prepare a report for your class as a whole or a written summary for your instructor.

1. Why do you think that the author of this reading gave so much information about Einstein's failure as a child and young man?

_____

_____

_____

_____

_____

2. Have you ever had a teacher who really believed in you? How did you respond to his or her expectations?

_____

_____

_____

3. Did you ever have a teacher you think may have underestimated your potential? How did you respond to his or her expectations?

_____

_____

READING 3

Learning the Student Role: Kindergarten as Academic Boot Camp

William E. Thompson and Joseph V. Hickey

The following reading is from a college sociology textbook. In it, the authors explain one view of the purpose and results of the kindergarten experience. What is the thesis statement for this reading? Also, as you read, think about what you know about the kindergarten experience. Do you agree with the purpose of kindergarten as presented here?

1   Education has been defined by classical and contemporary sociologists as one of the major social institutions. Its most important function has been and remains today that of socializing people into becoming productive members of society through a formalized, standardized procedure.

socializing
Preparing to fit in and to get along with others

2   Harry Gracey's research on kindergarten in a suburban school district in New York reveals that schools are large bureaucratic institutions. In the social organization of the schools, kindergarten is generally considered a year of preparation. A booklet prepared for parents by the staff of the school system that Gracey studied described the kindergarten experience as one that would "stimulate the child's desire to learn and cultivate skills . . . for learning in the rest of [the] school career." But Gracey found that kindergarten's most critical function was to teach children the "student role."

3   The unique job of the kindergarten in the educational division of labor seems . . . to be teaching children the student role . . . the repertoire of behavior and attitudes regarded by educators as appropriate to children in school. . . .

4   By the end of the school year, the successful kindergarten teacher has a well-organized group of children. They follow classroom routines automatically, having learned all the command signals and the expected responses . . . in our terms, [they have] learned the student role.

5   The children have learned to go through routines and to follow orders with unquestioning obedience, even when these make no sense to them. They have been disciplined to do as they are told by an authoritative person without significant protest.

6   According to Gracey, children who submit to school-imposed discipline become defined as "good students," while those who refuse to submit become known as "bad students," "troublemakers," or "problem children." He also surmised that children's creativity, initiative, and spontaneity are systematically eliminated, while unquestioned obedience to authority and rote

learning of meaningless material are encouraged and demanded. He concluded that learning the student role means "doing what you're told and never mind why."

anticipatory socialization
Advance preparation for people to function appropriately in adult life

7   Gracey contended that while kindergarten is designed to teach the student role, it may also be viewed as anticipatory socialization for adult life. Many children "will more than likely find themselves working in large-scale bureaucratic organizations, perhaps on the assembly line in the factory, perhaps in the paper routines of the white collar occupations, where they will be required to submit to rigid routines imposed by 'the company' which may make little sense to them." He concluded that those who learn to conform in school may also become successful bureaucratic functionaries as adults.

THOMPSON AND HICKEY, *Society in Focus*

| **Exercise 10** | ## Work with Words |

Use context clues, word-part clues, and if necessary the dictionary to choose the best definitions of the words that are italicized in the following sentences from Reading 3.

1. Harry Gracey's research on kindergarten in a suburban school district in New York *reveals* that schools are large bureaucratic institutions. (par. 2)

   reveals
   a. covers up
   b. shows
   c. criticizes

2. According to Gracey, children who *submit* to school-imposed discipline become defined as "good students," while those who refuse to *submit* become known as "bad students," "troublemakers," or "problem children." (par. 6)

   submit
   a. challenge
   b. disagree with
   c. give in

3. He concluded that those who learn to *conform* in school may also become successful bureaucratic functionaries as adults. (par. 7)

   conform
   a. be leaders
   b. be comfortable
   c. follow the rules

4. Gracey *contended* that although kindergarten is designed to teach the student role, it may also be viewed as anticipatory socialization for adult life. (par. 7)

contended
a. argued
b. disagreed
c. resented

Exercise 11 ## Identify Main Ideas and Thesis Statements

Choose the best answers to the following multiple-choice questions about Reading 3.

1. Which of the following sentences would be the best thesis statement for the reading?

   a. Kindergarten's most critical function is to teach the "student role," which is doing what you're told and never mind why.
   b. Kindergartens "stimulate the child's desire to learn."
   c. Those who learn to conform in school may also become successful adults.

2. Which of the following sentences would be the best main idea for paragraphs 3 through 5?
   a. The successful kindergarten teacher has a well-organized group of children.
   b. In an effective kindergarten class, the children follow classroom routines automatically after learning all the command signals and expected responses.
   c. The unique job of kindergarten seems to be teaching children the behavior and attitudes regarded by educators as appropriate to children in school.

3. Which of the following sentences would be the best main idea for paragraph 7?
   a. Many children will find themselves working in large-scale bureaucratic organizations when they grow up.
   b. Kindergarten may also be viewed as anticipatory socialization for adult life.
   c. Kindergarten children are required to submit to rigid routines imposed on them.

Exercise 12 ## Check Your Understanding

Write brief answers to the following questions about Reading 3.

1. What did the booklet that was prepared for parents say that children would learn in kindergarten?

The booklet said kindergarten would stimulate "the child's desire to learn and cultivate skills."

2. What kind of behaviors is Harry Gracey referring to when he uses the words "student role"?

He is referring to appropriate behaviors such as going through routines and following orders with unquestioned obedience.

3. Why does Harry Gracey think that kindergarten eliminates children's creativity, initiative, and spontaneity?

He thinks creativity, initiative and spontaneity are eliminated b/c the students are taught unquestioned obedience to authority and rote learning.

4. What kind of work does Harry Gracey say that kindergarten might prepare children for?

He says that kindergarten prepares children for work in bureaucratic organizations where workers are required to follow rigid routines.

| Exercise 13 | **Make Connections: Collaborative Activity** |

Write short answers to the following questions based on Reading 3, your experience, and your observations. Then, to extend this exercise, discuss your answers with your class group. Working together, prepare a report for your class as a whole or a written summary for your instructor.

1. Do you think that kindergarten should be mostly about teaching children how to behave in school? Explain your answer.

_____

_____

_____

2. What do the authors and Harry Gracey seem to think about the real purpose of kindergarten, which they've identified as teaching children the "student role"?

_____

_____

_____

3. How important do you think it is that people learn to conform to set rules without questioning them?

_____

_____

_____

4. What do you think are the most important things to teach children in kindergarten?

_____

_____

_____

READING 4

Aztec Education on the Eve of the Spanish Conquest
Enrique Dávalos

Enrique Dávalos is a Mexican scholar who has studied and written about Aztec society in Mexico before it was conquered by the Spanish in the sixteenth century. In the following reading, he explains how the Aztec educational system worked. As you read, pay particular attention to the ways that the school system was different from ours today as well as the ways it was similar.

1   It was the beginning of the Modern Age in Europe when the Spanish conquerors penetrated the lands of the Americas 500 years ago. The Europeans at the time had almost no public schools for children. They were surprised to learn the news sent by Hernan Cortes, the conqueror of Mexico, about the schools that Indians had for almost all their children. In Spain, the Catholic queen and king were just beginning to build the first public schools to teach basic skills in religion and literacy, while sophisticated educational institutions had been already created by the Aztecs for both boys and girls. The Aztecs, the people who dominated Mexico before the European invasion, had goals for their schools that were similar to those of our modern schools: they were designed to transmit cultural values and skills in a setting expressly created for children to prepare them for their future. At this time, the Europeans still used monasteries as schools for everybody regardless of age, including children, young adults, and old people. In fact, during the Middle Ages the Europeans didn't recognize that childhood was a special period of our life; they considered children "small adults," and they believed that it was best for children to learn to act like adults as soon as possible. In their books about education they wrote, "The well-behaved child is

the one who behaves like an old man." In contrast to the European schools, the Aztec schools were complex, diverse, and focused on the education of the new generation of young people.

2   The Aztecs ruled an empire from their fascinating capital city in the valley where Mexico City is now located. The Aztec capital, Tenochtitlán, was one of the largest cities in the world by 1500, having approximately one-quarter million people. The city was established on a lake called Texcoco. The city had a system of canals; both people and goods were transported by canoes. (After the Spanish conquest, the lake was dried out by building immense tunnels because the Spaniards did not know how to use the lake for agriculture, transportation, and the distribution of goods as the Aztecs had done.) Tenochtitlán was a multicultural city divided into *barrios,* or neighborhoods where people with different languages, religions, and professions lived. Each *barrio* had its own school called *telpochcalli.*

3   Aztec children began to attend the *telpochcalli*-school in their own neighborhood when they were about seven years old. Boys left their parents' house and made school their new home. Yet they returned during the day to eat with their parents and help them with some work. School girls spent more nights in their parents' home, but they also moved to the *telpochcalli.*

4   We don't know exactly what students learned in Aztec schools, but we do know that they studied two basic subjects. Religion was probably the most important subject, but "religion" in Aztec culture had a broad meaning. It included learning the history of gods and peoples, the use of different customs and ceremonies, and basic knowledge of how the whole universe works, from the movement of the stars to the organization of an ant hill. Every neighborhood had a specific profession that everybody learned and performed. Therefore, a second subject that children had to learn in the *telpochcalli* was the necessary skills to master their parents' profession. For example, a school in a merchant *barrio* would teach the children about trade routes, rules of buying and selling, and the use of money, like cacao-seeds and shells. In the same way, in Atempan, the famous *barrio* of physicians, boys and girls acquired medical skills and learned how to prepare medicinal plants.

5   Since the Aztecs ruled an empire based on political and military domination, boys were strongly encouraged to learn how to fight and behave in a war. An important skill that boys needed to learn was how to capture an enemy in the battlefield without killing him in order to later offer his body to the gods. On the other hand, our knowledge about the activities of girls in schools is more limited; in fact, some Spanish historians wrote that Indian women did not attend schools at all. But these reports are incorrect; the Spanish did not think that education of women was important or necessary, so they overlooked it among the Aztecs. In fact, we know that young women were taught that housekeeping was another kind of battle that they

needed to master. They also received training in how to raise and educate children, and they were especially prepared for the most crucial and difficult of the battles: pregnancy and childbirth. A strict division of labor between women and men was reflected in the different training provided for boys and girls in the schools.

division of labor The system of dividing who does what work

6   Children also learned manners and what was expected of them socially in the *telpochcalli.* Schools were annexed to temples, and both priests and priestesses played a key role in the children's education. Sexuality was, for example, an important issue in schools. In fact, each *telpochcalli* was divided into two centers, one for boys and one for girls. When students became older, priests asked them to control their sexual drives and concentrate their energies on productive work. However, the priests were also tolerant of students' desires, particularly when boys and girls attended a nocturnal school called *cuicacalli,* house of dance and music. For several months, students of both sexes studied together from sunset to midnight. They learned how to play music, dance, sing, and prepare performances for religious ceremonies. After classes, some students decided that they wanted to spend the night together, and they did. These relations could sometimes become more permanent love affairs, and they could even end in a marriage. Teachers and priests were tolerant if the relationship was discrete and was not clearly opposed to kinship rules that banned some sexual relations. In any case, after several years, students left the school to get married. At this point, a new stage of life began for an Aztec.

nocturnal Having to do with night

7   In addition to the *telpochcalli,* the Aztecs had a second kind of school called *calmecac.* It was not administered by the *barrios* but by the central government of the city. *Calmecac* was attended by both boys and girls and was designed to prepare the children of the elite to be the future religious, political, and military leaders of the empire. In *calmecac* the education was more intense than in *telpochcalli* in the fields of religion, philosophy, ethics, cosmology, and the learning of the complex systems of writing and reading. Learning reading and writing was particularly difficult since the ideographic codices required that the students have an extraordinary ability to memorize texts, numbers, dates, and the meanings of symbols. Discipline in a *calmecac* was more rigid than in a *telpochcalli* and included severe physical punishments, long fasts, permanent vigils, and constant self-sacrifices—pricking the body and extracting blood to offer to the gods. Education in a *calmecac* also incorporated the learning of rigid manners of dressing, walking, talking, eating, and laughing; these manners were symbols that would distinguish people of the empire's elite from common people.

ethics Rules of behavior; set of standards or values

ideographic codices The written documents of the Aztec who used graphic symbols for their writing

8   In addition, education in *calmecac* required absolute chastity for both men and women. Breaking this regulation could be punished, even with execution. There was, however, a sexual "compensation" for male students who graduated from *calmecac* because later they would have more opportunities to marry more than one wife. In fact, some important leaders had

chastity The condition of not having sexual relations

50 or more wives. This privilege was not granted to the women of the *calmecac*. They were expected to remain virgins until they left the *calmecac* and got married, because they could only marry one man at a time. The Aztecs were a patriarchal society in which women were not expected to become political or military rulers. However, the Aztecs had at least two queens who ruled the empire, and women who graduated from a *calmecac* could aspire to become religious leaders and occupy the highest positions in some temples and schools.

9   In general, children from the upper classes attended *calmecac*, while children of common people enrolled in *telpochcalli*. Therefore, the educational system functioned as a way of reproducing and maintaining the different social classes, as it often does today. Some children from the lower classes were accepted in *calmecac* in the same way that Harvard University today accepts a small group of students who do not come from an elite background. In this way, *calmecac* created the illusion that everybody had the opportunity to move up the social pyramid. This illusion, however, hid the fact that the few exceptions did not change the general rule that education for the elite was different from education for common people.

10   The sophisticated educational system in Aztec society was working and evolving into more complex arrangements when the Spaniards arrived in Mexico. After Cortes's army defeated the Aztecs, they destroyed the Indian empire and dismantled the Aztec schools. According to the Spaniards, those schools were "a creation of the Devil." Because of the conquest, Mexicans lost their educational systems without gaining any alternative education because the Spanish, with few exceptions, did not care about educating the Indian people. Under several centuries of Spanish domination, Mexicans lost their schools and therefore some of their cultural identity. The consequences are still present in modern Mexican society.

| Exercise 14 | ## Work with Words |

Use context clues, word-part clues, and if necessary, the dictionary to write in the definitions of the italicized words in the following sentences from Reading 4.

1. The Aztecs, the people who dominated Mexico before the European invasion, had goals for their schools that were similar to those of our modern schools: they were designed to *transmit* cultural values and skills in a setting expressly created for children to prepare them for their future. (par. 1)

   transmit _____

2. Tenochtitlán was a multicultural city divided into *barrios,* or neighborhoods where people with different languages, religions, and professions lived. (par. 2)

barrios _____

3. Each *barrio* had its own school called *telpochcalli.* (par. 2)

telpochcalli _____

4. Children also learned manners and what was expected of them socially in the telpochcalli. Schools were *annexed* to temples and both priests and priestesses played a key role in the children's education. Sexuality was, for example, an important issue in schools. (par. 6)

annexed _____

5. In this way, calmecac created the illusion that everybody had the opportunity to move up the social pyramid. This *illusion,* however, hid the fact that the few exceptions did not change the general rule that education for the elite was different from education for common people. (par. 9)

illusion _____

| Exercise 15 |

Identify Topics, Main Ideas, and Thesis Statements

Choose the best answers to the following multiple-choice questions about Reading 4.

1. What is the topic of this reading?
   a. the Aztec schools
   b. the Spanish schools
   c. the *telpochcalli*

2. What is the best thesis statement for the whole reading?
   a. The Aztecs had complex and diverse schools whose goals were to transmit cultural values and skills in institutions designed to educate all children.
   b. During the Middle Ages the Europeans didn't recognize that childhood was a special period of our life; they considered children as "small adults" and they believed that it was best for children to learn to act like adults as soon as possible.
   c. Under several centuries of Spanish domination, Mexicans lost their schools and therefore some of their cultural identity.

3. What is the best main idea statement for paragraph 2?

   a. The Aztec capital, Tenochtitlán, was one of the largest cities in the world by 1500, having approximately one-quarter million people.
   b. The Aztecs ruled an empire from their fascinating capital city in the valley where Mexico City is now located.
   c. Tenochtitlán was a multicultural city divided into *barrios,* or neighborhoods where people with different languages, religions, and professions lived.

4. What is the best main idea statement for paragraph 5?
   a. Since the Aztecs ruled an empire based on political and military domination, boys were strongly encouraged to learn how to fight and behave in a war.
   b. Thus, a strict division of labor between women and men was reflected in the different training provided for boys and girls in the schools.
   c. Yet, these reports are incorrect, probably because the Spanish themselves did not think that the education of women was important or necessary.

5. What is the best main idea statement for paragraph 7?
   a. In addition to the *telpochcalli*, the Aztecs had a second kind of school called *calmecac*.
   b. In *calmecac* the education was more intense than in *telpochcalli* in the fields of religion, philosophy, ethics, cosmology, and the learning of the complex systems of writing and reading.
   c. *Calmecac* was attended by both boys and girls, and was designed to prepare the children of the elite to be the future religious, political and military leaders of the empire.

| Exercise 16 |

Check Your Understanding

Write brief answers to the following questions about Reading 4.

1. Why were the Spaniards surprised by the Aztec educational system?

   _____

   _____

   _____

   _____

2. What were the two different kinds of schools that the Aztecs had, and whom did each of the schools serve?

   _____

   _____

3. What were the boys taught in the *telpochcalli,* and what were the girls taught? Why was their education so different?

_____

_____

_____

4. How were the marriage arrangements different for men and women of the elite classes in Aztec society?

_____

_____

5. In what ways were the *calmecac* similar to our elite universities like Harvard?

_____

_____

_____

6. What was the consequence of the Spaniards' dismantling of Aztec schools?

_____

_____

| Exercise 17 | **Make Connections: Collaborative Activity**

Write short answers to the following questions based on Reading 4, your experience, and your observations. Then, to extend this activity, discuss your answers with your class group. Working together, prepare a report for your class as a whole or a written summary for your instructor.

1. If you lived during the time of the Aztec empire, which of the two types of schools would you prefer to attend? Why?

_____

_____

2. Dávalos states that the purpose of Aztec schools was similar to the purpose of our schools today—to transmit cultural values and skills. Do you agree that this is the purpose of our schools? Explain your answer.

_____

_____

LANGUAGE TIP

Follow Directions

Most people, no matter how much education they have, have difficulty following directions. For some reason we all think we understand what we're supposed to do before we carefully listen to or read directions. For example, how often have you filled out a form incorrectly only because you didn't take your time? How often have you answered a test question incorrectly because you didn't take the time to read the question carefully, to be sure you understood before leaping on to the next step of actually writing? Let's see how well you follow directions now.

| Exercise 18 | ### Follow Directions |

Carefully follow all of the directions below. Be sure to read *all* the directions (1–7) before you do anything.

1. On a separate piece of paper, write your name in the top right corner.

2. Under your name, write today's date.

3. Put a circle around the date.

4. In the bottom right corner, write your birthday.

5. In the middle of the paper, draw a square.

6. Inside the square draw five zeros.

7. Don't do any of the things listed in numbers 1–6. Just sit and fold your hands on your desk.

How did you do following the directions? Congratulations if you read all the way to number 7 before you began to do anything!

Chapter Review

To aid your review of the reading skills in Chapter 3, study the Put It Together chart.

Put It Together: *Topics and Main Ideas*	
Skills and Concepts	*Explanation*
Topics (see pages 124–127)	A topic answers the question, "What is the reading about?" in a few words.
Main Ideas (see pages 125–132)	The main idea explains what the author is saying about a topic. It should be stated as a complete sentence.
Thesis Statements (see page 139)	A thesis statement expresses the main idea of an essay or longer readings, such as sections of a textbook that include several paragraphs.

To reinforce your learning before taking the Mastery Tests, complete as many of the following activities as your instructor assigns.

Reviewing Skills

Answer the following skills-review questions.

1. Explain how to identify a *topic* in a paragraph or longer passage.

_____

_____

2. Explain how to identify the *main idea* or a *thesis statement* in an essay or textbook section.

_____

_____

Collaborating

Brainstorm in a group. Have someone record all of the ways a teacher can help motivate students to learn. Then create a chart about motivational approaches. On the left, list each method of motivation. On the right, list what the group thinks the outcomes, or results, would be of this method. Consider that some methods would offer rewards and positive reinforcements, while others would emphasize negative consequences for failure.

Method of Motivation   *Outcomes*

1. _____   1. _____

   _____   _____

Method of Motivation	*Outcomes*
2. _____	2. _____
_____	_____
3. _____	3. _____
_____	_____
4. _____	4. _____
_____	_____
5. _____	5. _____
_____	_____

Writing

Choose one of the following topics to write about. Your instructor will tell you how much to write, and how to organize your writing.

1. What helps motivate you to learn?

2. Describe an unpleasant experience you had in school and how it affected your learning.

3. Describe a pleasant experience you had in school and how it affected your learning.

Extending Your Thinking

What kinds of problems and/or excellent programs exist in your local high school or grade school? Find an article or other source of information about these problems or programs. You might use any of the following:

■ article in a local newspaper or magazine

■ local Web site on the computer

■ local TV or radio news report

■ interview with high school students, parents, or school staff

Share the information you gather with your class group.

Visiting the Web

The following Web sites provide more information on learning and education.

1. *The National Library of Education*
   http://www.ed.gov/NLE

From the world's largest federally funded library, this site is devoted solely to education. NLE is the federal government's main resource center for education information.

2. *Rethinking Schools*

http://www.rethinkingschools.org
This online urban educational journal contains educational material and useful links for educators and students interested in public school reform.

3. *Center for Public School Renewal*

http://comnet.org/cpsr/
This is the Web site of an organization for teachers and community leaders promoting teacher-led schools and charter schools. The site includes interesting material about education.

4. *Coalition of Essential Schools (CES)*

http://www.essentialschools.org
The site of a national grassroots school-reform network. In its vision of education, students are active learners; school schedules and routines help teachers and students know each other well and work in an atmosphere of mutual trust and high expectations.

Name _____ Date _____

In Praise of the F Word Mary Sherry

The following reading suggests a different approach for motivating students: a "healthy fear of failure." As you read, look for main ideas and think about whether you agree or disagree with Sherry's thesis. Do you think that students get passing grades when they don't deserve them? Do you think that students would do better if teachers were stricter about grades and flunked students more often?

1 Tens of thousands of 18-year-olds will graduate this year and be handed meaningless diplomas. These diplomas won't look any different from those awarded their luckier classmates. Their validity will be questioned only when their employers discover that these graduates are semiliterate.

semiliterate Not able to read well enough to function well in everyday life

2 Eventually a fortunate few will find their way into educational-repair shops—adult-literacy programs, such as the one where I teach basic grammar and writing. There, high-school graduates and high-school dropouts pursuing graduate-equivalency certificates will learn the skills they should have learned in school. They will also discover they have been cheated by our educational system.

3 As I teach, I learn a lot about our schools. Early in each session I ask my students to write about an unpleasant experience they had in school. No writers' block here! "I wish someone would have had made me stop doing drugs and made me study." "I liked to party and no one seemed to care." "I was a good kid and didn't cause any trouble, so they just passed me along even though I didn't read well and couldn't write." And so on.

4 I am your basic do-gooder, and prior to teaching this class I blamed the poor academic skills our kids have today on drugs, divorce and other impediments to concentration necessary for doing well in school. But, as I rediscover each time I walk into the classroom, before a teacher can expect students to concentrate, he has to get their attention, no matter what distractions may be at hand. There are many ways to do this, and they have much to do with teaching style. However, if style alone won't do it, there is another way to show who holds the winning hand in the classroom. That is to reveal the trump card of failure.

5 I will never forget a teacher who played that card to get the attention of one of my children. Our youngest, a world-class charmer, did little to develop his intellectual talents but always got by. Until Mrs. Stifter.

6 Our son was a high-school senior when he had her for English. "He sits in the back of the room talking to his friends," she told me. "Why don't you move him to the front row?" I urged, believing the embarrassment would get him to settle down. Mrs. Stifter looked at me steely-eyed over her glasses. "I don't move seniors," she said. "I flunk them." I was flustered. Our son's academic life flashed before my eyes. No teacher had ever threatened him with

that before. I regained my composure and managed to say that I thought she was right. By the time I got home I was feeling pretty good about this. It was a radical approach for these times, but, well, why not? "She's going to flunk you," I told my son. I did not discuss it any further. Suddenly English became a priority in his life. He finished out the semester with an A.

7   I know one example doesn't make a case, but at night I see a parade of students who are angry and resentful for having been passed along until they could no longer even pretend to keep up. Of average intelligence or better, they eventually quit school, concluding they were too dumb to finish. "I should have been held back," is a comment I hear frequently. Even sadder are those students who are high-school graduates who say to me after a few weeks of class, "I don't know how I ever got a high-school diploma."

8   Passing students who have not mastered the work cheats them and the employers who expect graduates to have basic skills. We excuse this dishonest behavior by saying kids can't learn if they come from terrible environments. No one seems to stop to think that—no matter what environments they come from—most kids don't put school first on their list unless they perceive something is at stake. They'd rather be sailing.

9   Many students I see at night could give expert testimony on unemployment, chemical dependency, abusive relationships. In spite of these difficulties, they have decided to make education a priority. They are motivated by the desire for a better job or the need to hang on to the one they've got. They have a healthy fear of failure.

10   People of all ages can rise above their problems, but they need to have a reason to do so. Young people generally don't have the maturity to value education in the same way my adult students value it. But fear of failure, whether economic or academic, can motivate both.

11   Flunking as a regular policy has just as much merit today as it did two generations ago. We must review the threat of flunking and see it as it really is—a positive teaching tool. It is an expression of confidence by both teachers and parents that the students have the ability to learn the material presented to them. However, making it work again would take a dedicated, caring conspiracy between teachers and parents. It would mean facing the tough reality that passing kids who haven't learned the material—while it might save them grief for the short term—dooms them to long-term illiteracy. It would mean that teachers would have to follow through on their threats, and parents would have to stand behind them, knowing their children's best interests are indeed at stake. This means no more doing Scott's assignments for him because he might fail. No more passing Jodi because she's such a nice kid.

12   This is a policy that worked in the past and can work today. A wise teacher, with the support of his parents, gave our son the opportunity to succeed—or fail. It's time we return this choice to all students.

SHERRY, "In Praise of the F Word"

Based on the context clues in the reading, write the meaning of each of the italicized words below.

1. Eventually a fortunate few will find their way into educational-repair shops—adult-*literacy programs,* such as the one where I teach basic grammar and writing. (par. 2)

   literacy programs _____

2. I am your basic do-gooder, and prior to teaching this class I blamed the poor academic skills our kids have today on drugs, divorce and other *impediments* to concentration necessary for doing well in school. (par. 4)

   impediments _____

3. However, if style alone won't do it, there is another way to show who holds the winning hand in the classroom. That is to reveal the *trump card* of failure. (par. 4)

   trump card _____

4. Flunking as a regular policy has just as much *merit* today as it did two generations ago. We must review the threat of flunking and see it as it really is—a positive teaching tool. (par. 11)

   merit _____

5. It is an expression of confidence by both teachers and parents that the students have the ability to learn the material presented to them. However, making it work again would take a dedicated, caring *conspiracy* between teachers and parents. . . . It would mean that teachers would have to follow through on their threats, and parents would have to stand behind them, knowing their children's best interests are indeed at stake. (par. 11)

   conspiracy _____

Choose the best answers to the following multiple-choice questions about the reading.

6. Employers are upset when they find out that some of their employees
   a. only have a high-school diploma.
   b. have a high-school diploma but can barely read.
   c. dropped out of high school and lied on their applications.

7. Why are some high-school graduates' diplomas meaningless?
   a. because teachers pass students who can't or won't do the work
   b. because the students were not very talented
   c. because parents forced the school to let their children graduate

8. Sherry formed her opinions about grading
   a. from her experience in teaching an adult literacy class.
   b. when she was a high-school student.
   c. from her experience in teaching an adult literacy class, and from a high-school English teacher's threat to flunk her son.

9. When Sherry asked her students to write about an unpleasant experience they had in school, which of the following complaints was *not* made?
   a. being passed for not making trouble
   b. not being stopped from taking drugs
   c. being forced to work hard for classes

10. How does Sherry suggest teachers get the attention of students who can't concentrate?
    a. Be a basic do-gooder.
    b. Teaching style alone will be enough of a motivator.
    c. Use effective teaching style and threaten failure.

11. What effect does passing students who aren't qualified have on them?
    a. They become motivated.
    b. They and their employers feel cheated.
    c. They have higher self-esteem.

12. Which of the following is *not* a problem that the night students had?
    a. chemical dependency and unemployment
    b. abusive relationships
    c. too much free time on their hands

13. What is the topic of the reading?
    a. meaningless diplomas
    b. importance of flunking kids who don't achieve
    c. angry students

14. What is the thesis of the reading?
    a. Fear of failure can motivate students to rise above their problems and to value education.
    b. Young people generally don't have the maturity to value education in the same way adult students value it.
    c. People of all ages can rise above their problems if they have a reason to do so.

15. What is the main idea of paragraph 3?
    a. As I teach, I learn a lot about our schools.
    b. "I wish someone would have had made me stop doing drugs and made me study."
    c. "I liked to party and no one seemed to care."

16. What is the main idea of paragraph 7?
    a. Most kids don't put school first on their list of priorities.
    b. Many students eventually quit school.
    c. Students are frequently not happy to have been passed along.

17. What is the main idea of paragraph 11?
    a. Flunking students was a regular policy two generations ago.
    b. We must see the threat of flunking as a positive teaching tool.
    c. Parents should not help their child pass by doing his or her homework.

Write short answers to the following questions based on your reading, your experience, and your observations.

18. Do you think fear of failure is a good way to motivate students? Explain your answer.

    _____

    _____

    _____

    _____

19. Have you ever received a better or worse grade than you deserved? How did this experience affect you?

    _____

    _____

    _____

    _____

20. How did your favorite teachers give grades? Do you think their grading system was good set? Explain your answer and give examples.

    _____

    _____

    _____

    _____

The Problems of Our Schools: Myths and Reality

[Adapted from] Jerome Skolnick and Elliott Currie

The following reading summarizes the analysis of the American public schools that sociologists Jerome Skolnick and Elliott Currie make in their book, Crisis in American Institutions. *As you read, think about the debate over our public schools. Try to determine the thesis statement of the reading as well as the main ideas of the paragraphs.*

1   Sociologists Jerome Skolnick and Elliott Currie point out in their book *Crisis in American Institutions* that we Americans are constantly hearing reports about the inadequacy of our schools. Bad schools get blamed for a long list of our country's problems, from uneven economic development to the violence in our cities and towns. However, this negative image of our schools is not based on fact.

2   Let's look at the facts. The schools have more children from a wider range of backgrounds, and with more problems, than ever before. Nevertheless, the scores of achievement tests, which had fallen during the 1970s, are not falling any more. Moreover, more American students go to college than in just about any other industrial country. Finally, our system of higher education is one of the best in the world, and it attracts students from all over the world.

3   Overall, the public schools are better than people think.

4   There are, however, a number of serious problems with American schools, but it is important to know which problems are real and which ones are not.

5   According to Jonathan Kozol's study of the schools in East St. Louis, our schools are deteriorating rather than getting better. "Savage" inequalities continue to divide our children into those who get a good education and those who do not. In his study, Kozol describes some of the specific problems of these schools, from backed-up sewage, clogged toilets, rusty appliances, poorly paid and overworked teachers, to rooms with no heat in the winter. These schools are not that different from many other schools in poor communities around the country.

6   Some people like to argue that the schools have plenty of resources and funds but that they squander those resources. They assert that the taxpayers' money is wasted on big bureaucracies and greedy, mediocre teachers. And while there are, of course, some school districts that waste money, the charge against the public schools in general is greatly exaggerated. David Berliner and Bruce Biddle, in their book *The Manufactured Crisis: Myths, Fraud, and the Attack on America's Public Schools*, show that school spending has increased, but it hasn't been for salaries of bureaucrats or

teachers. The additional money has gone to pay for new responsibilities that we have given the schools—nutrition programs, school safety programs, day-care programs, medical care programs. Schools have been given these responsibilities because our society has not provided an adequate health care system or social service system for families and children. So, while school spending has increased, the money has been used to fund a series of important services to solve problems in our society that schools were not asked to solve in the past.

7   Much of the public believes that the schools are inadequate and even dangerous. The answer to this perception has been the growing popularity of the idea of "privatizing" the schools, sometimes called school "choice." One version of this idea is to give parents "vouchers" that would allow them to send their children to any school that they want to. The school would re-ceive money from the state to pay for educating the child. Opponents of the "school choice" system argue that it will lead to a two-tiered school system, with one set of schools for the privileged and one for the poor. They say it will allow wealthy and middle-class parents to pay a little extra to put their children into private schools (the voucher that comes from tax dollars would pay the rest). Then, once their children are no longer in the public schools, these parents will not be concerned about those schools or the children who remain in them.

Adapted from Skolnick and Currie, *Crisis in American Institutions*

Use context clues from the reading to write in your words the definitions of the italicized words.

1. The schools have more children from a wider *range* of backgrounds, and with more problems, than ever before. (par. 2)

    range _____

2. According to Jonathan Kozol's study of the schools in East St. Louis, our schools are *deteriorating* rather than getting better. "Savage" in-equalities continue to divide our children into those who get a good education and those who do not. In his study, Kozol describes some of the specific problems of these schools, from backed-up sewage, clogged toilets, rusty appliances, poorly paid and over-worked teachers, to rooms with no heat in the winter. (par. 5)

    deteriorating _____

3. Some people like to argue that the schools have plenty of resources and funds but that they *squander* those resources. (par. 6)

squander _____

4. They assert that the taxpayers' money is wasted on big bureaucracies and greedy, *mediocre* teachers. (par. 5)

   mediocre _____

5. Opponents of the "school choice" system argue that it will lead to a *two-tiered* school system, with one set of schools for the privileged and one for the poor. (par. 7)

   two-tiered _____

Choose the best answers to the following multiple-choice questions about the reading.

6. Which of the following sentences would be the best thesis statement for the reading?
   a. Americans are constantly hearing reports about the inadequacy of our schools.
   b. The scores of achievement tests, which had fallen during the 1970s, are not falling any more.
   c. The public schools are better than people think even though there are a number of serious problems.

7. Which of the following statements is *not* true about the American education system?
   a. More American students go to college than in any other industrial country.
   b. Our system of higher education is one of the best in the world.
   c. Most high-achieving American high school graduates go to colleges and universities in other countries.

8. Which of the following is the best topic for paragraph 5?
   a. inequality among public schools
   b. backed-up sewage
   c. schools in East St. Louis

9. Which of the following is the best main idea sentence for paragraph 5?
   a. Jonathan Kozol's study of the deteriorating schools in East St. Louis brings attention to one of the real problems.
   b. "Savage" inequalities continue to divide our children into those who get a good education and those who do not.
   c. These schools are not that different from many other schools in poor communities around the country.

10. What is the topic of paragraph 6?
    a. squandered money
    b. school funding and where it goes
    c. criticisms of the schools

11. Which of the following is the best main idea sentence for paragraph 6?
    a. While school spending has increased, the money has been used to fund a series of important services to solve problems in our society that schools were not asked to solve in the past.
    b. Some people like to argue that the schools have plenty of resources and funds but that they squander those resources.
    c. They assert that the taxpayers' money is wasted on big bureaucracies and greedy, mediocre teachers.

12. Which of the following are *not* additional expenses of increased spending of most of America's public schools?
    a. salaries for bureaucrats and teachers
    b. funding to solve problems of our society
    c. funding for school safety programs

Write brief answers to the following questions about the reading.

13. What are some of the positive achievements of American public schools?

    _____

    _____

    _____

    _____

14. What services has increased school funding paid for?

    _____

    _____

15. What, according to the reading, are the real problems of the U.S. public schools?

    _____

    _____

16. How does the system of school vouchers work?

    _____

    _____

Name _____ Date _____

17. Why, according to the reading, would the wealthy and middle-class parents stop being concerned with the poor public schools and the children who remain in them?

_____

_____

_____

_____

Write short answers to the following questions based on your reading, your experience, and your observations.

18. Many people argue that the "school choice" or school "voucher" system would help make the schools that are not doing well improve because they would have to compete for students. Do you agree? Explain your answer.

_____

_____

_____

_____

19. Thinking of your own experience with schools, what were the "bad" aspects of schools, and what do you think were the causes of the problems?

_____

_____

_____

_____

20. What were the good aspects of schools, and what do you think contributed to them?

_____

_____

_____

_____

Chapter 4

Unstated Main Ideas

Challenges in Education

Education is the process through which we discover that learning adds quality to our lives.

—William Glasser

- In what ways do you think education might be considered a process that adds quality to your life?

- The students in the photo are studying together. In what ways do you think studying with and getting to know other people with the same goals helps you to become a better student?

Getting Ready to Read

Why do some people do well in school and others do not? What behaviors, both in and out of the classroom, help us to do well in school? What behaviors hold us back? Some people believe that the home environment is most important for preparing students to do well; others believe that what happens in the classroom itself is most important. The answers to these questions are vital to us as individuals and to our society as a whole. After all, the purpose of schools is to help us prepare for life, to fit into our society, to be productive and aware citizens. How can we be sure that our schools are doing a good job?

In this chapter you will read and think about student behaviors and teacher behaviors, and what is necessary for students to be successful. As you do, you will improve your reading skills by learning how to

- identify unstated main ideas
- write main idea sentences in your own words

READING 1

Why Some Students Get A's Alex Thio

In the following reading from his sociology textbook, Alex Thio discusses some new ideas about why some students are motivated to do well in school. As you read, think about whether you agree with the ideas presented. Why are some students motivated to learn and others not? What do you think is important for students to want to do well in school? The teacher? The home environment? Or?

1 The search for a magic-bullet explanation for academic success continues. Usually parents get the credit or the blame. Sometimes it's laid off on schools or bureaucrats or even genetics. Now there's another entrant in the sweepstakes: the peer group. A new study of 20,000 high-school teens has concluded that the kids who kids hang out with have the greatest influence on an adolescent's classroom performance. According to the study, this is not good news. The prevailing attitude among students is that "getting by" is good enough. "There is," the study concludes, "substantial pressure on students to underachieve."

2 The study, published last month [October, 1997] in a new book called *Beyond the Classroom*, is the work of three academics, Temple University psychologist Laurence Steinberg, Stanford sociologist Stanford Dornbusch, and Bradford Brown, a psychologist at the University of Wisconsin. Together, they researched nine public high schools in California and Wisconsin. They polled students, interviewed families and observed classrooms. They compared the academic careers of students who began high school with equivalent grades

but who had different sorts of friends in the years that followed. They found that the youngsters with "more academically oriented" friends did better over the course of school, and that kids who hung out with more delinquent types were more likely themselves to get into trouble.

account for
Explain

3   Their findings help to account for ethnic differences in students' academic achievement. "The conventional explanation for why black and Latino kids do poorly in school and Asian-Americans perform at the highest levels is that it's their home environment. Our data suggest that might not be the case," Steinberg says. The researchers found that Asian parents were not unusually involved in their children's education. Indeed, black parents often were much more concerned. Still, Asian children had far more success in school.

4   Why? Asian students in the study found it harder to join popular crowds of "slackers," so they tended to form academically focused peer groups. Once in these crowds, Asian students studied together and pressed each other to earn A's. The opposite was true for black and Latino students. The groups they joined tended to sneer at academic accomplishment, sometimes dismissing it as "thinking white."

dismissing
Rejecting

5   These are powerful influences for parents and teachers to contend with. The authors offer no easy solutions. They suggest, unsurprisingly, that parents should "know your child's friends and steer children early in their development toward youngsters who value achievement and school."

THIO, *Sociology*

| Exercise 1 | ## Recall and Discuss |

Answer these questions about Reading 1, and prepare to discuss them in class.

1. What, according to the study the author discusses, has the greatest influence on whether kids do well in school? Do you agree? Explain.

   Peer presre from fom

2. Why do Asian students tend to do better in school than kids from other ethnic groups?

   They prese to each other to get A's

main ideas: Education
←There are several
reason why some
students excel over
other.

3. Why do African-American and Latino students tend to do worse?

They look down each other

_____

_____

4. Based on the findings from this study, how could schools organize activities that would encourage students to do better?

_____

_____

_____

5. Where do you think the pressure to underachieve comes from? Explain.

_____

_____

_____

Unstated Main Ideas

In Chapter 3 you identified topics and main ideas that were stated directly in the paragraph or passage. The main idea, as you remember, is simply a general statement, or assertion, the writer wants to make about the topic. However, as a reader you will find that main ideas are not always so obvious. Sometimes the main idea is not stated at all, and you need to arrive at the main point the writer is trying to make based on the information you are given. Sometimes authors deliberately avoid stating main ideas, or theses, to force readers to think critically about the information presented and to come to their own conclusions.

unstated main idea
The main idea of a reading that the reader must figure out because there is no main idea sentence

To decide on an **unstated main idea**, you should follow three basic steps.

1. Identify the topic.
2. List the points made about the topic.
3. Add up the points listed to arrive at the main idea.

Read the following paragraph and see if you can decide what the unstated main idea is by following these three steps.

Forty percent of Finns aged 24 to 65 have a college degree compared with 12 percent in the United States. Understandably, Finns are, per

capita, the greatest consumers of literature in the world. School attendance is compulsory up to age 16, an earlier age than in Belgium, but
schooling is rigorous. High school students attend classes 38 hours a
week, compared with about 25 hours in the United States. Finnish students are also required to take more courses, including two foreign languages. All higher education is free, with most financial support coming
from the state and the rest from private industries (Peltonen, 1993).
(Thio, *Sociology*)

What is the topic? *education in Finland*

What are the points made about the topic?

- *40 percent of Finns have college degrees versus 12 percent in the United States*
- *Finns consume the most literature (read the most) in the world*
- *Schooling is rigorous (very demanding)*
- *High school students are in class 38 hours a week versus 25 in the United States*
- *Finns take more courses, including two foreign languages*
- *All higher education is free*

Add up the points listed to arrive at the main idea:
What is the main idea? *Finland has an outstanding educational system.*

Sometimes authors seem to state more than one main idea within a single paragraph. Sometimes the ideas even contradict each other. As you
read you must think actively about the ideas presented. If you are asked
to identify the main idea in a paragraph where there appears to be more
than one, your statement of the main idea may need to include both
ideas. For example, read the following paragraph about the Japanese educational system.

The Japanese youngsters' academic excellence cannot be attributed to the
schools alone. Japanese mothers play a crucial role in their children's education, not only constantly encouraging hard work but also rendering help
with homework. After-school classes, called jukus ("cram shops"), also contribute substantially, as they are attended by more than one-quarter of all
primary pupils and more than one-half of all secondary students. Since so
many students are involved in this supplementary learning, Francis
McKenna concludes that the quality of Japanese schooling is actually lower
than popularly believed. (Thio, Sociology)

Which of the following sentences is the better statement of the main idea
of this paragraph?

_____ 1. The success of Japanese students may be due to the time they spend studying outside school rather than to the quality of the schools themselves.

_____ 2. After-school classes are the main reason why Japanese students are so successful academically.

You should have chosen sentence 1 as the better statement of the main idea for the paragraph. Sentence 2 emphasizes the contribution of extra hours to Japanese students' success, but the paragraph as a whole does not try to prove that this is the main reason, or the only reason, for their success. Also, this statement does not include the doubts raised in the last sentence of the paragraph about the quality of regular Japanese schools.

Exercise 2

Identify Unstated Main Ideas

For each of the following paragraphs, choose the sentence that is the better statement of the paragraph's main idea.

1. The public schools, supported by public funds, have the responsibility to teach skills needed in public life—among them the use of the English language. They also must inculcate an appreciation of all the cultures that have contributed to this country's complex social weave. To set one ethnic group apart as more worthy of attention than others is unjust, and might breed resentment against that group. (Mujica, "Bilingualism's Goal")

   _____ a. All cultures need to be appreciated by the schools, and all students need to be given a good education that includes English.

   _____ b. Special treatment of one ethnic group is not fair and causes resentment.

2. [His students'] life stories were amazing, and Crowfoot alone had heard every one. He struck up a conversation with a chunky kid in the front row and found himself listening to the dreams of a Salvadoran boy who hoped someday to become a cop. He complimented the artwork of the student who couldn't seem to shut up in class and found himself the confidant of a frustrated adolescent whose Guatemalan mother so feared the lure of gangs that she wouldn't let him out of the house. Someone stuck a wad of chewing gum into the hair of a tattooed class bully and, as he leaned forward to help remove it, he found himself unexpectedly moved by the gleam of hot tears welling in the boy's eyes. (Hubler, "Fledgling Teacher Gets Tough Lessons, Unexpected Rewards")

———— a. There were a lot of students in Crowfoot's class.

———— b. Crowfoot learned a lot about his students, and sometimes they did not fit the ideas that he had about them before he knew them better.

3. There has been phenomenal growth in the number of children who receive their formal education at home. Today there are about 500,000 such children, compared with only 12,500 in the late 1970s. Most of the home schooling parents are fundamentalist Christians who believe that religion is either abused or ignored in the public school. Other parents reject public education because of poor academic standards, overcrowding, or lack of safety. Most homeschooling parents have some college, with median incomes between $35,000 and $50,000. Over 90 percent are white. (adapted from Thio, *Sociology*)

——✓— a. More parents are choosing homeschooling for their children, and they are doing so for a variety of reasons.

———— b. Parents often reject public education because of the problems they observe there: poor academic standards, overcrowding, and lack of safety.

4. On a cloudy winter afternoon, Florann Greenberg, a teacher at P.S. 14 in New York City, noticed that her first-grade class was growing fidgety. One girl, dropping all pretense of work, stared at the snow falling outside the schoolroom windows. Annoyed, Greenberg asked her, "Haven't you seen snow before?" The girl whispered, "No." Her classmates began shaking their heads. Then it dawned on Greenberg: of course these children had never seen snow; almost all were immigrants from Colombia and the Dominican Republic. Immediately, she changed the lesson plan. New topic: What is snow? How is it formed? How do you dress in the snow? What games do you play? (Gray, "Teach Your Children Well")

———— a. Many children have never seen snow and are surprised and fascinated when they see it in New York City for the first time.

——✓— b. Teachers like Florann Greenberg need to recognize the diversity of their students' experience and to plan lessons accordingly.

5. Younger students sometimes have emotional problems in their educational environment. The stress of taking exams and of meeting deadlines can cause difficulty for those not used to responsibility and intense work. On the other hand, older students with children or with experi-

ence in jobs or the military adapt to pressure and stress more easily. A student who is also the parent of three children, for example, knows that grades, exams, and reports are not the most important aspects of life. Older students are also less likely to be intimidated by instructors or professors. (Levine and Adelman, *Beyond Language*)

_____ a. Younger students sometimes have emotional problems in
their educational environment.

___✓___ b. Older students are likely to handle the stress of being a
student better than young students.

READING 2

The Best Teacher in America

A. Jerome Jewler and John N. Gardner

The following reading is about Jaime Escalante, the math teacher who was made famous by the movie about his accomplishments, Stand and Deliver. *Escalante had incredible success with his students who were from Mexican-American families in East Los Angeles. As you read, notice what Escalante did and believed that made him such an exceptional teacher. Also, think about who your favorite teacher was, and why you liked that teacher so much. What qualities do you think make a good teacher?*

The film *Stand and Deliver* was based on the true story of Jaime Escalante's successes as a teacher in East Los Angeles.

1   Jaime Alfonso Escalante Gutierrez was born in 1930 in Bolivia and was educated in La Paz. Although he describes himself as "a somewhat undisciplined young man," he nevertheless excelled in school and went on to a
teacher training college because his family could not afford to send him to
engineering school. For twelve years as a high school teacher in La Paz, he
gained a reputation for excellence, creating a team of science students that
consistently won city-wide science contests.

2   In 1963 he and his family emigrated to the United States. Barred from
teaching because he did not hold a U.S. degree, he worked as a cook and
at other jobs while slowly earning night school credits at California State
University, Los Angeles. After ten years, in 1974, he was finally hired to teach
basic mathematics at Garfield High School, a predominantly Hispanic barrio
school in East Los Angeles.

barrio   A neighborhood with many residents whose families come from Latin America

3   In 1978 he began teaching an advanced placement (AP) calculus
course. Four years later, when all eighteen of his students passed the AP examination for college calculus (seven with perfect scores), the Educational
Testing Service, which administers the test, concluded that some of his students had copied their answers and forced twelve of them to retake the
test. All twelve passed a second time. With this incident, Escalante's program drew local, state, and national attention, including the dramatization
of the story in the 1988 film *Stand and Deliver.* By 1988–89 over 200 students were enrolled in the AP calculus program.

4   Jaime Escalante believes that motivation is the key to learning. Here's
what he has to say:

criterion   Reason

5   I do not recruit students by reviewing test scores or grades, nor are
they necessarily among the "gifted" or on some kind of "high IQ
track." . . . My sole criterion for acceptance in this program is that the
student wants to be a part of it and sincerely wants to learn math. I
tell my students, "The only thing you need to have for my program—
and you must bring it every day—is *ganas* [desire, or will to suc-
ceed]." If motivated properly, any student can learn mathematics. . . .

6   From the beginning, I cast the teacher in the role of the "coach"
and the students in the role of the "team." I made sure they knew
that we were all working together. . . .

7   I often break the students into groups to solve lecture problems. . . . After school, the students almost always work in teams. . . .

status   Level

8   The key to my success . . . is a very simple time-honored tradition: hard work, and lots of it, for teacher and student alike. . . .
When students of any race, ethnicity, or economic status are expected to work hard, they will usually rise to the occasion. . . .
They rise, or fail, to the level of the expectations of those around
them, especially their parents and their teachers.

JEWLER AND GARDNER, *Your College Experience*

| Exercise 3 | **Work with Words** |

Use context clues, word part clues, and if necessary the dictionary to write the definitions of the italicized words in the following sentences from Reading 2.

1. Although he describes himself as "a somewhat undisciplined young man," he nevertheless *excelled* in school and went on to a teacher training college because his family could not afford to send him to engineering school. (par. 1)

   excelled _____

2. *Barred* from teaching because he did not hold a U.S. degree, he worked as a cook and at other jobs while slowly earning night school credits at California State University, Los Angeles. (par. 2)

   barred _____

3. After ten years, in 1974, he was finally hired to teach basic mathematics at Garfield High School, a *predominantly* Hispanic barrio school in East Los Angeles. (par. 2)

   predominantly _____

4. Four years later, when all eighteen of his students passed the AP examination for college calculus (seven with perfect scores), the Educational Testing Service, which *administers* the test, *concluded* that some of his students had copied their answers and forced twelve of them to *retake* the test. (par. 3)

   administers _____

   concluded _____

   retake _____

| Exercise 4 | **Identify Unstated Main Ideas** |

For each of the following paragraphs from Reading 2, choose the better main idea statement from the two sentences given. The main idea may be stated or unstated in the paragraph.

1. Paragraph 2

   _____ a. He worked as a cook and at other jobs while slowly earning night school credits at California State University, Los Angeles.

   _____ b. After immigrating to the United States, Escalante worked hard many years before he got his job as a teacher at Garfield High School.

2. Paragraph 3

_____ a. Escalante's program received nationwide attention when his students were accused of cheating on the AP calculus exam, but all passed it again when they had to take it over.

_____ b. In 1978 he began teaching an advanced placement (AP) calculus course.

3. Paragraph 4

_____ a. According to Escalante, any student can learn mathematics if motivated properly.

_____ b. Escalante does not recruit students by reviewing test scores or grades.

4. Paragraphs 7 and 8

_____ a. Escalante finds it easy to focus student attention on the challenge of the AP test and its rewards of possible college credits.

_____ b. Escalante has his students work in teams because he feels they study and learn best in groups.

5. The main idea of the whole reading:

_____ a. When students of any race, ethnicity, or economic status are expected to work hard, they will usually rise to the occasion.

_____ b. The film *Stand and Deliver* was based on the true story of Jaime Escalante's success as a teacher in East Los Angeles.

| Exercise 5 | ## Check Your Understanding

Write brief answers to the following questions about Reading 2.

1. List the things about Escalante's teaching that made him such a special teacher.

_____

_____

_____

_____

2. Why did the authorities think his kids cheated on their advanced placement exam?

_____

_____

_____

© 2002 by Addison-Wesley Educational Publishers Inc.

Exercise 6

Make Connections: Collaborative Activity

Write short answers to the following questions based on Reading 2, your experience, and your observations. Then, to extend this exercise, discuss your answers with your class group. Working together, prepare a report for your class as a whole or a written summary for your instructor.

1. Why do you think Escalante's students were so successful?

_____

_____

_____

_____

2. Have you ever had a class that you thought was hard but that you did very well in? How did you do it? What kind of help did you have?

_____

_____

_____

_____

_____

_____

Writing Main Idea Sentences

unstated main idea sentence Your sentence for stating the main idea of a paragraph when the author does not directly state the main idea

To identify an unstated main idea, you may need to write that idea in your own words. This is an **unstated main idea sentence**. To formulate an unstated main idea sentence, follow the steps for finding the main idea, then add one step, as follows:

1. Identify the topic.
2. List the points made about the topic.
3. Add up the points listed to arrive at the main idea.
4. Include the topic in the unstated main idea sentence, which explains what the author is saying about the topic.

For example, read the following paragraph.

Among the students in continuing education programs are blue-collar workers seeking a promotion, a raise, or a new career; homemakers preparing to enter the job market at middle age; retired people seeking to pursue interests postponed or dormant during their working years; and people who want to enrich the quality of their personal, family and social lives. Most of these adults are serious students, as 60 percent are enrolled in a degree program. (Thio, Sociology)

What is the topic?

adults returning to school or, more specifically, reasons why adults return to school

What is the main idea?

Adults return to college for many different reasons.

Because the main idea is not stated in this paragraph, you need to write it in a complete sentence of your own. Notice that the words used for the topic of the paragraph are included in the unstated main idea sentence.

LANGUAGE TIP

Complete Sentences

When you are asked to write the main idea for a paragraph or for a longer passage you've read, be sure you write that idea as a complete sentence. A complete sentence is a subject and verb combination that can stand on its own. For example, the following group of words is a complete sentence: "I arrived at school early." It has a subject, *I*, and a verb, *arrived*, and it is a complete thought that makes sense by itself. However, if we change this group of words to say, "If I arrive at school early," *I* is the subject, and *arrive* is the verb, but this group of words is still not a complete sentence. The word *If* at the beginning sets up a condition that isn't completed in the sentence. It's not a complete thought, so it's not a sentence. The sentence would be complete if it were worded something like this: "If I arrive at school early, I will have time to review my work." Likewise, "Men riding in a car" and "Because he doesn't like anchovies" are groups of words that do not form complete sentences. They would be sentences if they were worded something like this: "Three men were riding to work in the car," and "James won't eat the pizza because he doesn't like anchovies."

Remember, a complete sentence must have a
1. subject,
2. verb,
3. complete thought that makes sense,
4. capital at the beginning, and
5. period, a question mark, or an exclamation point at the end.

Exercise 7   ## Identify and Write Complete Sentences

Decide whether each of the following groups of words is a complete sentence or not. Write "C" on the blank before each complete sentence and "I" before an incomplete sentence. If your answer is "I," rewrite the group of words so it forms a complete sentence. The first one has been done for you.

____*I*____ 1. People who want to enrich the quality of their personal, family, and social lives.

People who want to enrich the quality of their personal, family, and

social lives often return to college after many years.

_____ 2. How Matthew earned a degree in mathematics.

_____

_____

_____ 3. After the final exam was over.

_____

_____

_____ 4. The graduation ceremony was conducted with great dignity.

_____

_____

———— 5. If you want to complete a B.A. degree in only four years.

_____

_____

———— 6. Who continue to study after high school than in any other
country.

_____

_____

Organize to Learn: Work in Groups

One of the most beneficial ways for many people to organize what they've learned involves working in groups. If you already know that you learn best by discussing what
you've read with other people or completing tasks—such as answering questions, organizing ideas graphically, or reviewing for a test—with a friend or two, working in
groups may be a strategy that you want to use regularly to improve your understanding
and ensure that you remember what you've learned. Many people find working in
groups an excellent learning and studying technique. Researchers have identified a
number of things that help small groups to be more effective, whether they are working
together at school or at work.

| Exercise 8 | ## Work with a Partner or a Group

Working with a partner or a group, answer the following questions and
prepare to discuss your answers in class.

1. Make a list of the advantages and disadvantages of studying in a
group, and of steps that you think people in groups could take to
make sure that the group functions well.

Advantages of Working in Groups	*Possible Problems of Working in Groups*	*Ways to Make Groups Work Well*

2. Employers today say that it is important for people to be able to work collaboratively on projects. Why do you think that this is true? Give some examples that you know of where people have to work in groups on their jobs.

_____

_____

_____

_____

READING 3

Participating in Small Groups
[Adapted from] Larry Samovar

The following reading discusses how small work groups function and how people within a group can work together. It also gives some guidelines for how a group of people can work well. As you read, think about the experiences you have had working in small groups, and try to identify the main ideas.

1 Learning to work with other people is one of the most important skills you can develop for your college career and for your lifetime of work. More and more often, students are required to work with their peers—other students in the class—to carry out a variety of tasks. In any of your classes, you may be asked to discuss an article together or to review information provided in a lecture. You may even be asked to do a project together or to write a paper together for which you will be graded as a group! Working collaboratively with other people is a skill that will often be required of you in your lifetime of work.

2 There are many advantages to working with other people, because several minds are better than one. At the same time, there can be disadvantages if the group doesn't work well together.

3 Experts who write about small-group communication agree on certain guidelines, or rules, that are important for members of small groups to follow. First of all, *the members of the group must be motivated to do their best for their group.* So it is important that everyone be prepared to contribute as much as he or she possibly can.

4 The two types of roles that all members of the group must play are (1) task roles and (2) supportive roles. *Task roles* are the responsibilities that group members have in order to work together and achieve their goal. *Supportive roles* involve the actions that individual members must take to make sure that everyone in the group gets along and works well together.

5 The two types of roles that you play overlap: One action may fulfill both roles. For example, a group member might say, "That's a good idea. I think we should write it down as part of our answer." This person is helping the

group carry out its assignment ("we should write it down as part of our answer") and at the same time is also being supportive of the other members of the group ("that's a good idea").

Task Roles

functional Useful

6   If you perform the following functional and task roles, you and your group will benefit.

1. Your group should decide on the steps you will follow to accomplish the assignment. If you are asked for the causes of a certain problem, concentrate on the causes. Don't allow yourselves to start talking about what might have happened if something had been different.

2. You need to be an active member of the group. Contribute as much as you can, but be brief and concise. Don't dominate your group by speaking more than everyone else or insisting that all of your ideas be used. Make sure that everyone has an opportunity to talk.

clarify Make clear

3. By asking questions you can be sure that you are all understanding the discussion in the same way. You might clarify your understanding by posing questions like, "I think that the author is saying that it helps children if they learn how to read in their first language before they try to learn how to read in a language that they don't understand. Do you think that was his point?" In this way, you both clarify what the author was saying, and you find out if your group needs to discuss the idea more before you all agree.

4. Be a leader when your group needs it. Don't expect one member of the group to make all the decisions. All members of the group can be a leader at different times. No one person has all the answers. That's why you are working in a group.

Supportive Roles

7   There are six maintenance and supportive roles that you should keep in mind when you are working in a group.

1. All of us are different. Each member of your group will have his or her own personality and areas of strengths. Members of your group may also come from different cultural backgrounds. Show respect for everyone in your group.

2. Even if everything that you say is polite, members of your group will also understand your body language. If you frown or make faces, or look at the ceiling when someone is talking, that person will understand that you disapprove or you are not interested in what he or she is saying.

3. Your feedback should be clear. You should give verbal and nonverbal responses when your group members are talking. You can make

Topic 1,
Working in group

friendly gestures like smiling or nodding your head so they know you are alert. You can also show that you are interested in what they are saying by interjecting supportive sounds ("Uh-huh," "I see what you're saying.").

Discuss what you need with other people

How do the "task roles" help the group function

How do the "Supportive role help the group function.

4. Keep a positive and constructive atmosphere. Tell members of your group when they do something well. Encourage each other. Especially encourage the members of the group who do not speak up as much. They may be just as prepared and they may have something valuable to say, but you won't know if you don't give them a chance by encouraging their participation.

5. Communication is a two-way process. Both the listener and the speaker are responsible. Listeners need to be alert and ask questions if they are unclear about what the speaker is trying to communicate. If there is someone in the group who disagrees with everyone else, make every effort to understand that person's point of view.

6. You may at times need to (a) seek other people's opinions, (b) help the group decide what to do next, (c) help the group stop and evaluate its progress, (d) recognize when members of the group are close to agreement, and (e) help keep the group spirit up.

Adapted from SAMOVAR, *Oral Communication*

Exercise 9

Work with Words

Use context clues, word part clues, and if necessary the dictionary to write the definition of the italicized words in the following sentences from Reading 3.

1. More and more often, students are required to work with their *peers*—other students in the class—to carry out a variety of tasks. (par. 1)

   peers _____

2. Working *collaboratively* with other people is a skill that will often be required of you in your lifetime of work. (par. 1)

   collaboratively _____

3. Experts who write about small-group communication agree on certain *guidelines*, or rules, that are important for members of small groups to follow. (par. 3)

   guidelines ___rules_____

4. Contribute as much as you can, but be brief and *concise*. (par. 6, item 2)

   concise ___brief to the point_____

5. Your *feedback* should be clear. You should give verbal and *nonverbal* responses when your group members are talking. (par. 7, item 3)

feedback ___respon_____

nonverbal _____

Write the Main Idea in Your Own Words

Write a main idea sentence in your own words for each of the following paragraphs for Reading 3. The main idea, or thesis, may or may not be stated. In either case, write the main idea in your own words so that the meaning of the paragraph is easier to understand. The first one has been done for you.

1. Paragraph 6, item 2

   Be an active member of your group but be sure that everyone else

   has a chance to contribute as well.

2. Paragraph 6, item 3

   _____

   _____

3. Paragraph 7, item 1

   _____

   _____

4. Paragraph 7, item 2

   _____

   _____

5. Paragraph 7, item 6

   _____

   _____

6. What is the thesis of Reading 3?

   _____

   _____

   _____

   _____

| **Exercise 11** | ### Check Your Understanding |

Write brief answers to the following questions about Reading 3.

1. How do the "task roles" help the groups function?

   _____

   _____

   _____

2. How do the "supportive roles" help the groups function?

   _____

   _____

   _____

| **Exercise 12** | ### Make Connections: Collaborative Activity |

Based on Reading 3, your experience, and your observations, write suggestions for improving the way your class groups function. Your suggestions can be for yourself, for members of your group, or for your class group as a whole. Remember to keep your comments positive.

   _____

   _____

   _____

   _____

   _____

   _____

   _____

READING 4

Reading, Writing, and . . . Buying?

Consumer Reports

This reading from Consumer Reports *discusses the increasing presence of advertising in the public schools. The authors question whether or not exposing children to commercial messages during school time is appropriate. Be an active reader. As you read, think about what you already know and your opinions about advertising in general, but especially in the schools.*

1   Gavin Wahl of Palisade, Colo., arrived home from first grade last year toting free book covers with ads for Frosted Flakes, Lay's potato chips, and deodorant. Then 6-year-old Gavin proclaimed Pizza Hut as his favorite pizza. "We don't even go to Pizza Hut," says George Wahl, Gavin's father. He attributes his son's comment to the school's Pizza Hut reading program, which rewards children with pizza coupons.

2   Gavin also told his parents about a school movie on tooth care. "I'm supposed to brush with Sparkle Crest," he said.

3   That was the last straw for his father. "He told me what to buy," George Wahl says in disgust. "Now the school is going to be a conduit for this kind of thing."

4   Advertising to kids is nothing new. But these days, there's a disturbing difference in the quantity and quality of such ads:

- This has become the "decade of sponsored schools and commercialized classrooms," according to a new study that tracked increased media reports of commercialism in the school by the University of Wisconsin at Milwaukee's Center for the Analysis of Commercialism in Education. The center is a nonprofit research group that receives support from Consumer's Union.

- Not only is advertising in schools pervasive, but some sponsored classroom materials give a biased view of public-policy issues. Workbooks that address global warming, for example, subtly steer class lessons in directions advantageous to the sponsor.

- Outside of school, marketers are milking the "nag factor." They're pitching to kids traditionally "adult" purchases such as cars, vacations, and telephone lines—and are even feeding kids arguments they can make—hoping parents will cave in to their kids' requests.

The Impact

5   No matter what parents may think of these practices, one thing is clear: Advertisers are winning. Spending by youngsters ages 4 to 12 has tripled in the 1990s, rising to $24.4 billion last year [1997], according to a leading market researcher, James U. McNeal of Texas A&M University. Moreover, last year children influenced purchases totalling nearly eight times that amount, McNeal says.

6   At a minimum, ads take power away from parents, says Diane Levin, a professor of education at Boston's Wheelock College who has studied how children respond to toy advertising. "The industry says parents need to decide what's appropriate," she says, "but then they go about using every marketing ploy they can to make it harder for parents to assert their authority." One example she cites: the gift registry at Toys 'R' Us, in which a child generates a list of favored toys by pointing at them with an electronic wand. The message to kids, she says, is that "anything that's out there I can want and nag to get. . . . "

7   Parents themselves don't like advertising's effect on children, according to a 1997 survey by Roper Starch Worldwide. Nearly 80 percent of adults said that marketing and advertising exploit kids by convincing them to buy things that are bad for them or that they don't need.

8   George Wahl is in this majority. The idea that Gavin will be "a Pepsi drinker for life, and this is something that was planted in his head when he was a toddler, to me that's offensive," he says.

Ad Campaigns

9   Market researchers probe virtually every aspect of kids' lives, going beyond how kids shop to sample their most intimate thoughts and feelings.

10   Last year, according to the child-marketing newsletter *Selling to Kids*, Roper Starch Worldwide and Just Kids Inc. studied kids' daydreams and fantasies, so that these could be incorporated into marketing and advertising programs. They found that 80 percent of U.S. kids daydream about helping people and 24 percent about protecting the environment. Such data, the newsletter says, can provide dividends for companies savvy enough to form the right strategic alliances with environmental groups.

11   Researchers even try to gauge how effectively kids nag their parents. Recently, *Selling to Kids* described a study by Western International Media, "The Nag Factor," which found that 3- to 8-year-olds were 14 percent more likely to get parents to buy a toy if they emphasized that the toy was important to them. "It's not just getting kids to whine, it's giving them a specific reason to ask for the product," a Western International official says in the newsletter.

12   Marketers also play on kids' emotional needs. . . . These needs include empowerment (because kids are lowest in society's power structure), peer approval, gender identification, and the desire to be a couple of years older.

gender identification
Identification as masculine or feminine

13   How do marketers view children? Brochures from industry conferences refer to goals such as "successful ways of reaching kids and their gatekeepers in schools." Other brochures say:

- "Today's savvy kids are tomorrow's loyal customers. It's not enough to throw crayons and a placemat at a child and expect any kind of loyalty. Kids need more sophisticated and challenging ways to learn about your product or service—and to remember you fondly for years to come."

- "Kids are intensely concerned about the environment. . . . Find out how you can put these findings to work for you in giving the 'cool' factor to your marketing strategy."

- "We will explore creating an intimate relationship with teens—one based on an intimate understanding of their lives and instincts, and reflecting them back in advertising."

Schools on the Block

penetrates
Influences

14 It's easy to understand why marketers focus on schools. Sponsoring educational programs achieves several goals: It builds good community relations by associating a company with a good cause; it penetrates a six-hour time period—9 A.M. to 3 P.M.—that's been traditionally off-limits to advertisers; and it gains priceless credibility for a company through association with trusted teachers. . . .

15   Here are some ways kids now receive commercial messages in school:

- Eight million students are required to watch Channel One, a news broadcast that includes commercials.

- More than half of American classrooms—25 million students—receive advertising-laden book covers, and 6 million schoolchildren receive advertising-filled cafeteria menus.

"Reading, Writing, and . . . Buying?" *Consumer Reports*

| Exercise 13 |

Work with Words

Use context clues, word part clues, and if necessary the dictionary to choose the best definitions of the italicized words in the following sentences from Reading 4.

1. Then 6-year-old Gavin proclaimed Pizza Hut as his favorite pizza. "We don't even go to Pizza Hut," says George Wahl, Gavin's father. He *attributes* his son's comment to the school's Pizza Hut reading program, which rewards children with pizza coupons. (par. 1)

   attributes
   a. believes the cause of
   b. refuses to believe
   c. recognizes the truth of

2. Not only is advertising in schools *pervasive*, but some sponsored classroom materials give a *biased* view of public-policy issues. Workbooks that address global warming, for example, subtly steer class lessons in directions advantageous to the sponsor. (par. 4, item 2)

   pervasive
   a. unimportant
   b. widespread
   c. inappropriate

   biased
   a. balanced
   b. prejudiced
   c. broad

3. . . . . they go about using every marketing *ploy* they can to make it harder for parents to *assert* their authority. (par. 6)

ploy
a. sneaky strategy
b. reasonable argument
c. piece of information

assert
a. lose
b. extend
c. defend or maintain

4. Market researchers probe virtually every aspect of kids' lives, going beyond how kids shop to sample their most *intimate* thoughts and feelings. (par. 9)

intimate
a. intimidating
b. reluctant
c. personal

5. Researchers even try to *gauge* how effectively kids nag their parents. (par. 11)

gauge
a. ignore
b. limit
c. measure

| Exercise 14 |

Identify Main Ideas

Choose the best main idea statement for each of the following paragraphs or groups of paragraphs from Reading 4.

1. Paragraphs 1–3
   a. Some parents are getting increasingly annoyed by the amount of commercial advertising directed at their kids in school.
   b. Gavin Wahl came home carrying book covers with ads for Frosted Flakes, Lay's potato chips, and deodorant.
   c. He attributes his son's comment to the school's Pizza Hut reading program, which rewards children with pizza coupons.

2. Paragraph 4, items 1–3
   a. This has become the "decade of sponsored schools and commercialized classrooms."
   b. Outside of school, marketers are milking the "nag factor."
   c. Although advertising is not new, marketers are using new strategies to target young people.

3. Paragraph 5
   a. Even though parents are not happy about it, advertisers are very successful.
   b. Spending by youngsters ages 4 to 12 has tripled in the 1990s.
   c. Last year [1997] children influenced purchases totalling nearly eight times the $24.4 billion that children themselves spent.

4. Paragraph 6
   a. The industry says parents need to decide what is appropriate for their children.
   b. The message to kids is that anything they want they should be able to get.
   c. Advertising takes power away from parents.

5. Paragraphs 9–12
   a. Advertisers found out about children's dreams of helping people and protecting the environment.
   b. Market researchers investigate every part of children's lives, including their most personal feelings.
   c. Researchers try to measure how effectively kids nag their parents.

| Exercise 15 |

Check Your Understanding

Write brief answers to the following questions about Reading 4.

1. What are the three ways that the quantity and quality of advertising to kids has changed recently?

   _____

   _____

   _____

   _____

2. How did the spending by children ages 4 to 12 increase in the 1990s?

   _____

3. What are some of the ways that marketers view children?

   _____

   _____

   _____

| **Exercise 16** | **Make Connections: Collaborative Activity** |

Write short answers to the following questions based on Reading 4, your own experience, and your observations. Then, to extend this exercise, discuss your answers with your class group. Working together, prepare a report for your class as a whole or a written summary for your instructor.

1. Why do you think this reading has the title "Reading, Writing, and . . . Buying?" Can we understand some of the author's position by the title alone?

_____

_____

_____

_____

2. What experience do you have or observations have you made about advertising and/or private sponsors of schools? Explain.

_____

_____

_____

_____

3. What is your opinion about the use of advertising and of corporate sponsors in the schools? Explain.

_____

_____

_____

_____

4. According to the reading, children need "peer approval." This means that they want to be approved of by other children their age. How do you think children get peer approval, and why are advertisers interested in it?

_____

_____

_____

_____

Chapter Review

To aid your review of the reading skills in Chapter 4, study the Put It Together chart.

Put It Together: *Unstated Main Ideas*	
Skills and Concepts	*Explanation*
Unstated Main Ideas (see pages 173–181)	An unstated main idea occurs when the author does not include a main idea sentence. To determine the unstated main idea, follow three basic steps: 1. Identify the topic. 2. List the points made about the topic. 3. Add up the points listed to arrive at the main idea.
Unstated Main Idea Sentences (see pages 181–182)	To write an unstated main idea sentence, you add another step to the three steps listed above. 4. Include the topic in an unstated main idea sentence, which explains what the author is saying about the topic.
Complete Sentences (see pages 182–184)	To write a complete sentence, remember that it must have a 1. subject 2. verb 3. complete thought that makes sense, 4. capital at the beginning, and a 5. period, a question mark, or an exclamation point at the end

To reinforce your learning before taking the Mastery Tests, complete as many of the following activities as your instructor assigns.

Reviewing Skills

Individually or in a group, read the following paragraph. Then follow the steps in "Put It Together" to write a complete sentence that states the unstated main idea for this paragraph.

In a 1990 Fortune magazine poll of its list of the 500 largest industrial corporations and the 500 largest service corporations, 98 percent of the companies responding contributed to public education. The principal form of assistance was contributing money (78 percent of the companies). Sizable percentages also provided students with summer jobs (76 percent), contributed materials or equipment to schools (64 percent), participated in school partnerships (48 percent), and encouraged employees to run for school boards (59 percent) or to tutor or teach (50 percent). (Mings, Study of Economics)

Unstated main idea sentence:

_____

_____

_____

Writing

In a paragraph, identify your strengths when working in a group. In a second paragraph, describe ways you think you can *improve* your group participation.

Collaborating

In your group, list as many factors as you can think of that are outside the classroom and can contribute to motivating students, helping them be successful in school. Also, list factors (outside the classroom) that you think demotivate students, making it difficult for them to be successful in school. Include in your two lists information that you have gathered from Chapters 3 and 4, as well as what you know, what you have experienced, and what you have observed. Your teacher may ask you to present your findings to the class.

Outside-the-Classroom Motivators	*Outside-the-Classroom Demotivators*
1. _____	1. _____
2. _____	2. _____
3. _____	3. _____
4. _____	4. _____
5. _____	5. _____

Extending Your Thinking

Find an article from a newspaper or magazine that describes someone who has overcome a very difficult educational situation or challenge. The story could be about a student, a teacher, a counselor, or an administrator. Clip out the article, and share it with your class group.

Write a main idea sentence for your article to share with your class group and to turn in to your instructor. Be sure that your main idea sentence is (1) a complete sentence and (2) a sentence that includes the important points that add up in your article.

Visiting the Web

The following Web sites provide more information on challenges in education

1. *Center on Media Education*

   http://www.cme.org
   This site alerts the public on excesses in marketing.

2. *Citizens' Campaign for Commercial-Free Schools*

   http://www.eskimo.com/~bassman/CCCS/homeroom.html
   The aim is to protect children and youth from commercial influences at school.

3. *Center for Commercial-Free Public Education*

   http://www.commercialfree.org/
   This Web site addresses the issue of commercialism in public schools.

4. *National Center for Fair & Open Testing (FairTest)*

   http://www.fairtest.org/
   Its mission is to end the abuses, misuses, and flaws of standardized testing and ensure that evaluation of students and workers is fair, open, and educationally sound.

5. *Group Work and Collaborative Writing*

   http://www-honors.ucdavis.edu/vohs/index.html
   This online book is dedicated to the use of group work with college students.

Name _____ Date _____

A Third of the Nation Cannot Read These Words   Jonathan Kozol

In the following reading, Jonathan Kozol does not state his main idea. He instead tells a story about a man who cannot read, and he allows you, the reader, to draw your own conclusions. As you read, put the pieces of the story together so that you can identify Kozol's main idea, or thesis.

meticulous Very neat

1   He is meticulous and well-defended.

2   He gets up in the morning, showers, shaves, and dresses in a dark gray business suit, then goes downstairs and buys a *New York Times* from the small newsstand on the corner of his street. Folding it neatly, he goes into the subway and arrives at work at 9 A.M.

3   He places the folded *New York Times* next to the briefcase on his desk and sets to work on graphic illustrations for the advertising copy that is handed to him by the editor who is his boss.

4   "Run over this with me. Just make sure I get the gist of what you really want."

5   The editor, unsuspecting, takes this as a reasonable request. In the process of expanding on his copy, he recites the language of the text: a language that is instantly imprinted on the illustrator's mind.

6   At lunch he grabs the folded copy of the *New York Times,* carries it with him to a coffee shop, places it beside his plate, eats a sandwich, drinks a beer, and soon heads back to work.

7   At 5 P.M., he takes his briefcase and his *New York Times,* waits for the elevator, walks two blocks to catch an uptown bus, stops at a corner store to buy some groceries, then goes upstairs. He carefully unfolds his *New York Times.* He places it with mechanical precision on a pile of several other recent copies of the *New York Times.* There they will remain until, when two or three more copies have been added, he will take all but the one most recent and consign them to the trash. . . .

8   He opens the refrigerator, snaps the top from a cold can of Miller's beer, and turns on the TV.

9   Next day, trimly dressed and cleanly shaven, he will buy another *New York Times,* fold it neatly, and proceed to work. He is a rather solitary man. People in his office view him with respect as someone who is self-contained and does not choose to join in casual conversation. If somebody should mention something that is in the news, he will give a dry, sardonic answer based upon the information he has garnered from TV.

10 He is protected against the outside world. Someday he will probably be trapped. It has happened before; so he can guess that it will happen again.

199

Defended for now against humiliation, he is not defended against fear. He tells me that he has recurrent dreams.

11 "Somebody says: WHAT DOES THIS MEAN? I stare at the page. A thousand copies of the *New York Times* run past me on a giant screen. Even before I am awake, I start to scream."

12 If it is of any comfort to this man, he should know that he is not alone. Twenty-five million American adults cannot read the poison warnings on a can of pesticide, a letter from their child's teacher, or the front page of a daily paper. An additional 35 million read only at a level which is less than equal to the full survival needs of our society.

KOZOL, *Illiterate America*

Based on the context clues in the reading and the dictionary definitions provided, choose the best definitions for the italicized words in the following sentences from the reading.

1. He places the folded *New York Times* next to the briefcase on his desk and sets to work on graphic illustrations for the advertising *copy* that is handed to him by the editor who is his boss. (par. 3)

   cop·y (kŏp′ē) *n., pl.* cop·ies. 1. An imitation or reproduction of an original; a duplicate: *a copy of a painting; made two copies of the letter.* 2. One specimen or example of a printed text or picture: *an autographed copy of a novel.* 3. *Abbr.* c., C. Material, such as a manuscript, that is to be set in type. 4. The words to be printed or spoken in an advertisement. 5. Suitable source material for journalism: *Celebrities make good copy.*

   a. an imitation or reproduction of an original
   b. the words to be printed or spoken in an advertisement
   c. suitable source material for journalism

2. "Run over this with me. Just make sure I get the *gist* of what you really want." (par. 4)

   gist (jĭst) *n.* 1. The central idea; the essence. See Synonyms at substance. 2. *Law.* The grounds for action in a suit.

   a. the central idea
   b. the grounds for action in a suit

3. The editor, unsuspecting, takes this as a reasonable request. In the process of expanding on his copy, he recites the language of the text: a language that is instantly *imprinted* on the illustrator's mind. (par. 5)

Name _____ Date _____

im·print (ĭm-prĭnt′) *tr.v.* im·print·ed, im·print·ing, im·prints. **1.** To produce (a mark or pattern) on a surface by pressure. **2.** To produce a mark on (a surface) by pressure. **3.** To impart a strong or vivid impression of: *"We imprint our own ideas onto acts"* (Ellen Goodman). **4.** To fix firmly, as in the mind: *He tried to imprint the number on his memory.* —im·print (ĭm′prĭnt′) *n.*

a. to produce (a mark or pattern) on a surface by pressure
b. to impart a strong or vivid impression on

4. He carefully unfolds his *New York Times*. He places it with mechanical *precision* on a pile of several other recent copies of the *New York Times*. (par. 7)

pre·ci·sion (prĭ-sĭzh′ən) *n.* **1.** The state or quality of being precise; exactness. **2.** *Mathematics.* The exactness with which a number is specified; the number of significant digits with which a number is expressed. —pre·ci·sion *adj.*
1. Used or intended for accurate or exact measurement: *a precision tool.*
2. Made so as to vary minimally from a set standard: *precision components.*
3. Of or characterized by accurate action: *precision bombing.*

a. exactness
b. the exactness with which a number is specified
c. used or intended for accurate or exact measurement

5. There they [the newspapers] will remain until, when two or three more copies have been added, he will take all but the one most recent and *consign* them to the trash. . . . (par. 7)

con·sign (kən-sīn′) *v.* con·signed, con·sign·ing, con·signs. —*tr.* **1.** To give over to the care of another; entrust. **2.** To turn over permanently to another's charge or to a lasting condition; commit irrevocably: *"Their desponding imaginations had already consigned him to a watery grave"* (William Hickling Prescott). **3.** To deliver (merchandise, for example) for custody or sale. **4.** To set apart, as for a special use or purpose; assign. See Synonyms at commit. —*intr. Obsolete.* To submit; consent. —con·sign′a·ble *adj.* —con′sig·na′tion (kŏn′sĭ-nā′shən, -sĭg-) *n.* —con·sig′nor or con·sign′er

a. entrust
b. set apart
c. commit

6. He is a rather *solitary* man. People in his office view him with respect as someone who is self-contained and does not choose to join in casual conversation. (par. 9)

sol·i·tar·y (sŏl′ĭ-tĕr′ē) *adj.* **1.** Existing, living, or going without others; alone: *a solitary traveler.* See Synonyms at **alone. 2.** Happening, done, or made alone: *a solitary evening; solitary pursuits such as reading and sewing.* **3.** Remote from civilization; secluded: *a solitary retreat.* **4.** Having no companions; lonesome or lonely. **5.** *Zoology.* Living alone or in pairs only: *solitary wasps; solitary sparrows.* **6.** Single and set apart from others: *a solitary instance of cowardice.* See Synonyms at **single. —sol·i·tar·y** *n., pl.*

   a. existing, living, or going without others; alone
   b. remote from civilization; secluded

7. If somebody should mention something that is in the news, he will give a dry, sardonic answer based upon the information he has *garnered* from TV. (par. 9)

   gar·ner (gär′nər) *tr.v.* **gar·nered, gar·ner·ing, gar·ners. 1.** To gather and store in or as if in a granary. **2.** To amass; acquire. See Synonyms at **reap. —gar·ner** *n.* A granary.

   a. gathered as in a granary
   b. acquired

8. Defended for now against *humiliation*, he is not defended against fear. He tells me that he has recurrent dreams. (par. 10)

   hu·mil·i·a·tion (hyōō-mĭl′ē-ā′shən) *n.* **1.** The act of humiliating; degradation. **2.** The state of being humiliated or disgraced; shame. **3.** A humiliating condition or circumstance.

   a. act of humiliating
   b. shame

Choose the best answers to the following multiple-choice questions.

9. What would be the best topic for this reading?
   a. The life of a secretly illiterate man
   b. The *New York Times* as status symbol
   c. Illiteracy in the United States

10. Which of the following was not a main point made about the topic?
   a. The man hides his inability to read in clever ways.
   b. The man is an illustrator.
   c. The man is poor because he can't read.

11. What is the main idea of the whole reading?
   a. A lot of people can't read well in the United States.
   b. It is difficult, and even painful, to have to hide the fact that you can't read.
   c. Eventually people who pretend they can read but cannot will be trapped and discovered.

Name _____ Date _____

12. What is the topic of paragraphs 1 through 9?
   a. The daily routine of an illiterate man
   b. The precision of the habits of an illiterate man
   c. The respect that an illiterate man gets from people in his office

13. What is the main idea of paragraphs 1 through 9?
   a. The man is aware of what's happening in the world because he watches television and listens carefully.
   b. The man has habits that make it look as if he can read and that help him find out what he needs to know without reading.
   c. The man reads the *New York Times* every day.

Write brief answers to the following questions about the reading.

14. What is the man in this reading afraid of?

   _____

   _____

15. Why does he carry the *New York Times* around with him all the time?

   _____

   _____

   _____

16. What are his bad dreams about?

   _____

   _____

   _____

17. What is Kozol referring to when he writes, "Someday he will probably be trapped"?

   _____

   _____

   _____

18. How many people in the United States, according to Kozol, have problems reading?

   _____

Write short answers to the following questions based on your reading, your experience, and your observations.

19. Have you ever been afraid that someone would find out that you don't know something that they expect you to know? Explain.

_____

_____

_____

20. Have you ever helped an adult (or a child) learn to read? Explain how you helped and what the experience was like.

_____

_____

_____

Blowing Up the Tracks   Patricia Kean

*In the following reading, educator Patricia Kean writes about
"tracking" in the public schools, the practice of placing students in
"ability groups." She begins with a description of two actual seventh-
grade classes. Read her account and see what she thinks about
tracking. She does not state her thesis, or main idea, at the beginning,
but instead waits for you to join her in evaluating what she observed.
As you read, consider what you know from your own experience and
observations about placing students in classrooms according to ability
groups.*

1   It's morning in New York, and some seventh graders are more equal than others.

2   Class 7–16 files slowly into the room, prodded by hard-faced men whose walkie-talkies crackle with static. A pleasant looking woman shouts over the din, "What's rule number one?" No reply. She writes on the board. "Rule One: Sit down."

3   Rule number two seems to be an unwritten law: Speak slowly. Each of Mrs. H.'s syllables hangs in the air a second longer than necessary. In fact, the entire class seems to be conducted at 16 RPM. Books come out gradually. Kids wander about the room aimlessly. Twelve minutes into class, we settle down and begin to play "O. Henry Jeopardy," a game which requires students to supply one-word answers to questions like: "O. Henry moved from North Carolina to what state—Andy? Find the word on the page."

4   The class takes out a vocabulary sheet. Some of the words they are expected to find difficult include "popular," "ranch," "suitcase," "arrested," "recipe," "tricky," "ordinary," "humorous," and "grand jury."

5   Thirty minutes pass. Bells ring, doors slam.

6   Class 7–1 marches in unescorted, mindful of rule number one. Paperbacks of Poe smack sharply on desks, notebooks rustle, and kids lean forward expectantly, waiting for Mrs. H. to fire the first question. What did we learn about the writer?

7   Hands shoot into the air. Though Edgar Allen Poe ends up sounding a lot like Jerry Lee Lewis—a booze-hound who married his thirteen-year-old cousin—these kids speak confidently, in paragraphs. Absolutely no looking at the book allowed.

8   We also have a vocabulary sheet, drawn from "The Tell-Tale Heart," containing words like "audacity," "dissimulation," "sagacity," "stealthy," "anxiety," "derision," "agony," and "supposition."

9   As I sit in the back of the classroom watching these two very different groups of seventh graders, my previous life as an English teacher allows me to make an educated guess and a chilling prediction. With the best of intentions,

Mrs. H. is teaching the first group, otherwise known as the "slow kids," as though they are fourth graders, and the second, the honors group, as though they are high school freshmen. Given the odds of finding a word like "ordinary" on the SAT's, the children of 7–16 have a better chance of standing before a "grand jury" than making it to college.

10   Tracking, the practice of placing students in "ability groups" based on a host of ill-defined criteria—everything from test scores to behavior to how much of a fuss a mother can be counted on to make—encourages even well-meaning teachers and administrators to turn out generation after generation of self-fulfilling prophecies. "These kids know they're no Einsteins," Mrs. H. said of her low-track class when we sat together in the teacher's lounge. "They know they don't read well. This way I can go really slowly with them."

11   With his grades, however, young Albert would probably be hanging right here with the rest of lunch table 7–16. That's where I discover that while their school may think they're dumb, these kids are anything but stupid. "That teacher," sniffs a pretty girl wearing lots of purple lipstick. "She talks so slow. She thinks we're babies. She takes a year to do anything." "What about the other one?" a girl named Ingrid asks, referring to their once-a-week student teacher. "He comes in and goes like this: Rail (pauses) road. Rail (pauses) road. Like we don't know what a railroad means!" The table breaks up laughing.

12   Outside the walls of the schools across the country, it's slowly become an open secret that enforced homogeneity benefits no one. The work of researchers like Jeannie Oakes of UCLA and Robert Slavin of Johns Hopkins has proven that tracking does not merely reflect differences—it causes them. Over time, slow kids get slower, while those in the middle and in the so-called "gifted and talented" top tracks fail to gain from isolation. Along the way, the practice resegregates the nation's schools, dividing the middle from the lower classes, white from black and brown. As the evidence piles up, everyone from the Carnegie Corporation to the National Governors Association has called for change.

homogeneity
Sameness

reflect   Show

13   . . . Because tracking puts kids in boxes, keeps the lid on, and shifts responsibility for mediocrity and failure away from the schools themselves, there is little incentive to change a nearly century-old tradition. "Research is research," the principal told me that day, "This is practice."

mediocrity
Something of low
quality

KEAN, "Blowing Up the Tracks"

Use context clues, word part clues, and if necessary the dictionary to write the definitions of the italicized words in the following sentences from or related to the reading.

Name _____ Date _____

1. Class 7–16 files slowly into the room, prodded by hard-faced men whose walkie-talkies crackle with static. A pleasant looking woman shouts over the *din*. . . . (par. 2)

   din _____

2. Kids wander about the room *aimlessly*. (par. 3)

   aimlessly _____

3. Paperbacks of Poe smack sharply on desks, notebooks rustle, and kids lean forward *expectantly*, waiting for Mrs. H. to fire the first question. (par. 6)

   expectantly _____

4. *Tracking*, the practice of placing students in "ability groups" based on a host of ill-defined criteria—everything from test scores to behavior to how much fuss a mother can be counted on to make—encourages even well-meaning teachers and administrators to turn out generation after generation of self-fulfilling prophecies. (par. 10)

   tracking _____

5. "What about the other one?" a girl named Ingrid asks, *referring to* their once-a-week student teacher. (par. 11)

   referring to _____

6. Along the way, the practice *resegregates* the nation's schools, dividing the middle from the lower classes, white from black and brown. (par. 12)

   resegregates _____

7. Though some fashionably progressive schools have begun to reform, tracking *persists*.

   persists _____

Choose the best answers to the following multiple-choice questions about the reading.

8. What is the best explanation of the sentence, "Given the odds of finding a word like 'ordinary' on the SAT's, the children of 7–16 have a better chance of standing before a 'grand jury' than making it to college." (par. 9)
   a. The best opportunity for these children is to stand before a grand jury.
   b. "Ordinary" is too easy to be on the SAT exam.
   c. The class is far too easy, making it more likely that the children will end up in jail than in college.

9. What is the main idea of paragraph 10?
   a. These kids know they're no Einsteins.
   b. Tracking . . . encourages even well-meaning teachers and administrators to turn out generation after generation of self-fulfilling prophecies.

10. What is the main idea of paragraph 11?
    a. I discover that while their school may think they're dumb, these kids are anything but stupid.
    b. With his grades, however, young Albert would probably be hanging right here with the rest of lunch table 7–16.

11. What is the main idea of paragraph 12?
    a. Tracking does not merely reflect differences—it causes them.
    b. Over time, slow kids get slower, while those in the middle and in the so-called "gifted and talented" top tracks fail to gain from isolation.

12. Which of the following statements best describes how Mrs. H. teaches the 7–16 group, the "slow group" of students?
    a. Starts class promptly, teaches material at or above grade level, challenges students to excel
    b. Takes 12 minutes to begin an activity, teaches material at about fourth-grade level, speaks slowly
    c. Spends the entire class focusing on sitting down and other disciplinary activities

13. Which of the following statements best describes how Mrs. H. teaches the 7–1 group, the honors group of students?
    a. Starts class promptly, expects students to be well prepared, teaches material at above grade level
    b. Makes sure students are escorted to the room, emphasizes discipline throughout the lesson
    c. Takes 12 minutes to begin an activity, teaches material at about seventh-grade level, speaks slowly

14. Mrs. H tells the author, "These kids know they're no Einsteins." They know they don't read well. This way I can go really slowly with them." The author is critical of these statements because she
    a. believes that if you have low expectations of students, they will live up to your expectations and do poorly.
    b. believes that these children could be Einsteins.
    c. believes the teacher does not care about the children.

Name _____ Date _____

15. At the 7–16 lunch table students talk about the teacher's approach to their group. Which statement best describes their response to the class?
    a. The students feel challenged by both Mrs. H. and her student teacher.
    b. The students think the student teacher does a much better job of teaching them than Mrs. H. usually does.
    c. They laugh at the teachers' slow speech and comment that they're being treated like "babies."

16. What is the overall main idea, or thesis, of the reading?
    a. The practice of tracking students does not benefit anyone, and it should be stopped.
    b. Tracking is okay for some students, but it is not so good for others; consequently, it is a necessary part of school programs.
    c. Tracking is helpful for all students to work at their own pace.

Write short answers to the following questions based on your reading, your experience, and your observations.

17. What is the point the author is trying to make by writing out a list of words in paragraph 4, and another list of words in paragraph 8? What do you think about the vocabulary portion of this Mastery Test?

    _____

    _____

    _____

    _____

18. Have you ever been in a class of students that was obviously grouped by tracking? What were the advantages? What were the disadvantages?

    _____

    _____

    _____

    _____

19. Do you think that tracking should continue in our schools? Why or why not?

    _____

_____

_____

_____

_____

20. What are the two meanings of "tracks?" And, why do you think this reading is called "Blowing Up the Tracks"?

_____

_____

_____

_____

_____

Chapter 5

Supporting Details

Popular Culture

These virtual reality games will constantly be improved on and upgraded, becoming better and more realistic until they will replace our actual experiences with digital ones.

—Marley Peifer, "The Reality of the Digital World: Video Games"

- Do you think that virtual reality will replace real experiences?

- How are our attitudes about life influenced by electronic entertainment like video games or mass media like popular magazines? Give examples to support your answer.

- What does the photo depict? Do you like these kinds of images? Explain your answer.

Getting Ready to Read

Our view of ourselves and where we fit in is increasingly influenced not just by our active experiences but by our passive experiences. In everything from action-packed video games to glamour-packed magazines at the checkout counter, we are all bombarded by the same images, the same symbols, the same superheroes, the same all-stars, and screen stars. We enjoy them and we share our enjoyment of them with most people in our society, and increasingly with people all over the world. This popular culture is mass-produced for us. We no longer create our culture; we consume it. In other words, a small group of people in the entertainment industry determine the popular culture. How many parents are telling the stories that they heard as children to their children? In contrast, how many children know only the stories they've seen on television or in videos? What cultural traditions have we maintained in our families and in our local communities? What traditions have we lost? Have we lost our ability to define our own dreams, even our selves?

In this chapter you will read about video games, teen magazines, and advertising to children, as well as about some aspects of our culture that we don't often consider as mass or popular culture—fairy tales. In the process, you will learn how to

- recognize supporting details for main ideas
- outline what you have read

READING 1

Violence and Video Games   Jenn Laidman

The following reading is from a Washington Times *article that was written two weeks after the 1999 tragedy in Littleton, Colorado, where two students killed twelve of their classmates and a teacher. When Americans learned that the students were addicted to violent video games, a heated national discussion about violence and video games began. What experiences have you had with video games? Do you or do your children play them? What kind of effect do you think they have on young people? As you read, consider whether you think violent video games contribute to crime.*

1   "Meet people from all over the world, then kill them"—An advertisement for the video game Subspace.
2   "More fun than shooting your neighbor's cat"—Point Blank ad copy.
3   "As easy as killing babies with axes"—Carmageddon ad slogan.
4   Violent video games are coming under increasing attack for desensitizing troubled youngsters to bloodshed while training them to be effective killers.

scapegoating
Blaming a problem
on a group of
people or things

But video game players maintain that blaming video games for school violence is scapegoating an industry for problems that start at home.

5   Video games are a common thread in at least two of five school massacres to take place in the past three years. The two students who killed 12 of their peers, a teacher, and themselves in Littleton, Colorado, . . . reportedly were devoted to violent video games. "They got on their home computers and linked them with modems. They had death matches with violent computer games, matching computer to computer," one Columbine High School student said. . . .

6   Parents of the three girls killed in Paducah, Kentucky, are suing makers of violent video games. They contend that Michael Carneal, the 14-year-old boy who killed three and wounded five in Paducah, was influenced by violent computer games such as "Doom," "Quake" and "Mortal Kombat." The $130 million lawsuit alleges that the teen was under the influence of violent pornography sites on the Internet and the 1995 Di Caprio film, "The Basketball Diaries." Attorneys in the federal lawsuit claim that video games trained him to be a proficient killer and desensitized him to what he was doing.

7   Researchers report that video games are used effectively by the military for training purposes. Lt. Col. David Grossman, author of the book *On Killing* and a former West Point psychology professor, worked with community members after attacks in Paducah, Kentucky, and Springfield, Oregon. He was on the scene immediately after two boys, 11 and 13, killed four students and a teacher in his hometown of Jonesboro, Arkansas. He likens the effect of video games to the military's efforts in reducing a young recruit's reluctance to kill. "In interactive, point-and-shoot video games, children are taught the motor skills of killing in a process that makes killing a reflexive response," he says. Michael Carneal hit eight students with eight shots. Five of those students were shot in the head and three in the upper torso. "This is an absolutely unprecedented marksmanship achievement," Col. Grossman says.

likens   Compares

reflexive
Automatic

8   University of Toledo psychology professor Jeanne Funk, whose work on video games and violence is recognized nationwide, says her research suggests that violent video games tend to draw children who already are troubled. "We've never found a positive relationship between a high preference for violent video games and positive self-concept," Miss Funk says. The fourth- through eighth-graders she studies seem to turn to violent video games when they feel they're not good at anything else, she says.

9   "Kids who preferred violent games tended to see their behavior as not as good as other kids'," Miss Funk says. They see themselves as poor students and poor athletes, with unsatisfying relationships with family and friends. These children have a lower ability to put themselves in another person's shoes, she says.

10   But preference for violent games isn't a clear signal of future behavior, Miss Funk says. "It is accompanied by other things: Kids who are failing in school, who are very alienated, who play video games all the time, who are nearly obsessed with violent media. Those are all problem indicators." . . .

11   Gregory W. Boller, a marketing professor at the University of Memphis in Tennessee, says his research among 18- to 24-year-olds shows that people who prefer violent video games feel helpless in other aspects of their lives. "The more powerless somebody feels themselves to be, the more interested they are in playing violent games," Mr. Boller says. . . .

12   Mr. Boller says advertising for video games is unprecedented in the themes it presents and the messages it sends. "I've never seen anything like it in the history of advertising," he says. "This is brand-new phenomena." For instance, an ad for a joystick that provides feedback says: "Psychiatrists say it's important to feel something when you kill." Another joystick advertisement states: "Great. You get better accuracy and control, but what are you going to do with all the extra bodies? Be the first on your block to make your neighbors say, 'What's that smell?'"

phenomena
Some things that are remarkable or extraordinary

simulations
Imitations or enactments

13   "We don't call them games, we call them murder simulations," Mr. Boller says. "Murder is not a game, nor is it entertaining, nor is it fun. It's frightening to me, and I have been in the [advertising] business for 17 years. I think this kind of advertising is irresponsible." . . .

LAIDMAN, "Violence, Video Games May Be a Volatile Mix"

| Exercise 1 | ## Recall and Reflect |

Answer these questions about Reading 1, and prepare to discuss them in class.

1. What do the three quotations from advertisements for video games at the very beginning of the reading tell us?

    It is telling the advertising are thrill +
    fun by the violence + killing

2. Why are parents of the three girls killed in Paducah, Kentucky, suing the makers of violent video games?

    Because they the boy are influenced
    by the violence video game to be
    a killer.

3. How did Michael Carneal allegedly learn to shoot? What evidence is given that he was an excellent marksman?

> *He learn shooting in the video game and shot 8 students vital bodies.*

4. What are some of the characteristics of people who are attracted to violent video games? Why do you think such people are attracted to violence?

> *The people attracted the video games are often in trouble, poor students, poor athletes, and unsatisfactory relationship with family.*

5. Do you think that it's right to sometimes blame video games when people commit violent crimes? Explain.

> *No, because sometimes not the f: of violent games*

6. What do you think the popularity of video games and of electronic entertainment tells us about our culture?

> *Not really but sometime yet.*

Supporting Details

In Chapters 3 and 4 you learned to identify main ideas in a variety of readings. A main idea is usually presented in a broad or general statement of the main point of the reading—what the reading says about the topic. It is also expressed through **supporting details,** which give additional information and are more specific. Some types of supporting details are:

supporting details
Details that give you additional information and are more specific than a general statement; examples or additional facts

- Examples. If the main idea is *people in the past used to entertain themselves more than we do today,* the supporting details might be examples of how they did that, such as

  singing and playing music
  dancing traditional dances
  telling stories
  drawing
  writing poetry

- Facts. Facts are forms of information that can be checked for accuracy. If the main idea is *Americans watch more television today than they ever did in the past,* the supporting facts would state how many hours Americans watch television, and perhaps how many television sets are in American homes.
- Reasons. Reasons answer the question "why." If a main idea is *I hate the shows my friends watch,* some reasons might be they are silly, they are always about the same thing, and they are childish.
- Descriptions. Descriptions help us form pictures in our minds, and can help us understand better what the writer is communicating to us. If a main idea is *the children were totally absorbed in the video game,* the writer may describe the scene by saying

> *Their concentration was so intense they forgot to blink their eyes.*
> *They hunched over the screen as though their lives depended on their virtual reality triumphs or failures.*
> *They held the excitement of the game in the tension of the muscles on their faces.*
> *They didn't even look up or respond in any way when their mother called them to dinner.*

The way a main idea is supported by specific details can be seen in sentences, paragraphs, and longer passages.

Recognizing Supporting Details in Sentences

Some sentences include both a general idea and supporting details. A writer may begin a sentence with a general idea and then give evidence. Normally you won't need to analyze a sentence this way, but you should know that frequently sentences have the same organization as paragraphs and longer readings. For example, read the following sentence:

> Our media culture glorifies violence through the images of violent actions such as assault, beatings, and murders that children see repeatedly in products such as video games, television shows, Hollywood movies, and on the internet.

What is the general idea of the sentence?

Our media glorify violence through images in products.

What are the supporting details? The supporting details are the responses to the following questions: What kinds of images? What kinds of products? What examples are given?

What kinds of images?
   assault
   beatings
   murders

What kinds of products?
 video games
 television shows
 Hollywood movies
 on Internet

| Exercise 2 |

Recognize Supporting Details in Sentences

Fill in the blanks about the sentences. What is the general idea? What are the supporting details?

1. The amount of violence children see on TV is astounding, as it is estimated that by the time they finish elementary school, they will see over 8,000 murders and 100,000 other violent acts.

   general idea: *The amount of violence children watch T.V is astounding,*

   supporting details: *by the end of elementary school,*

   a. *8,000 murders*

   b. *100,000 other violent acts*

2. Violence on television has two effects on children: the immediate effect lasts for about twenty minutes, and the long-term effect shapes the behavior of people later in life.

   general idea: *Violence on televison has two effects on children.*

   supporting details:

   a. *Immediate effect-lasts about 20 minutes*

   b. *long term effect shapes behavior later*

3. Games that children used to play, such as "Paintball" and "Cowboys and Indians," were not as violent as some of today's video games, such as "Doom" and "Blood."

   general idea: *Games that children used to play were not as violent as today's video games,*

   supporting details:

   a. *Old games; "paint ball," "cowboys + Indians"*

   b. *Video games; "Doom," "Blood"*

general statement
The main idea or broadest statement of a passage

specifics Detailed information

Separating General from Specific

The main idea of a paragraph or essay is a broad or **general statement.** The details that support it are **specifics.** The more detailed the information, the more specific it is. Let's look at a statement about our shared culture, or the nature of modern life:

> We live our lives by having more indirect, imaginary, and simulated experiences through playing video games, watching television, going to theme parks, going on the Internet, and going to the movies.

The general statement is: *We live our lives by having indirect experiences.*
The specific information is the list of types of indirect experiences:

playing video games

watching TV

going to theme parks

going on the internet

going to the movies

Exercise 3

Recognize General Statements and Specific Details

Read the following sentences, then identify the general statements versus the specific details.

1. In shooter video games, players are not responsible for what they do because the wound heals with the touch of a button, and the scream is silenced.

   general statement: _Many shows are self-help shows._

   specific details: _Help people attain personal freedom_
   Help people attain financial freedom.

2. Oprah has a variety of goals for helping people. Helping Habitat for Humanity build houses for the homeless and contributing funds for scholarships are just two of her projects.

   general statement: _In shooter video games players are not Responsible for what they do._

   specific details: _the wound heals with the touch of a button. The scream is silenced._

3. Many of the talk shows are "self-help" shows devised to help people attain personal and financial freedom.

   general statement: _Oprah has a variety of goals for helping people._

   specific details: _Helping Habitat for Humanity build houses for the homeless contributing funds for scholarships._

Recognizing Supporting Details in Paragraphs

In paragraphs, the general statement, or the main idea, is often given in the first few sentences, and then the writer supports the idea with more specific details. The best process to follow for finding important supporting details is to

- identify the main idea
- look for the additional important information about the main idea

These supporting details could be

- examples
- additional facts
- reasons
- descriptions

Read the following paragraph, which is from testimony presented to the U.S. Senate hearing on "Marketing Violence to Children." This testimony was made shortly after the tragic killing of twelve Columbine High School students by two fellow students in Littleton, Colorado.

Those shocked about the recent tragedy in Littleton, and the ones in Jonesboro and Springfield before it, have not been paying attention. Children growing up today are swimming in a culture of violence that has its effects—from subtle to deadly—on every child, family, and school. Every ten seconds a child is abused or neglected in this country. Every hundred minutes a child is killed by a firearm, that is fourteen children a day, equal to the number of children that died in Littleton. (Levin, "Marketing Violence to Children")

What is the main idea, or the general statement, of the paragraph?
Children growing up today are swimming in a culture of violence.

What are the supporting details? That is, how is the main idea supported with specific examples and facts?

Tragedies in Littleton, Jonesboro, and Springfield (examples)

Every 10 seconds a child is abused or neglected (facts)

Every 100 minutes a child is killed by a firearm (facts)

| Exercise 4 | **Identify Main Ideas and Supporting Details** |

For each of the following paragraphs, write the main idea, then list the major supporting points. The first one has been done for you.

1. Video games are not all bad. In fact, there are many benefits to playing these electronic games. Playing increases young people's motor
skills. It gives them practice in problem solving. It can improve their
ability to see spatial relationships in their minds. It can be therapeutic
for children who have attention deficit disorders. Playing video games
has been given credit for helping the reaction times of senior citizens,
and even for leading to higher self-esteem among elderly people.
(adapted from Laidman, "Violence, Video Games May Be a Volatile
Mix")

   main idea: _There are many benefits to playing video games._

   supporting details: _Examples of benefits_

   increases motor skills

   practice in problem solving

   improves ability to see spatial relationships

   therapeutic for children with attention deficit disorders

   helps reaction times of seniors

   leads to higher self-esteem for elderly

2. Interactive video games are a huge industry. Annual video game
revenue exceeds $18 billion worldwide. U.S. video game revenues
of $10 billion per year are double what is spent on movies annually,
according to Media Scope, a nonprofit organization concerned with
the media's portrayal of, and impact on, children. (Laidman, "Violence,
Video Games May Be a Volatile Mix")

   main idea: _Interactive video games are a huge industry,_

   supporting details: _Facts about profits_

   Annual revenue exceeds $18 billion worldwide,
   U.S. Revenue of $10 billion are double what is spent
   on movies,

3. Mr. Boller says advertising for video games is unprecedented in the
themes it presents and the messages it sends. "I've never seen anything like it in the history of advertising," he says. "This is a brand-
new phenomena." For instance, an ad for a joystick that provides
feedback says: "Psychiatrists say it's important to feel something
when you kill." Another joystick advertisement states: "Great. You get
better accuracy and control, but what are you going to do with all the
extra bodies? Be the first on your block to make your neighbors say,
'What's that smell?'" (Laidman, "Violence, Video Games May Be a
Volatile Mix")

main idea: *Video game advertizing is unprecedented in the themes it presents o the messages it sends*

supporting details: *Examples of joystick advertisements*

"It's important to feel something when you kill." "but what are you going to do with the extra bodies?"

4. Video games are consuming a larger amount of time every year. Virtually all children now play video games. The average seventh grader is playing electronic games at least four hours per week, and about half of those games are violent. Even though the number of hours spent playing video games tends to decline in the high school and college years, a significant portion of students are playing quite a few video games. In 1998 3.3 percent of men entering public universities in the United States reported playing video games more than 15 hours per week in their senior year in high school. In 1999 that percentage jumped to a full 4 percent. (Anderson, "Impact of Media Violence on Kids")

main idea: *Video games are consuming a larger amount of time every year.*

supporting details: *Facts about time spent playing video games*

Average 7th grader spends 4 hr per week 3.3% of men entering university played more than 15 hr per week in their senior year in high school. The 3.3% jumped to 4% in 1999.

Using Supporting Details to Find the Unstated Main Idea

In Chapter 4 you learned how to find the unstated main idea of paragraphs and longer passages: First list the points made about the topic, then add them up to arrive at the main idea. Basically, this process means that you recognize the supporting details in a reading and then, based on those details, you decide what the main idea is. You will be practicing this skill in much of the reading that you will be doing for college classes, as you read for pleasure, and as you read for your professional work as well.

LANGUAGE TIP

Facts

Facts are one important type of supporting detail. In general, facts are statements that can be proven, but there are many different kinds of facts, including

- *statistics*—which provide information in number form,
- *events*—which are examples of things that have happened or will happen,
- *dates*—which tell when something happened or will happen,
- *lists*—which put similar items together to show spatial or time relationships among the items.

Exercise 5   ## Identify the Facts and the Main Idea

Identify what kind of fact is being used in each of these examples: statistics, events, dates, or lists. Each example may use more than one kind of fact. Then add up the facts to arrive at the unstated or stated main idea

1. Rapper Lauryn Hill became the first hip-hop artist to ever win Album of the Year. Last year, actor Warren Beatty crafted his satire "Bulworth" around rap's language of protest. Martha Stewart, the woman who teaches Americans about good taste, appeared at the MTV Music Awards with rapper Busta Rhymes. (Adapted from Scott, "Rap Goes from Urban Streets to Main Street")

   type of facts: _Events_

   main idea: _Hip hop has become very important in U.S. popular culture._

2. The hip-hop label Def Jam took in nearly $200 million in 1998. Rap sold more than 81 million CDs, tapes and albums in 1998, compared with 72 million for country and western. Rap sales increased 31 percent from 1997–98, in contrast to 2 percent gains for country, 6 percent for rock and 9 percent for the music industry overall. (Adapted from "Live and Kicking")

   type of facts: _Statistics_

   main idea: _Hip-hop, or rap, sells better than country music + its sales are increasing more rapidly than the sales of the music industry as a whole._

3. Once the three networks [ABC, CBS, and NBC] fought only among themselves for audience leaderships. . . . But since the early 1980s the Big Three networks have faced five dangerous competitors whose com-

bined and growing strength has stolen many of the networks' viewers.
These are
a. cable television
b. a growing number of independent TV stations, which have developed strong audience appeal . . .
c. home video, which viewers watch instead of television
d. the aggressive young Fox network
e. appearance in 1995 of two additional broadcast networks, WB Television (Warner Brothers) and UPN, United Paramount Network.
(Agee, Ault, and Emery, Introduction to Mass Communications)

type of facts: ___list___

main idea: _The three main idea networks have much more competition for viewer's time than they did in the past._

READING 2

Video Games: The Reality of the Digital World
Marley Peifer

*The following reading was written by a high school sophomore whose
friends spend many hours playing video games. This essay is his
analysis of what those games can do to young people. You will notice
as you read that he takes a strong position about the games, but he
does not focus only on the violence problem. Notice his other
arguments for why the games are bad, and consider whether or not
you agree with his position.*

1   As we enter the twenty-first century, technology becomes more advanced
and more incorporated into our daily lives. It makes our lives easier, longer,
and more luxurious. Different machines have been designed to do just
about anything—wash your car for you, do math for you, wash your clothes,
and there are even machines that entertain and exhilarate you. They're
known as video games. They provide the addicting, time-consuming, and
complete waste-of-time digital experiences that glue you to the screen and
have you coming back for more. Video games are now replacing reading,
art, and other wholesome activities that benefit the mind and body.

exhilarate Thrill

2   As these electronic games replace more traditional pastimes, there is a
noticeable decrease in the creativity and attention span of the kids that play
them. A child, after playing video games for three hours, may have difficulty
stopping the game and starting to read a book instead. After being immersed in a fast-paced game, children are often incapable of concentrating
long enough to read. They quickly lose attention on the book and begin to
fidget with something. While playing the game their mind is bombarded

with countless images from the screen, images realistic enough that no imagination is required. However, reading requires imagination and thought to understand and register what is being read. Some children may also have difficulty paying attention to a teacher speaking after playing a video game for a while.

3   A child who plays video games all the time becomes less social. Instead of going and playing with his friends, he'd rather sit cooped up in his room playing video games on his personal television. These days the typical slumber party, instead of consisting of social activities such as board games or talking, consists of several-hour video game playing marathons that may last well into the night. In this circumstance, even though the group of friends is spending time together, they are not interacting socially with each other. So actually, there is little difference between this activity and really being alone.

4   As soon as a child starts one of these video games, she may become totally immersed in a world very similar yet different from the real one. While the video world may look and sound realistic, no one really dies, and you can always start over. Modern video games are designed to cater *to* your sense of sight, hearing, and even, with new controllers called "Rumble Packs" that shake in your hands, your sense of touch. All these senses are stimulated while you play the game, adding to the sensation of being in a different world. In this different world, you can be a hero, you can have amazing and superhuman powers, you can do the impossible, you can beat any odds, you can do anything. In this digital world, you can do all the things you've always wanted to do but couldn't in the real world. It's no wonder, then, that many people prefer this artificial world to reality. A young boy who is unfit physically may escape his shortcomings in sports by playing video games. In the game he can be an all-star home-run hitter or the MVP (most valuable player) for a World Cup soccer team. However, all the action occurs on the screen, and his actual physical fitness may actually deteriorate. People who have few talents and don't stand out in the real world can take solace in this digital world, where they can excel. It's not surprising that people who play video games a great deal may find the "real world" boring, for they are unable to fly around or shoot people like they can in the game.

5   The amount of time that people waste playing video games is alarming. Many games, such as "Mario 64," have 100 or more levels, with each level taking close to an hour to complete. Imagine the constructive things that could be done in the time it would take to beat the game. Recent statistics show the average seventh grader plays four hours of video games a week, which in most cases is more time than is spent on homework and reading combined. Actually, since this figure is only an average for all seventh graders, and includes girls, who do not play nearly as much as boys,

cater to   Please

take solace   Feel better

excel   Do well

the amount of time that serious video game players spend is far more than four hours a week. In some cases, twenty hours a week would be more like it.

6   As if the games in general weren't already bad enough, approximately half of all video games have a violent theme. For example, in Sony PlayStation's "Resident Evil" the objective is to kill all the zombies and other horrible creatures before they dismember you and feast upon your flesh. However, don't worry, because you can fight back with a rocket launcher that splatters pieces of your foes on the walls. Or you can use a flame thrower that melts the zombies' flesh from their bones. Sometimes you don't even have to fight the zombies—they'll just gnaw on each other's limbs, gushing blood on the floor. How can someone behave normally after being submitted to hours of this carnage? The real answer is they can't. Studies have shown that exposure to these video games causes a great increase in aggressive thinking. It's no wonder an individual who has witnessed countless deaths in a game becomes desensitized and can even consider taking a life as no big deal.

carnage   Slaughter or massacre

7   In recent years, great leaps forward have been made in technology. Significant advances have been made in the fields of medicine, science, and business. But let's not forget the advances in video games. They're becoming ever more realistic and always faster. So what does the future hold? In the not so distant future we must expect graphics so realistic they can't be differentiated from the real thing. The games will be so indepth they might take more than a year to beat. Also, virtual reality technology, which is now in a mere embryonic stage, will become so advanced that you might not know whether you're in a game or not. The development of this new breed of super indepth, super realistic video games could be the downfall of creativity and thought for the future generations. These virtual reality games will constantly be improved on and upgraded, becoming better and more realistic until they will replace our actual experiences with digital ones. Yet, hopefully, we will know when to stop.

PEIFER, "Video Games: The Reality of the Digital World"

| Exercise 6 |

Work with Words

Use context clues, word part clues, and if necessary the dictionary to write the definitions of the italicized words in the following sentences from Reading 2.

1. Video games are now replacing reading, art, sports and other *wholesome* activities that benefit the mind and body. (par. 1)

wholesome—healthy, beneficial to the mind & body.

2. After being *immersed* in a fast-paced game, children are often incapable of concentrating long enough to read. (par. 2)

*unable to
do something.
or feel emotion.*

immersed – totally involved

3. In the game he can be an all-star home-run hitter or the *MVP* (most valuable player) for a World Cup soccer team. (par. 4)

MVP – most valuable player

4. However, all the action occurs on the screen, and his actual physical fitness may actually *deteriorate*. (par. 4)

deteriorate – get worse → not as good as someone.

5. However, don't worry, because you can fight back with a rocket launcher that splatters pieces of your *foes* on the walls. (par. 6)

foes – enemies

Exercise 7

Identify Main Ideas and Supporting Details

For the following groups of sentences from, or related to, Reading 2, write "MI" for the main idea sentence and "SD" for the sentences that provide supporting details.

1. __MI__ a. As these electronic games replace more traditional pastimes, there is a noticeable decrease in the creativity and attention span of the kids that play them.

__SD__ b. A child, after playing video games for three hours, may have difficulty stopping the game and starting to read a book instead.

__SD__ c. After being immersed in a fast-paced game, children are often incapable of concentrating long enough to read.

__SD__ d. While playing games their mind is bombarded with countless images from the screen, images realistic enough that no imagination is required.

2. __SD__ a. These days the typical slumber party, instead of consisting of social activities such as board games or talking, consists of several-hour video game playing marathons that may last well into the night.

__SD__ b. In this circumstance, even though the group of friends is spending time together, they are not interacting socially with each other.

_____ SD c. So actually, there is little difference between this activity and really being alone.

_____ MI d. A child who plays video games all the time becomes less social.

3. _____ SD a. His actual physical fitness may actually deteriorate.

_____ SD b. They can take solace in the digital world, where they can excel.

_____ MI c. People who feel they don't have talents and don't stand out in the real world can do all the things they've always wanted to do in this digital world.

_____ SD d. You can beat any odds; you can do anything.

4. _____ SD a. While it may look and sound realistic, no one really dies, and you can always start over.

_____ SD b. Modern video games are designed to cater to your sense of sight, hearing, and even, with new controllers called "Rumble Packs" that shake in your hands, your sense of touch.

_____ MI c. As soon as a child starts one of these video games, she may become totally immersed in a world very similar yet different from the real one.

_____ SD d. In the game he can be an all-star home-run hitter or the MVP for a World Cup soccer team.

5. _____ SD a. In Sony PlayStation's "Resident Evil" the objective is to kill all the zombies and other horrible creatures before they dismember you and feast upon your flesh.

_____ SD b. You can fight back with a rocket launcher that splatters pieces of your foes on the walls.

_____ SD c. Or you can use a flame thrower that melts the zombies' flesh from their bones.

_____ MI d. Video games seem to be getting more and more violent.

6. _____ SD a. People of all ages will be seduced by these games, and instead of drawing a picture or acting in a play, millions will be playing video games.

_____ SD b. The games will be so indepth they might take more than a year to beat.

_SD_ c. In the not so distant future we must expect graphics so realistic they can't be differentiated from the real thing.

_MI_ d. The development of this new breed of super indepth, super realistic video games could be the downfall of creativity and thought for the future generations.

Exercise 8   ## Check Your Understanding

Write brief answers to the following questions about Reading 2.

1. What are the characteristics of video game playing that cause young people to lose their ability to pay attention to reading or to teachers?

When young people get used to fast paced exciting entertainment, they lose the ability to pay attention to a book or a teacher b/c they can't concentrate on anything for long periods.

2. Why do children who play video games become less social?

They would rather play games than visit their friends + they can lose interest in "real" social activities.

3. What kinds of young people, according to Peifer, appear to be most attracted to video game playing? And why is this so?

He thinks that people who have few talents + don't stand out in the real worlds are attracted to video games b/c they can be successful in the digital world.

4. List Peifer's main reasons for saying that video games are bad.

- People lose the ability to concentrate + to be creative.
- People lose the ability to be social.
- People waste a terrible amount of time.
- Video games are becoming more + more violent.

Exercise 9   ## Make Connections

Write short answers to the following questions about video games based on your reading, your experience, and your observations.

1. What experience do you have either directly or indirectly with video games?

   My experience with video game that is fun to play with when I have free time.

2. Who do *you* think is most attracted to playing video games? Do you agree with Peifer's assessment that young people who don't stand out are most attracted to these games? Why or why not?

   No, blc I also knew some friends are they did stand out, they also attract to video game in some how.

3. What does Peifer think about the future and video games? Do you agree with his vision? Explain your answer.

   Yes, because even we play video game is not good, but if you know when you stop then is a good thing to do.

Organize to Learn: Outline

When you are reading information that includes a lot of details, it is helpful to organize that information in some way so it will be easier to remember. Making an outline is one good method. Outlines include the most important points of a reading in a way that provides you with a visual framework for studying and remembering information. This framework shows the main idea, and important supporting details.

To set up your outline,
1. identify the topic and the main idea (or thesis for longer readings).
2. identify the supporting points for those ideas.

For example, in the following two paragraphs, pay particular attention to (1) the main idea, and (2) the supporting details.

> The Center for Successful Parenting was created in 1997 to make available more than forty years of clinical research on the adverse effects of media violence on the nation's juvenile population. The founders believe that America's children live in a society that glorifies aggressive behavior. Even if children are not influenced to commit violence

continued

themselves, they may live in fear of violent acts by their schoolmates, friends, and neighbors. At the same time, children are desensitized to these violent realities. The Center believes that there are two ways to go about changing this situation. One plan is to make all parents and grand-parents in America aware of the fact that media violence is a huge and growing problem that must be addressed now. Another plan is to give parents and grandparents some helpful guidelines for helping children to live happy, secure, and safe lives.

There are five ways for parents to help combat the negative effects of media violence in their home. First, provide a Media Free zone in your home where children can read, talk, and play games. Second, do not put a television in your child's bedroom. Third, read to your children. Fourth, refuse to expose younger children to violent content in movies, television shows, and video games. Fifth, check Moviereport.com. Moviereport.com is a Web site run by the Center for Successful Parenting that has reviews of movies and video games for parents to look at before they take their children to a movie or buy them a video game. The reviews are done by experts who look at con-tent in movies and games. The Web site is an excellent resource for those parents who wish to become informed about a movie or game. (Stoughton, "Media Violence and What Is Being Done About It")

Now, we'll go through the process of writing an outline for these paragraphs.

1. First we need to ask the question, what is the topic of the reading?

    The Center for Successful Parenting and the effects of media violence on children

2. Next, we need to ask, what is the main idea?

    The Center for Successful Parenting makes available the research on media violence and its

    effects on children and it helps parents combat the negative effects of media violence in

    their home.

3. Finally, we need to ask, what are the important supporting points? In the main idea sentence, we can notice that the first point is *the effects of violence on children.* So for our outline we could list the supporting details that prove this point. Notice that in an outline we use Roman numerals (I, II, III, etc.) to signal broad categories and capital letters (A, B, C, etc.) to indicate supporting details under those categories.

    > _I. The effects of media violence on children_
    > _A. Children may commit violence or live in fear of violence_
    > _B. Children are desensitized to violence_

continued

The second point of the main idea sentence is *ways to combat the negative effects of media violence.* So for our outline we would list the supporting details for that point.

II. Five ways to combat media violence
    A. Provide a Media Free Zone in your home.
    B. Do not put a television in your child's bedroom.
    C. Read to your children.
    D. Refuse to expose younger children to violent movies, television shows, and video games.
    E. Check Moviereport.com for reviews of movies and video games.

We can put these pieces together to form a single outline of the two paragraphs.

topic: The Center for Successful Parenting and the effects of media violence on children

main idea: The Center for Successful Parenting makes available the research on the effect of violence on America's children, and it wants to help parents combat the negative effects of media violence in their home.

I. Effects of violence on children
    A. Children may commit violence or may live in fear of violence.
    B. Children are desensitized to violence.

II. Five ways to combat effects of media violence
    A. Provide a Media Free Zone in your home.
    B. Do not put a television in your child's bedroom.
    C. Read to your children.
    D. Refuse to expose younger children to violent movies, television shows, and video games.
    E. Check Moviereport.com for reviews of movies and video games.

Exercise 10   ## Outline

Read the following paragraphs. Then follow the model for outlining to fill in the spaces of the outline provided for you.

Media violence is an issue that has recently become one of the leading questions in government, the court systems, and our society at large. In the wake of recent "school killings," the media have been under the scrutiny of many authorities. Studies have been done that conclusively correlate violence in the media with violent behavior exhibited in society. The surgeon general, the attorney general, and the Office of the President all have released statements concerning the negative effect that violence in the media has on our society. The American Medical Association calls "media violence" one of the largest threats to our national health.

"Media violence" is the term given to any form of media that graphically portrays, glorifies, and promotes violence. Action movies, for instance, often portray violence in such a way that it becomes attractive to people, especially the young. Some music lyrics and video games do the same. The media, by glorifying perverse actions, help to encourage aggressive behavior among children and adolescents. The fact that, as a society, we are inundated and fascinated with violence has an effect on the younger population called "desensitization." This term is basically applied to a child or adolescent who, through repeated and prolonged exposure to violence, becomes indifferent to it. It simply becomes a part of his or her life. Study after study has been done to confirm the belief that exposure to violent media influences human behavior. There is no question about this fact from a scientific standpoint, as it has been proven beyond a doubt. So if this is true, how is society responding? (Stoughton, "Media Violence and What's Being Done About It")

---

topic: _____

main idea: _Media violence is a major social issue._

I. Media violence - a major social issue

   A. _____

   B. Surgeon general—negative effect

   C. _____

II. Media violence - any media that graphically portrays, glorifies and promotes violence

   A. Action movies

   B. _____

   C. _____

III. Media violence - "desensitization" of children

   A. _____

   B. Confirmed by "study after study"

READING 3

Advertisement: How the Industry Hits Its Target
Selling to Kids

The following reading appeared in the journal Selling to Kids, *which is written for advertisers and companies that need to know how to get kids to buy their products. As you read, see if you recognize advertising techniques that you are familiar with. Consider why the information in this article would be important for companies who want to continue to sell more and more of their products. Also, notice what kind of supporting details the author gives to back up the main idea, or thesis.*

1   If you're not already marketing to ethnically diverse kids, it's later than you think. African-, Hispanic- and Asian-American populations are growing at least three to five times the rate of the general population, says Robert McNeil, Jr., president and CEO of Images USA, a marketing agency that specializes in the ethnic market. In fact, in less than 10 years, half of the U.S. population under 21 will be non-white. Already in California, half of kids under 18 and 65% of those under 10 are non-white, McNeil says, citing U.S. census numbers. "Any marketer who's not paying attention to cultural and ethnic differences is missing the boat" and is probably seeing that inattention affect the bottom line. . . .

2   If population-growth stats [statistics] aren't enough to convince you, take a look at spending patterns. In 1998, Hispanic teens spent $20 billion, 14% of the total $140 billion spent by all teens, and at $375 a month, 7.8% more than the average teen, according to Teenage Research Unlimited. *Latin Girl* magazine found that the 2.4 million Hispanic female teens spend up to $400 each month just on beauty products.

3   "Many people think [these populations] can be reached from the general market," but there are opportunities in targeting them specifically, says Carrales [an advertising executive]. Burger King and McDonald's are among the companies that agree. They know, for example, that African Americans and Latinos tend to consume more fast food and they're more value-conscious than general-market consumers who spend less per transaction, says McNeil. Latinos, in particular, make a fast-food restaurant visit into a family experience. They tend to order more side dishes. So the restaurants have added specialty items and flavoring geared to these groups and created advertising that shows families enjoying them.

4   Ethnic groups also are more loyal to brands than the general market is, says Charles Nicolas, Burger King spokesman. To target them, the company works with agencies that specialize in ethnic advertising. On African-American-directed ads, Burger King has worked with UniWorld Group in New York for

at least 13 years, he says. And Bromley-Aguilar and Associates in San Antonio handles its Hispanic-directed ads.

5   But most of the ads targeted to Hispanics are "just general market ads that have been dubbed," Carrales says. With the emergence of Hispanic networks like Univision and Telemundo, however, dubbing's not enough. Effective advertising to ethnic groups includes the right music, look of the kids, the way copy is delivered, colorfulness and vibrancy. There has to be cultural relevancy, she says.

6   McNeil adds that marketers who are doing this right hone in on the lifestyles of specific targets in their ads. More than choosing actors who represent the ethnicity of the targets, honing in means paying attention to nuances. For example, he says, you can't just target Hispanics as if they're a single group. You're talking to Cubans in Florida, Mexicans in Southern California and Texas, and Puerto Ricans on the East Coast, each with different dialects and accents.

proprietary
Privately owned

7   Quaker Oats Co. is one of the clients for which Carrales creates "mom-targeted, kid-friendly" ads. Because "Hispanic moms tend to be more indulgent" than the average mom, the ads have to appeal to kids who will drive the request. Carrales uses clients' proprietary research as well as some informal studies she conducts at Dallas-area ethnic schools with which she has relationships and that can use support. For example, in exchange for time spent with the kids on advertising, she has supplied her client's Gatorade for a school's field day, and she speaks at Career Days. The relationship works because "we're very careful about not taking up" learning time, she says.

Speaking "Spanglish"

assimilate Adopt
new customs, fit in

8   With all this effort to inject Hispanic culture into marketing, it's important to know that many Hispanic parents influence their kids to speak English at home and assimilate the American lifestyle, McNeil says. Parents want them to learn to speak without an accent because they see that as the key to the greatest economic and educational opportunities. But by the time kids reach their teens, they often reach back to their roots and begin using Spanish again because it's hip. That's especially true, Carrales says, with the popularity of so many Hispanic musicians who've crossed into the mainstream such as Ricky Martin, Jennifer Lopez, Marc Antony and Enrique Iglesias. Not to mention the Taco Bell chihuahua.

close-knit Close

9   Rupa Ranganathan, SVP (Senior Vice President) of Strategic Research Institute, which runs ethnic-marketing conferences agrees: Kids are clinging to their Hispanic heritage because it has become cool to be ethnic. Many marketers, she says, are using 'Spanglish,' a mix of Spanish and English to tap into cultural pride. Ads that speak 'Spanglish' or Spanish can appeal to the whole family and they should, because Hispanic families are close-knit and more likely than other groups to watch television together. A recent

Kaiser Family Foundation study found that Hispanic- and African-American kids spend more time watching television every day, with African Americans watching the most.

Amount of Daily TV Hours by Race/Ethnicity

	Ages 2 to 7	Ages 8 to 18
White	1:43	2:47
Black	2:46	4:41
Hispanic	2:20	3:50

SOURCE: Kaiser Family Foundation

Selling to Kids, "Think Eth-Nickelodeon"

Exercise 11

Work with Words

Use context clues, word part clues, and if necessary, the dictionary to choose the best definitions of the following italicized words from Reading 3.

1. Already in California, half of kids under 18 and 65% of those under 10 are non-white, McNeil says, *citing* U.S. census numbers. (par. 1)

   citing
   a. quoting
   b. underestimating
   c. ignoring

2. "Any marketer who's not paying attention to cultural and ethnic differences is missing the boat" and is probably seeing that *inattention* affect the *bottom line*. . . . (par. 1)

   inattention
   a. with attention
   b. lack of attention
   c. attention orientation

   bottom line
   a. minimum level
   b. lowest point
   c. profits

3. McNeil adds that marketers who are doing this right *hone in on* the lifestyles of specific targets in their ads. (par. 6)

   hone in on
   a. pay special attention to
   b. open up their focus on
   c. take in

4. More than choosing actors who represent the ethnicity of the targets, honing in means paying attention to *nuances*. For example,

he says, you can't just target Hispanics as if they're a single group. You're talking to Cubans in Florida, Mexicans in Southern California and Texas, and Puerto Ricans on the East Coast, each with different dialects and accents. (par. 6)

nuances
a. important matters
b. specific information
c. the whole group

5. Because "Hispanic moms tend to be more *indulgent*" than the average mom, the ads have to appeal to kids, who will drive the request. (par. 7)

indulgent
a. extending time
b. permissive
c. strict

6. [Hispanic children returning to their roots] is especially true, Carrales says, with the popularity of so many Hispanic musicians who've crossed into the *mainstream* such as Ricky Martin, Jennifer Lopez, Marc Antony, and Enrique Iglesias. (par. 8)

mainstream
a. singing group
b. widely accepted group
c. targeted ethnic group

| Exercise 12 | ## Identify Main Ideas and Supporting Details |

For the following groups of sentences from or related to Reading 3, write "MI" for the main idea sentence and "SD" for the sentences that provide supporting details.

1. _____ a. In less than ten years, half of the U.S. population under 21 will be non-white.

_____ b. Already in California, half of kids under 18 and 65 percent of those under ten are non-white.

_____ c. If you are not marketing directly to ethnically diverse kids, you are losing profits.

2. _____ a. You should be marketing to this group of young people because of their spending patterns.

_____ b. In 1998, Hispanic teens spent $20 billion, 14 percent of the $140 billion spent by all teens.

_____ c. Hispanic teens spent $375 a month, 7.8 percent more than the average teen.

_____ d. *Latin Girl* magazine found that the 2.4 million Hispanic female teens spend up to $400 each month just on beauty products.

3. _____ a. African Americans and Latinos tend to consume more fast food.

_____ b. African Americans and Latinos are more value-conscious than general-market consumers, who spend less per transaction.

_____ c. It is important to target these populations directly, looking at their specific purchasing characteristics.

_____ d. Latinos, in particular, make a fast-food restaurant visit into a family event and tend to order more side dishes.

4. _____ a. Smart companies work with advertisement agencies that specialize in ethnic advertising.

_____ b. On African-American-directed ads, Burger King has worked with UniWorld Group in New York.

_____ c. Bromley-Aguilar and Associates in San Antonio handles its Hispanic-directed ads.

5. _____ a. The ads need to include the right music.

_____ b. The kids need to look right.

_____ c. There needs to be colorfulness and vibrancy.

_____ d. Ads targeted at Hispanics have to have cultural relevancy.

6. _____ a. Carrales knows that Hispanic moms are more indulgent than other moms, and the kids often get what they want their mom to buy, so she designs her advertising towards the kids.

_____ b. She has relationships with the schools.

_____ c. In exchange for time spent with the kids on advertising, she has supplied her client's Gatorade for a school's field day.

7. _____ a. It is cool to be ethnic.

_____ b. Many Hispanic musicians are popular among all groups.

_____ c. The Taco Bell chihuahua is popular among all groups.

Outline

Based on Reading 3, choose the best answers to the questions. Then fill in the spaces of the outline model below.

1. What is the topic of the reading?
   a. how the industry hits its target
   b. advertising to ethnic minority kids
   c. advertising to ethnic minorities

2. What is the best main idea statement for the reading?
   a. It is important for advertisers to target the young ethnic minorities, and to adapt their approach to reach this audience.
   b. Advertisers have always targeted young ethnic minorities.
   c. If you're not already marketing to ethnically diverse kids, it's later than you think.

Now fill in the outline.

topic: _____

main idea: _____

_____

_____

I. _Reasons for targeting ethnically diverse young people to spend money_ _____

   A. _____

   B. _____

   C. _____

II. _Some characteristics and special approaches to reach this audience._ _____

   A. _Fast food_ _____

      1. _____

      2. _____

   B. _Brand loyalty - Agencies to target certain ethnic groups._ _____

      1. _____

      2. _____

C. *Ads targeted to the Hispanic market - Cultural Relevance*

  1. *Dubbing not enough*

  2. *Right music*

  3. _____

  4. _____

  5. _____

  6. _____

D. _____

  1. _____

  2. _____

  3. *Puerto Ricans on the East Coast*

E. *Kid friendly marketing*

  1. _____

  2. _____

F. *Hip to be ethnic*

G. *Amount of TV watching*

  1. White: _____

  2. Black: _____

  3. Hispanic: _____

Exercise 14 **Make Connections: Collaborative Activity**

Write short answers to the following questions about advertising based on your reading, your experience, and your observations. Then, to extend this exercise, discuss your answers with your class group. Working together, prepare a report for your class as a whole or a written summary for your instructor.

1. What special advertising techniques have you noticed that are directed at a specific audience (such as children, seniors, ethnic groups, etc.)? List the techniques and the audience they address.

_____

_____

_____

2. If you worked for an ad agency, what suggestions would you make for targeting a specific audience? Explain what product you are selling, what audience you have chosen, and what you would do to sell to that group.

_____

_____

_____

READING 4

Teen Girl Magazines: The Good, the Bad, and the Beautiful
Elena Peifer

In the following reading, Elena Peifer discusses what teen girl magazines mean for teenage girls—how they influence them for better and for worse. As you read, consider what you know about adolescent girls, and analyze whether her assessments of the magazines and of their reading audience seem justified. Also, note how she develops her thesis and her supporting points.

1 Almost every day the average teenage girl is judged and criticized by other teenage girls, on clothes, complexion, hair, makeup, and figure. But where does the teenage girl's idea of beauty come from? One of the answers is magazines. Magazines such as *Teen, Seventeen, YM (Young and Modern),* and *Teen People* have models on every page, pictures of the perfect body, smoothest hair, and flawless features. When we teenage girls see these flawless faces and gorgeous bodies, an idea of the perfect woman gets placed in our heads, and this idea sticks.

2 The ideal of the 110-pound, size-three, C-cup, five-foot nine-inch blond woman is one that many of us will go to extremes to achieve. We will deprive ourselves of food in pursuit of this image. When we can't reach this unrealistic goal, too many of us end up binge eating because we're depressed. Then, in order not to gain weight, we are likely to purge ourselves of the food we consumed. So the destructive cycle of eating disorders begins. As if disrupting our eating habits is not bad enough, we will wear uncomfortable clothes to look "better," high-heeled shoes to look taller, too-tight jeans to look smaller, dyed hair to be blond, and uncomfortably revealing outfits to look more like the young women in the magazines. But why exactly do we teenage girls torture ourselves so to change our looks and try to take on the supposed perfection of the models in magazines? What is in these magazines that appeals so much to girls who are becoming young women?

consumed Ate

disrupting
Radically changing

3   Horoscopes, advice, beauty and body tips, questions and answers on all topics, and interesting and informative articles are some of the things you will find in the many magazines targeted at teenage girls. In some of the many articles they have about anorexia, bulimia, and other eating disorders, the magazines tell about the devastating effects—medical and psychological—of those disorders along with firsthand accounts of people who have suffered from them. Yet, on just about every page, there are young women who are so thin they look as if they have those very disorders. Other interesting stories that these magazines sometimes have are firsthand accounts of "shopaholics," or compulsive buyers, while on just about every page there are advertisements practically screaming, "Buy, buy, buy." Ads for clothes, bathing suits, makeup, hair care, nail care, and "feminine needs" are everywhere. These ads lead teenage girls to believe that if we manage to obtain all of these products, we will somehow be transformed into the glamorous women in the magazines who, because they are "beautiful," must also be happy. The advertisements thrust on young women the idea that we need—in fact, that we must have—all of these beautifying products to be socially accepted.

devastating
Extremely damaging

4   Although magazines create impossible desires for young women, there are also many features that will help us through this awkward stage of life. In traditional cultures, there are coming-of-age ceremonies that provide very clear guidelines and rituals for how we are supposed to act as we experience our adolescence; however, American girls in our times are left to fend for ourselves during the stage between childhood and womanhood. Magazines such as *Seventeen* have articles about some of the life-altering decisions that must be made during this time, decisions such as whether or not to have sex, do drugs, concentrate in school and go to college. These articles are supplemented with advice columns with names like "Beauty," "Boys," and "Saying Goodbye," which go over teenagers' problems and their solutions.

life-altering
Life-changing

5   Sometimes teenagers, like all other people, want to forget our problems, even if it means laughing at other people's misfortunes. Columns that poke fun at other people are "Trauma-rama," "Most Mortifying Moments," and "Why Me?" It's hard for teenage girls to find our way in life, so we sometimes want to read about someone else who has had bad or embarrassing experiences. More importantly, however, magazines publish articles on hard-to-deal-with, widespread experiences—divorce, domestic violence, difficult breakups, peer pressure, and even rape. These articles show young women that we are not alone in dealing with these problems and refer us to people who can help. Family members are the hardest people to talk to about these problems, and sometimes these articles can explain to teen girls some possible ways to inform our families about what we're going through.

6   With parents, friends, teachers, and peers telling the young women of today who to be and how to act, it is easy for girls to get lost trying to find who we truly are. In the adolescent girl's search for her identity, the teen magazines can be both bad and good. On the one hand, they instill in our minds an unrealistic and unachievable goal of beauty. On the other hand, they help us find ourselves and understand better how to accomplish our goals in life. If we can find a way to tune out the messages from the models and ads, or if the magazines themselves would rule them out, I think these magazines would be mostly beneficial in allowing young women to take advantage of learning from others' mistakes. After all, we would all like to learn from mistakes without making them ourselves.

PEIFER, "Teen Girl Magazines: The Good, the Bad, and the Beautiful"

Exercise 15   ## Work with Words

Use context clues, word part clues, and if necessary the dictionary to write the definitions of the italicized words in the following sentences from Reading 4.

1. The ideal of the 110-pound, size-three, C-cup, five-foot nine-inch blond woman is one that many of us will go to extremes to achieve. [Young women] will deprive themselves of food *in pursuit of* this image. (par. 2)

    in pursuit of _____

2. What is in these magazines that *appeals* so much to girls who are becoming young women? (par. 2)

    appeals _____

3. In some of the many articles they have about *anorexia, bulimia,* and other eating disorders, the magazines tell about the devastating effects—medical and psychological—of those disorders along with firsthand accounts of people who have suffered from them. (par. 3)

    anorexia and *bulimia* _____

4. In traditional cultures, there are *coming-of-age ceremonies* that provide very clear guidelines and rituals for how we are supposed to act as we experience our adolescence; however, American girls in our times are left to fend for themselves during the stage between childhood and womanhood. (par. 4)

    coming-of-age ceremonies _____

    _____

5. If we can find a way to tune out the messages from the models and ads, or if the magazines themselves would rule them out, I think these magazines would be mostly *beneficial* in allowing young women to take advantage of learning from others' mistakes. (par. 6)

beneficial _____

Exercise 16   ## Identify Main Ideas and Supporting Details

For the following groups of sentences from or related to Reading 4, write "MI" for the main idea sentence and "SD" for the sentences that provide supporting details.

1. _____ a. Teenage girls sacrifice their health and comfort trying to achieve the right look.

   _____ b. Young women will deprive themselves of food in pursuit of this image.

   _____ c. We will wear uncomfortable shoes to look taller, too-tight jeans to look smaller, died hair to be blond, and uncomfortably revealing outfits.

2. _____ a. In some of the articles about anorexia and bulimia, the magazines tell about the devastating effects—medical and psychological—of those disorders along with first-hand accounts of people who have suffered from them.

   _____ b. Other interesting stories that these magazines have are about "shopaholics," or compulsive buyers, while on just about every page there are advertisements practically screaming, "Buy, buy, buy."

   _____ c. There are important articles from which we can learn a lot, but there are also models and advertisements that seem to represent the unrealistic expectations the articles warn us about.

3. _____ a. These articles are supplemented with advice columns with names like "Beauty," "Boys," and "Saying Goodbye," which go over teenagers' problems and their solutions.

   _____ b. Magazines such as *Seventeen* have articles about some of the life-altering decisions that must be made during this time, decisions such as whether or not to have sex, do drugs, concentrate in school and go to college.

   _____ c. There are also many features in these teen magazines that can help us through this awkward stage of life.

4. _____ a. These articles show young women that they are not alone in dealing with these problems.

_____ b. The magazines help girls forget their problems, but they also help them deal with the very real problems that they have.

_____ c. Magazines publish articles on hard-to-deal-with, widespread experiences—divorce, domestic violence, difficult breakups, peer pressure, and even rape.

Exercise 17   ## Outline

Based on Reading 4, choose the best answers to the questions. Then fill in the spaces of the outline model below.

1. What is the topic of the reading?
   a. magazines
   b. teen magazines
   c. teen magazines for girls

2. What is the best main idea statement for the reading?
   a. Teen magazines appeal to girls because they have so many glamorous photos.
   b. If we could find a way to tune out the messages from the models and ads, teen magazines would be mostly beneficial for young women.
   c. Teen magazines contradict themselves.

Now fill in the outline.

topic: _____

main idea: _____

_____

_____

I. Trying to reach the idea of beauty set by the magazines

   A. *Eating disorders (anorexia, binge eating, purging)*

   B. _____

II. Differences between the lessons of the articles and the advertisements

   A. _____

   B. *Articles about shopaholics/pictures and ads of things to buy on every page*

III. Good features

   A. <u>*Articles about important decisions we have to make*</u>

   B. _____

   C. _____

IV. Bad and good sides, but mostly beneficial

   A. <u>*Instill in our minds unrealistic goals*</u>

   B. _____

| Exercise 18 |

Make Connections

Write short answers to the following questions about magazines and advertisements based on your reading, your experience, and your observations.

1. What kinds of magazines do you read? What kinds of articles and advertisements do they have?

_____

_____

_____

_____

2. Do your magazines have both a positive and negative side as Peifer states the teenage girl magazines do? Explain.

_____

_____

_____

_____

Chapter Review

To aid your review of the reading skills in Chapter 5, study the Put It Together chart.

Put It Together: *Supporting Details*

Skills and Concepts	Explanation
Supporting Details (see pages 215–217)	Supporting details give additional information about the main idea and are more specific. They can be examples, reasons, facts, and even descriptions.
General Statements and Specific Information (see pages 217–221)	The main idea of a paragraph or essay is a broad, general statement. Specifics are the details that support the general statement.
Outlining (see pages 229–232)	Outlining is a useful technique for organizing information that you need to remember. When you outline, you follow four basic steps: 1. Determine the topic. 2. Determine the main idea(s). 3. Determine the supporting points for the main idea(s). 4. Arrange the information in outline form (see pages 230–231).

To reinforce your thinking before taking the Mastery Tests, complete as many of the following activities as your instructor assigns.

Reviewing Skills

Answer the following skills-review questions individually or in a group.

1. What is the format that you should follow to write an outline? On a separate piece of paper make a diagram of an outline. (see pp. 230–231)

_____

2. When is it helpful for you to outline a reading? _____

_____

Writing

On a separate piece of paper write a paragraph or more answering the following question: What are your favorite ways to spend time that involve mass culture—that is, culture produced for millions of people to enjoy? Explain why you spend your time in this way, why it appeals to you.

Collaborating

Brainstorm in a group all of the ways that all of us are consumers of mass entertainment. Make a list, and then fill out the chart of the benefits and disadvantages of each type of entertainment. Try, as a group, to decide which types of mass entertainment have the most benefits and the fewest disadvantages.

Type of Entertainment	*Benefits*	*Disadvantages*

Extending Your Thinking

To answer the following questions, you will have to do a little research. Then prepare to share the information you gather with your class group.

1. Go to the library or a store and flip through some popular magazines. Write down the types of articles the magazine has, and the types of advertisements. Use this information to explain who the target audience is.

2. Visit a fast food restaurant. Study the menu, and observe the people who go to the restaurant. How does the restaurant market its products to its customers? Consider the food offerings and, if you are familiar with them, the television commercials.

3. Play a video game. Describe the objectives of the game and the effects of the game on you. Determine in what ways the game is beneficial and in what ways it may be damaging. Explain your reasons.

Visiting the Web

The following Web sites provide more information on various aspects of popular culture.

1. *Media Matters*

   http://www.aap.org/advocacy/mediamatters
   National public education campaign of the American Academy of Pediatrics about the influence that media (television, movies, computer and

video games, Internet, advertising, popular music, etc.) have on child and adolescent health. Issues of concern include the use of tobacco, alcohol and other drugs; aggression and violence; sex and sexual exploitation; obesity and poor nutrition.

2. *The Rape of Our Youth*

http://it.stlawu.edu/~advertiz/children/
This excellent Web site focuses on the effect of television advertising on children; interesting information and links are provided.

3. Seventeen, *Self-Image, and Stereotypes*

http://www.rethinkingschools.org/Archives/14_02/sev142.htm
A high school teacher explains his unit on advertising and media literacy—and why some students wanted to cancel their subscription to *Seventeen* after taking his course.

Diana: The People's Princess   Kelly Mayhew

In the following reading, Dr. Kelly Mayhew examines why people all over the world were enthralled and inspired by the late Princess Diana. What do you remember about her? Did you enjoy watching programs about her or looking at magazine articles about her? As you read, consider what made her so fascinating. Notice how the details that Mayhew provides support the thesis that she develops.

1   When she appeared at the top of the aisle in Westminster Abbey, she was a fairy tale come true: yards of ivory silk billowing to the floor, pearl beading down the bodice of her gown, huge puffy sleeves, and that face peering out through the gauzy fabric of her veil. Lady Diana Spencer was soon to be Princess Di; a woman was about to become an image. No matter that some thought her prince looked more like a frog than a man, here was a flesh and blood girl about to walk down the aisle of a fantasy held by countless women in England, Europe, and the United States. In America, in fact, little girls and their mothers got up at the crack of dawn to watch this most magical wedding. Why was there such a fuss? After all, royals have been marrying each other for centuries—ever since there were royals who needed new bloodlines and new political alliances. Princess Di was seen as special because she represented not only a modern-day princess, but a collective fantasy come true.

2   What is a collective fantasy? It is a fantasy, a desire, an image, held by many. Little boys in this society may grow up fancying themselves the next Michael Jordan, Oscar de la Hoya, or Mark McGwire. Men revisit these images when they watch a ballgame or read the sports page. Girls grow up surrounded by images of courtship and marriage: Barbie has Ken, and Cinderella has her prince. These are powerful fantasies because they are given to us at such an early age. By adulthood, most of us know that they are indeed fairy tales, but the images are still very powerful.

3   Princess Diana was a particularly potent fairy tale because she seemed more "common" than the rest of the royals. She was not a princess before she got married, and she did not come from some "foreign" country. Instead, she came directly out of Merry Ol' England and was the daughter of the Royal Family's riding master. For those Americans for whom the English nobility is a mystery, Diana's beginnings seemed quite humble. While she was a "Lady," she also worked at a preschool and lived on her own. Who can forget the photographs of Diana playing with the children she took care of after her engagement was announced? There she was, a fresh-faced nineteen-year-old who seemed so much like one of "us," not afraid to wade into a sea of preschoolers and get her clothes dirty.

4   The engagement pictures furthered the "common" image of the soon-to-be princess. While Charles looked stiff, Diana glowed and appeared to be quietly giddy with her good fortune. Her gorgeous sapphire-and-diamond

ring set off her short, stubby nails, nails that topped hands that had done work. Already, people felt that Diana would be one of them and thus, was *their* princess. Her behavior at the Cinderella-like wedding supported the people's assumptions: as she rode down the street in the open carriage, she waved and nodded with more warmth than other royals had displayed. Many women felt as if they were there with her, as if she were generously sharing this most intimate of days with them. Diana seemed to invite the "common" folks to experience her fantasy wedding with her. She was the flesh and blood embodiment of all the fairy-tale princesses. That she also looked nervous, a bit awkward, and extremely young added to her allure.

5   As she grew into her role as a princess of England, and as her dress size shrank, Princess Diana maintained her generosity of spirit. Although reports from the palace indicated that her marriage to Charles was not idyllic, Princess Di, in her public appearances at hospitals, parades, and schools never let on that her prince was indeed rather froglike. Try as the media might to paint her as a party girl or a clothes-horse, Diana kept the goodwill of the British people, probably because she went among them so frequently. Pregnant, nursing, battling bulimia, dealing with marital difficulties, Diana always seemed to be able to make herself available to her public. And in public, she was not too shy to shake hands, hold babies, and hug the elderly or infirm. She even took her public role on the road by visiting the poor and common in India, Africa, and elsewhere. Through her public role, Diana nourished the collective fantasy surrounding her. She was seen as a working princess: as someone who gave back to her subjects even as she lived in a palace and wore incredible clothes and jewels.

infirm   Sick

6   For, of course, she had to look the part. Many people didn't seem to mind that as England experienced a terrible recession, Diana wore designer fashions. After all, this was her bargain. Play the part of fairy-tale princess and wear the clothes. Giant hats and plunging necklines, her experiments with fabrics and patterns in some odd ways made her seem more like regular women. How does one develop a fashion sense? One experiments, one makes faux pas, one laughs about one's mistakes. One is not stuffy, like the queen or Princess Anne. One is like everybody else, like common women let loose in a department store or at the hairdresser's salon.

recession   A period of bad economic times

faux pas Embarrassing mistake

7   The rest of Princess Di's story was again, quite common, in a fairy-tale sort of way. After having two strong boys, the glitter was stripped away from the princess's marriage. How do we know this? Aside from the revelations of the tabloids, Princess Di's painful weight loss spoke of a deep sadness. Such sadness again made her appear to her subjects to be just like them. Unlike royals past, Diana found forgiveness from the public when she sought a separation. It didn't matter to her that someday Charles would be king of England. What mattered was that he had hurt her and that she could no longer live with that. Her separation and impending divorce, rather than making her seem less Cinderella-like, made her more so. Princess Diana

was a modern princess whose own life mirrored the lives of her subjects. This made her more human. That her pain was played out in palaces and on expensive yachts was to be expected.

8   Princess Diana's death was like a terrible negative of her wedding: a mangled black car in a tunnel at night with her playboy lover. The whiteness and lightness of the one canceled out by the darkness of the other. And ironically, she appeared to have been killed by the very media that nurtured her fairy-tale image. The very media that sold more magazines, more newspapers, more feature television stories about Diana than about anyone else in the twentieth century were the indirect cause of her death. And that media continue to spin Diana's life as a fantasy, shared by all. She was a princess, after all.

MAYHEW, "Diana: The People's Princess"

Based on the context clues, word part clues, and if necessary the dictionary, choose the best definition for the meaning of each of the italicized words in the following sentences from the reading.

1. After all, royals have been marrying each other for centuries—ever since there were Royals who needed new bloodlines and new political *alliances*. (par. 1)

   alliances
   a. partnerships
   b. resources
   c. subjects

2. Little boys in this society may grow up *fancying* themselves the next Michael Jordan, Oscar de la Hoya, or Mark McGwire. (par. 2)

   fancying
   a. knowing
   b. imagining
   c. considering

3. Men *revisit* these images when they watch a ballgame or read the sports page. (par. 2)

   revisit
   a. visit again
   b. think about again
   c. confuse

4. Princess Diana was a particularly *potent* fairy tale because she seemed more "common" than the rest of the royals. (par. 3)

   potent
   a. unlikely
   b. weak
   c. powerful

5. Although reports from the palace indicated that her marriage to Charles was not *idyllic*, Princess Di, in her public appearances at hospitals, parades, and schools never let on that her prince was indeed rather froglike. (par. 5)

   idyllic
   a. difficult
   b. perfect
   c. valid

6. She was the flesh and blood embodiment of all fairy-tale princesses. That she also looked nervous, a bit awkward, and extremely young added to her *allure*. (par. 4)

   allure
   a. fortune
   b. wisdom
   c. attraction

7. Aside from the *revelations* of the tabloids, Princess Di's weight loss spoke of a deep sadness. (par. 7)

   revelations
   a. detailed diet plan
   b. secrets that are told to the public
   c. public information

8. Through her public role, Diana *nourished* the collective fantasy surrounding her. (par. 5)

   nourished
   a. added to
   b. noticed
   c. disliked

For the following groups of sentences from or related to the reading, write "MI" for the main idea sentence and "SD" for the sentences that provide supporting details.

9. _____ a. Princess Di was seen as special because she represented not only a modern-day princess, but a collective fantasy come true.

   _____ b. No matter that some thought her prince looked more like a frog than a man, here was a flesh and blood girl about to walk down the aisle of a fantasy held by countless women.

   _____ c. In America, little girls and their mothers got up at the crack of dawn to watch this most magical wedding.

10. _____ a. Princess Diana was a particularly important fairy tale because we could all relate to her.

_____ b. She was not a princess before she got married.

_____ c. Her beginnings seemed quite humble.

_____ d. She was a fresh-faced nineteen-year-old who seemed so much like one of "us," not afraid to wade into a sea of preschoolers and get her clothes dirty.

11. _____ a. While Charles looked stiff, Diana glowed and appeared to be quietly giddy with her good fortune.

_____ b. Her gorgeous sapphire-and-diamond ring set off her short, stubby nails, nails that topped hands that had done work.

_____ c. That she also looked nervous, a bit awkward, and extremely young added to her allure.

_____ d. Diana seemed to invite the "common" folks to experience her Cinderella-like wedding with her.

12. _____ a. In her public appearances at hospitals, parades, and schools, she never let on that her prince was indeed rather froglike.

_____ b. Princess Di was seen as a working princess with a generosity of spirit, as someone who gave back to her subjects.

_____ c. Pregnant, nursing, battling bulimia, dealing with marital difficulties, Diana always seemed to be able to make herself available to her public.

_____ d. And in public, she was not too shy to shake hands, hold babies, and hug the elderly or infirm.

13. _____ a. Her sadness made her appear to her subjects to be just like them.

_____ b. Princess Di's weight loss spoke of a deep sadness.

_____ c. Princess Diana was a modern princess whose life mirrored the lives of the common people.

_____ d. The public could forgive Diana when she sought separation from Charles because he had hurt her.

Choose the best answers to the following multiple-choice questions based on the reading.

14. What do girls grow up dreaming about?
    a. the same fantasies as boys
    b. courtship and marriage
    c. images

15. What is a "collective fantasy"?
    a. Barbie and Ken
    b. Oscar de la Hoya, Michael Jordan, and Mark McGwire
    c. a desire, or an image, held by many

16. Which of the following is *not* a reason why people loved Diana even when she spent so much money on clothes while many people were struggling to earn a living?
    a. She kept up her image as a modern-day fairy tale.
    b. She was like everybody else, like common women.
    c. She never made a mistake or experimented with her clothes.

17. Why did the media follow her everywhere, including on the night she died?
    a. Because stories about her sold and made a lot of money for them
    b. Because they didn't like Prince Charles
    c. Because they wanted to find out why she was getting a divorce

18. Mayhew writes that "Princess Diana's death was like a terrible negative of her wedding" in order to emphasize what?
    a. That the media was probably partially responsible for her death
    b. How terrible her death was compared to how beautiful her wedding was
    c. Her life as a collective fantasy

Write short answers to the following questions about heroes and public figures based on your reading, your experience, and your observations.

19. Why do you think people like to have heroes and heroines, or to have fantasies to dream about?

    _____

    _____

    _____

20. What public figure(s) do you most admire? Why?

    _____

    _____

    _____

Some Day My Prince Will Come

Kelly Mayhew and Elena Peifer

In the following reading, Kelly Mayhew and Elena Peifer take a look at fairy tales, why we enjoy them, and the lessons that we learn from them. As you read, pay close attention to the main ideas that they present and their supporting details. Also, consider whether or not you agree with their analysis.

1   Fairy tales have captivated peoples' imaginations for centuries. Stories of princes saving princesses, fairy godmothers, wolves, goblins, evil queens, stepmothers, and stepsisters have been written, told, and acted out in various versions in most parts of the world. In the United States in the 1930s, Walt Disney began to bring fairy tales alive in the form of animation, starting with *Snow White and the Seven Dwarfs* in 1935. The children of today still watch these films, along with other classics such as *Sleeping Beauty, Cinderella, The Little Mermaid,* and *Beauty and the Beast,* thanks to the ever-present VCR. Although the films take place in different locations, and the stories are different, they have many similarities. They are all about the plight of a young woman of noble birth who has problems, frequently caused by the presence of an evil character who wants to keep her from fulfilling her dreams. These problems are later swept away by her Prince Charming, who comes to save her in some way. Since this formula has been told and retold for centuries, fairy tales continue to attract our attention because they are predictable and comforting, and we tend to believe that if we live by the formula, our dreams will come true.

2   Let's take a look at the basic formula of romantic fairy tales. First, there is the romantic ideal they depict, which is that there is a Prince Charming who will sweep the princess off her feet. Cinderella dances all night with her prince, who can't keep his eyes or hands off her. Snow White's prince can't help but kiss her when he sees her lying in her glass coffin. And Sleeping Beauty's prince comes running to her rescue just at the mere mention of her name and her predicament. These are powerful ideas and dreams that meet a deep need in people to feel loved and needed. And when people—in particular women—grow up, they may hold onto this unfulfillable and unrealistic dream and believe that there is a real Prince Charming out there who will save them, marry them, and live happily ever after with them. We know from these tales how romances should end; unfortunately, though, fairy tales never continue on to show the complexities, both the joys and sorrows, of marriage.

3   Next is the concept of a "damsel in distress" whom Prince Charming must save. This is important because it represents the image of the weak woman, the one who can't care for herself and who needs a man to save

her. In his eyes she is worth saving only because he has an idea of her beauty and of how she will follow and obey him, which is a powerful image, for men in particular. Sleeping Beauty, lying beautifully asleep for 100 years, is a good example of the "damsel in distress." The prince's kiss is *so* powerful, that it literally reanimates her, it wakes her up, it makes her able to move again. This type of story reinforces the idea that women are whole only through the help and support of a man, that somehow a woman is helpless, not capable, and even not alive unless she has a man at her side. This idea of the helpless woman is not good for women to believe in because it renders them helpless and unwilling to live their lives on their own terms. And for men, it enforces the notion that a woman cannot survive without a man, which gives men a lot of power in their relationships.

4   The power of the man-hero is made very clear in fairy tales if we look at who the prince rescues the princess from. He has to save her from some truly evil characters. Often this character is connected in some way to one of the other main characters. For instance, in Cinderella, there are Cinderella's evil stepmother and stepsisters, and in Snow White, there is the queen, who is also Snow White's stepmother. The evil character is frequently a woman who is deeply jealous of the young, beautiful heroine and who will stop at nothing to see her brought down or even killed. Symbolically, we have a war going on here between youth and age and between weakness and power. As Susan Douglas argues in her book *Where the Girls Are: Growing Up Female with the Mass Media,* powerlessness is rewarded in fairy tales, and activity is punished. What does this mean? It means that women—usually the wicked witches—who have power or who want it are evil, nasty creatures who must be stopped. These fairy tales tell us that power in women is wrong. This is why it is almost always a man—the prince, for example—who thwarts the wicked plans of the evil stepmother/ queen by rescuing the princess and rewarding her powerlessness. Although the fairy godmothers have some power, in Disney movies they are usually portly and comical figures. The main group of women with power are the evil women, and they fail over and over again.

5   The versions of fairy tales that we have available to us send extremely strong messages. The repetition of the fairy-tale formula has a great deal to do with how girls and boys grow up viewing each other and imagining their eventual relationships. The damsel in distress, Prince Charming, and evil queen/stepmother characters tell us a lot about how we view women, men, and romance. People often like to dismiss (or not recognize) the importance of these stories and movies. Some say that they are just "entertainment," but any story that we hear over and over again influences us. Haven't most girls dreamed of finding their Prince Charming? Haven't most boys thought that they could come to the aid of a (helpless) girl?

MAYHEW AND PEIFER, "Some Day My Prince Will Come"

Name _____ Date _____

Based on the context clues, word part clues, and if necessary the dictionary, choose the best definition for the meaning of each of the italicized words in the following sentences from the reading,

1. They are all about the *plight* of a young woman of noble birth who has problems, frequently caused by the presence of an evil character who wants to keep her from fulfilling her dreams. (par. 1)

   plight
   a. character
   b. health
   c. difficult situation

2. Since this formula has been told and retold for centuries, fairy tales continue to attract our attention because they are *predictable* and comforting, and we tend to believe that if we live by the formula, our dreams will come true.

   predictable
   a. always retold
   b. possible to know what will happen
   c. comfortable to hear

3. First, there is the romantic ideal they *depict*, which is that there is a Prince Charming who will sweep the princess off her feet. (par. 2)

   depict
   a. show
   b. reinforce
   c. invent

4. And when people—in particular women—grow up, they may hold onto this *unfulfillable* and unrealistic dream and believe that there is a real Prince Charming out there who will save them, marry them, and live happily ever after with them. (par. 2)

   unfulfillable
   a. possible to carry out
   b. impossible to carry out
   c. difficult to carry out

5. We know from these tales how romances should end; unfortunately, though, fairy tales never continue on to show the *complexities*, both the joys and sorrows, of marriage. (par. 2)

   complexities
   a. complications, many parts
   b. problems
   c. pains and satisfactions

6. This type of story *reinforces* the idea that women are whole only through the help and support of a man. (par. 3)

   reinforces
   a. makes stronger
   b. introduces
   c. ignores

7. The prince's kiss is so powerful, that it literally *reanimates her*, it wakes her up, it makes her able to move again. (par. 3)

   reanimates her
   a. thrills her
   b. brings her back to life
   c. turns her into an animal

8. This idea of the helpless woman is not good for women to believe in because it *renders* them helpless and unwilling to live their lives on their own terms. (par. 3)

   renders
   a. helps
   b. makes
   c. encourages

For the following groups of sentences from or related to the reading, write "MI" for the main idea sentence and "SD" for the sentences that provide supporting details.

9. _____ a. Cinderella dances all night with her prince.

   _____ b. Snow White's prince can't help but kiss her.

   _____ c. Sleeping Beauty's prince comes running to her rescue.

   _____ d. There is the romantic ideal that there is a Prince Charming.

10. _____ a. There is the concept of a "damsel in distress" whom the Prince Charming must save.

   _____ b. Sleeping Beauty, lying beautifully asleep for 100 years, is a good example of the "damsel in distress."

   _____ c. Frequently fairy tales portray the image of the weak woman who can't care for herself and needs a man to save her.

   _____ d. The prince's kiss is SO powerful that it wakes her up and makes her able to move again.

11. _____ a. In *Cinderella*, there are Cinderella's evil stepmother and stepsisters.

_____ b. In *Snow White,* there is the queen, who is also Snow White's stepmother.

_____ c. The evil character is frequently a woman who is deeply jealous of the young, beautiful heroine and who will stop at nothing to see her brought down or even killed.

_____ d. In *Sleeping Beauty,* the evil character is also a witch.

12. _____ a. Walt Disney began to bring fairy tales alive in the form of animation in the 1930s, and American audiences have been watching them ever since.

_____ b. Some of the most recent Disney animated films are *The Prince of Egypt* and *Mulan.*

_____ c. The children of today still watch these films, along with other classics such as *Sleeping Beauty, Cinderella, The Little Mermaid,* and *Beauty and the Beast,* thanks to the ever-present VCR.

_____ d. *Snow White and the Seven Dwarfs* was produced in 1935.

13. _____ a. People can take some strange lessons from fairy tales.

_____ b. Women are weak.

_____ c. Men can save women from their weak condition, and will be the heroes.

_____ d. Women with power are evil, and they lose in the end.

Choose the best answers to the following multiple-choice questions about the reading.

14. What is the main idea, or the thesis, of "Some Day My Prince Will Come"?
   a. People have always loved fairy tales.
   b. Fairy tales teach us to have dreams that are unrealistic, and to think of women as weak.
   c. People all over the world love to watch Disney animated fairy tales.
   d. The bad woman in the fairy tales is usually a stepmother or witch.

15. Which of the following is *not* true about fairy tales?
    a. There is usually a "damsel in distress."
    b. There is usually a Prince Charming.
    c. All of the good characters are thin.
    d. The evil women lose in the end.

16. Which of the following is *not* a reason the authors give for why people love fairy tales?
    a. They captivate our imaginations and give us dreams.
    b. The originally unfortunate heroine wins in the end.
    c. We know the formula, and we are comfortable with it.
    d. We love to sit around and hear a good story at night.

17. What idea do we get about men from fairy tales?
    a. Men are expected to save women, who are weaker.
    b. Men will also get help when they need it.
    c. Men may have problems also.
    d. Men fall in love with women once they know them well.

18. What idea do we get about women from fairy tales?
    a. Women can lead independent lives.
    b. Women can go to sleep and wake up 100 years later.
    c. Women should be active in creating their own lives.
    d. Women are weak and need a man.

Write short answers to the following questions about fairy tales and dreams based on your reading, your experience, and your observations.

19. What are your two favorite fairy tales or favorite stories? Why do you like them?

    _____

    _____

    _____

    _____

20. We all have dreams about how our lives will be. Where do you think those dreams come from?

    _____

    _____

    _____

    _____

Chapter 6

Major and Minor Supporting Details

Television in Our Society

In the last Nielsen survey of American viewers, the average family was watching television seven hours a day. This has never happened before in history. No people has ever been entertained for seven hours a day. This all-pervasive diet of instant imagery must have changed us in profound ways.

—Pete Hamill, "Crack and the Box"

- How much television do you watch? In what ways do you think we have changed since we've started watching so much television?

- Whose photo is shown here? Do you think most Americans would recognize them? Why?

Getting Ready to Read

Just about every American household has one or more television sets. Almost without exception, we watch it for hours every day. Sometimes the programs are educational, but more frequently they are purely for entertainment. Have you ever thought about how beneficial or detrimental television viewing might be to our lives? Have you ever thought about which types of shows contribute something to the quality of our lives and which shows do not? In this chapter you will be thinking about some of the many kinds of television programming that we have to choose from—the possible good and the possible bad of our television habit. As you do, you will improve your reading skills by learning how to

- distinguish major supporting details from minor supporting details
- use outlines to visualize the distinction
- mark texts to distinguish major and minor supporting details
- organize main ideas and supporting details into maps
- write summaries that capture, in your own words, main ideas and major supporting details

READING 1

The Oprah Hour, the Oprah World

Craig Stoughton

In the following reading, Stoughton presents an extremely positive picture of Oprah Winfrey's career in television and of her many other activities. As you read, think about what you already know about Oprah, and decide whether you agree with him. Also, consider how Stoughton supports his thesis with details about Oprah's show and about her life.

1   It is Monday afternoon, 4 P.M. Millions of people are sitting in front of their television sets, waiting for a woman to appear. Many of them watch this woman because she is entertaining, many watch her because they seem to know her somehow. To these people, this woman is a best friend and confidant. Her name is Oprah Winfrey and she is the most popular woman in the history of television. In fact, she may be the single most well known woman in the world, especially now that Princess Diana is no longer alive. Her show is the most consistently highest ranked among all talk shows, and Oprah herself is the single richest female media personality in America. The Oprah Winfrey show is such a success because of Oprah herself. It doesn't seem to matter what the topic of the show is or what guests appear, Oprah's personality and on-camera presence keep viewers coming back day after day.

confidant A person you share your secrets with

innumerable
Uncountable, very many

2   At precisely 4 P.M., Monday through Friday, Oprah appears on innumerable television sets. First, before the live action starts, a theme song is heard. Oprah sings her own song, in which the main lyrics are, "I will rise." Various photographic stills of Oprah are flashed on the screen. Some of these snapshots include Oprah hugging a distraught fan, Oprah laughing with that signature smile, Oprah dancing with her hands clapped together, Oprah bent down on one knee like a preacher holding a young girl's hand. All of these images are there to relax the television viewing audience, and to assure them that Oprah is a kind, caring, fun-loving individual who really is "real."

3   When Oprah first appears, she sets the stage and the mood for what is to come. The show begins after a brief commercial break with an excited-looking Oprah running onto the set to the cheers of a very enthusiastic audience. Oprah gives audience members high fives, on her face is a huge grin as she prances onto the stage. The applause goes on for a moment or two as Oprah bows, and then the cheering dies out. Speaking loudly into her hand-held microphone, Oprah greets the audience in a very friendly manner and points out some things about the audience that she finds funny. Often she relates to the audience something that occurred to her backstage. After cheerfully bantering with the audience, Oprah explains what she has in store for them today. Sometimes she has a celebrity guest, other times she has on a "regular" person whose story has inspired her. Her celebrity guests have included stars like Michael Jackson and Tina Turner; her "regular" guests have shared their triumphs, and problems. On other shows she picks a topic like how to handle your money and invites financial experts on the show. They may cover such skills as how to save money at the grocery store or how to balance your checkbook.

lurid   Shocking

4   Oprah seems genuine in her pursuit of helping people. Before the 1995 season, Oprah made a pledge to her viewers that instead of having lurid and provocative topics, she would refocus her show on more positive areas. Since then her shows have mainly centered around positive issues. Many are "self-help" shows devised to help people attain personal and financial freedom. On others she invites celebrities to discuss how they have become so successful. In all of these shows Oprah seemingly has the audience's welfare in mind.

philanthropic
Showing concern for people; giving money to the needy

5   In 1998 Oprah began what is known as the Angel Network. This program has many philanthropic goals, for example, pairing up with Habitat for Humanity in building houses for those who are homeless, contributing to college funds and scholarships (Oprah herself is a huge donator to the United Negro College Fund), and generally helping people out.

6   Along with being a media star and philanthropist, Oprah has revolutionized the publishing business with Oprah's Book Club. She picks a book every month or so and asks her viewers to read the book. After a couple of weeks, she usually invites the author of that book on the show for a chat. Oprah has even had the book club meet in her house. Bookstores now

feature an Oprah's Book Club stand where a consumer can find current and past club selections. Each selection now has Oprah's club name on its cover. Most selections go straight to the number one slot on the New York Times Bestseller list.

7   Oprah is not only a television star, she is also a multimedia personality. She has starred in many movies. In 1986 she played an important supporting role in Steven Spielberg's film adaptation of the book *The Color Purple.* For her performance, Oprah was nominated for an Academy Award. Since then she has had numerous television and movie roles, most notably on a television miniseries, "The Women of Brewster Place," and recently she produced and starred in another film adaptation of one of her favorite books, Toni Morrison's *Beloved.*

8   Oprah's mission to help people is expressed at the end of each of her shows in a prerecorded segment called "Remembering Your Spirit." During this segment Oprah gives advice, or she has viewers discuss different issues in their lives that they are struggling or have struggled with and relate how they have found help. It seems that in the past fourteen years, Oprah has found her spirit on the show, and her audience has been on that journey with her, with everybody involved learning more about themselves during the process.

STOUGHTON, "The Oprah Hour, the Oprah World"

| Exercise 1 | ## Recall and Discuss |

Answer these questions about Reading 1, and prepare to discuss them in class.

1. What does Oprah do at the beginning of the show to make her viewers relax and to show that she really cares?

   _____

   _____

   _____

   _____

2. What are some of Oprah's accomplishments other than her talk show?

   _____

   _____

3. Have you ever watched Oprah? What do you think of her show?

   _____

   _____

4. Do you watch any television talk shows? Which ones? Why do you like them?

_____

_____

Major and Minor Supporting Details

In addition to recognizing main ideas and supporting details, as you practiced in Chapter 5, it is important to know how to distinguish major supporting details from minor supporting details. As you know, the main idea is the overall general statement, or main point the author is trying to make.

Major Supporting Details

major supporting details Details, examples, or reasons that the author gives to support the main idea statement, or thesis

The supporting details that you learned about in Chapter 5 can be considered **major supporting details,** the most important examples, facts, reasons, or descriptions that the author gives to support the main idea statement, or thesis.

Minor Supporting Details

minor supporting details Additional points that provide more information or examples to support major supporting details

The **minor supporting details** are additional points that support major supporting details. They can give

1. more information to explain the major supporting details.
2. more examples to illustrate major supporting details.
3. more specifics to make the material more interesting.

In some readings, minor supporting details offer important information essential to your understanding. For example, when you are studying for a biology exam, you will need to learn and remember minor supporting details. In other situations, such as when you are reading a magazine article for pleasure or to understand general trends, minor supporting details are extras that may make the reading more pleasurable or more convincing but need not be remembered.

The following passage is an example of a paragraph with important major and minor supporting details about the Oprah Winfrey Show.

At precisely 4 P.M., Monday through Friday, Oprah appears on innumerable television sets. First, before the live action starts, a theme song is heard. Oprah sings her own song, in which the main lyrics are, "I will rise." Various photographic stills of Oprah are flashed on the screen. Some of these snapshots include Oprah hugging a distraught fan, Oprah laughing with that signature smile, Oprah dancing with her hands clapped together, Oprah bent down on one knee like a preacher holding a young girl's hand. All of these images are there to relax the television viewing audience, and to assure them that Oprah is a kind, caring, fun-loving individual who really is "real." (Stoughton, "Oprah Hour")

First, we should answer the question, what is the topic of the paragraph?

The introduction to the Oprah Winfrey show

Next, what is the main idea?

All of the images at the beginning of the show relax and assure the audience that Oprah is a kind, caring, fun-loving individual who really is "real".

Looking carefully at the paragraph, we should ask, what are the major supporting details?

1. The theme song

2. The photographic stills

Checking the paragraph again, we should further ask, how is each major supporting detail backed up with minor supporting details?

The theme song: (a) Oprah sings it herself, (b)the main lyrics are "I will rise".

The photographic stills of Oprah: (a) hugging a fan, (b) laughing, (c)dancing, (d) bent on one knee holding a girl's hand

Working with Main Ideas and Major and Minor Supporting Details

Recognizing main ideas and major and minor supporting details is an essential skill you are now mastering. You can reinforce your understanding of a reading as well as aid your studies by learning some ways of organizing information that reflect the relationships between main ideas, and major and minor supporting details. To do this, it is helpful to outline, create maps, and mark texts.

outline A form of organizing information using numbers and letters and spatial layout to indicate levels of supporting details

Using an Outline

In Chapter 5, you practiced making **outlines** to organize the information you learn using roman numerals and letters to indicate levels of information. Outlining is a great way to see which supporting details are major and which are minor, because an outline shows how the details relate to each other in a spatial way. If still more detail is needed, use regular numbers under the capital letters. Here is an example:

topic: expressed in a few words, not a complete sentence

main idea: expressed as a complete sentence

I. major supporting detail
   A. minor supporting detail
      1. more minor detail
      2. more minor detail
   B. minor supporting detail

Using the information in Reading 1 about the beginning of Oprah's show, we can identify the major and minor supporting details as follows:

topic: *The Introduction to the Oprah Show*

main idea: *All of the images at the beginning of the show relax and assure the audience that Oprah is a kind, caring, fun-loving individual who really is "real."*

I. *Theme song*
   A Oprah sings
   B. Lyrics: "I will rise"

II. *Photographic stills of Oprah*
   A. Hugging a fan
   B. Laughing
   C. Dancing
   D. Holding a girl's hand
      1. Like a preacher
      2. Bent on one knee

Exercise 2

Outline Major and Minor Supporting Details

For the following paragraphs, complete the short outlines by writing in the appropriate places the stated or unstated main idea, the major supporting details, and the minor supporting details. Some of the information has been provided.

1. When Oprah first appears, she sets the stage and the mood for what is to come. The show begins after a brief commercial break with an excited-looking Oprah running onto the set to the cheers of a very enthusiastic audience. Oprah gives audience members high fives, on her face is a huge grin as she prances onto the stage. The applause goes on for a moment or two as Oprah bows, and then the cheering dies out. Speaking loudly into her hand-held microphone, Oprah greets the audience in a very friendly manner and points out some things about the audience that she finds funny. Often she relates to the audience something that occurred to her backstage. After cheerfully bantering

with the audience, Oprah explains what she has in store for them today. Sometimes she has a celebrity guest, other times she has on a "regular" person whose story has inspired her. Her celebrity guests have included stars like Michael Jackson and Tina Turner; her "regular" guests have shared their triumphs, and problems. On other shows she picks a topic like how to handle your money and invites financial experts on the show. They may cover such skills as how to save money at the grocery store or how to balance your checkbook. (Stoughton, "Oprah Hour")

main idea: *When Oprah first appears, she sets the stage and the mood for what is to come.*

I. *Oprah running onto the set and starting the show*

    A. _____

    B. *High fives*

    C. _____.

    D. *Shares something funny that occurred backstage*

II. *Explains the day's program*

    A. _____

        1. *Michael Jackson, Tina Turner*

        2. *Regular guests: share triumphs and problems*

    B. *Sometimes a special topic, like finances*

        1. _____

        2. _____

2. No one can ever accuse Oprah of hoarding money. She's got the wealth and, boy, does she enjoy spreading it around. This was illustrated loudly and clearly when she turned up at an auction in New Lebanon, N.Y., and spent a whopping $470,000 in a couple of hours. Without batting an eye, she forked over $220,000 for one antique work counter alone. . . . Oprah even took time out during her lavish weekend-long 40th birthday celebration in Los Angeles to treat a dozen of her girlfriends to a Beverly Hills shopping spree. After picking up a $1,300 lunch tab, Oprah and her all-girl group piled into two limos and headed for Santa Monica's trendy Montana Avenue shopping district, where she blew $35,000 in less than two hours, buying dresses, jewelry, a purse, a pantsuit and presents for her nieces. ("Who Wants to Be a Billionaire?")

main idea: *Oprah spends a lot of money with no problem.*

I. *Auction in New York*

    A. _____

    B. _____

II. _____

    A. _____

    B. *$35,000 shopping spree in Santa Monica*

       1. *Dresses*

       2. _____

       3. _____

       4. _____

       5. _____

3. As Oprah explains, "My mission is to use my position, power and money to create opportunities for other people. I firmly believe that none of us in this world have made it until the least among us have made it." Here are some of the causes Oprah favors, and the ones she hopes her fans will support:

   - Oprah's Angel Network: Oprah guides this collective of fans to perform thousands of acts of charity and kindness each year. Projects have included collecting more than $3.5 million in spare change to fund scholarships for needy students, donating music equipment to choirs, and helping to build homes for the poor.

   - The National Child Protection Act: This is part of Oprah's effort to help protect children from abuse. She worked long and hard on the political campaign to pass this act, and eventually won over President Clinton and the Senate Judiciary Committee with her lobbying. The main purpose of this act is to establish a national database of child abusers to prevent them from repeating their actions.

   - A Better Chance: Oprah endorsed this organization in 1997 when she began acting as a spokesperson. She also contributed $1 million of her own money to the group, which has helped 9,000 students go to college since its start 37 years ago. (Choueke, "She Gives from the Heart")

main idea: _____

I. Oprah's Angel Network: raised #3.5 million

    A. _____

    B. _____

    C. _____

II. _____

    A. won support

        1. President Clinton

        2. _____

    B. purpose of the act - establish national database of child abusers to prevent them from repeating their crime

III. A Better Chance—College Scholarships

Organize to Learn: Make a Map

In addition to outlining, another way to organize information for learning is to create a visual pattern that diagrams information, such as the map shown here. Notice how the information in a paragraph or in a longer passage can be organized visually so that you immediately understand the relationships between the main idea, the major supporting details, and the minor supporting details. As you practice mapping and outlining, you will probably find that you like one technique more than another. Sometimes, though, a map can show some relationships better than an outline. For example, if something is causing something else to happen, you can use arrows to show the cause-and-effect relationship. Some people even draw little cartoons to help them organize and remember information. Now take a look at the sample map.

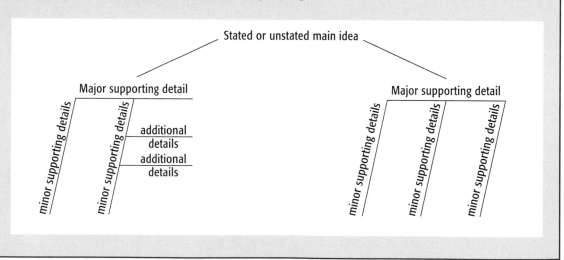

The information from the paragraph about the introduction to Oprah's show (page 263), mapped in the pattern shown, would look like this:

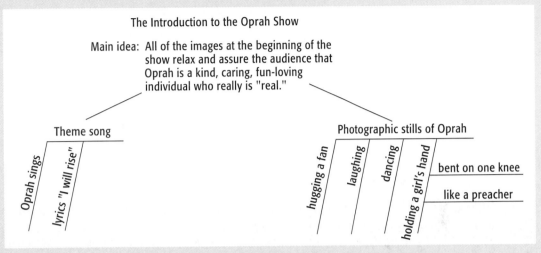

The Introduction to the Oprah Show

Main idea: All of the images at the beginning of the show relax and assure the audience that Oprah is a kind, caring, fun-loving individual who really is "real."

Theme song

Oprah sings

lyrics "I will rise"

Photographic stills of Oprah

hugging a fan

laughing

dancing

holding a girl's hand

bent on one knee

like a preacher

In this map, the information is shown in a spatial way. The main idea is at the top. The two major supporting details are diagrammed next to each other, below the main idea. The minor supporting details branch off from the major supporting details, just below them. Because there are two minor details for the theme song, there are two branches under it. Because there are four minor details for the photographic stills of Oprah, there are four branches under it. Notice that even more minor details describe Oprah's position as she was holding the child's hand.

Each map will look different, because it is shaped to suit the information you are working with. Some maps will have branches, and some may use arrows.

| Exercise 3 | ## Map Major and Minor Supporting Details |

For the following paragraphs or groups of paragraphs, complete the maps that show the relationships between the main idea and the major and minor supporting details.

1. From the beginning, television captured the imagination and the pocketbooks of its viewers, who loved the combination of the new with the familiar. People watched the small screen as radio personalities of the 1930s and 1940s made their way in front of the cameras. Radio stars Milton Berle, George Burns, and Gracie Allen took to the new medium with a whole new flair. Advertisers eagerly paid broadcasting companies for the right to sell their products on the air. Every show had a sponsor, and the sponsor's name was prominent in the title of the show. In these early years, companies such as Colgate, Buick, and Texaco produced the variety shows. (Lindsay, "Television and Popular Culture")

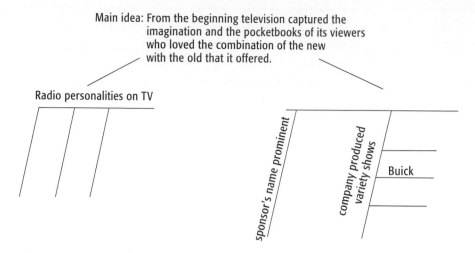

Main idea: From the beginning television captured the imagination and the pocketbooks of its viewers who loved the combination of the new with the old that it offered.

Radio personalities on TV

sponsor's name prominent

company produced variety shows

Buick

2. In the 1950s television was a simple affair: you could be entertained with a wholesome diet of variety shows or family shows. *The Ed Sullivan Show* was one of the most popular shows of the period, and although Ed was not a skilled performer, he brought important personalities to his show. By showcasing such musical talents as the Beatles, Elvis Presley, Lena Horne, and Duke Ellington, Ed showed that the average viewer would want to watch entertainers from different backgrounds and races. At the same time, in the America of the 1950s, most of the population held traditional, somewhat conservative beliefs, and television mirrored this image we had of ourselves. The program *Leave It to Beaver* portrayed a "typical" American family. Ward worked at the office, and June took care of the family and the house. When Wally or Beaver would get into trouble, Ward would step in, deliver a lecture, and everything was settled by the end of the half-hour show. (Lindsay, "Television and Popular Culture")

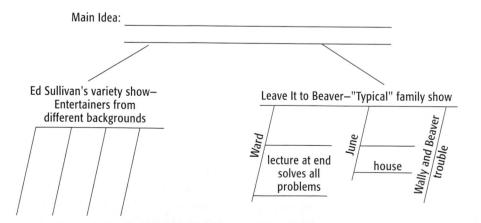

Main Idea: _____

Ed Sullivan's variety show—
Entertainers from
different backgrounds

Leave It to Beaver—"Typical" family show

Ward

lecture at end
solves all
problems

June

house

Wally and Beaver
trouble

3. Television advertising has evolved over time. Originally the emphasis of the ads was to simply describe the usefulness of the product. The assumption was direct: people would buy a product that they thought they could use. Commercials were originally sold in sixty-second intervals. Gradually, the approach changed. Networks began shrinking the ad time to thirty-second spots. The sponsors followed by producing more visual images and less narrative. Ad agencies also began to concentrate on the feelings they wanted viewers to associate with the product, like feeling hip, young, and sexy. This strategy was so successful that it is still in use today. (Lindsay, "Television and Popular Culture")

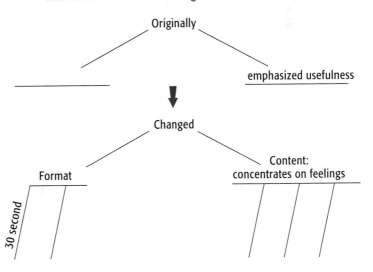

Main idea: Television advertising has evolved over time.

Originally

emphasized usefulness

_____

Changed

Format

Content: concentrates on feelings

30 second

Marking Main Ideas and Major and Minor Supporting Details

marking
Underlining, highlighting, numbering readings to indicate main ideas, and major and sometimes minor supporting details

In Chapter 3, you practiced **marking** main ideas to help you organize to learn. Marking can also help you distinguish major and minor supporting details and remember the major ones. Underline main ideas, then number major supporting details. You can even put lowercase letters in front of minor supporting details if you wish. If you mark your text in this way, you will find it easy to locate the important information when you are reviewing or studying for a test. Notice how the following paragraph can be marked.

<u>African-American viewers watch much more television and have tastes in programming that are very different from those of their white counterparts.</u> According to recent studies, African-American households *(1)* watched 40 percent more television than white households in the last part of 1998. *(a)* They watched 70.4 hours a week, compared with *(b)* 50.2 hours for non-blacks. *(2)* But the different preferences are pretty obvious. *(a)* "The Steve Harvey Show" ranked first for African-American households, but placed 127th among white viewers. *(b)* The "Jamie Foxx Show" was second among black viewers, but 120th among white viewers. (Adapted from Trescott, "For Blacks, 50 Years on TV Fringes")

| Exercise 4 | ## Mark Main Ideas and Major and Minor Supporting Details |

Underline the main ideas, number the major supporting details, and if appropriate, put letters in front of the minor supporting details for the following paragraphs

1. The power of television to influence contemporary life is astounding, . . . especially in sports. It often dictates the hour at which events take place and when the game action will halt for commercials. National political conventions are staged and timed like theatrical performances to lure a TV audience. Protest demonstrations that would pass almost unnoticed gain national exposure when a television news crew arrives and photographs protesters shaking their fists at the camera. In the home, the program listings influence meal- and bed-times. Parents may use the TV set as a babysitter, relieved that it keeps the children quiet, and too often unconcerned about the ideas and images they are absorbing (Agee, Ault, and Emery, *Introduction to Mass Communications*).

2. Although television programming can occasionally be excellent, usually it is junk designed to make a profit, not to provide quality entertainment or education. In fact, television has become a kind of drug for some adults to escape the realities of daily life with a regular diet of television that includes game shows, soap operas, reruns of old movies, ridiculous

situation comedies, talk shows, sexually oriented "reality" programs, and violent police shows. Because the station's purpose is not so much to entertain us as it is to make money, all these shows are all interrupted constantly by commercials. A situation comedy may have as many as twenty-five commercials in a single one-half-hour period.

3. The television industry represents a huge amount of money to be spent and to be made. Advertisers know that commercials on television sell their products, so they are willing to pay huge sums to broadcast their commercials on popular shows. Today the typical thirty-second spot for the Super Bowl costs more than a million dollars. NBC paid over a billion dollars for the television rights for the Summer Olympic Games in 2000 and the Winter Olympic Games in 2002. Stars in sitcoms such as *Friends* can make more than a million dollars per episode.

Writing Summaries

summary A piece of writing that is a shorter version of what someone else has written

Summaries explain the content of a passage, essay, or reading in an abbreviated form that does not use the same words the original author used. Students and professional workers are often asked to write summaries of important information. You might, for example, be asked to research a topic—such as television commercials—and report your summarized findings to your fellow students or to your employer. Writing a summary is also an excellent way to organize the material that you have read for future review and testing

To write a summary you will need to use the skills you have just practiced—you need to identify the main ideas and major and minor supporting details and to decide whether to include the minor details in your summary. Sometimes minor details are very important, but very often they are not necessary. You can decide on the importance of minor supporting details based on your purpose for reading and your purpose for summarizing. Usually minor supporting details are not needed because a summary, after all, is supposed to be quite a bit shorter than the original reading.

Paraphrasing

paraphrase Putting what someone else has written in your own words

Paraphrasing is putting what someone else has written in your own words. In some ways it is similar to stating main ideas in your own words. To paraphrase effectively, follow these steps:

1. First read and understand the information that you want to put into your own words.
2. Try to substitute words that are familiar to you for words that are not familiar.
3. Write down only one or two of the very important words that help explain the idea.
4. Turn your paper over and try to write the sentence in your own words.
5. Don't get discouraged. Paraphrasing is a skill that takes a lot of practice. You won't sound like a professional writer to begin with, but you're not supposed to be!

Let's look at a few examples. If the following is the original sentence from someone else's writing, then what words are absolutely necessary for you to keep when you rewrite the idea?

Gruesomely violent video games, movies, and television shows are showing kids that violence is fun.

You would probably pick *violent video games, movies and TV,* so you might state this idea in your own words by writing the following: *Children learn that it's okay to enjoy violence from violent video games, movies and TV.*

Now try another example. Read the following sentence, and decide which words you would keep when you rewrite the idea.

It's incorrect to assume that violence in the United States is caused by violence on television, because people in Japan and Britain see just as much violence, but there is not anywhere near as much crime in those countries.

What words are absolutely necessary? *Violence, United States, TV, Japan, and Britain*

So how might you state this idea in your own words? An example would be: *Although the television shows in Japan and Britain are as violent as the ones we have, those countries have less crime, so maybe we can't blame violent crime on violent TV.*

| Exercise 5 | ## Paraphrase

Rewrite each of the following sentences in your own words.

1. Incredible as it may seem, most children will see over 8,000 murders and 100,000 other violent acts by the time they are eleven years old.

   _____

   _____

2. Before the opening of "Star Wars" in 1999, the Star Wars toys sold surpassed $4.5 billion. (Diane Levin, "Marketing Violence to Children")

_____

_____

3. Today, instead of experiencing life first-hand by taking a walk, talking to friends, playing sports, or fishing, increasing numbers of people simply watch TV for several hours a day.

_____

_____

4. The show begins after a brief commercial break with an excited-looking Oprah running onto the set to the cheers of a very enthusiastic audience. (Stoughton, "The Oprah Hour, the Oprah World")

_____

_____

5. The television industry represents a huge amount of money to be spent and to be made.

_____

_____

LANGUAGE TIP

Paraphrasing and Plagiarizing

If you take words directly from another text, you must use quotation marks (" ") and include the source of your information. If you use other people's sentences or phrases without giving them credit, you may be accused of "copying," or "plagiarizing," work. One of the most important rules in American colleges and universities is *don't copy other people's work!*

Many students say, "But I can't explain it as well as this writer." This may be true, but the only way you can learn to write better is if you practice. If you need to use some of the author's words, put quotation marks around them and give the source.

| Exercise 6 | Avoid Plagiarism |

Write short answers to the following questions.

1. What is plagiarism?

_____

_____

2. How can you as a student avoid plagiarizing when you write?

_____

_____

The Structure of a Summary

You can begin a summary different ways, but an effective method gives the main idea and the source of information in the first sentence. Many professors and employers want to know the main idea of the text you're summarizing, who wrote it, and where and when it was published at the very beginning of the summary. Remember, it is very important to use your own words. Once you have figured out how to write the main idea in your own words, you can write the first sentence of the summary by using the phrase, "According to *(name of author)* in the *(article, passage, or book)* entitled *(title here)*, *(main idea here),* published in *(date here)*."

For example, you may have decided that the main idea of an article, written in your own words, is *Television programming has always been closely tied to selling products.*

Let's say that the article that you are summarizing is written by Lois White. The title of the article that you're summarizing is "TV That Sells" and it appears in the June 1, 2000, issue of a newspaper called *The Daily News.* You would write your first sentence something like this: *According to Lois White, in her Daily News article for June 1, 2000, "TV That Sells," television programming has always been closely tied to selling products.*

To write an effective summary, follow these steps:

1. Carefully read and make sure you understand the material you are going to summarize.
2. Determine the main idea, or thesis. Write that main idea in a sentence using your own words. Very often, when you write the main idea sentence, you will give credit to the author whose work you are summarizing and will mention the title of the reading, or article or book.
3. Decide what major supporting details you need to include.
4. Decide whether or not to include minor supporting details. Usually you do not need to include this level of details.
5. Write the summary in your own words, beginning with your main idea sentence and including the major supporting details. Use complete sentences.
6. Remember, it is easier to use your own words if you are not looking directly at the passage while you write! Don't copy! If you use the author's language, be sure to put quotation marks around those words.

In a summary, you are giving the information or opinion of another writer in an abbreviated form. You are not giving your own opinion. Unless your instructor asks you to do so, do not inject your ideas into your summary.

| **Exercise 7** | # Write Main Idea Sentences for Summaries |

Rewrite the following main idea sentences to give credit to the author and refer to the source. Use the format "*According to*" —————————. The first one is done for you. (These are not real authors or real sources. We've created them to give you practice.)

1. Americans watch television for many reasons, not the least of which is to escape the boredom of their daily lives. (based on an article titled "TV: The Electronic Drug" by John Doe, which appeared in *The Herald Examiner* newspaper on December 20, 2000)

   According to John Doe, in his Herald Examiner article for December 20, 2000,

   "TV: The Electronic Drug," Americans watch TV for many reasons, and one of

   the most important reasons is "to escape the boredom of their daily lives."

2. We would be surprised if we ever counted the number of commercials we see by just watching a single half-hour sitcom. (based on an article titled "Situation Comedies" by Cathy Romano, which appeared in *The Daily News*)

   _____

   _____

   _____

3. Television improves the quality of life of many Americans, especially of seniors. (based on a chapter on mass media in the textbook titled *Mass Media* by Ross Clark)

   _____

   _____

   _____

   _____

4. Parents simply need to make clear decisions about when and what children can watch on television. (based on a statement by Libby Drake, which appeared in her book *All You Need to Know About Raising Children*)

   _____

   _____

   _____

   _____

5. *Sesame Street* was one of the best and most educational programs to ever be aired on television. (based on a statement by Jane Graham, which appeared in an article entitled "Educational TV" in *The Daily News*)

_____

_____

_____

Going Through the Steps of Writing a Summary

Now you know the steps for writing a summary (p. 278), how to write a main idea sentence in your own words (p. 276), and how to give credit to the author and source (pp. 277, 278). So now let's walk through the steps of writing a summary of Reading 1.

What is the main idea of the reading?

People like Oprah Winfrey because in her talk show and her many other activities, we believe that she cares and that she makes a positive impact on our lives.

What are the major supporting details?

Her talk show
  Makes us comfortable
  Emphasizes positive and helpful topics
Her interest in helping people
  Angel network
  Oprah Book Club

Do you want to include any minor supporting details?

We don't need to include minor supporting details because it would make our summary too long, and those details aren't essential for understanding the general idea of the reading.

Using the main idea sentence and the major supporting details, your summary should look something like the following. Notice how the major supporting details work to make the main idea convincing. Notice also that it is important to give the author and the source in the summary.

According to Craig Stoughton, in his article, "the Oprah Hour, The Oprah World," people like Oprah Winfrey because in her talk show and her many other activities, we believe that she cares and that she makes a positive impact on our lives. On her talk show she makes us comfortable and she emphasizes positive and helpful topics. She also shows her real interest in helping people through projects such as the Angel Network and the Oprah Book Club.

Exercise 8	## Write a Summary

Read the following excerpt from the textbook *Introduction to Mass Communications* about Spanish-language television. Follow the steps on page 278 and write a summary on a separate piece of paper.

Millions of American viewers are unaware that a thriving television world exists in their country in addition to the English-language programs they watch. It consists of Spanish-language networks and local stations.

Two over-the-air Spanish networks and one principal cable network serve millions of Spanish viewers with wide-ranging programming built around novelas [soap operas], sports, . . . and an increasing amount of news. They are:

Univision. This is the dominant, more prosperous of the over-the-air networks. It owns and operates eleven full-power stations in major Hispanic markets, such as Miami, Los Angeles, and New York, and delivers programs to affiliates elsewhere. One of its primary attractions is the Mexican novelas it shows. These continuing dramatic stories are the most popular programming among Hispanic viewers.

Telemundo. Much smaller in audience size and handicapped by financial and programming difficulties, this over-the-air network is making a comeback after emerging from Chapter 11 bankruptcy. It owns and operates seven full-power and nine low-power stations. Like Univision, it concentrates on building a younger audience.

Galavision. This cable network serves more than a million households, providing a schedule of entertainment, news, and Mexican football.

The Nielsen organization now produces rating information for the Hispanic networks that reflects their growth as the Hispanic population increases. (Agee, Ault, and Emery, *Introduction to Mass Communications*)

READING 2	

Trouble on the Air Aline Franco

In the following reading, Franco analyzes the history and current state of talk shows. Based on the title, "Trouble on the Air," what can you guess are some of her conclusions? As you read, consider how she supports her position with major and minor supporting details, and think about what you know about talk shows. Do you agree that the newer group of talk shows are "trouble"?

alternative
Another choice; using
new ideas

1   In 1967 *The Phil Donahue Show* aired in Dayton, Ohio, as a new daytime talk alternative. Donahue's show offered a completely different kind of program than the "women's shows" that were popular until that time. On Monday of his first week he interviewed an atheist, exploring why he no longer believed in God. On Tuesday he interviewed single men about what they looked for in women. On Wednesday he showed a film of a baby being born. On Thursday he sat in a coffin while talking to a funeral director. And on Friday he held up an anatomically correct doll without its diaper. When Donahue asked his viewers to call to give their opinions about the show, he got a tremendous response.[1] The country learned that women were interested in things other than how to bake perfect cookies and keep their houses spotlessly clean.

2   For eighteen years after that first day, Donahue's shows dealt with issues of concern to all Americans, and his show was the most popular of the daytime talk shows. He addressed a wide variety of important topics and invited guests who were specialists on these topics and who were passionate

advocate   A person
who speaks or writes
to support a cause

advocates for one side or the other. For example, on one show he and his guest Ralph Nader talked about consumer rights, how the government does and does not protect the consumer from fraudulent business practices, and what each of us can do to protect ourselves and to make wise choices. On another show, they discussed gender roles—the roles that men and women are expected to fill in our society—and where we get our ideas about whether or not we want to accept the roles assigned to us by our sex. On yet another show, they even talked about the political events of the day: the U.S. involvement in the Vietnam War, the positions of those who opposed the war as well as the positions of those who supported it.

3   Donahue's show dealt with issues that were important to the lives of the daytime women viewers. But his most original contribution was in setting up the viewing audience itself to participate in the shows. The women watching the show were part of the conversation and could be heard by everyone who tuned in across the country. Donahue even introduced the concept of call-ins, which, in effect, expanded the conversation beyond the studio audience. Viewers at home could literally join in on the discussion by

calling into the show and adding their point of view to the mix. The information was often very useful and women were able to give their opinions about everything, including politics and sex.

4   Finally, in 1985, *The Oprah Winfrey Show* gave Donahue some competition. Oprah's style was more intimate; people loved it, and her ratings soared. Her show passed Donahue's in popularity. While Donahue uncovered and explored issues, Winfrey shared and understood them in a personally more involved way. Both of these talk show hosts helped raise our consciousness about important issues such as the dynamics of domestic violence, the consequences of divorce on the family, and the challenges facing women who wanted to reenter the workforce after being full-time mothers and homemakers. Although they had their share of shows that were sensational—one example would be Oprah's program on satanism or her outrageous 1993 interview with Michael Jackson, and Donahue's penchant for shows featuring male strippers—both hosts focused mostly on important and relevant topics and more often than not dealt with those topics in ways that were useful and interesting. They helped pave the way for many more talk shows that unfortunately didn't live up to the largely serious and sensitive precedent set by Donahue and Winfrey.

5   Phil Donahue's last show was on May 3, 1996. Although Oprah's show topped Donahue's ratings by wide margins, during his career as a talk show host, he had won twenty Emmy's and the prestigious Peabody Award. And when he taped the last show, he commented, "We never thought we'd last twenty-nine days and we've lasted twenty-nine years."[2]

6   Unfortunately, the content and quality of a more recent generation of talk shows—successors to *The Oprah Winfrey Show* and *The Phil Donahue Show*—have deteriorated. Geraldo Rivera's consistently sensational talk show, *Geraldo,* first aired on CBS in 1987. Viewers could depend on seeing the outrageous: Geraldo getting into fist fights with guests, Geraldo knocked down by a boxer in a bikini, Geraldo hit over the head with a chair by a skinhead. But Geraldo's popularity waned with ongoing competition from Oprah and with new competition from Jerry Springer. Geraldo went off the air in 1998.

7   Currently, Jerry Springer's show is perhaps the most outrageous and one of the most popular and influential of all. Premiering in September 1991, it airs all over the United States and in more than forty foreign countries. He has been called "the king of trash TV" because his shows provide a steady diet of violence, profanity, and sensational titles such as "I'm pregnant by my brother." Guests verbally and sometimes physically attack one another, and bouncers run up to the stage to break up fights. Yet television audiences love the Springer show, and millions tune in nightly. Where Donahue's and Winfrey's shows usually seek to educate and inform, Springer's shows seek to excite and to make the people watching them feel superior to those exposing their lives on the airwaves. The shows have a carnival quality to them.

8   Jerry Springer, Jenny Jones, Sally Jessy Raphael . . . the list goes on. The current crop of television talk shows, while entertaining and lucrative to their networks and hosts, have, in many critics' opinions, lowered public standards and people's ability to converse civilly with one another. Teachers sometimes complain that their students don't know how to have a mature discussion about a controversial subject about which there may be different opinions because of these shows. Rather, students "act out," become outrageous, use profanity, and attack each other as if they were on television.

9   We've come a long way from the early days of the *Donahue* show. For better or for worse, television talk shows represent a large portion of our television fare. In one way, they demonstrate how much people want to talk to—or at least at—each other. We can thank Phil Donahue for getting the ball rolling. Perhaps it's time to catch the ball and to throw it in a fresh, more positive direction.

Notes

1. Jeanne Albronda Heaton and Nona Leigh Wilson, "Talk TV: Tuning in Trouble," *Ms. Magazine,* September 1999.

2. "The Challengers" in *The Many Faces of Oprah* (Boca Raton, Fla.: American Media Specials Inc.), vol. 1, no. 7 (April 2000).

FRANCO, "Trouble on the Air"

Exercise 9	## Work with Words

Use context clues, word part clues, and if necessary the dictionary to write the definitions of the italicized words in the following sentences from Reading 2.

1. On Monday of his first week he interviewed an *atheist*, exploring why he no longer believed in God. (par. 1)

   atheist _____

2. On another show, they discussed *gender roles*—the roles that men and women are expected to fill in our society—and where we get our ideas about whether or not we want to accept the roles assigned to us by our sex. (par. 2)

   gender roles _____

3. They helped pave the way for many more talk shows that unfortunately didn't live up to the largely serious and sensitive *precedent* set by Donahue and Winfrey. (par. 4)

   precedent _____

4. Where Donahue's and Winfrey's shows usually *seek* to educate and inform, Springer's shows *seek* to excite and to make the people watching them feel superior to those exposing their lives on the airwaves. (par. 7)

   seek _____

5. The current crop of television talk shows, while entertaining and *lucrative* to their networks and hosts, have, in many critics' opinions, lowered public standards and people's ability to *converse civilly* with one another. Teachers sometimes complain that their students don't know how to have a mature discussion about a controversial subject about which there may be different opinions because of these shows. (par. 8)

   lucrative _____

   converse _____

   civilly _____

| Exercise 10 | ## Identify Main Ideas and Major and Minor Supporting Details |

For the following groups of sentences, write "MI" for the main idea sentence, "Major SD" for the major supporting details, and "Minor SD" for the minor supporting details.

1. _____ a. Donahue's most original contribution was in setting up the viewing audience itself to participate in the shows.

   _____ b. Donahue even introduced the concept of call-ins, which, in effect, expanded the conversation beyond the studio audience.

   _____ c. Viewers at home could literally join in on the discussion by calling into the show and adding their point of view to the mix.

2. _____ a. On Monday of his first week he interviewed an atheist, exploring why he no longer believed in God.

   _____ b. The shows for the first week of his program made it very clear that his approach to daytime "talk" was special for that time.

   _____ c. Donahue's show offered a completely different kind of program than the "women's shows" that were popular until that time.

   _____ d. On Tuesday he interviewed single men about what they looked for in women.

   _____ e. On Wednesday he showed a film of a baby being born.

   _____ f. On Thursday he sat in a coffin while talking to a funeral director.

   _____ g. And on Friday he held up an anatomically correct doll without its diaper. When Donahue asked his viewers to call to give their opinions about the show, he got a tremendous response.

| Exercise 11 | ## Mark Main Ideas and Major and Minor Supporting Details |

Underline the main ideas, number the major supporting details, and put letters in front of the minor supporting details for paragraphs 1, 2, 3, and 6 from Reading 2.

| Exercise 12 | ## Outline |

Based on Reading 2, choose the best answers to the questions. Then, following the model, fill in the spaces of the outline provided for you.

1. What is the topic of the reading?
   a. Daytime talk shows
   b. Phil Donahue
   c. The new generation of talk shows

2. What is the best main idea sentence for the reading?
   a. Daytime talk shows started dealing with issues that were important to women viewers with Phil Donahue and Oprah Winfrey, but the more recent group of talk shows emphasize the outrageous and the sensational.
   b. The sensational talk shows are popular because they make a lot of money and because that is the kind of entertainment people want to watch.
   c. *The Oprah Winfrey Show* has been the most popular talk show, overall, for many years.

Now fill in the outline.

topic: _____

main idea: _____

_____

_____

_____

_____

_____

I. Phil Donahue Show

   A. Daytime talk alternative

      1. _____

      2. _____

      3. _____

      4. _____

      5. _____

   B. Dealt with issues of concern

      1. Consumer rights

      2. _____

      3. _____

II. _____

    A. Call ins

    B. _____

III.   - competition

        1. More intimate - shared and understood

        2. Became more popular than Donahue

IV. Both shows: _____

    A. _____

    B. _____

V. Recent generation of talk shows

    A. Geraldo Rivera - outrageous

        1. _____

        2. _____

        3. _____

    B. Jerry Springer

        1. Most popular

        2. Most outrageous

            a. _____

            b. _____

VI. Effects of recent talk shows

        1. Lose our ability to converse civilly

        2. Students _____

        3. We need to change the direction of talk shows to something more positive.

Exercise 13 | ## Write a Summary

Using the main idea and the major supporting details identified in your outline, write a summary of Reading 2. Remember to refer to the author and title of the reading in your main idea sentence.

Exercise 14 | ## Make Connections: Collaborative Activity

Write short answers to the following questions based on your reading, your experience, and your observations. Then, to extend the exercise, discuss your answers with your class group. Working together, prepare a report for your class as a whole or a written summary for your instructor.

1. Why do you think daytime talk shows are so popular?

_____

_____

_____

2. What do you think daytime talk shows should emphasize? Explain why.

_____

_____

_____

READING 3

Crack and the Box   Pete Hamill

How much television do you watch? Do you think you are a television "addict"? In the following reading, Pete Hamill compares watching television to being addicted to drugs. What are his points of comparison? Is he convincing? As you read keep in mind his thesis, and his major and minor supporting details.

1   One sad, rainy morning last winter I talked to a woman who was addicted to crack cocaine. She was twenty-two, stiletto-thin, with eyes as old as tombs. She was living in two rooms in a welfare hotel with her children, who were two, three, and five years of age. Her story was the usual tangle of human woe: early pregnancy, dropping out of school, vanished men, smack and then crack, tricks with johns in parked cars to pay for the dope. I asked her why she did drugs. She shrugged in an empty way and couldn't really answer beyond "makes me feel good." While we talked, . . . the children ignored us. They were watching television. . . .

2   Television, like drugs, dominates the lives of its addicts. And though some lonely Americans leave their sets on without watching them, using them as electronic companions, television usually absorbs its viewers the way drugs absorb their users. Viewers can't work or play while watching television; they can't read; they can't be out on the streets, falling in love with the wrong people, learning how to quarrel and compromise with other human beings. In short, they are asocial. So are drug addicts.

3   One Michigan State University study in the early eighties offered a group of four- and five-year-olds the choice of giving up television or giving up their fathers. Fully one-third said they would give up Daddy. Given a similar choice (between cocaine or heroin and father, mother, brother, sister, wife, husband, children, job), almost every stone junkie would do the same.

4   There are other disturbing similarities. Television itself is a consciousness-altering instrument. With the touch of a button, it takes you out of the "real" world in which you reside and can place you at a basketball game, the back alleys of Miami, the streets of Bucharest, or the cartoony living rooms of Sitcom Land. Each move from channel to channel alters mood, usually with music or a laugh track. On any given evening, you can laugh, be frightened, feel tension, thump with excitement. You can even tune in *MacNeil/Lehrer* [a program on public television which is now called *The NewsHour With Jim Lehrer*] and feel sober.

5   But none of these abrupt shifts in mood is earned. They are attained as easily as popping a pill. Getting news from television, for example, is simply not the same experience as reading it in a newspaper. Reading is active. The reader must decode little symbols called words, then create images or ideas and make them connect; at its most basic level, reading is an act of the imagination. But the television viewer doesn't go through that process. The words are spoken to him or her by Dan Rather or Tom Brokaw or Peter Jennings. There isn't much decoding to do when watching television, no time to think or ponder before the next set of images and spoken words appears to displace the present one. The reader, being active, works at his or her own pace; the viewer, being passive, proceeds at a pace determined by the show. Except at the highest levels, television never demands that its audience take part in an act of imagination. Reading always does.

decode Figure out

passive Not active

6   In short, television works on the same imaginative and intellectual level as psychoactive drugs. If prolonged television viewing makes the young passive (dozens of studies indicate that it does), then moving to drugs has a certain coherence. Drugs provide an unearned high (in contrast to the

earned rush that comes from a feat accomplished, a human breakthrough earned by sweat or thought or love).

alienated from
Separated from

7　And because the television addict and the drug addict are alienated from the hard and scary world, they also feel they make no difference in its complicated events. For the junkie, the world is reduced to him or her and the needle, pipe, or vial; the self is absolutely isolated, with no desire for choice. The television addict lives the same way. Many Americans who fail to vote in presidential elections must believe they have no more control over such a choice than they do over the casting of *L.A. Law.*

8　The drug plague also coincides with the unspoken assumption of most television shows: Life should be easy. The most complicated events are summarized on TV news in a minute or less. Cops confront murder, chase the criminals, and bring them to justice (usually violently) within an hour. In commercials, you drink the right beer and you get the girl. Easy! So why should real life be a grind? Why should any American have to spend years mastering a skill or craft, or work eight hours a day at an unpleasant job, or endure the compromises and crises of a marriage?

enhance　Improve

9　The doper always whines about how he or she feels; drugs are used to enhance feelings or obliterate them, and in this the doper is very American. No other people on earth spend so much time talking about their feelings; hundreds of thousands go to shrinks, they buy self-help books by the millions, they pour out intimate confessions to virtual strangers in bars or discos. Our political campaigns are about emotional issues now, stated in the simplicities of adolescence. Even alleged statesmen can start a sentence, "I feel that . . . ." when they once might have said, "I *think* . . . ." I'm convinced that this exaltation of cheap emotions over logic and reason is one by-product of hundreds of thousands of hours of television.

10　Most Americans under the age of fifty have now spent their lives absorbing television; that is, they've had the structures of drama pounded into them. Drama is always about conflict. So news shows, politics, and advertising are now all shaped by those structures. Nobody will pay attention to anything as complicated as the part played by Third World debt[1] in the expanding production of cocaine; it's much easier to focus on Manuel Noriega,[2] a character right out of *Miami Vice,* and believe that even in real life there's a Mister Big.

11   What is to be done? Television is certainly not going away, but its addictive qualities can be controlled. It's a lot easier to "just say no" to television than to heroin or crack. As a beginning, parents must take immediate control of the sets, teaching children to watch specific television *programs,* not "television," to get out of the house and play with other kids. Elementary and high schools must begin teaching television as a subject, the way literature is taught, showing children how shows are made, how to distinguish between the true and the false, how to recognize cheap emotional manipulation. All Americans should spend more time reading. And thinking.

12   For years, the defenders of television have argued that the networks are only giving the people what they want. That might be true. But so is the Medellin Cartel.[3]

Notes

1. Many countries in the Third World owe billions of dollars to American and European banks. Because of having to pay interest on this debt, these countries are becoming poorer, and it is because of poverty that many farmers turn to growing drug-related crops.

2. Manuel Noriega was the dictator of Panama who was involved in drug trafficking.

3. The Medellin Cartel is the most powerful drug ring in Colombia.

Hamill, "Crack and the Box"

| Exercise 15 |

Work with Words

Use context clues, word part clues, and if necessary the dictionary to choose the best definitions of the italicized words in the following sentences from Reading 3.

1. Viewers can't work or play while watching television; they can't read; they can't be out on the streets, falling in love with the wrong people, learning how to quarrel and compromise with other human beings. In short, they are *asocial.* (par. 2)

asocial
a. not social or able to get along with people in a variety of ways
b. not able to go to parties
c. not able to be in a good argument

2. There are other disturbing similarities. Television itself is a *consciousness-altering* instrument. With the touch of a button, it takes you out of the "real" world in which you reside and can place you at a basketball game, the back alleys of Miami, the streets of Bucharest, or the cartoony living rooms of Sitcom Land. (par. 4)

   consciousness-altering
   a. able to make conscious
   b. able to make unconscious
   c. able to change your consciousness

3. Drugs provide an unearned high (in contrast to the earned rush that comes from a *feat* accomplished, a human breakthrough earned by sweat or thought or love). (par. 6)

   feat
   a. task
   b. extraordinary accomplishment
   c. unearned "high"

4. The drug plague also *coincides with* the unspoken assumption of most television shows: Life should be easy. (par. 8)

   coincides with
   a. conflicts with
   b. contradicts
   c. corresponds to

5. The doper always whines about how he or she feels; drugs are used to enhance feelings or *obliterate* them, and in this the doper is very American. (par. 9)

   obliterate
   a. cover up
   b. repair
   c. destroy

Exercise 16

Identify Main Ideas and Major and Minor Supporting Details

For the following groups of sentences, write "MI" for the main idea sentence, "Major SD" for the major supporting details, and "Minor SD" for the minor supporting details.

1. _____ a. Reading is active.

   _____ b. The reader must decode little symbols called words, then create images or ideas and make them connect.

   _____ c. At its most basic level, reading is an act of the imagination.

   _____ d. Getting information from television is not the same as getting information from books.

   _____ e. The television viewer is passive.

   _____ f. The words are spoken to him or her by Dan Rather.

   _____ g. There isn't much decoding to do or time to think before the next set of images goes up.

   _____ h. The viewer proceeds at the pace set by the show.

   _____ i. The reader proceeds at his or her own pace.

2. _____ a. Because the television addict and the drug addict feel separated from the world, they also feel that they make no difference in the world.

   _____ b. The world for the junkie is reduced to his or her need to get high.

   _____ c. The junkie does not think about the world or people in his or her life.

   _____ d. The television addict lives just like the junkie.

   _____ e. The television addict often doesn't vote for president because he/she feels that voting won't make any difference.

3. _____ a. Cops confront murder, chase criminals, and bring them to justice in one hour.

   _____ b. The most complicated events are summarized on television in a minute or less.

   _____ c. If you buy the right things, you will succeed.

   _____ d. If you drink the right beer, you'll get the girl.

   _____ e. Television shows that life should be easy.

| Exercise 17 | ## Mark Main Ideas and Major and Minor Supporting Details |

Carefully reread Reading 3, then go back and underline the main ideas. You will probably not need to underline a main idea for every paragraph because you are focusing on the most important ideas in the whole reading. For paragraph 11, underline the main idea and number the major supporting details, and put letters for the minor supporting details.

| Exercise 18 |

Outline

Based on Reading 3, choose the best answers to the questions. Then, following the model, fill in the spaces of the outline provided for you.

1. What is the topic of the reading?
   a. Drug addiction
   b. Television addiction
   c. The passivity of watching television

2. What is the best main idea sentence for the reading?
   a. Television, like drugs, dominates the lives of its addicts.
   b. Television itself is a consciousness-altering instrument.
   c. Television works on the same level as psychoactive drugs.

Now, fill in the outline.

topic: _____

main idea: _____

I. *Don't function normally in life*
   A. *Can't work*

   B. _____
   C. *Can't read*
   D. *Not social*

   1. _____

   2. *Not falling in love*

   3. _____

II. *Consciousness-altering*

   A. _____

   1. _____

   2. _____

   3. *Streets of Bucharest*
   4. *Sitcom land*
   B. *In one evening: laugh, be frightened,* _____ *be excited, be sober*

III. *Reading is active, TV is passive*
   A. *Reading is active*

   1. _____

   2. *Create images*
   3. *Use imagination*

B. _____

    1. Words spoken to

    2. Images change rapidly

    3. Pace determined by show

    4. Almost never demands audience participation

IV. Alienated from the world, feel not able to have control

V. Leads to assumption: Life should be easy

    A. _____

    B. _____

    C. Commercials - will solve your problems

VI. Focused on feelings

VII. Drama - conflict; little interest in more serious stuff

    A. Most shows framed by "dramatic" structure

    B. Not much attention to serious issues

        1. Third World debt - not interesting

        2. Manuel Noriega - interesting because he's like TV shows

VIII. Solutions

    A. _____

    B. _____

       _____

    C. _____

Exercise 19

Write a Summary

Using the main idea and the major supporting details identified in your outline, write a summary of Reading 3. Remember to refer to the author and title in your main idea sentence.

Exercise 20

Make Connections

Write short answers to the following questions based on your reading, your experience, and your observations.

1. When do you watch television, and why do you watch at those hours?

    _____

    _____

    _____

2. Have you ever stopped watching television? What was the experience like?

_____

_____

_____

3. Do you agree with Hamill that television is like drugs? Explain your answer.

_____

_____

_____

_____

4. Do you think it's a good idea to restrict the amount of television that children watch? Explain your answer.

_____

_____

_____

_____

READING 4

Sports and Television: Isolation or Community?
Jim Miller

In the following reading, Miller sketches the history of sports and how communities built around sporting events have changed with the advent of newspapers, radios, and television. He argues that television is not always as isolating an activity as many would claim. As you read, notice how he develops his point by first explaining the position of people who probably do not agree with him, and then stating his case. How does he support his thesis with major and minor supporting details? Consider your experiences with sports and with watching sports on television. Does your experience parallel the scenes described here by Miller?

1 A fat man with a big beer belly in boxer shorts and a dingy white tank top is sitting in a well-worn easy chair staring at younger men in better shape play a game. He is chugging a "tall boy" and his coffee table is cluttered with empty beer cans, a pizza box, and a crumpled sports page. Perhaps he stops

gazing at the TV during commercials just long enough to bark orders at his sullen wife in the kitchen or tell the kids to shut up. Every day he goes from a job he hates to the isolation of his living room. He has no control at work and lives through the actions of others on the TV while at home. He is the model for a society of watchers, a nation of passive consumers of packaged events who have lost touch with their community, family, and perhaps even themselves.

bemoan Complain about

2   We all know this picture and have heard the critics bemoan the loss of community and human interaction since the advent of TV. Everyone watches the tube, yet few people defend its benefits. But is this really the true state of affairs in American homes or is there something else going on? TV, while certainly a central force in our culture, has not completely eliminated our social life, but it has transformed it and created both isolation and new forms of community activity. In sum, TV has sold us more isolation and, paradoxically, a grander promise of being part of something larger than ourselves. The phenomenon of watching sports on TV is a perfect illustration of the contradictory nature of the consumer spectacle in America.

3   In the past, people participated in sporting events together as a form of social activity. Baseball teams formed as clubs in the nineteenth century, and the whole idea of spectator sports as we know it today did not exist. It was only in the twentieth century, with the rise of consumer culture, that the sporting event became a very profitable form of business. Slowly, baseball, boxing, and other events moved out of the town park and into the stadium. With the rise of the news media, people across the country could read about ballgames that took place in other cities, and, with the advent of radio, they could listen to them as they were played. This certainly turned more people into consumers than participants, but it also drew more people together in a new way. In the African-American community, for example, sports became a symbol of racial pride and accomplishment. Spectators of Negro League baseball shared in the display of black excellence and artistry. Blacks who huddled around radios and listened to Joe Louis fight became part of a larger community of listeners hanging on his every move. Listeners or viewers outside the black community were exposed to evidence of the humanity and achievement of blacks at a time when the idea of black equality was revolutionary. Thus, as older forms of community vanished, something new was created.

competitive individualism
Valuing oneself over others; anxious to defeat or be better than others

4   In the post–World War II era, with the invention of television and the explosion of the business of sports, more and more people started watching sports. Now a big-money industry and a large part of economic life in America, sports is used to sell products and encourage more consumption. Corporations and politicians use it to promote patriotism, competitive individualism, and the values of the marketplace that have been responsible for the gradual loss of community in American life. Many social critics see

sports as nothing more than a useless diversion at best and a form of pro-paganda and indoctrination at worst. We sit alone in dark rooms, being en-couraged to buy more, compete with our neighbors, and win at all costs by athletes at the expense of all other values. Or do we?

5   Certainly watching sports on TV is a consumer activity that, at one level, promotes the values of the marketplace, but encourages other things as well. Just as sports tells us to win, it forces us to identify with a team. A team, in concept, is a community in microcosm. For a team to do well, peo-ple must cooperate. The ideas of equality and teamwork exist side by side with the notion of competitive individualism. Even the fan is part of the team, and to want to be part of a team is to desire connection with some-thing larger than oneself—a group, a community, a city, humanity.

microcosm Small version

6   Perhaps even the act of watching is less isolated than the critics would have us think. Do not many people watch together? How many football Sun-days are nothing more than an excuse to eat and talk with friends? How many people forget the score as the barbecue proceeds and the conversation turns to other matters. If so, then the ritual of watching is less an isolating event than an excuse to invent community where it is not. And even when the focus is on the game, the noise of the crowd, and the play of the team, we enjoy having interests in common and connections with other people. I would not argue that the celebration of winning the World Series can replace more genuine forms of connection with others, but I do think that the core of what we love about such moments is that they make us feel a part of some-thing larger that we love. So, the fat man in the chair may not be such a de-pressing sight. As a sports fan, along with millions of other sports fans, he can, at least in part, represent the desire for more community in America today.

MILLER, "Sports and Television"

| Exercise 21 |

Work with Words

Use context clues, word part clues, and if necessary the dictionary to write the definitions of the italicized words in the following sentences from Reading 4.

1. We all know this picture and have heard the critics bemoan the loss of community and human interaction since the *advent* of TV. (par. 2)

   advent _____

2. TV, while certainly a central force in our culture, has not completely eliminated our social life, but it has *transformed* it and created both isolation and new forms of community activity. (par. 2)

   transformed _____

3. In sum, TV has sold us more isolation and, *paradoxically,* a grander promise of being part of something larger than ourselves. (par. 2)

paradoxically _____

4. Now a big-money industry and a large part of economic life in America, sports is used to sell products and encourage more *consumption.* (par. 4)

consumption _____

5. Many social critics see sports as nothing more than a useless *diversion* at best and a form of propaganda and *indoctrination* at worst. (par. 4)

diversion _____

indoctrination _____

6. Perhaps even the act of watching is less *isolated* than the critics would have us think. Do not many people watch together? (par. 6)

isolated _____

Exercise 22

Identify Main Ideas and Major and Minor Supporting Details

For the following group of sentences, write "MI" for the main idea sentence, "Major SD" for the major supporting details, and "Minor SD" for the minor supporting details.

_____ 1. It was only in the twentieth century, with the rise of consumer culture, that the sporting event stopped being a neighborhood affair.

_____ 2. Baseball, boxing, and other events moved out of the town park and into the stadium.

_____ 3. With the rise of the news media, people across the country could read about ballgames that took place in other cities.

_____ 4. With the advent of radio, they could listen to them as they were played.

_____ 5. The twentieth century has seen more people turn into consumers of sports rather than participants in sports, but it also drew people together in a new way.

_____ 6. In the African-American community, for example, sports became a symbol of racial pride and accomplishment.

_____ 7. Spectators of Negro League baseball shared in the display of black excellence and artistry.

_____ 8. Blacks who huddled around radios and listened to Joe Louis fight became part of a larger community of listeners hanging on his every move.

_____ 9. Listeners or viewers outside the black community were exposed to evidence of the humanity and achievement of blacks at a time when the idea of black equality was revolutionary.

Exercise 23

Map Main Ideas and Major and Minor Supporting Details

On a separate piece of paper, and using the information in the sentences in Exercise 22, create a map that visually shows the information and the relationships of the main idea, major supporting details, and minor supporting details.

Exercise 24

Outline

Based on Reading 4, choose the best answers to the questions. Then, following the model, fill in the spaces of the outline provided for you.

1. What is the topic of the reading?
   a. Consumerism and television
   b. Sports and television
   c. Television and baseball

2. What is the best main idea statement for the reading?
   a. Perhaps even the act of watching sports on television is less isolated than critics think.
   b. The fat man in the chair may not be such a depressing sight after all.
   c. Watching sports on television is a consumer activity that can be isolating, but it encourages other things as well, even a sense of community.

Now fill in the outline.

topic: *Sports and television*

main idea: *Watching sports on TV is a consumer activity that can be isolating, but it encourages other things as well, even a sense of community.*

I. TV has transformed our social life. Not as bad as critics say. Sports is an example

II. The history - evolution from participant sport to consumer sports

A. Profitable business

    1. _____

    2. _____

    3. _____

B. _____

    1. Negro League baseball

    2. _____

    3. Those outside black community learned about achievements of black athletes.

III. Television - negative aspects

A. _____

B. Encourages consumption

C. Promotes corporations and politicians

D. Promotes competitive individualism

E. _____

IV. _____

A. People must cooperate on a team.

B. Fan is part of team - a connection to a community.

V. Football Sundays - a new kind of community

A. _____

    1. Barbecue

    2. Conversation

B. A connection with people

    1. _____

    2. _____

| Exercise 25 | ## Write a Summary |

Using the main idea and the major supporting details identified in your outline, write a summary of Reading 4. Remember to refer to the author and the title in your main idea sentence.

| Exercise 26 | Make Connections: Collaborative Activity |

Write short answers to the following questions based on your reading, your experience, and your observations. Then, to extend this exercise, discuss your answers with your class group. Working together, prepare a report for your class as a whole or a written summary for your instructor.

1. Do you or does someone you know enjoy watching sports on TV? Which sports? With other people or alone?

_____

_____

_____

_____

2. Do you agree with Miller's thesis that watching sports on TV allows us to be part of a community? Explain.

_____

_____

_____

_____

3. Do you think that the positive aspects of TV that Miller discusses outweigh the negative aspects that Hamill discusses in Reading 3 (pp. 289–292)? Explain your opinion.

_____

_____

_____

_____

Chapter Review

To aid your review of the reading skills in Chapter 6, study the Put It Together chart.

Put It Together: *Major and Minor Supporting Details*

Skills and Concepts	*Explanation*
Major Supporting Details **(see pages 265–266)**	Major supporting details are the most important • examples, • facts, • reasons, or • descriptions that the author gives to support the main idea statement or thesis.
Minor Supporting Details **(see pages 265–266)**	Minor supporting details are additional points that give • more information to explain major supporting details • more examples to illustrate major supporting details • more specifics to make material more interesting.
Outline (see pages 266–270)	Organize the information you learn using numbers and letters and spatial layout to indicate levels of information
Maps (see pages 270–273)	Diagram the relationships between ideas and information in a visual way
Mark (see pages 273–275)	Underline main ideas, and number major supporting details. Write on a text to help you remember the information.
Paraphrase **(see pages 275–278)**	Put an idea that someone else has written in your own words
Summarize **(see pages 275–281)**	Put what someone else has written in a shorter version and in your own words Steps for writing a summary 1. Read and understand the reading you are going to summarize. 2. Determine the main idea or thesis. Write it in your own words, referring to the author and the source of the reading. 3. Decide on major supporting details to include. 4. Decide whether you need to include minor supporting details. (Usually you do not.) 5. Write the summary in your own words; don't give your opinions unless you are asked. 6. Don't copy.

To reinforce your thinking before taking the Mastery Tests, complete as many of the following activities as your instructor assigns.

Reviewing Skills

Answer the following skills-review questions individually or in a group.

1. What is the format you should follow to design a map of a reading?

_____

_____

_____

2. When do you think it is helpful for you to map a reading? When might it be better to map than to outline?

_____

_____

Collaborating

Brainstorm in a group the names of all the talk shows that you can think of. Make a list of these names and add their characteristics. Then, as a group, decide which talk shows are, in your opinion, better, and list the reasons why.

Name of Talk Show	*Thought-Provoking, Meaningful Content*	*Sensational, Outrageous Content*

Extending Your Thinking

To answer the following questions, you will have to do a little research. Then, prepare the information you gather to share with your class group.

1. Watch a half-hour situation comedy. Take notes on how many commercials there are, and what they are for. How much time is dedicated to the show? How much time is dedicated to the commercials? Who are the targets of the commercials (young, old, men, women, etc.)? What do your observations tell you about the priorities of the broadcasters?

2. Watch a TV talk show and take notes on the topics and the guests. Are the topics useful and helpful, or are the topics outrageous, presented just for the sake of entertaining but having no informational value? Do the guests present themselves in a dignified and thoughtful way? Do you think that the show helps people deal with life or not? How valuable do you think the show was? Explain your opinions.

Writing

On a separate piece of paper, write a paragraph or more answering one of the following questions.

1. What do you think could be done to create the best possible television talk show? What would its content be?

2. What is your favorite television program and why?

Visiting the Web

The following Web sites provide more information on various aspects of television.

1. *Oxygen:*

   http://www.oxygen.com
   This Web site co-founded by Oprah Winfrey provides information on various aspects of television including self-help, parenting advice, lifestyle tips, meeting places, news, features, advice columns, and much more.

2. *TV is a Drug:*

   http://www.loyola.edu/dept/philosophy/techne/tvkenedy.htm
   This Web site suggests that TV is an addictive drug that is destroying our lives. Information and links are provided.

3. *TV-Turnoff Network:*

   http://www.tvturnoff.org
   This Web site encourages children and adults to watch less television in order to promote healthier lives and communities.

Fighting over Sneakers Richard Campbell

The following reading from a communications textbook discusses the impact that advertising and brand names have had on American young people. The example the author uses is the popularity of certain kinds of basketball shoes and the tactics that some poor young people have used in order to get those very expensive shoes. As you read, think about how important brand names are to you. Look for Campbell's thesis for this reading, and consider the major and minor supporting details that support his thesis.

1　During the 1950s and 1960s, most serious basketball payers wore simple canvas sneakers—usually Converse or Keds. Encouraged by increasing TV coverage, interest in sports exploded in the late 1960s and 1970s, as did a wildly competitive international sneaker industry. First Adidas dominated the industry, then Nike and Reebok. The Great Sneaker Wars have since continued unabated, although they may have peaked at the 1992 Olympics when pro-basketball stars Michael Jordan and Charles Barkley—Nike endorsers—refused to display the Reebok logo on their team jackets at the awards ceremony. Reebok had paid dearly to sponsor the Olympics and wanted the athletes to fall in line. A compromise was eventually worked out in which the two players wore the jackets but hid the Reebok name.

unabated　As strong as ever

2　Although the Olympic incident seems petty, battles over brand-name sneakers and jackets in the 1980s were a more dangerous "game." Advertisers found themselves embroiled in a controversy that, for a time, threw a bright and uncomfortable spotlight on the advertising industry. In many poor and urban areas throughout the United States, kids and rival gangs were fighting over and stealing brand-name sportswear from one another. Particularly coveted and targeted were $100-plus top-of-the-line basketball shoes, especially the Nike and Reebok brands heavily advertised on television. A few incidents resulted in shootings and killings. Articles in major newspapers and magazines, including *Sports Illustrated* ("Your Sneakers or Your Life") took advertisers to task. Especially hard hit was Nike, which by the early 1990s controlled nearly 30 percent of the $5.5 billion world sneaker market. Nike's slogan—"Just do it"—became a rallying cry for critics who argued that while for most middle-class people, the command simply meant get in shape, work hard, and perform, for kids from poorer neighborhoods, "Just do it" was a call to arms: "Do what you have to do to survive."

controversy　Public argument

coveted　Desired (something that belongs to someone else)

3　The problem was exacerbated during the 1980s by underlying economic conditions. As the gap between rich and poor grew, advertisements suggested that our identities came from the products that we own. It is not surprising, then, that the possession of a particular brand-name product became increasingly significant for kids who felt they did not own much.

Having the "right" sneaker or jacket came to represent a large part of their identities. For some groups and gangs, such possession became a requirement for membership.

4   The controversy over brand-name products has raised serious concerns about the moral responsibilities of agencies and advertisers. On one hand, Nike and other advertisers have become a lightning rod for the problems of a consumer culture that promises the good life to everyone who "just does it." On the other hand, criticisms of advertising have often stopped with the ads and have not examined whether they *cause* the violence or are simply *symptoms* of the inequities in contemporary America. Although many critics vilified Nike at the time, few were willing to discuss the drawbacks of capitalism and consumerism in general.

mandate Require

5   Fights over sneakers and jackets generate significant questions at the heart of our consumer culture. Does brand-name advertising unrealistically raise hopes about attaining the consumer "dreams" that some ads promise? Who should share the ultimate responsibility for violence that takes place in the name of a coveted shoe or jacket? As a society, should we mandate noncommercial messages and public-service announcements that offer alternative visions? While we need to debate these issues vigorously as individuals and as a society, in some communities kids and adults have already acted. Although brand-name products continue to sell well, an alternative attitude rejects such labeling and opts for cheaper generic products and used rummage-sale clothing. Posing a challenge to the advertising industry, this attitude undermines the view that brand-name identification is a requirement of our times.

CAMPBELL, *Media and Culture*

Use the context clues, word part clues, and if necessary the dictionary to choose the best definition for each of the italicized words in the following sentences from the reading.

1. Although the Olympic incident seems *petty,* battles over brand-name sneakers and jackets in the 1980s were a more dangerous "game." (par. 2)

   petty
   a. unimportant
   b. important
   c. necessary

2. Advertisers found themselves *embroiled* in a controversy that, for a time, threw a bright and uncomfortable spotlight on the advertising industry. (par. 2)

embroiled
a. involved in celebration
b. involved in conflict
c. confused

3. In many poor and urban areas throughout the United States, kids and *rival* gangs were fighting over and stealing brand-name sportswear from one another. (par. 2)

rival
a. friendly
b. enemy
c. executive

4. Particularly coveted and targeted were $100-plus top-of-the-line basketball shoes, especially the Nike and Reebok brands heavily advertised on television. A few incidents resulted in shootings and killings. Articles in major newspapers and magazines, including *Sports Illustrated* ("Your Sneakers or Your Life") *took advertisers to task.* (par. 2)

took advertisers to task
a. praised advertisers
b. criticized advertisers
c. looked for publicity

5. The problem was *exacerbated* during the 1980s by underlying economic conditions. As the gap between rich and poor grew, advertisements suggested that our identities came from the products that we own. (par. 3)

exacerbated
a. relieved
b. made worse
c. complemented

6. Although many critics *vilified* Nike at the time, few were willing to discuss the *drawbacks* of capitalism and consumerism in general. (par. 4)

vilified
a. said bad things about
b. said good things about
c. made suggestions about

drawbacks
a. advantages
b. disadvantages
c. details

7. On the other hand, criticisms of advertising have often stopped with the ads and have not examined whether they cause the violence or are simply symptoms of the *inequities* in contemporary America. (par. 4)

    inequities
    a. inequalities
    b. wealth
    c. high standard of living

For the following groups of sentences, write "MI" for the main idea sentence, "Major SD" for major supporting details, and "Minor SD" for minor supporting details.

8. _____ a. At that time, the basketball players wore simple canvas shoes, but those times have changed.

    _____ b. The 1950s and 1960s were simpler times for our athletes and for our young people.

    _____ c. Today, with the help of advertising, many young people feel that they have to own a pair of expensive Nikes or Adidas.

9. _____ a. In many poor and urban areas throughout the United States, kids and rival gangs were fighting, stealing, and sometimes killing for brand-name sportswear.

    _____ b. The battles over brand-name sneakers and jackets became a dangerous game.

    _____ c. Articles about the incidents appeared in major newspapers and magazines, including *Sports Illustrated.*

10. _____ a. As the gap between rich and poor grew, advertisements suggested that our identities came from the products that we own.

    _____ b. The possession of a particular brand-name product became more important for kids who felt they did not own much.

    _____ c. Having the right sneaker or jacket was important to these children.

11. _____ a. The controversy over brand-name products has raised serious questions about the moral responsibilities of advertisers.

    _____ b. Young people getting killed for basketball shoes is just one example of the problems that we face.

_____ c. Some critics think that advertisers are responsible for our problems as a consumer culture.

12. _____ a. As a society, we should mandate noncommercial messages and public-service announcements that offer alternative visions.

_____ b. In some communities people are taking a stand against brand-name products.

_____ c. These examples show us that we really don't "have to have" those expensive products.

Choose the best answers to the following multiple-choice questions about the reading.

13. What is the main idea, or thesis, of "Fighting Over Sneakers"?
   a. The advertising industry has created a need for brand-name products that has even led to violence.
   b. Nikes are better shoes than Adidas for aspiring young athletes.
   c. Young people cannot have a good opinion of themselves if they don't own brand-name sneakers and jackets.

14. Which of the following is not true about the 1992 Olympics?
   a. Reebok sponsored the Olympics.
   b. Reebok wanted the athletes to wear Reebok jackets.
   c. The athletes were happy to wear the Reebok jackets.

15. What is the primary reason the author gives that young people feel they must own brand-name sneakers?
   a. The more expensive sneakers help them play better ball.
   b. Having the right sneaker came to represent a large part of their identities.
   c. They can tell the difference between cheap products and well-made products.

16. What idea do you get about advertising from the reading?
   a. Advertising influences our society in bad ways.
   b. Advertising is simply doing an important job informing the consumer.
   c. Advertising helps companies make the profits that they deserve.

17. It is clear that the author believes which of the following?
   a. Consumer culture is healthy and good for the economy.
   b. Consumer culture creates problems.
   c. The answers to the problems of consumer culture are simple.

Write short answers to the following questions about advertising and brand-name products, based on your reading, your experience, and your observations.

18. What are some of the best advertisements that you have ever seen on television? Briefly describe them.

_____

_____

_____

19. What advertisements do you think have influenced you most to buy a product, or at least to want to buy it? Explain.

_____

_____

_____

Get Rich Quick!   Shawna Livingston

In the following reading, Shawna Livingston describes some of the game shows that have become so popular. She argues that these shows encourage and reflect an attitude that we should be able to get rich quick with just a little luck. And we can do just that on television shows. As you read, notice how Livingston supports her position with major and minor details. Also, consider what you think about these kinds of shows. Do you agree with Livingston?

1   Unlike any other time in history, Americans today have expectations of instant gratification—the idea that if we want something we should be able to have it immediately. The most convincing evidence of this is the latest fad, television shows with cash prizes of a million dollars or more. These new shows have titles such as "Greed," "Who Wants to Be a Millionaire?" and the notorious "Who Wants to Marry a Multi-Millionaire?" Almost every network television channel now features a version of these shows; the high ratings and the names seem to indicate a shift in our cultural values.

shift Change

2   Many of us are descendants of people who lived through hard financial times, like the Great Depression of the 1930s, during which millions of people were unemployed and homeless. Thrift, hard work, and patience used to be the American values that led to financial success. Now the belief is, eat, drink, and spend a lot, for tomorrow we may win a million dollars. More and more people are being drawn to gambling, lotteries, and big-money game shows instead of planning for the future wisely. The work ethic is being sacrificed for the small—very small—chance of winning immense wealth.

benign Not harmful

3   "Who Wants to Be a Millionaire?" seems to be the most benign, or least damaging, of these new game shows so far, even though it is really about greed and instant gratification. A contestant is chosen after giving the correct answer in the least amount of time. A typical question would be, "Put the following movies by Denzel Washington in chronological order." Once selected from that pool, the contestant proceeds to answer questions with the help of three aids called "lifelines," each of which can be used only once. When a contestant uses the lifeline called "50/50," half of the answers disappear from the screen, thus increasing the odds of picking the correct answer. Another lifeline available allows the contestant to phone a friend or family member for assistance. The third lifeline allows the contestant to ask the audience to suggest an answer. These last two lifelines make the show appear to value people helping each other.

chronological In order by date

4   Like "Who Wants to Be a Millionaire?" the show "Greed" has a qualifying round. However, "Greed" works differently in that a team is created during the qualifying round, with the captain being the contestant who came closest to the answer. An actual question was, "According to the January 2000 Roper

Poll, what percentage of Americans believe a woman will be president during their lifetime?" After the team reaches $100,000, the members can decide to stop and keep that amount or go on to the next level, competing for $200,000. During that round, one of the contestants' stations makes a loud noise indicating that the "Terminator" (computer) has selected that player to challenge a teammate in a cutthroat elimination match. The winner gets to continue with the team. This cutthroat format defies the definition of team-work instilled in most of us during our childhood. "Greed" seems to diverge even more from traditional values in that way.

5   An example of how far people will go to attain quick wealth was the two-hour show "Who Wants to Marry a Multi-Millionaire?" In this show, fifty women competed in a beauty pageant format that included swimsuit and evening gown competitions. Instead of being scored by a panel of judges, they were selected by the eligible bachelor. The identity of the mystery mul-timillionaire prize, Rick Rockwell, was not revealed to the contestants until the final stage. Marriage, once shown on television as a highly valued institu-tion representing a deep commitment and love, was used as a vehicle to get rich quick in this show. Darva Conger, a nurse, was the lucky bride. Shortly after winning, Darva Conger was signing annulment papers to void the mar-riage. Reportedly, Conger will be allowed to keep the $35,000 engagement ring, the Isuzu Trooper, and any money she may have collected from giving interviews, and she does not have to reimburse anyone for the Caribbean honeymoon cruise. Not much thrift, hard work, and patience were required for her to endure the two-hour show that increased her wealth.

6   Some people might claim that shows like these are to blame for Amer-ica's current values. However, the popularity of these shows indicates that they are merely a reflection of our changing values and interests. The added attraction to watching these shows is that although instant gratification in this large amount is not available to most people, the show gives them something to dream about. People watch these shows to come closer to their fantasies of instant riches; they want to be that successful contestant who wins large amounts of money.

LIVINGSTON, "Get Rich Quick!"

Use context clues, word part clues, and if necessary the dictionary to write the definitions of the italicized words in the following sentences from the reading.

1. Unlike any time in history, Americans today have expectations of *instant gratification*—the idea that if we want something we should be able to have it immediately. (par. 1)

   instant gratification _____

2. Almost every network television channel now *features* a version of these shows; the high ratings and the names seem to indicate a shift in our cultural values. (par. 1)

features _____

3. *Thrift,* hard work, and patience used to be the American values that led to financial success. (par. 2)

thrift _____

4. More and more people are being *drawn to* gambling, lotteries, and big-money game shows instead of planning for the future wisely. (par. 2)

drawn to _____

5. "Who Wants to Be a Millionaire?" seems to be the most *benign,* or least damaging, of these new game shows so far, even though it is really about greed and instant gratification. (par. 3)

benign _____

6. Once selected from that *pool,* the contestant proceeds to answer questions with the help of three aids called "lifelines," each of which can be used only once. (par. 3)

pool _____

7. This cutthroat format *defies* the definition of teamwork instilled in most of us during our childhood. (par. 4)

defies _____

8. An example of how far people will go to *attain* quick wealth was the two-hour show "Who Wants to Marry a Multi-Millionaire?" (par. 5)

attain _____

For the following groups of sentences, write "MI" for the main idea sentence, "Major SD" for the major supporting details, and "Minor SD" for the minor supporting details.

9. _____ a. The most convincing evidence of this is the latest fad, television shows with cash prizes of a million dollars or more.

_____ b. These new shows have titles such as "Greed," "Who Wants to Be a Millionaire?" and the notorious "Who Wants to Marry a Multi-Millionaire?"

_____ c. Unlike any time in history, Americans today have expectations of instant gratification—the idea that if we want something we should be able to have it immediately.

10. _____ a. During a certain round, one of the contestants' stations makes a loud noise indicating that the "Terminator" (computer) has selected that player to challenge a team-mate in a cutthroat elimination match.

_____ b. The winner of the match gets to continue with the team. The loser is out.

_____ c. Teammates work together most of the time, but some-times they actually compete against each other.

_____ d. The cutthroat format of "Greed" diverges from our idea of teamwork.

11. _____ a. A contestant is chosen after giving the correct answer to a question in the least amount of time.

_____ b. A typical question would be, "Put the following movies by Denzel Washington in chronological order."

_____ c. "Who Wants to Be a Millionaire?" is perhaps the least cutthroat of the new game shows.

12. _____ a. Instead of being scored by a panel of judges, they were selected by the eligible bachelor.

_____ b. They did swimsuit and evening gown competitions.

_____ c. The show "Who Wants to Marry a Multi-Millionaire?" demonstrated how far people will go to get rich quick, as well as the change in our attitude toward marriage.

_____ d. Fifty women competed in a variety of activities to win the pageants.

13. _____ a. Darva Conger was chosen to "marry a millionaire," and although she didn't stay married, she did very well.

_____ b. Marriage, once shown on television as a highly valued in-stitution representing deep commitment and love, was used as a vehicle to get rich quick on "Who Wants to Marry a Multi-Millionaire?"

_____ c. Conger will reportedly keep the $35,000 engagement ring, the Isuzu Trooper, and any money that she has made from giving interviews.

Choose the best answers to the following multiple-choice questions about the reading.

14. What is the main idea, or thesis, of "Get Rich Quick"?
    a. Almost every network television channel now features a version of game shows.
    b. Americans have expectations of instant gratification, and the popular game shows reflect this assumption.
    c. Thrift, hard work, and patience used to be the American values that led to financial success.

15. Which of the following is not true about game shows?
    a. Many of them have a cutthroat format.
    b. They reinforce the American value that hard work leads to financial success.
    c. They are very popular and have extremely high ratings.

16. What does Livingston believe that dreaming of winning big on a game show is similar to?
    a. Gambling and betting on the lottery
    b. Playing sports
    c. Planning your future

17. "Who Wants to Marry a Multi-Millionaire?" is an example of what?
    a. Good television programming
    b. A viable way to find a husband
    c. Marriage used as a vehicle to get rich quick

18. Why does Livingston conclude that people watch these shows?
    a. Because they like to practice answering the questions.
    b. Because it gives them something to dream about.
    c. Because they enjoy seeing the contestants try to answer the questions.

Write short answers to the following questions about game shows based on your reading, your experience, and your observations.

19. Have you ever dreamed of getting rich quick? How did you think you would do it? How would you spend the money?

    _____

    _____

    _____

    _____

20. Do you think that Livingston is correct when she says that we expect "instant gratification"—that we expect to get our way or get what we want easily and quickly? Why or why not? Give examples of how we know that we have to work hard for our goals if you disagree. Give examples of how we get things easily if you agree.

_____

_____

_____

_____

Chapter 7

Patterns of Organization

Families in History and Around the World

All happy families resemble one another; every unhappy family is unhappy in its own fashion.

—Leo Tolstoy

- What do you think is the relationship of the people in the picture to each other? What are they doing?

- What is the meaning of the quotation under the picture? Do you agree? Why or why not?

Getting Ready to Read

What is a family? What do you think a family should be like? If you think about your own family, your friends' families, and other families you know, you will recognize that there are lots of different kinds of families. Who are the members of these families? You probably know some single-parent families, some blended families, some families that include grandparents, and some families made up of both biological parents and their children.

In this chapter you will read and think about family life in the United States, how it has changed over the past few centuries, and how it is different from family life elsewhere in the world. As you do, you will improve your reading skills by learning how to

- recognize patterns of organization, including examples and listing, chronological order, definition, and classification
- recognize transitional words and phrases in sentences, between sentences, and between paragraphs, that can help you identify patterns of organization
- organize what you have read using patterns of organization

READING 1

My Husband's Nine Wives   Elizabeth Joseph

In the following reading, Elizabeth Joseph writes about her experience in a rather unusual marriage relationship. Her family practices polygamy; that is, her husband had six other wives when she married him, and now he has nine wives. Read to see why she thinks this is an ideal relationship for herself and her children.

1   I married a married man.

2   In fact, he had six wives when I married him 17 years ago. Today, he has nine.

3   In March, the Utah Supreme Court struck down a trial court's ruling that a polygamist couple could not adopt a child because of their marital style. Last month, the national board of the American Civil Liberties Union, in response to a request from its Utah chapter, adopted a new policy calling for the legalization of polygamy.

paradox
Something that is different from what is expected

mandates Requires

4   Polygamy, or plural marriage, as practiced by my family is a paradox. At first blush, it sounds like the ideal situation for the man and an oppressive one for the women. For me, the opposite is true. While polygamists believe that the Old Testament mandates the practice of plural marriage, compelling social reasons make the lifestyle attractive to the modern career woman.

5   Pick up any women's magazine and you will find article after article about the problems of successfully juggling career, motherhood, and mar-

riage. It is a complex act that many women struggle to manage daily; their frustrations fill up the pages of those magazines and consume the hours of afternoon talk shows.

6   In a monogamous context, the only solutions are compromises. The kids need to learn to fix their own breakfast, your husband needs to get used to occasional microwave dinners, you need to divert more of your income to insure that your preschooler is in a good day-care environment.

7   I am sure that in the challenge of working through these compromises, satisfaction and success can be realized. But why must women only embrace a marital arrangement that requires so many trade-offs?

8   When I leave for the 60-mile commute to court at 7 A.M., my 2-year-old daughter, London, is happily asleep in the bed of my husband's wife, Diane. London adores Diane. When London awakes, about the time I'm arriving at the courthouse, she is surrounded by family members who are as familiar to her as the toys in her nursery.

9   My husband, Alex, who writes at night, gets up much later. While most of his wives are already at work, pursuing their careers, he can almost always find one who's willing to chat over coffee.

10   I share a home with Delinda, another wife, who works in town government. Most nights, we agree we'll just have a simple dinner with our three kids. We'd rather relax and commiserate over the pressures of our work day than chew up our energy cooking and doing a ton of dishes.

11   Mondays, however, are different. That's the night Alex eats with us. The kids, excited that their father is coming to dinner, are on their best behavior. We often invite another wife or one of his children. It's a special event because it only happens once a week.

12   Tuesday night, it's back to simplicity for us. But for Alex and the household he's dining with that night, it's their special time.

13   The same system with some variation governs our private time with him. While spontaneity is by no means ruled out, we basically use an appointment system. If I want to spend Friday evening at his house, I make an appointment. If he's already "booked," I either request another night, or if my schedule is inflexible, I talk to the other wife and we work out an arrangement. One thing we've all learned is that there's always another night.

14   Most evenings, with the demands of career and the literal chasing after the needs of a toddler, all I want to do is collapse into bed and sleep. But there is also the longing for intimacy and comfort that only he can provide, and when those feelings surface, I ask to be with him.

intimacy Closeness

15   Plural marriage is not for everyone. But it is the lifestyle for me. It offers men the chance to escape from the traditional, confining roles that often isolate them from the surrounding world. More important, it enables women, who live in a society full of obstacles, to fully meet their career, mothering, and marriage obligations. Polygamy provides a whole

confining Restricting

solution. I believe American women would have invented it if it didn't already exist.

JOSEPH, "My Husband's Nine Wives"

Exercise 1 | ## Recall and Discuss

Answer these questions about Reading 1, and prepare to discuss them in class.

the custom or practice of having more than one husband or wife at the same time

1. Why does Joseph think that polygamy is an attractive lifestyle for the modern career woman?

Joseph thinks polygamy is an attractive lifestyle b/c it provides for greater child care & free time, allowing for more time & energy one can use pursuing one's career.

2. What does she mean when she says her husband is already "booked"?

only "Booked" Already "booked" means her husband is busy at that time. He has another commitment.

3. What does she mean when she says, "Polygamy provides a whole solution"?

She means that fewer compromises must be made in this arrangement due to the flexibility it provides.

4. How do women or men you know manage the responsibilities of marriage, family, and career? Contrast their situation with the one Joseph describes.

They really care their husband and their children.

Patterns of Organization

patterns of organization The ways details are put together to support main ideas

In Chapters 5 and 6 you learned to distinguish between main ideas and the many supporting ideas in paragraphs and essays. These supporting ideas are often organized according to certain **patterns of organization.** Writers choose a particular pattern of organization because it helps them present their ideas and information in a clear way. Recognizing these patterns makes it easier for readers to understand what the writer is trying to tell us. Four of the most common ways to organize information are by examples, chronological order, definition, and classification.

Examples

examples A pattern of organization that provides instances of the main idea, introduced with phrases like "for example" and "for instance"

enumeration A pattern of organization that lists examples using numbers

One of the most commonly used ways to organize information is by **examples,** which explain a more general idea by providing instances of it. In Chapter 5 you learned that examples are one type of supporting detail. One way to present examples is to list and number them. This variation is called **enumeration.**

In Sentences

Examples are easily recognized in sentences where they are introduced by a phrase like "such as" and are separated by commas. For instance, read this sentence and identify the different types of families.

> Families in America today include a wide variety of models, such as the <u>traditional extended family</u>, the <u>single-parent family</u>, the <u>nuclear family</u>, and the <u>blended family</u>.

Each of the underlined terms in this sentence is a separate example of a kind of family in today's society. Notice that the examples here are separated by commas, but in some cases longer examples are separated by semicolons.

In Paragraphs

In a paragraph or a longer passage, an example could be one sentence or several sentences long. Examples in sentences—which can be major or minor supporting details—are often used to support the main idea statement of a paragraph. In the following paragraph, the main idea is stated in the first sentence, "Families around the world choose to raise their children in various ways." The writers then use examples from the United States and Western Europe, from Africa and India, to support their main idea. Notice that each example is introduced by its location in a different part of the world.

Families around the world choose to raise their children in various ways. In the United States and in Western European societies, the biological parents traditionally have assumed the responsibilities of child rearing, but this is only one of the many variations in the world. In the Baganda tribe of Central Africa, the biological father's brother is responsible for child rearing. The Nayars of southern India assign this role to the mother's eldest brother. (Adapted from Appelbaum and Chambliss, *Sociology*)

Once you recognize that this paragraph is organized to give examples, you can arrange that information into a map showing the major and minor supporting details. In Chapters 5 and 6 you already learned to organize supporting details into maps and outlines. The map of this paragraph would look like this:

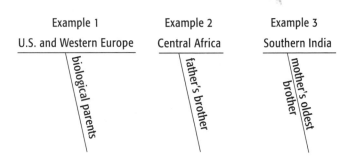

Sometimes writers list examples by number. In the following paragraph, the benefits of extended families are *enumerated*.

In many parts of the world, the extended family, in which grandparents, aunts, uncles, and children all live together, is the most common family structure. The extended family structure has been successful because it provides many benefits for families such as (1) economic advantages, because it is cheaper to house and to feed many people who all live together; (2) work distribution advantages, because there are more people to share in household tasks such as cooking, cleaning, and taking care of children; and (3) social advantages, because with so many family members around, no family members are lonely or left alone if they need help taking care of themselves due to sickness or old age.

When examples are enumerated, they are easy to outline. For the preceding paragraph, a brief outline might look like this:

topic: Benefits of extended families

main idea: The extended family structure has been successful because it provides many benefits for families.

  I. Economic
     A. Cheaper to live together
     B. Cheaper to eat together

II. Work distribution; share in tasks
   A. Cooking and cleaning
   B. Taking care of children

III. Social
   A. No one lonely
   B. If sick or old, taken care of

Lists of examples are not always numbered. In the following excerpt, the author presents the sources available to a family caring for an aging parent, signaling each one with a design figure called a *bullet*.

No one can, or should, take care of another person without help. Here are three important sources for finding help:

- Government/community agencies
- Medical facilities and businesses catering to older people and caregivers
- Relatives, friends, coworkers and neighbors

(Smith, *Caring for Your Aging Parents*)

| Exercise 2 | ## Identify Examples |

In the following paragraphs, underline the main idea. Then on a separate sheet of paper, make a map, outline, or bulleted list that shows the important examples in the paragraph.

1. In traditional European peasant societies, the firstborn son inherited the family land, so second and third sons had to look for other ways to earn a living. In sixteenth-century Spain there were more options open to them. First, they could join the Church. Second, they could become a paid soldier. And finally, they could join the expeditions of exploration to the New World.

2. Historically, men's most important role within the family structure was to provide food for the family. This they did by hunting, fishing, and raising sheep or cattle. In addition, they were frequently responsible for the agricultural tasks that required heavy physical labor.

3. First of all, the family, because of the strong feelings it generates, is a powerful source not just of love and care but *also* of pain and conflict. . . . In most families, there are instances of conflict and violence, such as anger, physical punishment of children, or spouses poking and slapping each other. In fact, the family is one of the few groups in society empowered by law or tradition to hit its members. It is, for example, legal for parents to spank their children as a form of punishment. Moreover, many husbands who strike their wives to "keep them in line" are not arrested, prosecuted, or imprisoned. (Thio, *Sociology*)

LANGUAGE TIP

Coordination

Coordination is one of the ways that information and ideas are combined in sentences. As you may have noticed, examples are often linked by the word *and*. *And* is a **conjunction,** a category of words that link or join ideas. **Coordinating conjunctions** join equal ideas. *And, but,* and *or* are the most frequently used coordinating conjunctions. Read over the following list of conjunctions and the explanations of their different meanings.

- *and*—indicates additional information
- *but*—indicates a contradiction, an exception, or unexpected information
- *or*—indicates that a choice must be made between two possibilities

Items presented in a series within a sentence are **coordinated** by these conjunctions. For example:

> Families in America include a wide variety of models, such as the traditional extended family, the single-parent family, the nuclear family, and the blended family.

Here the list of examples is marked by a comma after each item and then by *and* between the last two items in the series.

As you learned in Chapter 5, a complete sentence is an independent clause. **Independent clauses**—subject/verb combinations that can stand alone as a sentence—can also be **coordinated,** or linked together, in a sentence. For example, the following is a compound sentence:

>   (subject) (verb)   (subject) (verb)
> The Roman family was an extended one, and the patriarch had the authority even to kill his sons.

As a reader you should recognize that two independent clauses joined by *and* are considered equally important.

Watch for the conjunctions that link ideas or clauses in sentences, because these small words can completely change the meaning of the entire thought. For example, notice how a change from *and* to *but* gives the following sentences very different meanings.

> Roman fathers had the right to kill their sons, but they almost never killed a child.

In this sentence, the emphasis is on how rare it was for a father to kill a son.

> Roman fathers had the right to kill their sons, and they occasionally did kill their own offspring.

In this sentence, the emphasis is on the fact that sometimes fathers actually did kill a son.

Exercise 3	## Check Coordination

In the following similar sentences, underline the conjunctions. Notice how changing the conjunction changes the meaning of the sentence. (Not all of the sentences are true, of course.)

1. In Brazil, the extended family was typical, and the oldest male was in charge.

2. In Brazil, the extended family was typical, but the oldest male was not in charge.

3. In Brazil, families were either extended families, or they were nuclear families.

Now complete the following sentences by adding the appropriate coordinating conjunction ("and," "but," "or") on the blank line.

4. Families establish their own habits, rules, ___*and*___ values over the years.

5. Marco had grown up in a very close-knit family, ___*but*___ as an adult he chose the single life.

6. As a child, you may learn to either love ___*or*___ hate large family gatherings for a variety of reasons.

Chronological Order

chronological order
A pattern of organization that provides information in time order, using words like *then, when, after, before,* and *later*

Chronological order organizes information according to the time at which events occur or occurred. It often shows how something developed over time or explains its history. This pattern is often used to narrate stories and to explain the steps in a process.

In Sentences

Chronological order in sentences may be signaled by dates or times. For example, the writer of the following sentence is concerned about the changes in the baby boom generation's attitude toward family between the 1960s and the 1970s.

> The large baby boom generation, which had been active in the 1960s, was moving on to marriage and parenthood by the end of the 1970s. (Skolnick and Skolnick, *Family in Transition*)

In Paragraphs

Chronological order may also be used to organize information in paragraphs and longer passages. For example, in the following paragraph each sentence begins with dates to keep the reader's focus on the changes in the family from one decade to another. In fact, the main idea of the paragraph is, "The American family has been changing over time," or "The American family has changed since the 1950s." The time clues—which help you figure out the main idea—have been underlined for you.

During the 1950s the Cleavers on the television show "Leave It to Beaver" epitomized the American family. In 1960, over 70 percent of all American households were like the Cleavers: made up of a breadwinner father, a homemaker mother and their kids. Today, "traditional" families with a working husband, an unemployed wife, and one or more children make up less than 15 percent of the nation's households. (Martin et al., *America and Its Peoples*)

Organize to Learn: Make a Time Line

One good way to organize information based on chronological order is to use a **time line,** which is a table listing important events by dates. With a time line, you can see the chronological relationship between events. For example, the following paragraph can be organized with a time line:

> According to the U.S. Census Bureau, since the 1950s both men and women have gradually been marrying the first time at a later age. In 1955, the average age to enter a first marriage for a man was 22.6 and for a woman 20.2. By 1970, men's average age was 23.2 and women's was 20.8. Ten years later, in 1980, the average age for men was 24.7 and for women 22.0. This gradual increase continued into the 1990s. In 1995, the average age for men to enter their first marriage was 26.9 and for women it was 24.5.

A time line for the information in this paragraph might look like this:

main idea: Since the 1950s, men and women have entered their first marriages later.

1955	Men married at age 22.6, women 20.2
1970	Men married at age 23.2, women 20.8
1980	Men married at age 24.7, women 22.0
1995	Men married at age 26.9, women 24.5

Exercise 4	## Make a Time Line

In the following excerpts, underline dates and words or phrases that indicate chronological order. Write the main idea and complete the time lines.

1. Developed largely after World War I came to an end in 1918, the U.S. custom of dating has spread to many industrial countries. It has also changed in the United States in the last two decades. Before the 1970s, dating was more formal. Males had to ask for a date at least several days in advance. It was usually the male who decided where to go, paid for the date, opened doors, and was supposed to be chivalrous. The couple often went to an event, such as a movie, dance, concert, or ball game.

   Today, dating has become more casual. In fact, the word "date" now sounds a bit old-fashioned to many young people. (Thio, *Sociology*)

   main idea: <u>Dating developed after 1918 in U.S,</u> <u>has spread to foreign countries, and,</u> <u>has undergone many changes since the 1970s.</u>

   time line:

   1918 <u>Spread and development of dating custom;</u> end of WWI

   Before 1970s <u>Dating was more formal.</u>

   Today <u>dating has more become casual.</u>

2. Families and individual family members have at certain times in history decided to move away from the areas where they were born. In the early 1800s, German peasants began migrating to the United States. In the 1840s, people from Ireland migrated because there was not enough food due to the failed potato crops. Later in the nineteenth century, Scandinavians came. Finally, in the 1890s and early twentieth century, many Eastern European families moved to the "New World," looking for better opportunities.

   main idea: <u>Throughout history, people have</u> <u>moved from the areas where they were born.</u>

   time line:

   Beginning of 1800s <u>German peasants migrate to U.S.</u>

   1840s <u>Ireland people migrated due to potato famine</u>

   Late 1800s <u>that Scandinavians came U.S</u>

   End of 1800s, early 20th century <u>many Eastern Europeans</u> <u>moved to U.S. seeking opportunities.</u>

Mixed Patterns of Organization

Longer passages often use more than one pattern of organization. Sometimes examples will develop a main idea, then a series of events is presented to make a point. As you read, you will need to be aware of the several different patterns an author can use to organize major and minor supporting details.

Transitions

As you have probably already noticed as you learned to identify examples and chronological order, certain words provide clues to which pattern of organization is being used. Words like "for example" and "for instance" are signals that the information is organized as supporting examples. Words like "first," "then," and "later" indicate an organization by chronological order. These small but important words, called **transitions,** link ideas and show the relationship between ideas. Recognizing common transitions will help you identify patterns of organization.

transitions Words that link ideas or show the relationship between ideas

Watch for the following transitions to help you recognize the introduction of examples.

- such as
- for example
- for instance
- in addition
- moreover
- also
- another

Watch for the following transitions to help you recognize material arranged in chronological order.

- then
- when
- after
- before
- later
- once
- while
- next
- first
- second
- finally
- last, at last

| Exercise 5 | **Choose Transitions** |

Choose the appropriate example or chronological-order transitions from the preceding lists in order to complete the following sentence sets.

1. *Examples:*

The tasks of the average medieval peasant woman were numerous. *For instance* she had to care for and raise the children. She *also* had to prepare the limited supply of food for each meal over an open hearth. *In addition* she did the laundry. *Moreover* keeping her home clean and orderly was difficult because her furniture was limited, and the floor was dirt covered with rushes or straw. The work was never done.

2. *Chronological order:*

Most medieval European couples married *after* a period of courtship. They may even have had sexual contact *before* marriage. *Once* they had decided to marry, they usually spoke their vows at the door of the village church. *Next* the priest pronounced them man and wife. *Then* the feast called a "bride ale" began.

| READING 2 |

Housework in Victorian America

James Kirby Martin et al.

The following reading from a college history textbook describes what life was like for the American housewife of 100 years ago. As you read it, think about how doing housework is different today. Notice the patterns of organization the authors use to develop their main ideas. You might expect a history text to use chronological order only, but does this one? What other patterns can you identify here?

1 Housework in nineteenth-century America was harsh physical labor. Preparing even a simple meal was a time- and energy-consuming chore. Prior to the twentieth century, cooking was performed on a coal- or wood-burning stove. Unlike an electric or a gas range, which can be turned on with the flick of a single switch, cast-iron and steel stoves were exceptionally difficult to use.

2 Ashes from an old fire had to be removed. Then, paper and kindling had to be set inside the stove, dampers and flues had to be carefully adjusted, and a fire lit. Since there were no thermostats to regulate the stove's temperature, a woman had to keep an eye on the contraption all day long. Any time the fire slackened, she had to adjust a flue or add more fuel.

3   Throughout the day, the stove had to be continually fed with new supplies of coal or wood—an average of 50 pounds a day. At least twice a day, the ash box had to be emptied, a task which required a woman to gather ashes and cinders in a grate and then dump them into a pan below. Altogether, a housewife spent four hours every day sifting ashes, adjusting dampers, lighting fires, carrying coal or wood, and rubbing the stove with thick black wax to keep it from rusting.

4   It was not enough for a housewife to know how to use a cast-iron stove. She also had to know how to prepare unprocessed foods for consumption. Prior to the 1890s, there were few factory-prepared foods. Shoppers bought poultry that was still alive and then had to kill and pluck the birds. Fish had to have scales removed. Green coffee had to be roasted and ground. Loaves of sugar had to be pounded, flour sifted, nuts shelled, and raisins seeded.

arduous Difficult   5   Cleaning was an even more arduous task than cooking. The soot and smoke from coal- and wood-burning stoves blackened walls and dirtied drapes and carpets. Gas and kerosene lamps left smelly deposits of black soot on furniture and curtains. Each day, the lamps' glass chimneys had to be wiped and wicks trimmed or replaced. Floors had to be scrubbed, rugs beaten, and windows washed. While a small minority of well-to-do families could afford to hire cooks at $5 a week, waitresses at $3.50 a week, laundresses at $3.50 a week, and cleaning women and choremen for $1.50 a day, in the overwhelming majority of homes, all household tasks had to be performed by a housewife and her daughters.

6   Housework in nineteenth-century America was a full-time job. Gro Svendsen, a Norwegian immigrant, was astonished by how hard the typical American housewife had to work. As she wrote her parents in 1862:

7   We are told that the women of America have much leisure time but I haven't yet met any woman who thought so! Here the mistress of the house must do all the work that the cook, the maid and the housekeeper would do in an upper class family at home. Moreover, she must do her work as well as these three together do it in Norway.

8   Before the end of the nineteenth century, when indoor plumbing became common, chores that involved the use of water were particularly demanding. Well-to-do urban families had piped water or a private cistern, but the overwhelming majority of American families got their water from a hydrant, a pump, a well, or a stream located some distance from their house. The mere job of bringing water into the house was exhausting. According to calculations made in 1886, a typical North Carolina housewife had to carry water from a pump or a well or a spring eight to ten times each day. Washing, boiling, and rinsing a single load of laundry used about 50 gallons of water. Over the course of a year she walked 148 miles toting water and carried over 36 tons of water.

9   Homes without running water also lacked the simplest way to dispose of garbage: sinks with drains. This meant that women had to remove dirty dishwater, kitchen slops, and, worst of all, the contents of chamberpots from their house by hand.

10   Laundry was the household chore that nineteenth-century housewives detested most. Rachel Haskell, a Nevada housewife, called it "the Herculean task which women all dread" and "the great domestic dread of the household."

detested Hated

11   On Sunday evenings, a housewife soaked clothing in tubs of warm water. When she woke up the next morning, she had to scrub the laundry on a rough washboard and rub it with soap made from lye, which severely irritated her hands. Next, she placed the laundry in big vats of boiling water and stirred the clothes about with a long pole to prevent the clothes from developing yellow spots. Then she lifted the clothes out of the vats with a washstick, rinsed the clothes twice, once in plain water and once with bluing, wrung the clothes out, and hung them out to dry. At this point, clothes would be pressed with heavy flatirons and collars would be stiffened with starch.

12   The last years of the nineteenth century witnessed a revolution in the nature of housework. Beginning in the 1880s, with the invention of the carpet sweeper, a host of new "labor-saving" appliances were introduced. These included the electric iron (1903), the electric vacuum cleaner (1907), and the electric toaster (1912). At the same time, the first processed and canned foods appeared. In the 1870s, H. J. Heinz introduced canned pickles and sauerkraut; in the 1880s, Franco-American Co. introduced the first canned meals; and in the 1890s, Campbell's sold the first condensed soups. By the 1920s, the urban middle class enjoyed a myriad of new household

conveniences, including hot and cold running water, gas stoves, automatic washing machines, refrigerators, and vacuum cleaners.

decline Go down

13   Yet despite the introduction of electricity, running water, and "labor-saving" household appliances, time spent on housework did not decline. Indeed, the typical full-time housewife today spends just as much time on housework as her grandmother or great-grandmother. In 1924, a typical housewife spent about 52 hours a week in housework. Half a century later, the average full-time housewife devoted 55 hours to housework. A housewife today spends less time cooking and cleaning up after meals, but she spends just as much time as her ancestors on housecleaning and even more time on shopping, household management, laundry, and childcare.

14   How can this be? The answer lies in a dramatic rise in the standards of cleanliness and childcare expected of a housewife. As early as the 1930s, this change was apparent to a writer in the *Ladies' Home Journal:*

15   Because we housewives of today have the tools to reach it, we dig every day after the dust that grandmother left to spring cataclysm. If few of us have nine children for a weekly bath, we have two or three for a daily immersion. If our consciences don't prick us over vacant pie shelves or empty cookie jars, they do over meals in which a vitamin may be omitted or a calorie lacking.

MARTIN ET AL., *America and Its Peoples*

| Exercise 6 | ## Check Your Understanding |

Choose the best answers to the following multiple-choice questions based on Reading 2.

1. What is the best main idea statement for the reading?
   a. Cleaning was even harder work than cooking for housewives in the nineteenth century.
   b. Housework in nineteenth-century America required harsh physical labor, and even the introduction of laborsaving devices did not lessen the workload significantly.
   c. The last years of the nineteenth century witnessed a revolution in the nature of housework.
   d. Standards of cleanliness have risen dramatically in American households.

2. What procedure was *not* included in preparing unprocessed foods for meals?
   a. Removing scales from fish
   b. Defrosting a frozen entree
   c. Killing a chicken or other poultry
   d. Roasting and grinding coffee beans

3. Before the end of the nineteenth century, the majority of American families got their household water from where?
   a. A hydrant
   b. A pump
   c. A well
   d. A nearby stream
   e. All of the above

4. According to this reading, what was the household chore that women hated most?
   a. Keeping a fire going in the stove
   b. Emptying chamberpots
   c. Doing laundry
   d. Scrubbing floors

5. Despite the introduction of laborsaving devices, why didn't time spent on household work decline?
   a. Standards of cleanliness rose dramatically.
   b. It took a lot of time to learn to use the new devices.
   c. Women didn't want to use the toasters, vacuum cleaners, and electric irons.
   d. The devices seldom worked as well as expected.

Exercise 7

Make Connections: Collaborative Activity

Write short answers to the following questions based on Reading 2, your experiences, and your observations. Then, to extend the exercise, discuss your answers with your class group. Working together, prepare a report for your class as a whole or a written summary for your instructor.

1. How do you divide the housework in your home? How many hours a week do the members of your household spend on housework? Is this more or less than the average of 52 hours in 1924 or 55 hours in 1974 reported in this reading?

   _____

   _____

   _____

2. List a number of the household duties you and members of your household regularly perform. How do those tasks compare to the duties of a housewife in the nineteenth century?

   _____

   _____

   _____

3. How do you think housework will change in the next 50 years? What new labor-saving device would you most like to see invented?

_____

_____

_____

| Exercise 8 | ### Identify Patterns of Organization

Read the following excerpts from Reading 2. Then identify the primary pattern of organization for each. Write your answer—examples or chronological order—in the space after each excerpt. Then write the main idea in a sentence. Finally, on a separate piece of paper, design your own map or make an outline of the excerpt.

1. The last years of the nineteenth century witnessed a revolution in the nature of housework. Beginning in the 1880s, with the invention of the carpet sweeper, a host of new "labor-saving" appliances were introduced. These included the electric iron (1903), the electric vacuum cleaner (1907), and the electric toaster (1912). At the same time, the first processed and canned foods appeared. In the 1870s, H. J. Heinz introduced canned pickles and sauerkraut; in the 1880s, Franco-American Co. introduced the first canned meals; and in the 1890s, Campbell's sold the first condensed soups. By the 1920s, the urban middle class enjoyed a myriad of new household conveniences, including hot and cold running water, gas stoves, automatic washing machines, refrigerators, and vacuum cleaners. (Martin et al., *America and Its Peoples*)

pattern of organization: _____

_____

main idea: _____

_____

_____

2. Cleaning was an even more arduous task than cooking. The soot and smoke from coal- and wood-burning stoves blackened walls and dirtied drapes and carpets. Gas and kerosene lamps left smelly deposits of black soot on furniture and curtains. Each day, the lamps' glass chimneys had to be wiped and wicks trimmed or replaced. Floors had to be scrubbed, rugs beaten, and windows washed. (Martin et al., *America and Its Peoples*)

pattern of organization: _____

_____

main idea: _____

_____

More Patterns of Organization

Now you are able to identify two of the most common patterns of organization: examples and chronological order. In the following sections you will become familiar with definition and classification, two closely related patterns that you will notice often in your reading.

Definitions

Definition is a frequently used pattern of organization in college textbooks. It answers the question, "What is it?" or "What does it mean?"

In Sentences

A sentence that develops a definition often introduces a term and then explains what it means. For example, the following sentence explains the meaning of "monogamy." The term is in *italics* to attract our attention to its importance, and the meaning is provided between the dashes.

> *Monogamy*—the marriage of one man to one woman—is the most common form in the world. (Thio, *Sociology*)

Clues in Verb Phrases   Watch for the following verb clues to help you recognize that the author has provided a definition. These verbs signal that a definition will follow:

- means
- refers to
- consists of
- is

Clues in Punctuation   Sometimes definitions are shown in these ways:

- *In parentheses*: "Polygamy (the practice of having more than one spouse at a time) is not very common in Western countries."
- *Between dashes*: "Polygamy—the practice of having more than one spouse at a time—is not very common in Western countries."
- *Immediately after the term between commas*: "Polygamy, the practice of having more than one spouse at a time, is not very common in Western countries."

Clues in Transitions   Some transitions also signal that a definition follows:

- that is
- namely
- in other words

definition
A pattern of organization that answers the question, "What is it?" or "What does it mean?" using words like "means," "refers to," and "is"

In Paragraphs

Sometimes a definition is so complex that it needs a paragraph or more of explanation. For example, in the following excerpt the authors try to define "family." In fact, the main idea of this excerpt is the definition of the family. Notice that "family" is not an easy word to define, and the authors approach it in several different ways.

What is a family? In everyday conversation we make assumptions about what families are or should be. Traditionally, both law and social science specified that the family consisted of people related by blood, marriage, or adoption. Some definitions of the family specified a common household, economic interdependence, and sexual and reproductive relations. . . .

Burgess and Locke defined the family as "a group of persons united by the ties of marriage, blood, or adoption; constituting a single household; interacting and communicating with each other in their respective social roles (husband and wife, mother and father, son and daughter, brother and sister); and creating and maintaining a common culture." This definition goes beyond earlier ones to talk about family relationships and interactions. (Lamanna and Riedmann, *Marriages and Families*)

Notice how definition as a pattern of organization can be outlined.

topic: Definition of the family

main idea: A family is defined as people related by blood, marriage, or adoption, although some experts have added additional characteristics to that list.

Additional characteristics (major supporting details):

I. Single household

II. Economic interdependence

III. Sexual and reproductive relations

IV. Communicating with each other in their roles (Burgess and Locke)

V. Maintaining a common culture (Burgess and Locke)

Exercise 9 | ## Identify Definitions

Circle the clues that indicate definitions in the following paragraphs. Underline the definition of each italicized word. Then complete the maps that follow.

1. A few societies have placed the mother at the head of the family. This type of family is called *matriarchal.* The husband usually goes to live

with the wife's family. Women may own the property, and pass it on to their daughters. A few tribes today are matriarchies. (Glazer, "Family")

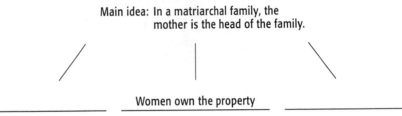

Main idea: In a matriarchal family, the mother is the head of the family.

Women own the property

2. There are also norms governing the number of spouses a person may have. *Monogamy*—the marriage of one man to one woman—is the most common form in the world. But many societies, especially small, preindustrial ones, approve of *polygamy,* marriage of one person to two or more people of the opposite sex. It is rare for a society to allow the practice of *polyandry,* marriage of one woman to two or more men. . . . A new variant of poiygamy has become increasingly common in the United States. Rather than having several spouses at the same time, many have one spouse at a time, going through a succession of marriage, divorce, and remarriage. Such practice is not really polygamy, but *serial monogamy,* marriage of one person to two or more people but only one at a time. (Thio, *Sociology*)

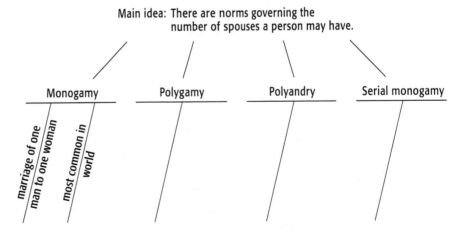

Main idea: There are norms governing the number of spouses a person may have.

Monogamy   Polygamy   Polyandry   Serial monogamy

marriage of one man to one woman   most common in world

| Exercise 10 | Identify Patterns of Organization in Sentences |

Decide whether each of the following sentences is organized primarily by examples, by chronological order, or by definition. Underline the clues that you used to decide. The first one has been done for you.

1. As families have become less traditional, the legal <u>definition</u> of a family has become much more flexible and nonspecific and is not limited to people linked by legal marriage, by blood, or by adoption. (Lamanna and Riedmann, *Marriages and Families*)

   pattern of organization: *definition*_____ *(The writers' focus in this sentence is on the different parts of "the legal definition of a family.")*

2. In the United States and Canada, the term *family* commonly means a group of related persons who share a home. (Glazer, "Family")

   pattern of organization: _____

3. The rate of divorce has more than doubled since 1965, peaking in 1979 and dropping slightly since then. (Lamanna and Riedmann, *Marriages and Families*)

   pattern of organization: ____*Time*_____

4. The study of the family does not fit neatly within the boundaries of any single scholarly field: genetics, physiology, archeology, history, anthropology, sociology, psychology, and economics all touch upon it. (Skolnick and Skolnick, *Family in Transition*)

   pattern of organization: _____

5. [Between] 1960 and 1993 the percent of children in one-parent families who were living with a never-married mother grew from 4 percent to 35 percent. (Wolf, *Marriages and Family in a Diverse Society*)

   pattern of organization: _____

6. Single-parent families, one-earner nuclear families, two-earner families and stepfamilies reflect the diversity of American families today.

   pattern of organization: _____

7. A society with the women in charge is called *matriarchal* (from words meaning "mother" and "ruler"). (Cavan, "Family")

   pattern of organization: _____

| Exercise 11 | Identify Patterns of Organization in Paragraphs |

Decide whether each of the following paragraphs is organized primarily by examples, by chronological order, or by definition. Find the main ideas and write them on the lines provided (they may be stated or un-stated). Circle the clues that you used to identify the pattern of organization. A paragraph may have more than one pattern of organization, so identify the one that is most important for supporting the main idea. The first one has been done for you.

1. Preparing a meal in the nineteenth century was no easy task. Women had to kill and pluck the chickens, remove the scales from fish, roast and grind the coffee, pound sugar, and sift the flour. (adapted from Martin et al., *America and Its Peoples*)

   pattern of organization: *Examples*

   (This paragraph is chiefly organized to provide examples of the various tasks—such as killing and plucking birds, roasting and grinding coffee, and sifting flour—that housewives had to perform 100 years ago.)

   main idea: *Housewives had to do a lot of different chores to prepare a meal prior to the 1890s.*

2. Families have been changing gradually over time, but in much of the world, the changes have followed the same basic steps. When families lived on farms, they were large because people needed children to help them with the work. Mothers spent their time taking care of the household. But in the last few hundred years people have been moving to urban areas where families have fewer children. Jobs have increasingly become available to women, and fewer women are able to stay at home and pass up the possibility of an added income to help support the family. Today, in most developed countries, the vast majority of women work.

   pattern of organization: _____

   main idea: _____

   _____

3. A primary group is a small group marked by close, face-to-face relationships. Group members share experiences, express emotions, and, in the ideal case, know they are accepted and valued. In many ways, teams and families are similar primary groups: joys are celebrated spontaneously, tempers can flare quickly, and expression is often physical. (Lamanna and Riedmann, *Marriages and Families*)

   pattern of organization: *definition*

   main idea: _____

   _____

4. In American society, life in many families is organized primarily around the *nuclear* family. A nuclear family is made up of parents and their children and spans only two generations. Nuclear families do not include extended family members such as aunts, uncles, and grandparents.

pattern of organization: _____

main idea: _____

_____

5. In a few societies the mother or grandmother has the stronger voice in making decisions. For example, among the Hopi Indians in the southwestern United States, the women of the family own the land. When a woman marries, her husband moves in with her family or into a house nearby. But the men work the land and also carry out important religious ceremonies. (Cavan, "Family")

pattern of organization: ___example_____

main idea: _____

_____

6. *Cohabitation* refers to two people living together in a sexual relationship without marriage. Two decades ago cohabitation was rare. In 1970 only 11 percent of people who married for the first time had prior experience with cohabitation. Today, almost half of people who enter first marriages have previously cohabited. The U.S. Bureau of the Census estimates that today there are 5 million cohabiting couples in the United States. . . . Of the cohabiting couples, 1.2 million have children under age fifteen living with them. (Wolf, *Marriages and Family in a Diverse Society*)

pattern of organization for the first sentence: ___definition____

pattern of organization for the rest of the paragraph: _____

main idea: _____

_____

classification
A pattern of organization that answers the question, "What kinds are there?" or "What type is it?" using terms like "another type" and "many kinds"

Classification

A pattern of organization closely related to definition is **classification.** Classification breaks a large category down into smaller categories. It answers the question, "What kinds are there?" or "What type is this?"

In Sentences

For example, the following sentence classifies types of families:

> After years of experience as a family therapist, Robbins decided that two types of families—abusive and addictive families—presented the most difficult challenges.

The large category—family—has been broken down into two smaller categories—abusive families and addictive families.

Clues in Verbs and Other Words   Classification is often signaled by verbs such as "classify" or "categorize." In their noun forms—"classification," "category"—these words also signal classification. Look for these clues, too: "another type," "one form," "additional sorts," "major kinds of," " groups," and "classes."

Classification and Definition   These two patterns of organization are closely related. Sometimes an author will define a term by describing its categories:

> A family is a group of people who are related. Their kinship can be established by blood or by marriage. Blood relatives include children and siblings. When children and siblings marry, they bring in-laws into the family, creating mothers-in-law, fathers-in-law, sisters-in-law, and brothers-in-law.

Notice how this author has defined *family* by describing two categories of family—*blood relatives* and *in-laws*.

In Paragraphs

Classification in paragraphs and longer passages is often used in combination with other patterns, particularly examples and definitions. Read the following paragraph to see how the authors use a variety of patterns, including classification.

The extended family consists of two or more closely related families who share a household and are economically and emotionally bound to others in the group. For example, among the Navajo, relationships among sisters and other family kin often take precedence over the husband-wife relationship, not only because these relationships are defined as more satisfying, but because women—not husbands and wives—live and work together and own property in common. Extended families take two major forms: *vertical extended families,* which include three or more generations—parents, their married children, grandparents, and so on—and *joint families,* consisting of siblings and their spouses and their children. (Thompson and Hickey, *Society in Focus*)

Notice that the authors begin with a definition of extended families, follow with examples, and end the paragraph with classification. They identify two different forms of the extended family, *vertical extended families* and *joint families*.

Exercise 12	## Identify Classification

Read the following paragraph and underline the four different types of child care that are classified here. Then list them.

Working parents have choices as to how they would like to have their children cared for while they are at work. Probably the most desirable way is to have a family member, such as a grandparent or aunt, care for the child. This kind of child care is particularly desirable if the relative can come to the children's home or if she lives with the family. Another type of child care is the hired "nanny" that lives with the family or comes into the home whenever the parents are at work. Of course, not every family can afford a live-in nanny. A third choice for child care is the licensed day-care home, where the parents drop the children off every day and pick them up at the end of the day. Many families actually prefer a fourth type of child care—the organized preschool—because of the educational and social benefits.

Types of child care

1. _____

2. _____

3. _____

4. _____

READING 3	

Marriage and Family: An Overview Robin Wolf

The following reading from a sociology textbook explains how our society has changed in the past fifty years and how those changes have affected the American family. As you read this selection, think about the patterns of organization that are used and the main ideas of the passage.

From Industrial to Postindustrial Society

1   The United States changed from an industrial society based on factory production, which had its heyday in the 1940s and 1950s, to a postindustrial society in the 1960s that is organized around information processing, advanced technology, and service jobs. A number of factors associated with this change altered American families.

altered   Changed

Female Employment

2   The expansion of service jobs drew married women into the work force. Female employment and financial independence made divorce possible for a greater number of people.

Delayed Marriage

3   In modern society, well-paid jobs for both men and women require higher education. Extended education is incompatible with early marriage, so three decades ago the marriage age began to rise. This encouraged cohabitation and premarital sexual expression.

The Sexual Revolution

4   Attitude change associated with the sexual revolution of the 1960s and 1970s encouraged cohabitation and probably also contributed to the rising divorce rate by making sexual relationships outside of marriage more acceptable. In addition, the oral contraceptive and legalized abortion separated sexual pleasure from reproduction.

Life Cycle Change

5   During the twentieth century the life cycle changed as life expectancy increased, fertility declined, and the number of years that women spent raising children also declined. This made it possible for more married women to seek paid employment and probably also contributed to the rise in the divorce rate. It is a challenge to choose a mate with whom to share a half century of married life.

Changes in Technology

6   Changes in technology made divorce and the employment of married women easier. Washing machines, fast food restaurants, microwave ovens, and prepared frozen entrees freed women to enter the labor force. Antibiotics and vaccinations reduced the time women spent caring for children with childhood diseases.

Was There a Golden Age?

nostalgically
Thinking about the
past pleasantly

7   Traditionalists observe these social changes and look nostalgically back at the family of the 1950s in which the mother kept house and looked after

the needs of the children and husband. However, social observers in every era look at family change, lament the discomfort it causes, and long for an earlier golden age when family life seemed more appealing. In reality, all periods of history challenge family members with problems and troubles. In the so called "golden age" of the 1950s, many wives felt frustrated by their inability to develop their talents in activities outside the home. It would probably be a mistake to judge the health of a family by the presence or absence of family tensions. Rather, the hallmark of a strong family is its ability to cope with difficult situations.

Harbor Not Haven

8 The family has traditionally been viewed as a "haven" or retreat from a harsh world. However, it is probably expecting too much of families to assume that they can satisfy all of the personal needs of their members. Schvaneveldt and Young suggest that it is more useful to view the family as a "harbor" rather than a "haven." A safe harbor provides its members with rest and security, but they can also set sail into the outside world and experience themselves as independent people. Marriage is coming to be seen as an institution that combines intimacy with autonomy, or self-direction. This image of the family is particularly useful for two-earner marriages and for stepfamilies in which children must relate to a complex array of family members in several nuclear families. Social change associated with the shift from an industrial to a postindustrial society often appears chaotic. Yet family change may represent a normal adjustment to new economic realities. Also, family change may, in part, reflect the attempts of family members to find a balance between autonomy on one hand and commitment and self-sacrifice on the other. In these changing times, it is not surprising that we have a growing diversity of family forms.

Structural Diversity Among Families

9 Families in the United States are becoming increasingly diverse in their structure. One-parent families, stepfamilies, two-earner families, and families with extended kin are becoming increasingly important. These family forms have increased in number in response to the recent social change discussed earlier.

One-Parent Families

10 Thirty percent of all families with children are one-parent families. Moreover, one-parent families are often a transitional state between first and second marriages, so that the number of people who have lived in one-parent families is far greater than the number who currently reside in one. It is estimated that over one-half of all children born in the early 1980s will live in a one-parent family before they reach age eighteen. One-parent families make up a significant portion of all families: one-fifth of white families,

one-third of Hispanic families, and six-tenths of African-American families. The loss of well-paid blue-collar (manual labor) jobs in the postindustrial era has hampered the ability of many men, particularly men of color, to support a family. The result has been a rising divorce rate and an increasing number of nonmarital pregnancies. . . .

hampered Made more difficult

11   [B]etween 1960 and 1993 the percent of children in one-parent families who were living with a never-married mother grew from 4 percent to 35 percent. In fact, the 5 million children living with never-married mothers in 1993 equaled the total number of children living in all one-parent families in 1960. Among low-income persons, non-marital parenthood, sometimes combined with cohabitation, has become an important family form.

12   Recently, the make-up of one-parent families has undergone a small but interesting change. Over the last two decades the number of one-parent families headed by fathers has tripled, so that father-headed families now make up 13 percent of all one-parent families. Fathers are becoming more likely to seek custody of their children, particularly when those children are older boys.

Stepfamilies

13 Stepfamilies are becoming an increasingly important family form. Half of all divorces involve a child under age eighteen. Three-fourths of divorced persons remarry, often bringing children with them. It has been estimated that one-third of all children will live in a stepfamily at some time before they reach age eighteen. Many of the traits that children exhibit in one-parent families are carried over into stepfamilies, such as taking responsibility for household chores. However, the autonomy that adolescents typically experience in one-parent families tends to disappear in stepfamilies. Children in stepfamilies are generally more closely supervised than those in one-parent families. The high school completion rate of children in stepfamilies is higher than that of children in one-parent families.

traits Characteristics

14   Although stepfamilies experience a good deal of stress as family members adjust to new roles in the family, most couples who remarry report that they are satisfied with their marriages. Moreover, some aspects of stepfamily life that were previously considered to be social problems, such as low cohesion (which refers to loose emotional connections between stepparents and stepchildren), are now considered to be a creative adaptation to the demands of relating to two families.

Two-Earner Families

15 The typical married couple today forms a two-earner family. In addition, cohabitors are most often found in a two-earner partnership. The working mother has become the norm even in families with young children. Because the purchasing power of wages earned by men declined after 1973, only with the entry of wives into the labor force have families been

norm Usual, standard

able to maintain their standard of living. Even families from traditional cultures, in which the wife was expected to remain at home to care for the family, tend to undergo change when they immigrate to the United States. Mexican-American wives and Southeast-Asian wives often find it necessary to seek employment in order to help support the family.

Families That Include Extended Kin

16 In American society, life in many families is organized primarily around the *nuclear family*. A nuclear family is made up of parents and their children and spans only two generations. In contrast, traditional societies consider the *extended family* to be of primary importance. The extended family includes those kin who extend outward from the nuclear family, such as grandparents, aunts, and uncles. Extended kin relationships have always been central in immigrant families, which were coping with a new environment, but have diminished in importance among white middle-class families. However, today extended kin relationships are once more growing in importance. Families are increasingly likely to provide housing to extended kin who have fallen on financial hard times. One-third of African-American families and one-fourth of white families include other adults in the household. Most often this other adult is a relative.

Cultural Diversity Among Families

17 It is not possible to study one version of "the family" in the United States as if it represented all families. Marital patterns and household composition vary with race and ethnicity, as does the meaning of "the family." For example, multiple roles have traditionally been the norm in African-American marriages, with women being wives, mothers and employees. In addition, the extended family is likely to be far more important to the functioning of African-American, Hispanic, and Asian families than to white families of European extraction. The economic marginality of many minority families means that they must rely on extended kin for security, for information on how to adjust to residence in a new country, and for such services as child care. Because family experiences of racial and ethnic groups vary, an examination of families in the United States would not be complete without taking into account ethnic and racial variation.

WOLF, *Marriage and Family in a Diverse Society*

| Exercise 13 |

Work with Words

Use context clues, word part clues, and if necessary the dictionary to write the definitions of the italicized words in the following sentences from Reading 3.

1. Extended education is incompatible with early marriage, so three decades ago the marriage age began to rise. This encouraged *cohabitation* and premarital sexual expression. (par. 3)

   cohabitation _____

2. However, social observers in every era look at family change, *lament* the discomfort it causes, and long for an earlier golden age when family life seemed more appealing. (par. 7)

   lament _____

3. The family has traditionally been viewed as a *"haven"* or retreat from a harsh world. (par. 8)

   haven _____

4. Marriage is coming to be seen as an institution that combines intimacy with *autonomy*, or self-direction. (par. 8)

   autonomy _____

5. One-parent families, stepfamilies, two-earner families, and families with extended *kin* are becoming increasingly important. (par. 9)

   kin _____

| Exercise 14 |

Check Your Understanding

Answer the following questions based on Reading 3.

1. Choose the best main idea sentence for the entire reading.
   a. The typical married couple today forms a two-earner family.
   b. The extended family includes those kin who extend outward from the nuclear family, such as grandparents, aunts and uncles, and these types of families have always been central in immigrant families.
   c. The traditional American family has been changing over the past 50 or 60 years, and today's families are increasingly diverse in their structure.

2. Find the best main idea sentence for paragraph 9, and write it here:

   _____

3. Find the best main idea sentence for paragraph 10, and write it here:

   _____

4. Which of the following statements would the author *not* agree with?
   a. The families of the 1950s were better than the families of today.
   b. People always think change is uncomfortable.
   c. In the 1950s women were not necessarily always happy with their roles as housewives.
   d. Families always face challenges.

5. According to the author, which of the following statements is *not* true?
   a. Families in the United States are more diverse than they were before.
   b. Families are changing because the times are changing.
   c. The changes in families are okay because families are adjusting to new realities.
   d. Family members are naturally dependent on their families for everything that they do.

Exercise 15   ## Identify Patterns of Organization

Read the following excerpts and identify the pattern of organization—examples, chronological order, definition, or classification. What clues helped you identify the pattern of organization? The first one has been done for you.

1. Changes in technology made divorce and the employment of married women easier. Washing machines, fast food restaurants, microwave ovens, and prepared frozen entrees freed women to enter the labor force. Antibiotics and vaccinations reduced the time women spent caring for children with childhood diseases. (Wolf, *Marriage and Family in a Diverse Society*)

   pattern of organization: *examples*

   clues: *list of examples divided by commas, use of the word "and"*

2. The United States changed from an industrial society based on factory production, which had its heyday in the 1940s and 1950s, to a postindustrial society in the 1960s that is organized around information processing, advanced technology, and service jobs. A number of factors associated with this change altered American families. (Wolf, *Marriage and Family in a Diverse Society*)

   pattern of organization: _____

   clues: _____

3. Between 1960 and 1993 the percent of children in one-parent families who were living with a never-married mother grew from 4 percent

to 35 percent. In fact, the 5 million children living with never-married mothers in 1993 equaled the total number of children living in all one-parent families in 1960. Among low-income persons, non-marital parenthood, sometimes combined with cohabitation, has become an important family form. (Wolf, *Marriage and Family in a Diverse Society*)

pattern of organization: _____

clues: _____

4. Families in the United States are becoming increasingly diverse in their structure. One-parent families, stepfamilies, two-earner families, and families with extended kin are becoming increasingly important. These family forms have increased in number in response to the recent social change discussed earlier. (Wolf, *Marriage and Family in a Diverse Society*)

pattern of organization: _____

clues: _____

5. A nuclear family is made up of parents and their children and spans only two generations. (Wolf, *Marriage and Family in a Diverse Society*)

pattern of organization: _____

clues: _____

Exercise 16

Make Connections

Write short answers to the following questions based on Reading 3, your experience, and your observations.

1. Briefly describe two families that you know. Who are the members of the family, and what is their relationship to one another?

_____

_____

_____

_____

2. Into which category of family described in Reading 3 do they fit?

_____

_____

| Exercise 17 | Make a Map, Time Line, or Outline |

1. On a separate sheet of paper, create a time line for the following paragraph, which is organized by chronological order.

> Over the last 50 years in China, family life has improved because more Chinese babies are living past the first year of life. The number of births has remained fairly constant, but in the early decades of the twentieth century, 27 to 30 infants died out of 1,000 births. In 1952, 18 infants died out of 1,000 births, and by the early 1970s, that figure had fallen to about 15 per 1,000 and was continuing to fall. ("China," *Encyclopedia Britannica*)

2. On a separate sheet of paper, design a map or outline that shows the main idea and the supporting details (examples) of the following paragraph.

> Changes in technology made divorce and the employment of married women easier. Washing machines, fast food restaurants, microwave ovens, and prepared frozen entrees freed women to enter the labor force. Antibiotics and vaccinations reduced the time women spent caring for children with childhood diseases. (Wolf, *Marriages and Family*)

| READING 4 |

Old Cultures and New International Families
Richard P. Appelbaum and William J. Chambliss

The following reading examines how old cultures are mixed with new in the increasing globalization of families. As you read, look for the various patterns of organization that are used in this sociology textbook.

1   Anthropologist Christine Ho (1993) has examined what she terms "international families," which result from globalization. Focusing on mothers who emigrate from the Caribbean to the United States, Ho documents how they often rely on child minding, an arrangement in which extended-family members and even friends cooperate in raising their children while they pursue work elsewhere, often thousands of miles away. The practice adds a global dimension to cooperative child-rearing practices that are a long-standing feature of Caribbean culture. The story of Anne-Marie, a woman who migrated from the impoverished Caribbean island of Trinidad in hopes of finding work in the United States, is illustrative.

2   Anne-Marie, the single mother of two infant sons, moved to New York City from Trinidad. She eventually got her "green card" permitting her to

work in the United States and managed to find a job doing clerical work in a bank. But for her first five years in the United States, Anne-Marie's sons remained behind in Trinidad, in the care of her mother. Eventually, once she was financially stable, Anne-Marie's sons joined her, accompanied by her mother and brother. The four then lived together in an extended-family household.

3   A few years later, Anne-Marie married a man who also came from Trinidad, and she and her new husband moved to Los Angeles in hopes that he would find work in the construction industry. Once again, until she could get reestablished, she left her sons behind in the care of her mother. After giving birth to a daughter, she sent for her sons and finally established a conventional nuclear family. This arrangement proved to be short-lived, however. In order to improve her career prospects, Anne-Marie decided to enroll in a year-long course in medical transcribing. Although her teenage sons were now old enough to be on their own after school, Anne-Marie wanted her daughter to get proper parental attention. The solution, once again, was child minding—this time by her husband's grandmother, mother, and younger sister, who lived in the Virgin Islands (also in the Caribbean). During the year of Anne-Marie's schooling, her infant daughter lived with her husband's extended family.

4   Seven years later, the situation once again changed. By now, Anne-Marie's sons had grown and moved away from Los Angeles, and she needed someone to provide after-school care for her daughter, now 8 years old, so she could work. Rather than rely on day care, Anne-Marie decided to send for her husband's sister from the Virgin Islands, the same young woman who had helped provide child minding seven years earlier. The sister moved to Los Angeles, where she joined Anne-Marie's again-extended family, resuming the care of Anne-Marie's daughter while going to high school. In a sense, Anne-Marie and her husband were now providing child minding for his younger sister, who was able to leave her own mother and grandmother in the Virgin Islands by joining her brother and sister-in-law in Los Angeles.

5   Nor were Anne-Marie, her husband, their daughter, and her husband's sister the only members of this extended family. Anne-Marie's husband had a daughter from a previous relationship, who spent summers with them, and three other children. The couple also had a host of relatives living in Trinidad, on the Virgin Islands, and in various places in the United States. Thus they had a large international family, an extended family spanning several countries, yet characterized by intense interactions, strong emotional ties, and a binding sense of mutual obligation.

6   Ho believes that such global family arrangements will enable Caribbean immigrants to avoid becoming fully "Americanized": international families and child minding are seen as providing a strong sense of continuity with

their original Caribbean culture. She predicts that Caribbean immigrants will retain their native cultures by regularly receiving what she characterizes as "cultural booster shots," accomplished through the constant shuttling back and forth of family members between the United States and the Caribbean. At the same time, Ho notes, this process also contributes to the "Americanization" of the Caribbean region, which may eventually give rise to an ever more global culture.

Appelbaum and Chambliss, *Sociology*

Exercise 18

Work with Words

Use context clues, word part clues, and if necessary the dictionary to write in the definitions of the italicized words in the following sentences from Reading 4.

1. Focusing on mothers who emigrate from the Caribbean to the United States, Ho documents how they often rely on *child minding,* an arrangement in which extended-family members and even friends cooperate in raising their children while they pursue work elsewhere, often thousands of miles away. (par. 1)

   child minding _____

   _____

   _____

2. Once again, until she could get *reestablished,* she left her sons behind in the care of her mother. (par. 3)

   reestablished _____

3. After giving birth to a daughter, she sent for her sons and finally established a *conventional* nuclear family. (par. 3)

   conventional _____

4. Ho believes that such global family arrangements will enable Caribbean immigrants to avoid becoming fully "Americanized": international families and child minding are seen as providing a strong sense of *continuity* with their original Caribbean culture. (par. 6)

   continuity _____

Exercise 19

Check Your Understanding

Choose the best answers to the following multiple-choice questions about Reading 4.

1. Why, based on anthropologist Ho's explanation, do you think international families exist?
   a. Some people like moving a long way away from their families.
   b. Sometimes people must move long distances away from family to get a job.
   c. Immigration authorities require families to remain separated.

2. Who cared for Anne-Marie's infant daughter during the year she went to school?
   a. her husband's extended family
   b. her older brothers
   c. her new husband

3. Which of these people was *not* mentioned as living as part of Anne-Marie's extended family?
   a. her mother-in-law
   b. her two sons
   c. her father

Choose the best way to complete the following statements about Reading 4.

4. Anne-Marie's family was often separated by great distances
   a. so they grew apart over the years.
   b. but they still maintained a close relationship.
   c. so they couldn't help each other in times of need.

5. Ho believes that this Caribbean family's global arrangements
   a. will help them maintain a sense of their own culture.
   b. will help them become Americanized more quickly.
   c. will lead to the breakup of the family.

| Exercise 20 | ## Identify Patterns of Organization |

Decide whether each of the following excerpts from Reading 4 is organized primarily by examples, by chronological order, or by definition. (Each pattern is used only once.)

1. Focusing on mothers who emigrate from the Caribbean to the United States, Ho documents how they often rely on child minding, an arrangement in which extended-family members and even friends cooperate in raising their children while they pursue work elsewhere, often thousands of miles away.

   pattern of organization: _____

2. The story of Anne-Marie, a woman who migrated from the Caribbean island of Trinidad in hopes of finding work in the United States, is illustrative.

   pattern of organization: _____

3. A few years later, Anne-Marie married a man who also came from Trinidad, and she and her new husband moved to Los Angeles in hopes that he would find work in the construction industry.

   pattern of organization: _____

| Exercise 21 | ## Make a Map or Time Line

On a separate sheet of paper, create a map or a time line to organize Paragraphs 2 through 4 of Reading 4.

| Exercise 22 | ## Make Connections

Write short answers to the following questions based on Reading 4, your experience, and your observations.

1. Are you part of a nuclear or extended family? What are the advantages of the type of family in which you live?

   _____

   _____

   _____

2. Have you had to live apart from other family members for a period of time? How did that affect your relationships? Why?

   _____

   _____

   _____

Chapter Review

To aid your review of the reading skills in Chapter 7, study the Put It Together Chart.

Put It Together: *Patterns of Organization*

Skills and Concepts	Explanation
Patterns of organization (see pages 322–323)	Patterns of organization are the ways details are arranged to support main ideas.
Examples (see pages 323–325)	Examples as a pattern of organization give one or more illustrations and are introduced with phrases like "for example," "for instance." Sometimes examples are enumerated—listed with numbers—or listed with bullets.
Chronological order (see pages 327–329)	Chronological order organizes information in time order and uses words like "then," "when," "after," "before," "later," as well as dates (Monday, March 1950, 1975, etc.).
Definition (see pages 337–339)	Definition as a pattern of organization organizes information to answer the question, "What is it?" and uses words like "means," "refers to," "is."
Classification (see pages 342–344)	Classification as a pattern of organization organizes information into categories to answer the question, "What kinds are there?" and uses words like "another type," "many kinds."
Transition (see pages 330–331)	Transitions are words that link ideas or show the relationship between ideas.

To reinforce your thinking before taking the Mastery Tests, complete as many of the following activities as your instructor assigns.

Reviewing Skills

List transitions and other clues to identify each of the following patterns of organization:

1. Examples: _____

_____

2. Chronological order: _____

_____

3. Definition: _____

_____

4. Classification: _____

_____

Writing

Write about your family history in a short paragraph that you organize by chronological order.

Collaborating

Share your family history with your class group. Create a time line for each family. Indicate where your families were in the same years. Discuss the results. Working together, prepare a summary of family history findings to submit to your instructor.

Extending Your Thinking

Find an article about families in a newspaper or magazine. Read it carefully. Write out the main idea, the most important pattern of organization, and the clues you used to identify it. Then map, outline, or make a time line of your article. Bring your article and your paper to class to share with your class group or to turn in to your instructor.

Visiting the Web

The following Web sites provide more information on families and parenting.

1. Parents Place

http://www.parentsplace.com
This Web site covers topics including potty training, childcare, parents going back to school, single parenting, advice on marriage, and advice from pediatricians.

2. Magic Carpet International Family Web Guide

http://www.ridethemagiccarpet.co.u/s/
This colorful site has informative links to sites in the U.S.A., the U.K., and Australia. It includes information for families ranging from self-help to finances to toddler games.

3. Family History—the Genealogy Home Page

http://www.genhomepage.com/
The genealogy home page lists worldwide sources for researching your family history. It includes newsgroups, an Internet genealogy guide, and guidance for how to get started on your search.

Marriage and Family Variations

Richard P. Appelbaum and William J. Chambliss

In the following reading from a college sociology textbook, the authors explain some of the different approaches to marriages, family, and child rearing in America and around the world. Notice how the authors organize the information using different patterns.

1   The notion of *marriage,* like that of *family,* is culturally constructed and open to change. Sociologists define *marriage* as *a culturally approved relationship, usually between two individuals, that provides for a degree of economic cooperation, intimacy, and sexual activity.* Marriages may be legitimized by legal or religious recognition, or simply by the norms of the prevailing culture (Parker, 1990). Although marriages usually involve partners of different sexes, same-sex marriages are becoming more common in the United States and other industrial societies, sometimes with legal recognition. The *nuclear family* is *a social group consisting of one or two parents and their dependent children.* The meaning of *nuclear family* has changed over time. During the 1950s, four out of five children grew up with two biological parents who were married to each other. Today only half of all children spend their childhood in such a family. Nuclear families are less than a quarter of all U.S. households (U.S. Bureau of the Census, 1995a; Whitehead, 1993). A significant number of families today have one or more of the following characteristics: a single parent (usually the mother); adopted children or children from previous marriages; mates who are not legally married; or same-sex couples . . .

2   A substantial minority of Americans live in *extended families, social groups consisting of one or more parents, children, and other kin, often spanning several generations, living in the same household.* An extended family may include grandparents, aunts, uncles, cousins, or other close relatives. Most northern European and American families are nuclear, while extended families are more common in eastern and southern Europe, Africa, Asia, and Latin America (Busch, 1990). In the United States, extended families are most likely to be found in lower-income households, in rural areas, among recent immigrants from countries where extended families are common, and among African Americans. Approximately one out of five whites and one out of four African Americans live in extended families (Ruggles, 1994). Economic necessity often contributes to the formation of extended families as a means of combining resources.

Cultural Variations in Marriage

3 Most societies have fairly clear norms regarding marriage, but the definitions of marriage vary greatly. The two basic cultural patterns are *monogamy,* in which *a person may have only one spouse at a time,* and *polygamy,* in which *a person may have more than one spouse at a time.* There are two types of polygamy: *polygyny,* in which *a man may have multiple wives,* and *polyandry,* in which *a woman may have multiple husbands.* In feudal Europe and Asia, monogamy prevailed, although in some parts of Asia wealthy men supported concubines (similar to mistresses) (Goody, 1983; Huber and Spitze, 1983). George Peter Murdoch's (1949) classic anthropological study of 862 preindustrial societies found that 16 percent had norms calling for monogamy, while 80 percent permitted polygyny. (Only 4 societies permitted polyandry.)

4 Some sociologists have suggested that, because divorce and remarriage are common in the United States and Western Europe, our marriage pattern should be labeled *serial monogamy, the practice of having more than one wife or husband but only one a time* (Goode, 1963). In most modern societies, there is a strong commitment to monogamy and to the selection of a lifelong mate, but in practice, many people have two or more marriages.

Child Rearing

5 There are significant cultural variations in who takes the responsibility for child rearing. The role of parent in the United States and in Western European societies is traditionally assumed by the biological parents, but this is only one of the many variations in the world. In the Baganda tribe of Central Africa, the biological father's brother is responsible for child rearing (Queen, Habenstein, and Adams, 1961). The Nayars of southern India assign this role to the mother's eldest brother (Schneider and Gough, 1974). "Child minding" is an arrangement common among Trinidadians and other Caribbean natives, in which extended-family members and friends cooperate in raising the children of a person who has migrated to another country, often the United States, in search of work (Ho, 1993). Five percent of all American children under 18 now live with their grandparents, often without the presence of either biological parent. This pattern is most common among African Americans, where 12 percent live with their grandparents. Among whites, the figure is 4 percent; among Hispanics, 6 percent.

APPELBAUM AND CHAMBLISS, *Sociology*

Based on the context clues in the reading, write the meaning of each of the italicized words.

Name _____ Date _____

1. The *nuclear family* is a social group consisting of one or two parents and their dependent children. (par. 1)

   nuclear family _a social group consisting of one or two parents and their dependent children._

2. A substantial minority of Americans live in *extended families,* social groups consisting of one or more parents, children, and other kin, often spanning several generations, living in the same household. (par. 2)

   extended families _social groups consisting of one or more parents, children, and other kin, often spawning several generations_

3. There are two types of polygamy: polygyny, in which a man may have multiple wives, and *polyandry,* in which a woman may have multiple husbands. (par. 3)

   polyandry _a marital relationship in which a woman may have multiple husbands._

4. In most modern societies, there is a strong *commitment* to monogamy and to the selection of a lifelong mate, but in practice, many people have two or more marriages. (par. 4)

   commitment _a strong bond or active loyalty._

5. The role of parent in the United States and in Western European societies is traditionally assumed by the biological parents, but this is only one of many *variations* in the world. (par. 5)

   variations _different types of one kind._

Write *true* or *false* before each of the following statements about the reading.

_F_ 6. The concept of marriage and family is very similar in all parts of the world and seldom changes.

_F_ 7. Today three-fourths of families in the United States are nuclear families.

_T_ 8. An extended family may include grandparents, aunts, uncles, cousins, or other close relatives.

_F_ 9. Serial monogamy is the practice of having more than one wife or husband at once.

_F_ 10. More Hispanic children than other groups of American children are raised solely by their grandparents.

_T_ 11. In one area of Central Africa, uncles are chiefly responsible for child rearing.

_T_ 12. Child minding is an arrangement common among the people of Trinidad and other areas of the Caribbean.

Choose the best way to complete the following statements about patterns of organization used in the reading.

13. The first half of paragraph 1, to the end of the sentence defining the nuclear family, is organized primarily by
    a. examples.
    b. chronological order.
    c. definition.

14. The second half of paragraph 1, beginning with the statement, "The meaning of nuclear family has changed over time," is primarily organized by
    a. examples.
    b. chronological order.
    c. definition.

15. Paragraph 2, after the initial definition of extended families, is primarily organized by
    a. examples.
    b. chronological order.
    c. definition.

16. Paragraph 3 is primarily organized by
    a. examples.
    b. classification.
    c. cause and effect.

17. Paragraph 5 is primarily organized by
    a. examples.
    b. chronological order.
    c. definition.

Write short answers to the following questions based on your reading, your experience, and your observation.

Name _____ Date _____

Answers vary
EX:

18. Do you agree that the marriage pattern in the United States should actually be called "serial monogamy?" Why or why not?

Yes, I agree b/c now in the USA many families are made up by one or both parents who have been married before once or more than once. No, b/c I don't believe there are many families that follow this pattern.

EX:

19. Why do you think that families in some areas of the world are primarily nuclear families and in other areas they are primarily extended families?

yes, I do b/c for example the author states on page 359 (paragraph two line five), "Most northern European & American families are unclear, while extended families are more common in eastern & Southern Europe, Africa, Asia, Latin America.

20. Why do patterns of marriage, family, and child rearing vary so much around the world?

_____

_____

_____

Swedish Approaches to Family Reform

William E. Thompson and Joseph V. Hickey

Patterns of family relations vary around the world. Many countries, however, are struggling with the issues of equal rights for women in the workplace and the changing role of women in the family. Sweden has long been considered a leader in making reforms for family life. Read the following report carefully, and compare Sweden's reforms with conditions in the United States. Also watch to see which patterns of organization the authors use to develop their points.

1   Some sociologists believe that if any nation deserves the "pro-family" label, it is Sweden. In the past century, the Swedish state, in cooperation with labor, industry, and the feminist and other social movements, has provided money and services to support family life and the employment of women. And to a lesser degree, it has sought to eliminate gender inequality and laws and customs that reinforce women's secondary place in society. As a result, wrote Joan Acker (1994:33), "Swedish women enjoy public programs and economic guarantees that have made Sweden a model for women in other countries."

2   Acker's study of Swedish reforms over the past few decades shows that many changes in the family were the result of conscious policy decisions. One of the most important began with labor shortages in the 1960s, which led the government to push for increased labor market participation of women. This was accomplished through a new tax policy that severely reduced tax deductions for wives and "encouraged" most to enter the workforce. The transition to work was also supported by the feminist movement, which saw work and financial independence as women's only hope of gaining equality with men (Acker, 1994:34).

3   To smooth the transition of women into the workforce, the Swedish government dramatically expanded welfare state services and new jobs—especially in a new sector called "caring work." These paid public sector jobs included nursing, child care, preschool teachers, and home helpers who make it possible for almost 90 percent of Swedish women to be gainfully employed—including similar percentages of women with children under 6 years of age.

4   The Swedish solution to the problem of successfully combining family and labor market work is the most advanced in the world. No longer is there a worker and housewife with separate but interdependent roles. Instead there are two workers—the classical, male-defined worker and a new worker in whose life the tasks of reproduction and production are intertwined (Acker, 1994:38).

Name _____ Date _____

5   The typical Swedish family today consists of two working parents, with the majority of women working part-time (67 percent of those with children) and more than 90 percent of men working full-time. To support women's and men's dual roles in the family and work, the state has devised a benefit package that *all* families receive regardless of class or income. Some of the benefits are public-supported child care, including day-care centers and licensed family care homes (organized by local communities), and parental leave insurance available to both men and women. Parents of a newborn are entitled to 360 days of leave at normal sick pay, new fathers are entitled to 10 days of parental leave, and parents have the legal right to "reduce their hours on the job to three-quarter of normal pay, until the child reaches eight years of age." Additionally, all families are entitled to a basic child allowance per year of around $900, as well as a housing allowance that is based on income and number of children in the family (Acker, 1994).

6   While Swedish attempts to balance family and work are the most progressive in the world, they remain an unfinished project. As Acker wrote (1994:40), "The new family model seems almost as firmly grounded in gender divisions as the old family model . . . The world of paid work is still primarily organized around the assumption of the male worker." For one thing, "Woman-friendly family work life coexists with sex segregation, a gendered wage gap, the concentration of women in low wage, low status jobs, and the same exclusions and invisibilities that women suffer in work organizations in the United States" (Acker, 1994:39).

7   As Acker's study found, most women are in part-time jobs and more than half of Swedish women were in just twelve occupations—most low-level service jobs. And as in other industrial nations, the top administrative posts are still dominated by men—with women occupying only 5 percent of upper management positions. Similarly, white collar women earn only about 75 percent of their male counterparts, and Swedish women continue to bear a disproportionate share of child care and other domestic duties. Full-time employed mothers had a 73-hour work week, 34 of these hours at home; the men's work week totaled 60 hours, about 41 hours in the workplace and 19 hours on domestic chores (Acker, 1994).

8   Despite these deficiencies, Acker insists that the way Swedish women combine family and employment is far superior to the situations in most other countries. Nevertheless, Swedish women are fully aware that pro-family legislation and benefits can be erased by global competition, economic recessions, downsizing, and high unemployment. As Acker (1994:48) noted:

9   In response, some Swedish women [are] organizing within political parties and unions, as well as outside traditional organizations, to save welfare state programs and to reverse the decline of political power . . . These women warn that they will form a new women's

party if the old parties do not actively work for women's interests. While the outcome is still unclear, the centrality of gender conflicts in welfare state politics is escalating in Sweden [as it is in the rest of the world].

THOMPSON AND HICKEY, *Society in Focus*

Based on context clues, word part clues, and if necessary the dictionary, write the definitions of the italicized words in the following sentences from the reading.

1. And to a lesser degree, it has sought to eliminate gender *inequality* and laws and customs that reinforce women's secondary place in society. (par. 1)

   inequality = difference in value or treatment

2. To smooth the *transition* of women into the workforce, the Swedish government dramatically expanded welfare state services and new jobs—especially in a new sector called "caring work." (par. 3)

   transition - State of change

3. The *typical* Swedish family today consists of two working parents, with the majority of women working part-time (67 percent of those with children) and more than 90 percent of men working full-time. (par. 5)

   typical - representing the most common form

4. Additionally all families are *entitled* to a basic child allowance per year of around $900, as well as a housing allowance that is based on income and number of children in the family. (par. 5)

   entitled - eligible for

5. For one thing, "Woman-friendly family work life coexists with sex segregation, a *gendered* wage gap, the concentration of women in low wage, low status jobs, and the same exclusions and invisibilities that women suffer in work organizations in the United States." (par. 6)

   gendered - based on the sex of individuals

Write *true* or *false* before each of the following statements about the reading.

   __T__ 6. For the past century Swedish government and social groups have worked to support family life and working women.

___T___ 7. Today the majority of Swedish women and men with children work outside the home.

___F___ 8. All Swedish families are entitled to a child allowance of around $9,000 per year.

___F___ 9. Swedish women are satisfied with their current status and do not need to seek additional changes.

___T___ 10. Acker, the source of the information in the reading, insists that Swedish women are much better off than women in most countries.

___T___ 11. Sweden has a benefit package for all families regardless of class or income.

___F___ 12. The job sector called "caring work" was devised to ensure that all Swedish men could find employment.

Choose the best way to complete the following statements based on the reading.

13. The main idea of the reading is
    a. American women have a better situation than Swedish women.
    b. Sweden has made considerable advances in pro-family issues, but it still has some work to do.
    c. Sweden is an outstanding model for women's and family issues and should be emulated all over the world.

14. Paragraph 2 is primarily organized by
    a. examples.
    b. chronological order.
    c. definition.

15. Paragraph 3 is organized by
    a. examples.
    b. chronological order.
    c. definition.

16. Paragraph 5 is primarily organized by
    a. examples.
    b. chronological order.
    c. definition.

17. Paragraph 6 is primarily organized by
    a. examples.
    b. classification.
    c. definition.

Write short answers to the following questions based on your reading, your experience, and your observation.

opinion 18. Acker believes that Sweden has created a model family and women's work environment. Do you agree or disagree? Why?

_____

_____

_____

Ex! 19. What U.S. government policies and programs exist now to help families?

Welfare; Food Stamps; Work Force Iniciative; etc.

_____

opinion 20. Make three suggestions for improving family and women's work policies in the United States.

1. _____

2. _____

3. _____

Chapter 8

Complex Patterns of Organization

The Family in the Community

The healthy family knows how to talk—and how to listen.

—*Curran*

- What are the father and son in the picture doing? What kind of relationship do you think they have?

- What does the quotation mean?

Getting Ready to Read

In Chapter 7 you read about some historical aspects of family life and various definitions of what a family is around the world. In this chapter you will read about families and child rearing in the United States today, the challenges of family life, and what makes a successful family. How do Americans of various cultures raise their children today? Are single parent families becoming more prevalent? Does it, as Hillary Clinton writes, take a village to raise a child? As you read about these issues, you will improve your reading skills by learning how to

- recognize complex, or paired, patterns of organization, including comparison and contrast, and cause and effect
- recognize transitional words and phrases in sentences, between sentences, and between paragraphs that can help you identify patterns of organization
- organize what you have read using patterns of organization

READING 1

It Takes a Village   Hillary Rodham Clinton

In her book It Takes a Village and Other Lessons Children Teach Us, *Hillary Rodham Clinton puts forth her ideas about the condition of American children and families today. She also makes many suggestions for what we can do to help strengthen families in our society. As you read, look for the main idea of the whole passage. How is it developed?*

bear Have

1   Parents bear the first and primary responsibility for their sons and daughters—to feed them, to sing them to sleep, to teach them to ride a bike, to encourage their talents, to help them develop spiritual lives, to make countless daily decisions that determine whom they have the potential to become. I was blessed with a hardworking father who put his family first and a mother who was devoted to me and my two younger brothers. But I was also blessed with caring neighbors, attentive doctors, challenging public schools, safe streets, and an economy that supported my father's job. Much of my family's good fortune was beyond my parents' direct control, but not beyond the control of other adults whose actions affected my life.

2   Children exist in the world as well as in the family. From the moment they are born, they depend on a host of other "grown-ups"—grandparents, neighbors, teachers, ministers, employers, political leaders, and untold others who touch their lives directly and indirectly. Adults police their streets, monitor the quality of their food, air, and water, produce the programs that appear on their televisions, run the businesses that employ their parents,

Copyright © August 5, 1995, Baby Blues Partnership. Reprinted with special permission of King Feature Syndicate.

and write the laws that protect them. Each of us plays a part in every child's life: It takes a village to raise a child. . . .

sage Wise person

3   The sage who first offered that proverb would undoubtedly be bewildered by what constitutes the modern village. In earlier times and places—and until recently in our own culture—the "village" meant an actual geographic place where individuals and families lived and worked together. To many people the word still conjures up a road sign that reads, "Hometown U.S.A., pop. 5,340," followed by emblems of the local churches and civic clubs.

fragmented Divided into separate pieces

4   For most of us, though, the village doesn't look like that anymore. In fact, it's difficult to paint a picture of the modern village, so frantic and fragmented has much of our culture become. Extended families rarely live in the same town, let alone the same house. In many communities, crime and fear keep us behind locked doors. Where we used to chat with neighbors on stoops and porches, now we watch videos in our darkened living rooms. Instead of strolling down Main Street, we spend hours in automobiles and at anonymous shopping malls. We don't join civic associations, churches, unions, political parties, or even bowling leagues the way we used to.

5   The horizons of the contemporary village extend well beyond the town line. From the moment we are born, we are exposed to vast numbers of other people and influences through radio, television, newspapers, books, movies, computers, compact discs, cellular phones, and fax machines. Technology connects us to the impersonal global village it has created.

refuge Safe place to hide

6   To many, this brave new world seems dehumanizing and inhospitable. It is not surprising, then, that there is a yearning for the "good old days" as a refuge from the problems of the present. But by turning away, we blind ourselves to the continuing, evolving presence of the village in our lives, and its critical importance for how we live together. The village can no longer be defined as a place on a map, or a list of people or organizations, but its essence remains the same: it is the network of values and relationships that support and affect our lives.

CLINTON, *It Takes a Village*

| Exercise 1 | **Recall and Discuss** |

Answer these questions about Reading 1, and prepare to discuss them in class.

1. In your own words, what is the main idea of this reading from Clinton's book?

   _____

   _____

   _____

2. Who was involved in raising you (mother? father? aunts? uncles? churches? social groups? Boy Scouts? 4-H clubs?)?

   _____

   _____

   _____

3. Do you think that you had a strong "network of values and relationships" that supported you and that continue to support you?

   _____

   _____

   _____

4. Do you agree with Clinton's idea that "it takes a village to raise a child"? Explain why or why not.

   _____

   _____

   _____

Paired Patterns of Organization

In Chapter 7 you learned to recognize and analyze examples, chronological order, definition, and classification as patterns of organization. You also noticed that some of these patterns are mixed in the paragraphs you read. In Chapter 8, you will become familiar with paired, or complex, patterns of organization: (1) comparison and contrast, and (2) cause and effect. What makes these patterns complex is the pairing of two different ideas.

Comparison and Contrast

comparison and
contrast
Statements that
answer the question,
"How are two things
alike or different?"

Comparison and contrast is a common paired pattern of organization. It answers the question, "How are two things alike or different?" To see how this pattern works, read the following excerpt, which compares how families use the television and other media. In the first paragraph you will notice two very different approaches to television use. This paragraph emphasizes the *contrast* between them. The second paragraph emphasizes the *similarities* of entertainment choices that families make.

In the United States today, families basically have two contrasting attitudes toward television. Many families allow the television to be on at any time of the day or night. Very often, members of these families watch television alone or don't interact with other family members while they are watching. The TV is used to have some kind of background noise in the house, or as a kind of electronic babysitter. Parents often turn it on to entertain "bored" children. In contrast, other families strictly control when the television will be watched and what programs can be watched. Often these families watch programs together and discuss them together. In these homes, the TV is rarely on if nobody is watching it. Instead of using it as an electronic babysitter, parents insist that children read or play actively rather than sit in front of a screen.

Regardless of their contrasting attitudes toward television viewing, families in America are choosing television and other passive activities, such as movie viewing, video games, and surfing the Web with unprecedented regularity. These activities are similar in their inactivity. Family members—young and old—watch rather than do. These passive forms of entertainment dull, rather than encourage, family interaction and community involvement.

The main idea of the first paragraph, expressed in the first sentence, clearly sets up the comparison/contrast pattern of organization.

> In the United States today, families basically have two contrasting attitudes toward television.

The phrase "two contrasting attitudes" tells us that the two types of attitudes are different from each other. Then the paragraph goes on to present different behaviors for each attitude toward television. Families with the first type of attitude

- allow the television to be on at any time of the day or night
- watch television alone or don't interact with other family members while they arc watching

- use the television for background noise
- use the television as an electronic babysitter

Families with the second type of attitude

- strictly control when the television will be watched and what will be watched
- watch programs together and discuss them
- do not leave the television on if nobody is watching
- do not use it as a babysitter, but insist that children read or play actively

The second paragraph introduces other forms of family entertainment—movies, video games, and the Web—describing them as similar. Like television viewing, these activities are passive.

In Sentences

Writers can use comparison and contrast in sentences to tell the reader both differences and similarities. For example, a writer might explain the *similarities* in two families' TV habits as follows:

> *Both* families enjoyed spending time together on Sunday afternoons watching football or baseball games on television.

In this sentence "both" indicates that the two families have been compared and that they have something in common—their TV habits.

On the other hand, a writer might explain the *differences* between two families' TV habits.

> My family left the television on all evening, whether anyone was watching or not, *but* I noticed my best friend's family turned the television on only for special programs on PBS or the Discovery Channel.

In this sentence, two different TV habits are presented: the writer's family and her friend's family. The word "but" is a signal that a contrast is coming.

Transitions and Other Words for Comparisons   Watch for clues that can help you recognize comparisons or contrasts in sentences or longer passages. Some are transitions, which, as you learned in Chapter 7, are words that link ideas.

Comparisons use words like the following: ~~similiary~~

- also
- both
- similarly
- alike
- as (the same as, as big as, as small as)

- same
- in comparison
- similar to

Transitions and Other Words for Contrasts   Transitions can also signal that the relationship between two words is a contrast.

Contrasts use words and phrases like the following:

- but
- yet
- although
- while
- instead of
- in contrast
- on the other hand
- however
- different from
- than (more than, less than, happier than)

In Paragraphs

In paragraphs, a writer can develop a number of points of comparison or contrast, all supporting one main idea. Consider all of the different kinds of things that are being compared and contrasted in the following paragraph, which describes two types of families, the slave family and the plantation master's family.

While slave parents who were able to spend time with their children loved them as much as the plantation masters loved their children, the slave family was as different from the master's family as anyone can possibly imagine. Of course, the master's family was well-fed, well-dressed, and lived in beautiful homes. In contrast, the slave families lived on an absolute minimum of food, were often provided one set of clothes for a year, and lived in shacks. The master's children were waited on hand and foot by slave mothers, whose own children had no one to tend to them. The chances were that the master's family was a nuclear family, which lived together until the children grew up and started their own families. In contrast, the slave family could be broken up at any time by the sale of the father, mother, or children.

The main idea of this paragraph appears in the second half of the first sentence:

The slave family was as different from the master's family as anyone can possibly imagine.

The author does recognize that there is one similarity between the families when she states that "slave parents who were able to spend time with their children loved them as much as the masters loved their children." However, if we look carefully at the rest of the paragraph, we can see that all the supporting details involve ways that these families are *different*. The emphasis, then, is on the *contrast* between the two types of families. For example, the master's family was

- well-fed
- well-dressed
- lived in beautiful homes

In contrast, the slave families

- lived on an absolute minimum of food
- were often provided one set of clothes for a year
- lived in shacks

The author continues to give examples of contrasts throughout the rest of the paragraph. When you look closely at this passage, you find the clue words "different from," "in contrast," and "while."

| Exercise 2 | ## Understand Comparison and Contrast |

The following excerpts all contain comparisons and/or contrasts. Read each one and then answer the questions that follow. The first one has been done for you.

1. We know much more now than we did even a few years ago about how the human brain develops and what children need from their environments to develop character, empathy, and intelligence. (Clinton, *It Takes a Village*)

   List the two things being compared:
   a. *what we know now about the human brain and children's needs*

   compared to
   b. *what we knew a few years ago about these topics.*

2. It is less respectable in Hispanic culture for a married woman to work outside the home than in either African-American or non-Hispanic white culture. (Wolf, *Marriages and Families in a Diverse Society*)

   The attitude toward married women working outside the home is being compared in
   a. *Hispanic Culture*

   to
   b. *neither A-A or Non H.*

3. Compared to families with young children, families with adolescents have been neglected. Even for the affluent sector, little work has been done on strengthening support networks for families during the stress of the great transition from childhood to adulthood. Still less attention has gone into strengthening networks for families who live in poverty or culturally different situations. Although adolescents are moving toward independence, they are still intimately bound up with the family, which is much more important to them than is evident. This is especially true in early adolescence. For that reason, we need to pay attention to the ways in which family relationships can be utilized to help adolescents weather the conditions of contemporary life. (Hamburg, "American Family Transformed")

This paragraph wants readers to focus on the needs of

a. families with ___*adolescent*___

rather than

b. families with ___*young children*___

In the middle of the paragraph, the author points out a contrast about adolescents.

a. adolescents ___*to money*___

but

b. ___*the move of the family.*___

HW: 377

Organize to Learn: Make a Chart

A useful way to check your comprehension after you've read a comparison and contrast paragraph or longer passage is to make a chart of the information presented. Follow these simple steps:

1. Determine the main idea.
2. Decide what is being compared or contrasted.
3. Put the names of what are being compared or contrasted on the top of two columns.
4. Determine the points on which the items are being compared.
5. List the likenesses and differences for each point under the correct columns.

Read the following paragraph about two different types of marriage systems.

The modern system of marriage agreements is now practiced by most people in most parts of the world, but a more traditional system is still

continued

used in some places. In the modern system, each person—the man and the woman—willingly agrees to marry. Usually in this system, the man proposes to the woman, and if she accepts, they inform their parents of their engagement and hope for their parents' support. In traditional systems, on the other hand—especially in Asia—it was not necessary for the woman to agree to marry. Usually the prospective husband or his family made the marriage arrangement with the prospective bride's father or parents.

Looking carefully at what is being compared or contrasted, we can identify *marriage systems* or *marriage agreements,* and we can identify the first sentence as the main idea:

> Main idea: The modern system of marriage agreements is now practiced by most people in most parts of the world, but a more traditional system is still used in some places.

Now we are ready to set up the chart with the points of similarities or differences. (In this case, of course, differences are emphasized.)

Marriage Systems Contrasted

Modern

- The man and the woman must agree to marry each other.
- The man proposes, and if the woman accepts, they tell the families.

Traditional (Especially in Asia)

- It was not necessary for the woman to agree.
- The man or his family made arrangements with the prospective bride's father.

| Exercise 3 | ## Make Charts |

Read the following two excerpts. The first compares and contrasts some of the experiences of children in two-parent versus single-parent families. The emphasis is on single-parent families; the comparison with two-parent families is sometimes implied rather than directly stated. As you read this excerpt, watch for the different points of comparison so that you can complete the accompanying chart. Then read the second excerpt, and complete the chart provided for that.

1. The family change perspective sees positive signs as well as drawbacks in one-parent families. One-parent families grant children more autonomy than two-parent families. That is, they allow children to make more decisions and have more control over their lives. This autonomy can have negative consequences when a teenager decides to put activities with peers ahead of studying. However, one-parent families also require responsibility for household chores from children of all ages. Children in one-parent families perform more housework than children in two-parent families. It has been suggested that single parents make an unspoken trade-off in which personal autonomy is granted in return for

help in running the household. Moreover, children in one-parent families tend to be more androgynous than children in two-parent families, in that they learn aspects of both traditional male and traditional female roles. Boys often learn to cook, and it is not unusual for teenage girls to work on Saturdays to earn spending money. These characteristics—household responsibility and androgyny—which one-parent families tend to foster in children, can be viewed as positive adaptations to new circumstances. (Wolf, *Marriages and Families in a Diverse Society*)

One-Parent Families versus Two-Parent Families

One-Parent Families	Two-Parent Families
Children have more autonomy - make more decisions (which is sometimes a problem).	Children make fewer decisions for themselves.
	Children have fewer household responsibilities.
Children are more "androgynous" - learn both traditional male and female roles (e.g., boys cook).	
	Missing some of the positive things that single-parent families have.

2. While slave parents who were able to spend time with their children loved them as much as the plantation masters loved their children, the slave family was as different from the master's family as anyone can possibly imagine. Of course, the master's family was well-fed, well-dressed, and lived in beautiful homes. In contrast, the slave families lived on an absolute minimum of food, were often provided one set of clothes for a year, and lived in shacks. The master's children were waited on hand and foot by slave mothers, whose own children had no one to tend to them. The chances were that the master's family was a nuclear family, which lived together until the children grew up and started their own families. In contrast, the slave family could be broken up at any time by the sale of the father, mother, or children.

Title _____

Slaves' families	Masters' families

Cause and Effect

cause and effect
Statements that answer why something is and explain results

Cause and effect statements answer two types of related questions. Causes answer *why* something is the way it is, or, "What happened to make something the way it is?" Effects usually explain the *results* of some action. They answer the question, "What were the consequences of something that happened?"

In Sentences

A single sentence may use either cause or effect or both. For example, a writer might say:

> The high rate of divorce today is caused by a lack of family values.

This writer is trying to explain *why* divorce rates are so high. He might go on to say:

> These high divorce rates have obvious negative effects on young people's attitudes toward marriage.

In this second sentence the writer is focusing on one of the *results* of divorce. Since cause and effect are such closely related ways of thinking about things, they may be combined in the same sentence or certainly in the same paragraph. For example, both cause and effect appear in the following:

> The high rate of divorce today is caused by a lack of family values, and it has obvious negative effects on the attitudes of young people toward marriage.

Word Clues for Causes   Watch for the following word clues that help you recognize cause statements in sentences or longer passages:

- because
- since
- the factors are
- is caused by
- the reason why

Some are verbs:

- contributes to
- leads to
- changes
- influences

Word Clues for Effects   *Effects* are also signaled by word clues. Some are transitions:

PO 381–386

- as a result
- therefore
- consequently
- thus
- so

In Paragraphs

Longer explanations of causes and effects may be a paragraph or more in length. Sometimes many factors contribute to one effect, and each factor needs to be examined in order to understand how a change occurs. All these factors are supporting points for the main idea of a paragraph.

For example, the main idea of a paragraph might be that there is no single reason why a couple decides to divorce; rather, many issues lead to this decision. The rest of the paragraph provides the supporting points, which are the varied reasons why people choose to divorce. Also, one cause may have many effects, and each effect needs to be explained. For example, a divorce may have many effects, including economic consequences for both partners, emotional responses of both partners, a need to change residences, and emotional responses of children.

In cause and effect paragraphs writers may also need to analyze a "chain" of interrelated causes and effects that unfold over time. Sometimes the writer will examine both immediate and underlying causes or immediate and long-range results.

| Exercise 4 |

Understand Cause and Effect

Read the following excerpt on the entry of mothers into the workplace. The author explains why women have made this choice. Then answer the questions below. Clue words have been underlined to assist you.

Another <u>factor reshaping</u> family life has been a massive influx of mothers into the work force. As late as 1940, less than 12 percent of white married women were in the work force; today the figure is nearly 60 percent and over half of all mothers of preschoolers work outside the home. The major <u>forces</u> that have <u>propelled</u> women into the work force include a rising cost of living which spurred many families to seek a second source of income; increased control over fertility through contraception and abortion, which <u>allows</u> women to work without interruption; and rising education levels, which <u>lead</u> many women to seek employment for intellectual stimulation and fulfillment. (Martin et al., *America and Its Peoples*)

1. What are three reasons (causes) why women have entered the work-force in such large numbers?

   a. _Rising cost of living_

   b. _increasing control over fertility,_

   c. _rising education level,_

2. To further explain each of the reasons for women entering the work-place, the author gives an effect of each. Fill in the accompanying chart with the causes you listed for Question 1 and the effect for each. One cause and its effect has been filled in for you.

Cause	Effect
a. _Rising cost of living_	a. Women needed to bring a second income into the family
b. _increasing control_	b. Allow women work without interruption.
c. _rising education level_	c. Make women lead to employment & intellectural.

3. Read one more cause and effect paragraph, and then write or copy the main idea and fill in the missing cause and missing effect in the chart that follows.

The status of women [in China] has been changed greatly. The marriage law promulgated in 1950 advocates equality of men and women and free-dom of marriage; marriages are no longer arranged by parents. Nurseries, kindergartens, public canteens, and homes for the aged have been widely established, gradually relieving women from family work and enabling them to participate in production. ("China," *Encyclopedia Britannica*)

---

main idea: _The marriage in china has been change in 1950._

Cause	Effect
a. _marriage law promulgated in 1950 men & wone freedon of marriage,_	a. Marriages are no longer arranged by parents
b. _Nurseries, and available care for the aged_	b. _gradually relieving women from family work & enabling them to participate in production._

Organize to Learn: Make a Concept Map

As you know, one good way to organize what you have read is to make a map of the information. These maps are sometimes called *concept maps* because they visually show the relationships among all the important ideas, or concepts, in a reading. Maps can be drawn in many sizes and shapes depending on the information being covered. For cause and effect, you probably want to indicate how the two are related. That is, you want the map to clearly show how the cause leads to the effect. This can be done by map layout, making it flow in a certain direction. The direction of flow can be emphasized with the use of arrows.

Exercise 5

Make a Concept Map

The map shown here is based on the first excerpt in Exercise 4. In this case the box on the far right is the result, and the arrows pointing to it are the three major effects of changes on women. On the far left are the causes for the effects that you identified in Question 2 of Exercise 4. Complete this concept map using your answers from Question 2 of Exercise 4.

Why Mothers Entered the Workforce

Cause		Effect		Result
Rising cost of living	→	*bring second income into family*	→	Mothers enter the workforce (1940 = 12% today = 60%)
Increasing control over fertility	→	Work without interruption	→	
Higher level of education	→	*Employment + intellectual*	→	

Exercise 6

Identify Patterns of Organization in Sentences

Decide whether each of the following sentences is primarily organized by *comparison and contrast* or *cause and effect*. Write out the clues that helped you identify the pattern of organization. The first one has been done for you, and an explanation follows.

1. As a result of their parents' inability to preserve their marriages or to marry at all, almost a quarter of U.S. kids live in single-parent households, the majority headed by females. (Black, "Single-Parent Family")

   pattern of organization: *Cause and effect*

   clues: *"As a result"*

   (This sentence is obviously organized by cause/effect because it states that single-parent homes are the result of parents' "inability to preserve their marriages or to marry at all." The phrase "as a result" at the beginning of the sentence gives us a definite clue that an effect will follow.)

2. Good families . . . share a common shortcoming—they can tell in a minute what's wrong with them, but they aren't sure what's right with them. (Curran, "What Good Families Are Doing Right")

   pattern of organization: _____

   clues: _____

3. According to Dr. Jerry M. Lewis—author of a significant work on families called *No Single Thread*—healthy spouses complement, rather than dominate, each other. (Curran, "What Good Families Are Doing Right")

   pattern of organization: _____

   clues: _____

4. If every parent spent a few minutes less a day on work-related tasks and spent that time with his or her child, children would benefit and families would be stronger.

   pattern of organization: _____

   clues: _____

Exercise 7

Identify Patterns of Organization in Paragraphs

For each of the following paragraphs, write out the main idea on the line provided. Decide whether each paragraph is primarily organized by *comparison and contrast* or *cause and effect*. Write the clues that helped you identify the pattern of organization. The first one has been done for you, and an explanation follows.

1. The increase in divorce has contributed to the feminization of poverty, the growing impoverishment of women and their children. Female-

headed families represent one-fourth of all families with children, yet they constitute over half (54 percent) of all poor families with children. Divorce often results in sharp downward social mobility for women with children. The poverty rate among single-mother families runs 45 percent, compared to a 6 percent poverty rate for two-parent families and an 18 percent poverty rate for single-father families. Although single-father families are less likely to live in poverty than single-mother families, the economic plight of all impoverished single parents and their children is a cause for concern. (Wolf, *Marriages and Families in a Diverse Society*)

main idea: *"The increase in divorce has contributed to the feminization of poverty, the growing impoverishment of women and their children."*

pattern of organization: *Cause and effect*

clues: *"Has contributed to," "results in"*

(The primary pattern of organization is cause and effect because the author's main purpose is to look at one result of increased divorce rates: poverty, particularly for women and children. Clues include "contributed to" in the first sentence and "results in" in sentence 3. Most of the rest of the paragraph gives statistics to show just how severe the problem of poverty is for divorced women and their children. Don't be misled by the comparison in the last sentence, introduced by "although"; this point is more of an afterthought than the main focus of the paragraph. Remember, as you learned in Chapter 7, patterns of organization are commonly mixed.)

2. The family is the first environment where an individual encounters drug use. Parents who smoke, drink alcohol, or use other drugs, will affect the formation and development of their children, even before they are conceived or born. Studies have found that the father's exposure to harmful substances at work, smoking cigarettes, drinking alcohol and using other drugs may contribute to low birth weight and other malformations in the baby. Young women, especially of low socioeconomic status, who abuse drugs and alcohol tend to be malnourished and lack access to prenatal health care—factors which can contribute to later fetal malformations during pregnancy. Families can also be gravely damaged or destroyed by excessive use of psychoactive substances by family members. The damage can result from the immediate effects of drug use, such as violence associated with intoxication, or from long-term effects, such as economic problems, discord and breakdown in communication resulting from drug dependence and impaired health. (Hsu, "Drug Use and the Family")

main idea: _____

_____

pattern of organization: _____

clues: _____

3. In American society, life in many families is organized primarily around the *nuclear family.* A nuclear family is made up of parents and their children and spans only two generations. In contrast, traditional societies consider the *extended family* to be of primary importance. The extended family includes those kin who extend outward from the nuclear family, such as grandparents, aunts, and uncles. Extended kin relationships have always been central in immigrant families which are coping with a new environment, but have diminished in importance among white middle-class families. However, today, extended kin relationships are once more growing in importance. Families are increasingly likely to provide housing to extended kin who have fallen on financial hard times. One-third of African-American families and one-fourth of white families include other adults in the household. Most often this other adult is a relative. (Wolf, *Marriages and Families in a Diverse Society*)

main idea: _____

_____

pattern of organization: _____

clues: _____

4. Most women in the labor force work primarily because the family needs the money and secondarily for their own personal self-actualization. Because of the decline in real family income from 1973 to 1988, most families find it essential for both parents to work to support them at a level that used to be achieved by one wage-earner, and in many families two earners are required to keep the family out of poverty. Most divorced, single, and widowed mothers must work to avoid poverty. (Scarr, Phillips, and McCartney, "Working Mothers and Their Families")

main idea: _____

_____

pattern of organization: _____

clues: _____

Summary Chart: *Patterns of Organization*

Pattern of Organization	Characteristics	Transitions and Other Clues
Examples	Gives instances or examples	*Transitions:* "such as," "for example," "for instance," "in addition," "moreover." *Other clues:* commas separate examples; when examples are listed, they are sometimes signaled by numbers or bullets.
Chronological order	Organizes information by time	*Transitions:* "then," "when," "after," "before," "later," "while." *Other clues:* dates (1942, October, etc.).
Definition	Answers the question, "What is it?" or "What does it mean?"	*Word clues:* "means," "refers to," "consists of," "is." *Other clues:* definitions are provided in parentheses between dashes, or between commas immediately after the term.
Classification	Answers the question, "What kinds are there?" or "What type is it?"	*Word clues:* "another type," "one form," "additional sorts."
Comparison and contrast	Answers the question, "How are two things alike or different?"	*Transitions for comparisons:* "also" "both," "similarly," "as," "same," "in comparison." *Transitions for contrasts:* "but," "yet," "although," "while," "instead of," "in contrast," "on the other hand," "however," "than."
Cause and effect	Answers the questions, "What happened to make something the way it is?" and "What were the consequences of something that happened?"	*Word clues for causes:* "because," "since," "the factors are," "is caused by," "reason why." *Word clues for effects:* "as a result," "the effects are," "therefore," "consequently"

The Single-Parent Family

Deborah Black

The following essay was written by Deborah Black, an older student who returned to college while she was raising three daughters by herself. She writes about the single-parent family and, because she is a single parent herself, she uses her own experience as an example. As you read, pay attention to the patterns of organization that Black uses.

1   As a result of their parents' inability to preserve their marriages or to marry at all, almost a quarter of U.S. kids live in single-parent households, the majority headed by females. David Blankenhorn, president of the Institute for American Values, a New York family-issues research group, says that as an expectation of childhood the experience of fatherlessness is approaching a rough parity with the experience of having a father.

parity   Equal level

2   Generally, children from single-parent families have more trouble while growing up and bear more scars than children from two-parent families. This is contrary to the longstanding opinion that children recover quickly from divorce and flourish in families of almost any shape. Sara McLanahan, a Princeton University sociologist who studies children of divorce as they enter adulthood, says, "Almost anything you can imagine not wanting to happen to your children is a consequence of divorce" (Magnet 44).

flourish   Do well

3   Children in single-parent families have less than one third of the median per capita income of kids from two-parent families. Seventy-five percent of single-parent children will sink into poverty before they reach eighteen years of age, versus 20% of the kids from two-parent families. Had family breakdown not deprived many families of a male breadwinner, the child poverty rate would have declined in the 80's.

deprived   Taken away

4   Growing up in a single-parent family marks not only the child's external economic circumstances, but also his or her psyche. A study from the National Center of Health Statistics has found that children from single-parent homes were 100 to 200% more likely than those from intact families to have emotional and behavioral problems and 50% more likely to have learning disabilities.

5   Judith Wallerstein, co-author of *Second Chances: Men, Women & Children a Decade after Divorce,* made some startling discoveries in her fifteen-year study of children of divorce. She was alarmed by the magnitude of pain and fear expressed by the children when their parents divorced. She believed these wounds would not heal and could be harmful years later.

magnitude   Quantity

6   Males in the study, even those who were bright, had difficulty learning and behaving well after divorce. Female children did much better, even better than girls from intact families. But Wallerstein found the girls' success tended to be "fragile." Says she: "These girls were on super behavior, con-

sciously trying to be good little girls at a high inner cost" (Magnet 44). By young adulthood males and females were having equal difficulty forming loving, intimate relationships.

7   Can the single parent provide a positive role model for male and female children? Joseph White in his book *The Psychology of Blacks: An Afro-American Perspective* tells us that the single parent can provide a positive role model for his or her children. He cites examples of black single-parent families who have used the extended family to help rear children who are fatherless or motherless. This extended family provides a safety net for these children of divorce and poverty. White feels that going to workshops, discussion groups, and community forums can help the single parent cope with his or her dual roles and responsibilities.

dual Double

8   The welfare system has a new program that is a valuable resource in providing troubled families with a chance for a better future. Project Independence is a program that gives a single parent an opportunity to further his or her education, thus enabling the parent to get not just a job but a career that will allow him or her to adequately provide for the family. This program provides child care, transportation, remediation, and financial aid. Additionally, single parents in this program receive food stamps, Medicaid, and a welfare check. The people who run this program are caring, dedicated individuals who encourage participants to set realistic goals and then help them to achieve these goals.

9   Being in this program has brought many changes in my life. After my divorce, I was alone, confused, and scared. I was undereducated and had no job skills that would make me marketable for employment. Like many people I thought that going on welfare was like admitting defeat. This program eliminated this viewpoint and gave me the opportunity to start a new life.

10   Can I be both mother and father to my three girls? The answer is yes. Though I never would have chosen this path, it is the one I have to travel. Much of the time I feel like I am experiencing multiple personalities: mother, father, and college student. One of the most important things to me is to be a good role model for my children. Every day they see me studying, working, and trying to get ahead. I also try to teach them how to be self-sufficient, how to cope with life's difficulties, and how to keep the lines of communication open between us.

11   The support systems that a parent enlists can help him or her to be a successful parent. Project Independence, Success at 6, Head Start, and Families First are important programs that can help struggling families in America. The success of future generations depends on our collective willingness to recognize the problems and support the solutions to them.

BLACK, "Single-Parent Family"

| Exercise 8 | **Check Your Understanding** |

Based on Reading 2, choose the best answers to the following questions.

1. What is the best main idea sentence for the reading?
   a. Almost a quarter of U.S. kids live in single-parent households, the majority headed by females.
   b. Even though raising a family as a single parent can be difficult, it can be done well if these parents have good support systems.
   c. Generally, children from single-parent families have more trouble while growing up and bear more scars than children from two-parent families.

2. Which of the following is *not* a problem that children necessarily have in single-parent families?
   a. Single-parent children are generally poorer.
   b. Single-parent children usually have bad parents.
   c. Single-parent children cannot find support in the extended family.

3. What surprised Wallerstein in her study on divorce? (Choose one.)
   a. Parents were less affected by divorce than children.
   b. Children experienced a great deal of pain and fear as a result of divorce.
   c. Wounds inflicted by divorce healed quickly in children.

4. Which of the following is *not* provided by Project Independence?
   a. child care
   b. education for single parents
   c. tutoring for the children

5. Why does Black feel she is a successful parent?
   a. Because she is a good role model for her children.
   b. Because her children are very dependent on her.
   c. Because her divorce improved her life.

| Exercise 9 | **Identify Patterns of Organization** |

Identify the primary pattern of organization (*cause and effect, chronological order, examples, classification, comparison and contrast,* or *definition*) and the main idea for the paragraphs from Reading 2. Write the main idea in a complete sentence.

1. Paragraph 2

   pattern of organization: _____

   main idea: _____

   _____

2. Paragraph 4

pattern of organization: _____

main idea: _____

_____

3. Paragraph 7

pattern of organization: _____

main idea: _____

_____

4. Paragraph 8

pattern of organization: _____

main idea: _____

_____

5. Paragraph 9

pattern of organization: _____

main idea: _____

_____

| Exercise 10 | **Make Connections: Collaborative Activity** |

Write short answers to the following questions based on Reading 2, your experience, and your observations. Then, to extend the exercise, discuss your answers with your class group. Working together, prepare a report for your class as a whole or a written summary for your instructor.

1. How can parents ease the pain of divorce for their children?

_____

_____

_____

2. What are some other things that single parents can do to make their family lives easier and to help them do a good job of raising their children?

_____

_____

_____

LANGUAGE TIP

Subordination

Sentences with comparison and contrast organization or cause and effect organization often use subordination within the sentence. *Subordination* is a way to combine two unequal ideas. Sentences with subordination have an independent clause and a dependent clause. As a reader, it is important for you to recognize the independent clause because it is usually the most important idea in the sentence. Remember, the *independent clause* can stand alone as a sentence; the *dependent clause* cannot. That's why it's called "dependent"; it is subordinate and it needs to be with the other part of the sentence.

The dependent clause begins with a subordinating conjunction, such as

- although
- even though
- since
- while
- whereas
- because

You will recognize some of these subordinating conjunctions as "clue" words for identifying patterns of organization.

For example, the word "although" in the following sentence is a subordinating conjunction beginning a dependent clause, and it also signals to the reader that this sentence is organized as a comparison and contrast.

> Although single-father families are less likely to live in poverty than single-mother families, the economic plight of all impoverished single parents and their children is a cause for concern. (Wolf, *Marriages and Families in a Diverse Society*)

The most important statement in this sentence is that "the economic plight of all impoverished single parents and their children is a cause for concern." The idea that follows the word "Although" ("single-father families are less likely to live in poverty than single-mother families") is not as important and therefore is presented as a dependent clause. It is not a complete thought by itself; it needs the rest of the sentence to complete the idea.

Subordinating conjunctions are especially helpful in explaining cause and effect relationships. "Because" and "since" are frequently used to begin dependent clauses. For example, in the following sentence the author of a marriage and family text explains why it will include the experiences of various ethnic and racial groups.

> Because family experiences of racial and ethnic groups vary, an examination of families in the United States would not be complete without taking into account ethnic and racial variation. (Wolf, *Marriages and Families in a Diverse Society*)

The first part of the sentence—"Because family experiences of racial and ethnic groups vary"—is a dependent clause. The sentence is not complete until the result is added in the independent clause that finishes the sentence.

continued

Dependent clauses can be found at the beginning or at the end of a sentence. In the following example, "because" begins the dependent clause in the middle of the sentence.

Most women in the labor force work primarily because the family needs the money. (Skolnick and Skolnick, *Family in Transition*)

In this case, the effect is given in the independent clause—"Most women in the labor force work"—and the reason why women work is given in the dependent clause at the end of the sentence. A similar sentence could be written with the dependent clause at the beginning.

Because families need money, most women work.

Exercise 11   **Check Subordination**

Underline the subordinating conjunction and the dependent clause in each of the following sentences. Then, circle the independent clause (the most important clause). The first one has been done for you.

1. Although stepfamilies experience a good deal of stress as family members adjust to new roles in the family, most couples who re-marry report that they are satisfied with their marriages.

2. Because women were able to decide when to have children, it became easier for them to work without interruptions.

3. Children can have a hard time adjusting to their parents' divorce even though children between ages 6 and 12 are generally flexible.

4. While children are taken care of by many adults in extended families, children in nuclear families must depend on only their parents.

5. Women have been forced to enter the workforce because men frequently do not earn enough money to support a family.

READING 3

Families and Diversity

William E. Thompson and Joseph V. Hickey

The following reading considers diverse families in America today. It examines the challenges they face and the results of their efforts. As you read, notice how the different patterns of organization are used to present the authors' ideas.

Minority Families

1   Minority families—some by choice and others in response to discrimination and out of economic necessity—contribute to family diversity . . . While myths abound that all minority families are extended families with strong social support networks, ethnicity, race, class, and gender contribute to considerable diversity among minority families (Roschelle, 1997).

2   Certainly, severe poverty influences minority families. For example, nearly one-third of all African Americans and Latinos live in poverty, and female-headed families represent almost three-quarters of all poor African-American families. And more than 60 percent of African-American children, in female-headed families, are currently classified by the government as poor (Danzinger and Gottshalk, 1995; Lichter, 1997; Roschelle, 1997).

3   Sharp declines in inner-city employment and cuts in government assistance to struggling families have taken an especially heavy toll on African-American and Latino families and have contributed to declining marriage rates, rising divorce rates, and a much greater number of female-headed households. Some of these trends have reinforced long-term pragmatic attitudes about the family among some minority groups. For example, instead of the traditional middle-class emphasis on the nuclear family and husband-wife relationships, many African-American families cope with scarcity and discrimination by seeking the assistance of extended families and fictive kin (close friends), as well as through flexible social networks (McAdoo, 1998).

4   Increasingly, African-American and some Latino families place more emphasis on childrearing than on marriage. As a consequence, more than 50 percent of all African-American women who head families have never married, and African-American mothers tend to be younger than their white counterparts (Taylor, 1990; Dickerson, 1995).

5   At first glance, two-parent African-American families, whose median adjusted incomes have grown relative to those of white families from 44 percent in 1949 to over 70 percent by the early 1990s, may appear to be like white middle-class families. But these families, accounting for almost half of all African-American families, provide much more progressive and flexible models of family life than the white majority. Of all families, they are the most egalitarian, with complementary and flexible family roles that allow for much greater participation of husbands in domestic and child-care responsibilities than is characteristic of most white families (Taylor, 1994).

6   Many African-American families also have stronger kin support systems—with many three-generation extended family households. Likewise, grandparents also may play greater roles in child care than they do in most white middle-class families. Because of economic marginalization and discrimination as well as cultural traditions, many Latino and Asian-American groups also emphasize extended families. During the past few decades,

many groups from around the world have used extended family networks and "circular migrations" to relocate from developing to developed countries, as well as to shift from rural to urban areas. But many remain anchored to kin in their home countries (Haberstein, 1998).

7   The strong emphasis on family is called familism, or a strong attachment and commitment to family and kin, which characterizes the attitudes of many Latino groups toward family life. This is especially true of recent immigrants from Central and South America who make great efforts to keep in touch with kin, including sending much of their pay to support relatives in their home communities (Ortiz, 1995; Vega,1995; Bacerra, 1998; McAdoo, 1998).

8   Despite powerful stereotypes of close-knit, "multi-generational" Asian-American families, there is considerable variation among Asian-American groups. Many recent immigrants from war-torn southeast Asia do indeed stress extended family networks, and some groups are strongly patriarchal. Many other Asian-American families who have been in the United States for generations, however, live in nuclear families and maintain kin ties that differ little from those of white middle-class Americans. On the surface, this is also true of many wealthy transplants and professionals from Hong Kong, Singapore, and other parts of Asia. Most of these families, however, maintain strong ties to widely dispersed kin throughout the Pacific, which may include regular family visitations and gifts, loans, and joint business ventures with relatives that most middle-class Americans would consider to be "distant kin" (Gelles, 1995; Wong, 1998).

Gay and Lesbian Families

9   One family type that has received little recognition until recently is the gay and lesbian family. By the mid-1990s, more than 1.5 million homosexual and lesbian couples lived together in stable and committed relationships, which a growing number of people recognize as "families." Philip Blumstein and Pepper Schwartz's (1983) research on American couples found that same-sex couples faced domestic concerns quite similar to those of their heterosexual counterparts—and they solved them in much the same ways.

THOMPSON AND HICKEY, *Society in Focus*

Exercise 12   ## Work with Words

Use context clues, word part clues, and if necessary the dictionary to choose the best definitions of the words that are italicized in the following sentences from Reading 3.

   1. For example, instead of the traditional middle-class emphasis on the *nuclear family* and husband-wife relationships, many African-American families cope with scarcity and discrimination by seeking

the assistance of extended families and *fictive kin* (close friends), as well as through flexible social networks. (par. 3).

nuclear family
a. husband, wife, and children only
b. husband, wife, and grandparents only
c. husband and wife only

fictive kin
a. made-up family members
b. close friends
c. African-American families

2. Of all families, they are the most *egalitarian,* with complementary and flexible family roles that allow for much greater participation of husbands in domestic and child-care responsibilities than is characteristic of most white families. (par. 5)

egalitarian
a. domestic
b. interested in equality
c. responsible

3. Many recent immigrants from war-torn southeast Asia do indeed stress extended family networks, and some groups are strongly *patriarchal.* (par. 8)

patriarchal
a. dedicated to their country
b. dominated by father
c. interested in networks

Exercise 13

Check Your Understanding

Answer the following questions about Reading 3.

1. In your own words, what is the main idea of this reading?

   _____

   _____

   _____

2. What are three challenges that diverse families encounter?

   a. _____

   b. _____

   c. _____

3. What are two ways diverse families respond to the challenges they face?

a. _____

b. _____

Exercise 14   ## Identify Patterns of Organization

Choose the best way to complete the following statements about Reading 3.

1. Paragraph 2 is organized primarily by
   a. definition.
   b. examples.
   c. cause and effect.

2. Paragraph 4 is organized primarily by
   a. cause and effect.
   b. comparison.
   c. definition.

3. Paragraph 5 is organized primarily by
   a. cause and effect.
   b. comparison and contrast.
   c. examples.

4. Paragraph 7 is organized primarily by
   a. cause and effect.
   b. definition.
   c. comparison and contrast.

5. Paragraph 8 is organized primarily by
   a. definition.
   b. cause and effect.
   c. comparison and contrast.

Exercise 15   ## Make Connections

Write short answers to the following questions based on Reading 3, your experience, and your observations.

1. Would you describe your family as having "familism" as defined in this reading? Explain your answer.

_____

_____

_____

2. What strengths in your family have helped it to meet challenges?

_____

_____

_____

3. Are gay and lesbian families accepted in your community? Do you think that they will be soon, if they aren't already? Explain your answer.

_____

_____

_____

| Exercise 16 |

Write a Summary

On a separate sheet of paper write a one paragraph summary of the information in Reading 3.

| READING 4 |

What Good Families Are Doing Right

Delores Curran

No matter what kind of family you have—nuclear, extended, single-parent—it is not easy to maintain a strong and healthy family today. The following reading by Delores Curran outlines some of the most important things that good families do. Probably most important is keeping lines of communication open.

1   I have worked with families for fifteen years, conducting hundreds of seminars, workshops, and classes on parenting, and I meet good families all the time. They're fairly easy to recognize. Good families have a kind of visible strength. They expect problems and work together to find solutions, applying common sense and trying new methods to meet new needs. And they share a common shortcoming—they can tell me in a minute what's wrong with them, but they aren't sure what's right with them. Many healthy families with whom I work, in fact, protest at being called *healthy.* They don't think they are. The professionals who work with them do.

2   To prepare the book on which this article is based, I asked respected workers in the fields of education, religion, health, family counseling, and voluntary organizations to identify a list of possible traits of a healthy family. Together we isolated fifty-six such traits, and I sent this list to 500 professionals who regularly work with families—teachers, doctors, principals,

members of the clergy, scout directors, YMCA leaders, family counselors, social workers—asking them to pick the fifteen qualities they most commonly found in healthy families.

3   While all of these traits are important, the one most often cited as central to close family life is communication: The healthy family knows how to talk—and how to listen.

4   "Without communication you don't know one another," wrote one family counselor. "If you don't know one another, you don't care about one another, and that's what the family is all about."

5   "The most familiar complaint I hear from wives I counsel is 'He won't talk to me' and 'He doesn't listen to me,' " said a pastoral marriage counselor. "And when I share this complaint with their husbands, they don't hear *me,* either."

6   "We have kids in classes whose families are so robotized by television that they don't know one another," said a fifth-grade teacher.

7   Professional counselors are not the only ones to recognize the need. The phenomenal growth of communication groups such as Parent Effectiveness Training, Parent Awareness, Marriage Encounter, Couple Communication, and literally hundreds of others tells us that the need for effective communication—the sharing of deepest feelings—is felt by many.

reveal To make known

8   Healthy families have also recognized this need, and they have, either instinctively or consciously, developed methods of meeting it. They know that conflicts are to be expected, that we all become angry and frustrated and discouraged. And they know how to reveal those feelings—good and bad—to each other. Honest communication isn't always easy. But when it's working well, there are certain recognizable signs or symptoms, what I call the hallmarks of the successfully communicating family.

The Family Exhibits a Strong Relationship Between the Parents

9   According to Dr. Jerry M. Lewis—author of a significant work on families, *No Single Thread*—healthy spouses complement, rather than dominate, each other. Either husband or wife could be the leader, depending on the circumstances. In the unhealthy families he studied, the dominant spouse had to hide feelings of weakness while the submissive spouse feared being put down if he or she exposed a weakness.

10   Children in the healthy family have no question about which parent is boss. Both parents are. If children are asked who is boss, they're likely to respond, "Sometimes Mom, sometimes Dad." And, in a wonderful statement, Dr. Lewis adds, "If you ask if they're comfortable with this, they look at you as if you're crazy—as if there's no other way it ought to be."

11   My survey respondents echo Dr. Lewis. One wrote, "The healthiest families I know are ones in which the mother and father have a strong, loving

relationship. This seems to flow over to the children and even beyond the home. It seems to breed security in the children and, in turn, fosters the ability to take risks, to reach out to others, to search for their own answers, become independent and develop a good self-image." . . .

The Family Listens and Responds

12 "My parents say they want me to come to them with problems, but when I do, either they're busy or they only half-listen and keep on doing what they were doing—like shaving or making a grocery list. If a friend of theirs came over to talk, they'd stop, be polite, and listen," said one of the children quoted in a *Christian Science Monitor* interview by Ann McCarroll. This child put his finger on the most difficult problem of communicating in families: the inability to listen.

13   It is usually easier to react than to respond. When we react, we reflect our own experiences and feelings; when we respond, we get into the other person's feelings. For example:

> *Tom, age seventeen:* "I don't know if I want to go to college. I don't think I'd do very well there."
>
> *Father:* "Nonsense. Of course you'll do well."

14   That's reacting. This father is cutting off communication. He's refusing either to hear the boy's fears or to consider his feelings, possibly because he can't accept the idea that his son might not attend college. Here's another way of handling the same situation:

> *Tom:* "I don't know if I want to go to college. I don't think I'd do very well there."
>
> *Father:* "Why not?"
>
> *Tom:* "Because I'm not that smart."
>
> *Father:* "Yeah, that's scary. I worried about that, too."
>
> *Tom:* "Did you ever come close to flunking out?"
>
> *Father:* "No, but I worried a lot before I went because I thought college would be full of brains. Once I got there, I found out that most of the kids were just like me."

15   This father has responded rather than reacted to his son's fears. First, he searched for the reason behind his son's lack of confidence and found it was fear of academic ability (it could have been fear of leaving home, of a new environment, of peer pressure, or of any of a number of things); second, he accepted the fear as legitimate; third, he empathized by admitting to having the same fear when he was Tom's age; and, finally, he explained why his, not Tom's, fears turned out to be groundless. He did all this without denigrating or lecturing.

denigrating Putting someone down

16   And that's tough for parents to do. Often we don't want to hear our children's fears, because those fears frighten us; or we don't want to pay attention to their dreams because their dreams aren't what we have in mind for them. Parents who deny such feelings will allow only surface conversation. It's fine as long as a child says, "School was okay today," but when she says, "I'm scared of boys," the parents are uncomfortable. They don't want her to be afraid of boys, but since they don't quite know what to say, they react with a pleasant "Oh, you'll outgrow it." She probably will, but what she needs at the moment is someone to hear and understand her pain.

17   In Ann McCarroll's interviews, she talked to one fifteen-year-old boy who said he had "*some* mother. Each morning she sits with me while I eat breakfast. We talk about anything and everything. She isn't refined or elegant or educated. She's a terrible housekeeper. But she's interested in everything I do, and she always listens to me—even if she's busy or tired."

18   That's the kind of listening found in families that experience real communication. Answers to the routine question, "How was your day?" are heard with the eyes and heart as well as the ears. Nuances are picked up and questions are asked, although problems are not necessarily solved. Members of a family who really listen to one another instinctively know that if people listen to you, they are interested in you. And that's enough for most of us.

Curran, "What Good Families Are Doing Right"

| Exercise 17 |

Work with Words

Use context clues, word part clues, and if necessary the dictionary to choose the best definitions of the words that are italicized in the following sentences from Reading 4.

1. And they share a common *shortcoming*—they can tell me in a minute what's wrong with them, but they aren't sure what's right with them. (par. 1)

   shortcoming
   a. arriving soon
   b. weakness
   c. strength

2. To prepare the book on which this article is based, I asked respected workers in the fields of education, religion, health, family counseling, and voluntary organizations to identify a list of possible *traits* of a healthy family. (par. 2)

   traits
   a. characteristics
   b. problems
   c. sources

3. "We have kids in classes whose families are so *robotized* by television that they don't know one another," said a fifth grade teacher. (par. 6)

   robotized
   a. synchronized
   b. made automatic
   c. brainwashed

4. But when it's working well, there are certain recognizable signs or *symptoms,* what I call the hallmarks of the successfully communicating family. (par. 8)

   symptoms
   a. successes
   b. results
   c. signs

5. He did all this without *denigrating* or lecturing. (par. 15)

   denigrating
   a. belittling
   b. lecturing
   c. denying

Exercise 18

Check Your Understanding

Choose the best way to complete the following statements about Reading 4.

1. The best main idea statement for the reading would be, "Good families
   a. have certain characteristics in common."
   b. can tell you what's wrong with them but are not sure what is right with them."
   c. listen to each other."

2. According to Curran, communication is key to a healthy family. The supporting examples that she gives include all of the following *except* (par. 3–6)
   a. they know how to talk and listen.
   b. they are robotized by television.
   c. they know one another.

3. Healthy families deal with conflicts by
   a. revealing their feelings honestly to other family members.
   b. covering up their anger.
   c. recognizing the need for conflict within close groups.

4. According to Dr. Lewis, healthy couples
   a. try to dominate each other.
   b. decide that no one is boss.
   c. complement rather than dominate each other.

5. In the healthiest families, the parents have
   a. a strong, loving relationship.
   b. have a dominating father who creates security.
   c. have a stay-at-home, full-time mother.

| Exercise 19 |

Identify Patterns of Organization

Identify the pattern of organization (cause and effect, definition, comparison/contrast, examples, chronological order, or classification) and the main idea for the following paragraphs.

1. Paragraph 2

   pattern of organization: _____

   main idea: _____

   _____

2. Paragraph 7

   pattern of organization: _____

   main idea: _____

   _____

3. Paragraph 9

   pattern of organization: _____

   main idea: _____

   _____

4. Paragraph 15

   pattern of organization: _____

   main idea: _____

   _____

Exercise 20

Make Connections

Write short answers to the following questions based on Reading 4, your experience, and your observations.

1. Which points from this article do you think are most important for explaining what good families are doing right? Explain your answer.

   _____

   _____

2. Which points are already being used in your family?

   _____

   _____

3. Which points would you like to add to the way your family interacts?

   _____

   _____

Exercise 21

Make a Map, Chart, Time Line, or Outline

Read the following paragraphs and identify the pattern of organization and the main idea. Then, on a separate sheet of paper, design a map, chart, time line, or outline that you think best visually represents the information.

1. The healthiest families I know are ones in which the mother and father have a strong, loving relationship. This seems to flow over to the children and even beyond the home. It seems to breed security in the children and, in turn, fosters the ability to take risks, to reach out to others, to search for their own answers, become independent and develop a good self image. (Curran, "What Good Families Are Doing Right")

   pattern of organization: _____

   main idea: _____

   _____

2. It is usually easier to react than to respond. When we react, we reflect our own experiences and feelings; when we respond, we get into the other person's feelings. (Curran, "What Good Families Are Doing Right")

   pattern of organization: _____

   main idea: _____

   _____

Chapter Review

To aid your review of the reading skills in Chapter 8, study the Put It Together Chart.

Put It Together: *Complex Patterns of Organization*	
Skills and Concepts	*Explanation*
Comparison and contrast (see pages 373–379)	Comparison and contrast answers the question, "How are two things alike or different?" They are introduced by words like "similarly" and "however."
Cause and effect (see pages 380–386)	Cause and effect answers the questions, "Why is something the way it is?" and "What were the results or consequences of something that happened?" Causes are introduced with phrases like "the reason why," and effects follow words like "as a result."

To reinforce your thinking before taking the Mastery Tests, complete as many of the following activities as your instructor assigns.

Reviewing Skills

Explain how to identify each of the following patterns of organization:

1. Comparison and contrast: _____

_____

2. Cause and effect: _____

_____

Writing

Write a cause and effect paragraph or a short essay explaining what you think makes a successful family.

Collaborating

Share your writing activity with your group, or discuss in your group the characteristics of a successful family. Then list these characteristics, and list, in contrast, the characteristics of an unsuccessful family.

	Successful Families		**Unsuccessful Families**
1.	_____		_____
2.	_____		_____
3.	_____		_____
4.	_____		_____

Extending Your Thinking

Interview the oldest person you know (a grandparent, great-grandparent, neighbor, etc.). Ask that person what life was like in his or her family when he or she was young. You might ask things like (1) Where did you live, in the city or in the countryside? (2) Who were the members of a typical family household? (3) Who did what kinds of work in and out of the home? and (4) What was the role of men and women in raising the children?

Write a paragraph or short essay in which you summarize what you learned about family life in the past.

Visiting the Web

The following Web sites provide more information on families and community services.

1. *Administration for Children and Families*

   www.acf.dhhs.gov/
   This is the homepage for the federal government's division of Health and Human Services that focuses on programs for children and families. It includes links to many services. It also has a separate subdivision for urban and minority families.

2. *Facts for Families*

   http://www.aacap.org/publications/factfam/
   On this Web site, the American Academy of Child and Adolescent Psychiatry provides free, up-to-date information on issues that affect children, teenagers, and their families. It also lists links to similar Web sites.

3. *The National Partnership for Women and Families*

   http://www.nationalpartnership.org/
   This site provides information on health care, work and the family, news and publications, legislation, and online resources.

Balancing Family and Work

William E. Thompson and Joseph V. Hickey

The following reading presents some of the issues that arise for contemporary American families as they attempt to balance the responsibilities of family and work. Do you think that employers, or the government, should provide more assistance for American families? As you read, notice the patterns of organization that the authors use to explain their ideas.

1   As we approach the twenty-first century, almost three of four married women with school-age children and more than 50 percent of women with preschool-age children are in the labor force. Further, more than 70 percent of employed mothers now work full time. The transition to coprovider families has not been without problems, and in many ways it remains an unfinished experiment (Collins and Coltrane, 1995; Hochschild, 1997).

2   In the past few decades women have entered the paid labor force in unprecedented numbers and have entered virtually every profession. Despite these efforts, women's domestic responsibilities have changed little. Working wives continue to carry a disproportionate share of family responsibilities, such as child care, shopping, and housework. While husbands are doing more around the house they remain "... pinch hitters or part-time players rather than regulars" (Furstenberg, 1988:209).

3   There has been some improvement in men's participation in child care and other domestic responsibilities—especially in television advertisements, where fathers "use the latest housecleaning products, change the baby's diaper, and even telephone young adults who have gone away to college" (Collins and Coltrane, 1995:431). In 1980 less than 15 percent of preschoolers were cared for by their fathers, while mothers worked. Today that figure is about 18 percent. When both parents are at home after work, however, women devote much more attention to child care than do men—about twice as much time—a situation that many women with economic resources and alternatives to marriage view as unjust and unacceptable (Lennon and Rosenfield, 1994).

4   When compared to domestic contributions of men in other industrial nations, American husbands rank somewhere in the middle. One survey found that American men averaged about one-half hour a day caring for children, which is less than many counterparts in Europe but considerably more than Japanese fathers, who "spent 3 minutes per day and 19 minutes per day on weekends on family work" (Ishii-Kuntz, 1993:47).

5   Gender inequality persists in other areas as well. Even when wives earn as much as or more than their husbands, many men still consider domestic

matters to be the wife's responsibility. In addition, many husbands continue to see their wives' jobs as competing with their needs and those of the children. And families have yet to receive much help from either the government or corporate America in the form of flexible work schedules, funding for quality day care, and maternity and family leave benefits (Aldous and Dumon, 1990; Menaghan and Parcel, 1990; Ross and Mirowsky, 1990).

6   Almost half of preschool-age children are cared for by relatives—some of it "tag team care" by parents. Twenty-one percent are looked after by nonkin and the rest spend their formative years in day-care centers, which are highly uneven in quality. Babysitters, nannies, and the much rarer on-site facilities are provided by 5,000 (out of 6 million) companies. Moreover, many facilities are unlicensed, overcrowded, and even dangerous. American businesses provide higher quality care, but they too are largely unregulated and of uneven quality (Collins and Coltrane, 1995; Garfinkel et al., 1996).

7   Nor has the government provided much help for working families with children. As Collins and Coltrane (1995) noted, although the Family Leave Act of 1993 took almost a decade to pass, it provided few substantive benefits; twelve weeks of *unpaid* parental leave for infant care or seriously ill family members and a few other minor concessions. Such benefits pale in comparison to family support policies in Sweden, which some sociologists believe is the most progressive and "family-friendly" environment in the industrial world (Acker, 1994; Coontz, 1997).

THOMPSON AND HICKEY, *Society in Focus*

Based on context clues, word part clues, and if necessary the dictionary, write the meaning of each of the italicized words in the following sentences from the reading.

1. The transition to *coprovider* families has not been without its problems, and in many ways it remains an unfinished experiment. (par. 1)

    coprovider families _____

2. In the past few decades women have entered the paid labor force in *unprecedented* numbers and have entered virtually every profession. (par. 2)

    unprecedented _____

3. One survey found that American men averaged about one-half hour a day caring for children, which is less than many *counterparts* in Europe but considerably more than Japanese fathers, who "spend 3 minutes per day and 19 minutes per day on weekends on family work." (par. 4)

    counterparts _____

Name _____ Date _____

4. Twenty-one percent are looked after by *nonkin* and the rest spend their formative years in day-care centers, which are highly uneven in quality. (par. 6)

   nonkin _____

5. As Collins and Coltrane noted, although the Family Leave Act of 1993 took almost a decade to pass, it provided few substantive benefits: twelve weeks of unpaid parental leave for infant care or seriously ill family members and a few other minor *concessions*. (par. 7)

   concessions _____

Write *true* or *false* before each of the following statements about the reading.

_____ 6. The majority of women with preschool-age children do not work outside the home.

_____ 7. Despite women's increasing role in the labor force, their responsibilities at home have remained about the same.

_____ 8. Many working women feel it is unfair that they spend about twice as much time on child care than their husbands do.

_____ 9. Japanese men are much more likely than American men to help with child care.

_____ 10. Many husbands still see their wives' jobs as competing with the needs of the family.

_____ 11. The author feels that day-care facilities in America are excellent.

_____ 12. The author suggests that the government should provide more assistance to families with children.

Choose the best way to complete the following multiple-choice statements about the reading.

13. The main idea of the reading is that
    a. gender inequality persists in many areas of employment.
    b. the transition to coprovider families has not been without its problems, and in many ways it remains an unfinished experiment.
    c. more than 70 percent of employed mothers now work full time.

14. "While husbands are doing more around the house they remain '. . . pinch hitters or part-time players rather than regulars.'" This sentence is organized primarily by
    a. comparison and contrast.
    b. chronological order.
    c. cause and effect.

15. "Despite these efforts, women's domestic responsibilities have changed little." This sentence is organized primarily by
   a. examples.
   b. chronological order.
   c. cause and effect.

16. Paragraph 4 is organized primarily by
   a. examples.
   b. chronological order.
   c. comparison and contrast.

17. Paragraph 5 is organized primarily by
   a. examples.
   b. cause and effect.
   c. definition.

18. Paragraph 7 is organized primarily by
   a. cause and effect.
   b. comparison and contrast.
   c. definition.

Write short answers to the following questions based on your reading, your experience, and your observations.

19. Why do you think there is such a difference between the time mothers and fathers spend in child rearing? How might this change?

   _____

   _____

   _____

20. Do you think that day-care programs in your area are of high quality? Why or why not?

   _____

   _____

   _____

From Father, with Love   Doris Kearns Goodwin

In this reading the author tells how baseball helped her form a bond with her father when she was growing up, and how she hopes her enthusiasm for this sport will have the same effect on her own family. What kinds of activities have helped your family form close relationships? As you read, notice how the author uses different patterns to organize her ideas.

1   The game of baseball has always been linked in my mind with the mystic texture of childhood, with the sounds and smells of summer nights and with the memories of my father.

2   My love for baseball was born on the first day my father took me to Ebbets Field in Brooklyn. Riding in the trolley car, he seemed as excited as I was, and he never stopped talking; now describing for me the street in Brooklyn where he had grown up, now recalling the first game he had been taken to by his own father, now recapturing for me his favorite memories from the Dodgers of his youth—the Dodgers of Casey Stengel, Zach Wheat, and Jimmy Johnston.

3   In the evenings, when my dad came home from work, we would sit together on our porch and relive the events of that afternoon's game which I had so carefully preserved in the large, red scorebook I'd been given for my seventh birthday. I can still remember how proud I was to have mastered all those strange and wonderful symbols that permitted me to recapture, in miniature form, the every movement of Jackie Robinson and Pee Wee Reese, Duke Snider and Gil Hodges. But the real power of that scorebook lay in the responsibility it entailed. For all through my childhood, my father kept from me the knowledge that the daily papers printed daily box scores, allowing me to believe that without my personal renderings of all those games he missed while he was at work, he would be unable to follow our team in the only proper way a team should be followed, day by day, inning by inning. In other words, without me, his love for baseball would be forever incomplete.

4   To be sure, there were risks involved in making a commitment as boundless as mine. For me, as for all too many Brooklyn fans, the presiding memory of "the boys of summer" was the memory of the final playoff game in 1951 against the Giants. Going into the ninth, the Dodgers held a 4–1 lead. Then came two singles and a double, placing the winning run at the plate with Bobby Thomson at bat. As Dressen replaced Erskine with Branca, my older sister, with maddening foresight, predicted the forever famous Thomson homer—a prediction that left me so angry with her, imagining that with her words she had somehow brought it about, that I would not speak to her for days.

5   So the seasons of my childhood passed until that miserable summer when the Dodgers were taken away to Los Angeles by the unforgivable O'Malley, leaving all our rash hopes and dreams of glory behind. And then came a summer of still deeper sadness when my father died. Suddenly my feelings for baseball seemed an aspect of my departing youth, along with my childhood freckles and my favorite childhood haunts, to be left behind when I went away to college and never came back.

6   Then one September day, having settled into teaching at Harvard, I agreed, half reluctantly, to go to Fenway Park. There it was again: the cozy ballfield scaled to human dimensions so that every word of encouragement and every scornful yell could be heard on the field; the fervent crowd that could, with equal passion, curse a player for today's failures after cheering his heroics the day before; the team that always seemed to break your heart in the last week of the season. It took only a matter of minutes before I found myself directing all my old intensities toward my new team—the Boston Red Sox.

7   I am often teased by my woman friends about my obsession, but just as often, in the most unexpected places—in academic conferences, in literary discussions, at the most elegant dinner parties—I find another woman just as crazily committed to baseball as I am, and the discovery creates an instant bond between us. All at once, we are deep in conversation, mingling together the past and the present, as if the history of the Red Sox had been our history too.

8   There we stand, one moment recollecting the unparalleled performance of Yaz[1] in '67, the next sharing ideas on how the present lineup should be changed; one moment recapturing the splendid career of "the Splendid Splinter,"[2] the next complaining about the manager's decision to pull the pitcher the night before. And then, invariably, comes the most vivid memory of all, the frozen image of Carlton Fisk as he rounded first in the sixth game of the '75 World Series, an image as intense in its evocation of triumph as the image of Ralph Branca weeping in the dugout is in its portrayal of heartache.

9   There is another, more personal memory associated with Carlton Fisk, for he was after all the years I had followed baseball, the first player I actually met in person. Apparently, he had read the biography I had written on Lyndon Johnson and wanted to meet me. Yet when the meeting took place, I found myself reduced to the shyness of childhood. There I was a professor at Harvard, accustomed to speaking with presidents of the United States, and yet, standing beside this young man in a baseball uniform, I was speechless.

10   Finally, Fisk said that it must have been an awesome experience to work with a man of such immense power as President Johnson—and with that, I was at last able to stammer out, with a laugh, "Not as awesome as the thought that I am really standing here talking with you."

11   Perhaps I have circled back to my childhood, but if this is so, I am certain that my journey through time is connected in some fundamental way to the fact that I am now a parent myself, anxious to share with my three sons the same ritual I once shared with my father.

12   For in this linkage between the generations rests the magic of baseball, a game that has defied the ravages of modern life, a game that is still played today by the same basic rules and at the same pace as it was played one hundred years ago. There is something deeply satisfying in the knowledge of this continuity.

13   There is something else as well which I have experienced sitting in Fenway Park with my small boys on a warm summer's day. If I close my eyes against the sun, all at once I am back at Ebbets Field, a young girl once more in the presence of my father, watching the players of my youth on the grassy field below. There is magic in this moment, for when I open my eyes and see my sons in the place where my father once sat, I feel an invisible bond between our three generations, an anchor of loyalty linking my sons to the grandfather whose face they never saw but whose person they have already come to know through this most timeless of all sports, the game of baseball.

Notes

1. Red Sox star Carl Yastrzemski.

2. Ted Williams, another famous Red Sox player.

GOODWIN, "From Father with Love"

Based on context clues, word part clues, and if necessary the dictionary, write the meaning of each of the italicized words in the following sentences from the reading.

1. The game of baseball has always been linked in my mind with the *mystic texture* of childhood, with the sounds and smell of summer nights and with the memories of my father. (par. 1)

   mystic texture _____

2. Riding in the trolley car, he seemed as excited as I was, and he never stopped talking; now describing for me the street in Brooklyn where he had grown up, now recalling the first game he had been taken to by his own father, now *recapturing* for me his favorite memories from the Dodgers of his youth—the Dodgers of Casey Stengel, Zach Wheat, and Jimmy Johnston. (par. 2)

   recapturing _____

3. But the real power of that scorebook lay in the responsibility it *entailed*. (par. 3)

   entailed _____

4. Suddenly my feelings for baseball seemed an *aspect* of my departing youth, along with my childhood freckles and my favorite childhood haunts, to be left behind when I went away to college and never came back. (par. 5)

   aspect _____

5. For in this linkage between the generations rests the magic of baseball, a game that *defied the ravages* of modern life, a game that is still played today by the same basic rules and at the same pace as it was played one hundred years ago. (par. 12)

   defied the ravages _____

Write *true* or *false* before each of the following statements about the reading.

_____ 6. The author has always linked her memories of baseball with her memories of her sister.

_____ 7. She kept daily scores and discussed them with her dad when he came home from work.

_____ 8. After her father died, the author avoided baseball for a while, but she came back to it when she was teaching at Harvard.

_____ 9. She never finds any women as crazily commited to baseball as she is.

_____ 10. The first baseball player she actually met in person was Lyndon Johnson.

_____ 11. The author believes that baseball may serve as a great link to bond parents and children.

_____ 12. She never takes her three sons to the ballpark because she is afraid it will make her miss her father.

Choose the best way to complete the following statements based on the reading.

13. The main idea of the reading is that
    a. women seldom enjoy sports like baseball as much as men do.
    b. baseball is the best sport for Americans, and everybody should learn to play it.
    c. for the author, baseball bonds the generations together, including her father, herself, and her own three sons.

14. Paragraph 5 is organized primarily by
    a. examples.
    b. chronological order.
    c. definition.

15. Paragraph 7 is organized primarily by
    a. comparison and contrast.
    b. chronological order.
    c. cause and effect.

16. Paragraph 8 is organized primarily by
    a. examples.
    b. comparison and contrast.
    c. cause and effect.

17. Paragraph 10 is organized primarily by
    a. comparison and contrast.
    b. chronological order.
    c. cause and effect.

Write short answers to the following questions based on your reading, your experience, and your observation.

18. Goodwin believes that baseball formed a lifelong bond between her father and herself. Why?

    _____

    _____

    _____

19. What are two activities that have helped your family to form bonds with each other? Explain.

    _____

    _____

    _____

20. What are some other examples you can think of where members of families share a common interest?

    _____

    _____

    _____

Chapter 9

Inferences,
Fact versus Opinion,
and Conclusions

Growing Up

"I get a little down, but I'm very good at hiding it. It's like I wear a mask. Even when the kids call me names or taunt me, I never show them how much it crushes me inside. I keep it all in."
—from an interview of fourteen-year-old Adam in William Pollack's Real Boys

- What does the fourteen-year-old mean when he says he wears a "mask"? Why does he wear a mask?

- What image of themselves are the young men in the photo trying to give?

Getting Ready to Read

Adolescence is a crucial period in everyone's life. It is when we "come of age," when we form our understanding of the world around us and our relationships to people. Many societies have special "coming of age" ceremonies, but in others there is no clear moment when the child turns into an adult, and there are no clear rules for how parents and children are supposed to behave during this "growing up" process. Researchers have been studying the adolescent years of boys and girls—young men and women—to try to develop some guidelines that will help them through this difficult passage to adulthood. Teenagers will be making crucial decisions about their attitude to education, to their friends and families, to drugs, to sex, to their bodies, to violence, to their work, to their lifestyle goals, and to their communities. We need to ask ourselves how do we best prepare our children to make good choices for now and for their life? What can and should parents do? Schools? Communities? The government?

In this chapter you will read about the challenges for parents and young people during these crucial years. In the process, you will improve your reading skills by learning how to

- recognize inferences and clues that inferences are based on
- distinguish between facts and opinions
- draw your own conclusions after comparing the opinions of others

READING 1

The Boy Code: "Everything's Just Fine"

William Pollack

The following reading is from the best-selling book Real Boys *by William Pollack, who is a Harvard Medical School child psychologist and researcher. In his book he addresses many of the problems boys have as they grow up to become men. He believes that boys are in serious trouble, including many boys who seem to be doing fine. As you read, think about why the boy in the story might be in trouble, and why he is acting as he does.*

1   Adam is a fourteen-year-old boy whose mother sought me out after a workshop I was leading on the subject of boys and families. Adam, she told me, had been performing very well in school, but now she felt something was wrong.

2   Adam had shown such promise that he had been selected to join a special program for talented students, and the program was available only at a different—and more academically prestigious—school than the one Adam

had attended. The new school was located in a well-to-do section of town, more affluent than Adam's own neighborhood. Adam's mother had been pleased when her son had qualified for the program and even more delighted that he would be given a scholarship to pay for it. And so Adam had set off on his new life.

3   At the time we talked, Mrs. Harrison's delight had turned to worry. Adam was not doing well at the new school. His grades were mediocre, and at midterm he had been given a warning that he might fail algebra. Yet Adam continued to insist, "I'm fine. Everything's just fine." He said this both at home and at school. Adam's mother was perplexed, as was the guidance counselor at his new school. "Adam seems cheerful and has no complaints," the counselor told her. "But something must be wrong." His mother tried to talk to Adam, hoping to find out what was troubling him and causing him to do so poorly in school. "But the more I questioned him about what was going on," she said, "the more he continued to deny any problems."

4   Adam was a quiet and rather shy boy, small for his age. In his bright blue eyes I detected an inner pain, a malaise whose cause I could not easily fathom. I had seen a similar look on the faces of a number of boys of different ages, including many boys in the "Listening to Boys' Voices" study. Adam looked wary, hurt, closed-in, self-protective. Most of all, he looked alone.

malaise Discomfort
fathom Understand

5   One day, his mother continued, Adam came home with a black eye. She asked him what had happened. "Just an accident," Adam had mumbled. He'd kept his eyes cast down, she remembered, as if he felt guilty or ashamed. His mother probed more deeply. She told him that she knew something was wrong, something upsetting was going on, and that—whatever it was—they could deal with it, they could face it together. Suddenly, Adam erupted in tears, and the story he had been holding inside came pouring out.

6   Adam was being picked on at school, heckled on the bus, goaded into fights in the schoolyard. "Hey, White Trash!" the other boys shouted at him. "You don't belong here with *us*!" taunted a twelfth-grade bully. "Why don't you go back to your own side of town!" The taunts often led to physical attacks, and Adam found himself having to fight back in order to defend himself. "But I never throw the first punch," Adam explained to his mother. "I don't show them they can hurt me. I don't want to embarrass myself in front of everybody."

7   I turned to Adam. "How do you feel about all of this?" I asked. "How do you handle your feelings of anger and frustration?" His answer was, I'm sad to say, a refrain I hear often when I am unable to connect to the inner lives of boys.

8   "I get a little down," Adam confessed, "but I'm very good at hiding it. It's like I wear a mask. Even when the kids call me names or taunt me, I never show them how much it crushes me inside. I keep it all in."

9   "What do you do with the sadness?" I asked.

10   "I tend to let it boil inside until I can't hold it any longer, and then it explodes. It's like I have a breakdown, screaming and yelling. But I only do it inside my own room at home, where nobody can hear. Where nobody will know about it." He paused a moment. "I think I got this from my dad, unfortunately."

11   Adam was doing what I find so many boys do: he was hiding behind a mask, and using it to hide his deepest thoughts and feelings—his real self—from everyone, even the people closest to him. This mask of masculinity enabled Adam to make a bold (if inaccurate) statement to the world: "I can handle it. Everything's fine. I am invincible."

persona   A public role or personality

feigned   Pretended

bravado   Show of false bravery

12   Adam, like other boys, wore this mask as an invisible shield, a persona to show the outside world a feigned self-confidence and bravado, and to hide the shame he felt at his feelings of vulnerability, powerlessness, and isolation. He couldn't handle the school situation alone—very few boys or girls of fourteen could—and he didn't know how to ask for help, even from people he knew loved him. As a result, Adam was unhappy and was falling behind in his academic performance.

13   Many of the boys I see today are like Adam, living behind a mask of masculine bravado that hides the genuine self to conform to our society's expectations; they feel it is necessary to cut themselves off from any feelings that society teaches them are unacceptable for men and boys—fear, uncertainty, feelings of loneliness and need.

14   Many boys, like Adam, also think it's necessary that they handle their problems alone. A boy is not expected to reach out—to his family, his friends, his counselors, or coaches—for help, comfort, understanding, and support. And so he is simply not as close as he could be to the people who love him and yearn to give him the human connections of love, caring, and affection every person needs.

15   The problem for those of us who want to help is that, on the outside, the boy who is having problems may seem cheerful and resilient while keeping inside the feelings that don't fit the male model—being troubled, lonely, afraid, desperate. Boys learn to wear the mask so skillfully—in fact, they don't even know they're doing it—that it can be difficult to detect what is really going on when they are suffering at school, when their friendships are not working out, when they are being bullied, becoming depressed, even dangerously so, to the point of feeling suicidal. The problems below the surface become obvious only when boys go "over the edge" and get into trouble at school, start to fight with friends, take drugs or abuse alcohol, are diagnosed with clinical depression or attention deficit disorder, erupt into physical violence, or come home with a black eye, as Adam did. Adam's mother, for example, did not know from her son that anything was wrong until Adam came home with an eye swollen shut; all she knew was that he had those perplexingly poor grades.

POLLACK, *Real Boys*

Exercise 1

Recall and Discuss

Answer these questions about Reading 1, and prepare to discuss them in class.

1. Why was Adam selected to join a special program for talented students?

   _____

   _____

   _____

2. What problems did Adam encounter in his new school?

   _____

   _____

   _____

3. Why did Adam not tell his mother what was happening at the new school?

   _____

   _____

   _____

4. Do you think that it was a good idea for Adam to "wear a mask"? Why or why not?

   _____

   _____

   _____

Recognizing Inferences

Like Adam, often writers (and speakers) do not state everything directly. Instead, they give you clues—pieces of information—so that you can make some reasonable assumptions or guesses about what they are trying to say. To understand this kind of communication, you must **infer,** or "read between the lines," think about what is being said, and come to your own conclusions. A writer or speaker who says something indirectly is *implying* meaning, and the reader or listener is *inferring* the meaning from the clues that are given.

infer Read between the lines to understand what a speaker or writer is saying indirectly

In Reading 1, Adam's mother inferred that something was wrong from the clue of her son's poor grades. The second clue was unmistakable—a black eye. Like Adam's mother, you make inferences every day of your life. The clues for these inferences often come from your understanding and experience and the situation around you. As an example, let's say you're watching a baseball game, the bases are loaded, and the team member who is up to bat strikes out. She says, "Oh, that's just great!" You will of course know, from inference, that she means, "That's just terrible!"

You base your inference on clues in the situation and on your own experience in similar situations. These situations are the *context*. In Chapter 2, you learned that context clues can help you guess a word's meaning from its surroundings. Context clues can help you with inferences, too. At the baseball game you know from the context—striking out when the bases are loaded—that the batter is upset and that she is using the word "great" to mean the opposite, "terrible." You no doubt received extra visual clues from the expression on her face and from the way she acted. She probably looked distressed instead of happy, and her body language probably showed disappointment instead of triumph.

Sometimes inferences can help you predict what will happen next in a situation or a story. For example, if your boss has just observed you arriving twenty minutes late for work for the third time this week, and he says with a frown, "Mark, see me in my office," what do you infer, or predict, he will say to you? It's not likely he's going to praise you! You know that being on time is expected in most jobs, plus you noticed his frown. Those context clues will lead you to infer that he is unhappy with your actions.

Making Inferences While Reading

Writers help us make inferences in many ways. Sometimes they present us with a lot of detailed information and then expect us to reach the same conclusions they did by inference. You practiced this skill of making inferences in Chapter 4 when you learned how to identify unstated main ideas in what you read. Read the following excerpt from a news story to see what you might reasonably infer.

WASHINGTON—[In Washington, D.C.] police have no gasoline for their cruisers. Health clinics have run out of drugs. Six blocks from the White House, firefighters ride trucks with no ladders and buy their own boots.

Potholes blister Embassy Row. The decrepit water-treatment plant threatens to spew sewage into the Potomac. Earlier this year, inmates set fire to their cells after the prison ran out of food. (Montgomery, "Short of Funds, the Nation's Capital Is Falling Apart")

What can we reasonably infer from this information?

Washington, D.C., is having serious trouble maintaining regular city services.

In this case this inference would also be the main idea for this passage. It is unstated, but the details, or clues, in the article add up to this conclusion. What clues do we have to make this inference?

(1) Police don't have gasoline, (2) health clinics don't have drugs,
(3) firefighters don't have ladders or boots, (4) the streets have potholes,
(5) the water-treatment plant doesn't work, (6) prison inmates ran out
of food.

This long list of examples shows that things are falling apart in that city.

You can also infer that these conditions are particularly disgraceful because they are in our nation's capital. This understanding is implied more subtly. The writer states that "six blocks from the White House" firefighters don't have the proper equipment. The firefighters' problems are no doubt true all over the city, but it looks worse when we realize how close this is to the home of the president of our country. Also, there are potholes on Embassy Row. If there are potholes in the finest streets—where ambassadors from countries all over the world reside—that is very embarrassing. From the details the writer includes and the way she states them, we can probably also conclude that she thinks these problems in our nation's capital should be remedied.

| Exercise 2 |

Recognize Inferences in Paragraphs

Read the following passages about the difficulties as well as some of the positive aspects of growing up in our communities and attending our schools, then circle the letter in front of each statement that you decide is a reasonable inference. There may be more than one. The first one has been done for you.

1. Even celebrities sometimes quietly give of themselves behind the scenes. In Joe Dumars's life, basketball and community responsibility came together early on. The Detroit Pistons' guard grew up in Natchitoches, La., the youngest of seven children. One day his father, a truck driver, cut an old door in half, nailed a bicycle rim to it and transformed the neighborhood. "We had the biggest yard, a basketball hoop, and it was just a magnet for all the kids in the area," he remembers. "It was always crowded, but everyone was made to feel welcome. My mother, Ophelia, made sure of that." (Alter, "Everyday Heroes")
   a. Dumars's father made a basketball hoop and a backboard out of an old door and a bicycle rim.
   b. Joe Dumars was the youngest of seven children.

c. Dumars's father knew his son would be a basketball star when he grew up.

(d.) Dumars's yard became a kind of neighborhood center.

(Statements a and d are the only reasonable inferences from the information provided in the paragraph. We are told that Dumars's father "cut an old door in half" and "nailed a bicycle rim to it." In the next sentence we discover that there was a basketball hoop in the yard, and we infer that this must have been what his father built. Statement d is supported by the clues that the basketball hoop "transformed the neighborhood," was "a magnet for all the kids in the area," and "it was always crowded, but everyone was made to feel welcome." Statement b is not an inference because it is a fact directly stated in the paragraph. There is not enough information in the paragraph to support statement c. His father might have hoped that Dumars would become a basketball star, but no information in the paragraph tells us that.)

2. In Denmark, a small Scandinavian country, parents have an interesting attitude toward teenagers and alcohol. Most families allow their teenagers to drink small amounts of alcohol at family dinners and at social occasions. This practice seems to make the consumption of alcohol a normal part of life, and Danish parents believe that if alcohol is not forbidden to their children, their children will not sneak off to drink alone. In addition, families, schools and Danish society in general all participate in the following tradition: When a class graduates from high school, they celebrate by visiting each of the classmates' homes to have a drink. Of course, after visiting between fifteen and thirty classmates' homes, you can imagine the condition of the students! To ensure the students' safety, the school organizes the activity by providing the class with a bus and a chauffeur to drive it.

    a. Teenagers are probably in fewer drunk driving accidents in Denmark than in the United States.

    b. Danish teenagers are different from teenagers in other parts of the world.

    c. Danish high school graduates get drunk after their graduation ceremony.

    d. Probably not many accidents in Denmark are caused by drunk students who are celebrating their high school graduation.

3. Frequently the children in middle- and upper-middle-class suburbs are busy people. They often leave school to be driven hurriedly to soccer or lacrosse practice three times a week and then to a game once a week on the weekend. They also very often take music lessons once a week near their home or across town, but they need to practice in between lessons, of course. In addition, they may study judo, karate, sewing, or they may be active in church youth organizations.

a. These children are probably driven around.

b. These children probably take the bus to all these activities.

c. There's a good chance that these children don't have very much free time to play.

d. These children study whenever they're not at organized activities.

4. Everything seemed fine for Camara when he came to this country from Kingston, Jamaica, several years ago. He was living with his mother and stepfather, taking tough courses and getting top grades at Thomas Jefferson. But after a bitter fight with his parents, he found himself out on the street. For four days, he lived and studied on the subway at night, getting off to go to school during the day.

   This would throw most kids for a loop. Even if they're not getting on well with their mothers and fathers, young people depend on parents to provide food and shelter and a certain degree of emotional support and stability. But after people at Thomas Jefferson helped Camara get settled in a homeless shelter, he pulled his grades back up, studied for his SATs, and applied for college admission. Rather than devastating him, the experience of being alone, with nowhere to spend the night but a subway car, seems to have strengthened Camara's resolve to study and make something of himself. (Shanker, "A Real Role Model")

   a. Camara's parents knew he could do well out on his own, so they threw him out of the house while he was still in high school.

   b. Camara had a special kind of inner drive and determination to be successful in school despite the circumstances of his life.

   c. Most young people who have the same problems as Camara are not as successful as he was.

   d. Camara's parents were unable to take care of him.

5. Since math is stereotyped as a male domain, boys benefit more than girls from math classes—they are spoken to more, are called on more, and receive more corrective feedback, social interaction, individual instruction, and encouragement. They learn more than what is in the textbook. By contrast, girls are mostly consigned to learning by rote the math in the text, with little exposure to extracurricular math and science. (Thio, *Sociology*, 5th ed.)

   a. Boys probably do better in math under these circumstances than do girls.

   b. Girls and boys are treated differently because they are perceived differently.

   c. Because boys are naturally better in math, they should get more attention than girls in math class.

   d. Feedback, individual instruction, and encouragement would make anybody good in math.

6. SOUTH BRUNSWICK, N.J. A tied soccer game between 8- and 9-year old boys ended in a brawl among their parents yesterday after a disagreement over where a coach was standing, police said. A shootout was to take place between the teams—one from Staten Island, N.Y., and the other from North Hunterdon—but before it could, a Staten Island coach argued that a North Hunterdon coach shouldn't be allowed to stand behind the goal.

shootout A means of breaking a tie in tournament soccer games; each team gets five direct kicks on goal

The argument escalated into a fistfight with as many as a dozen parents and coaches involved. No children were involved, South Brunswick police officer Jim Ryan said. Even after police arrived, parents were still yelling at each other, he said. Ryan said a coach and a parent claimed to have been assaulted, but no one was seriously injured or arrested, police said. Both teams were escorted from the field, and neither was declared the game winner, Ryan said.

The fight was the latest case of parental rage at youth sporting events this year [2000]. In August, a hockey dad was indicted on manslaughter charges in the beating death of another father at a game in Massachusetts, and a baseball coach was accused of breaking an umpire's jaw after a disputed call in Florida in June. ("Parents in Brawl at Kids' Soccer Game")

   a. The Staten Island coach was right.
   b. The parents can get more worked up at the sporting events than their children.
   c. The children don't care about winning the game.
   d. The children in these games may be influenced by the way their parents are acting at these games, and may eventually have more violent reactions at sports events themselves.

7. Often the children of immigrants who have lived in the United States for a while rebel against their parents' old-fashioned values and rules. Some Vietnamese mothers, for example, would like their daughters to date—once they are in their twenties and old enough to date—only Vietnamese men who would agree to having their wife's mother live with them if the couple gets married. (Adapted from Pipher, *Reviving Ophelia*)

   a. Young American men would not likely want their mother-in-law to live with them.
   b. These mothers probably don't want their daughters to become too Americanized.
   c. These mothers' expectations are unreasonable in an American cultural context.
   d. The daughters of Vietnamese immigrants need to be more obedient.

Organize to Learn: Separate Personal Opinion from Reasonable Inferences

Quite naturally, you will have your own feelings and opinions about what you read. Did the behavior of the soccer parents (Exercise 2, number 6) disgust you? Did you have a strong reaction to the ideas of the Vietnamese mothers (Exercise 2, number 7)? Your feelings and opinions are valid responses to what you read, but you must not let them get in the way of understanding what the author is saying or implying. If you do not keep personal opinion separate from reasonable inferences, you risk listening to yourself instead of learning from, or "listening" to, the author.

For example, in Exercise 2, number 4, the author writes,

> But after a bitter fight with his parents, he found himself out on the street. For four days, he lived and studied on the subway at night, getting off to go to school during the day.

What was your opinion about these events? It might have been something like one of the following:

1. Parents should never throw their children out, no matter how big the disagreement.
2. He should have *taught* his parents a lesson by just hiding out for a while so they could worry about him.
3. Why should he still care about doing well in school? His parents obviously don't care what happens to him.
4. I know what it is like to be on the streets when you are a kid; it can really be tough.
5. I don't approve of the parents' throwing their child out of the house, but I understand how parents' exasperation with teenage acting out can make them take drastic steps.

You may have had these or other opinions about Camara's situation, and that's fine. As you learned in the PRO reading system, you should always be involved with what you read. Reflect on what you've read, make connections with your prior reading and experiences, and form your own opinions about it. The only caution is to not confuse *your* opinions with inferences suggested by the author. The way to do that is to stick to the clues. For any reasonable inference that you make, be sure there are clues in the reading that lead to that inference.

Read the following paragraph and then see if you know which of the statements that follow is a personal opinion and which is a reasonable inference. In the blank put an "I" for an inference and "O" for a personal opinion.

> Authorities have become convinced that reformatories have failed as rehabilitation centers and instead have become crime schools in which teenagers learn how to become more effective criminals. A study con-

continued

ducted by the U.S. Department of Justice in 1987 showed that 49.7 percent of all juveniles in detention facilities had been arrested six or more times. Half of that number had been arrested eleven or more times. Acting on this belief, the Commonwealth of Massachusetts closed all five of its reform schools in 1972 and placed its young criminals in small, community-based programs. (Newton, *Teen Violence: Out of Control*)

_I_ The number of juveniles who are repeatedly arrested and returned to reformatories indicates that reformatories are failing to achieve their goal of deterring young people from returning to crime.

This inference is reasonably based on the clues: "49.7 percent of all juveniles in detention facilities had been arrested six or more times"; half of those people "had been arrested eleven or more times"; and "reformatories have failed as rehabilitation centers."

_O_ It's obvious that many of these juveniles cannot be helped, and they should simply be treated as adults in the courts.

Although the paragraph clearly seems to say that reformatories do not keep the majority of youths from committing additional crimes, there are no clues that prove that they simply cannot be helped by any means, and there is no mention of adult courts. This statement is clearly an opinion, perhaps based on other data and experience.

Exercise 3   ### Identify Personal Opinion or Reasonable Inference

Continue to identify personal opinions and reasonable inferences about the paragraph above. Write "O" for opinion or "I" for reasonable inference. Remember, a reasonable inference has supporting clues in the excerpt itself.

_O_ 1. The community-based programs in Massachusetts are definitely the best way to deal with youthful offenders.

_I_ 2. The Commonwealth of Massachusetts believed that placing young criminals in small, community-based programs would be more effective than placing them in reform schools.

_O_ 3. The State of New York has the best reform schools in the country.

_I_ 4. Teenagers who serve time in reformatories often commit crimes after they're released.

_O_ 5. Juvenile delinquents should receive the same sentences as adults.

_I_ 6. Juvenile crime is a problem in the United States today.

Finding Inferences in Longer Passages

Inferences in longer passages are sometimes easier to identify than those in short passages because there are more clues. You still go through the same process: add up the information you are given directly in the piece, consider all the clues you are given about what is implied, and then infer what the writer is saying. In narratives, or stories, clues will lead you to predict what will happen next. These clues include what has already happened and the character of the people in the story, but your own experiences will help you predict, too.

READING 2

Codes of Conduct   Geoffrey Canada

The following reading tells the story of how Geoffrey Canada and his brothers learned how to resolve a conflict with some other boys in their neighborhood. Canada's mother taught her children an important lesson on the day he describes. As you read, see if you can predict how the conflict will be resolved. What do you think his mother wanted her children to learn from this experience? Mark some clues as you read.

1   Down the block from us was a playground. It was nearby and we didn't have to cross the street to get there. We were close in age. My oldest brother, Daniel, was six, next came John who was five, I was four and my brother Reuben was two. Reuben and I were unable to go to the playground by ourselves because we were too young. But from time to time my two oldest brothers would go there together and play.

2   I remember them coming inside one afternoon having just come back from the playground. There was great excitement in the air. My mother noticed right away and asked, "Where's John's jacket?"

3   My brother responded, "This boy . . . this boy he took my jacket."

4   Well, we all figured that was the end of that. My mother would have to go and get the jacket back. But the questioning continued. "What do you mean, he took your jacket?"

5   "I was playing on the sliding board and I took my jacket off and left it on the bench, and this boy he tried to take it. And I said it was my jacket, and he said he was gonna take it. And he took it. And I tried to take it back, and he pushed me and said he was gonna beat me up."

6   To my mind John's explanation was clear and convincing, this case was closed. I was stunned when my mother turned to my oldest brother, Daniel, and said, "And what did you do when this boy was taking your brother's jacket?"

7   Daniel looked shocked. What did he have to do with this? And we all recognized the edge in my mother's voice. Daniel was being accused of something and none of us knew what it was.

8   Daniel answered, "I didn't do nuthin; I told Johnny not to take his jacket off. I told him."

9   My mother exploded. "You let somebody take your brother's jacket and you did nothing? That's your younger brother. You can't let people just take your things. You know I don't have money for another jacket. You better not ever do this again. Now you go back there and get your brother's jacket."

10   My mouth was hanging open. I couldn't believe it. What was my mother talking about, go back and get it? Dan and Johnny were the same size. If the boy was gonna beat up John, well, he certainly could beat up Dan. We wrestled all the time and occasionally hit one another in anger, but none of us knew how to fight. We were all equally incompetent when it came to fighting. So it made no sense to me. If my mother hadn't had that look in her eye, I would have protested. Even at four years old I knew this wasn't fair. But I also knew that look in my mother's eye. A look that signified a line not to be crossed.

11   My brother Dan was in shock. He felt the same way I did. He tried to protest. "Ma, I can't beat that boy. It's not my jacket. I can't get it. I can't."

12   My mother gave him her ultimatum. "You go out there and get your brother's jacket or when you get back I'm going to give you a beating that will be ten times as bad as what that little thief could do to you. And John, you go with him. Both of you better bring that jacket back here."

13   The tears began to flow. Both John and Dan were crying. My mother ordered them out. Dan had this look on his face that I had seen before. A stern determination showed through the tears. For the first time I didn't want to go with my brothers to the park. I waited a long ten minutes and then, to my surprise, John and Dan triumphantly strolled into the apartment. Dan had John's jacket in his hand.

CANADA, *FistStickKnifeGun*

| **Exercise 4** | **Identify Inferences** |

Use the clues from Reading 2 to support your answers to each of the following questions about inferences.

1. Why did the boys' mother send them back to get the jacket themselves?

   Because his mother want them to bring back after they let some one

2. Why did she make the oldest son, Daniel, get the jacket even though it wasn't his?

   Because she did not have any money to buy another jacket

3. Why were the boys scared about going back to the playground?

they thought they were going to beat up.

4. How do you think they got the jacket?

they might of just tooken the jacket ftten away

5. Write your personal opinion of this situation. Was the mother right or wrong to send her sons back to get the jacket?

_____

_____

_____

Now read the rest of the story to find out what happened and to check if your inferences about what happened are correct. See if the rest of the story changes your personal opinion about whether the mother was right or wrong.

Codes of Conduct (Continued)

14   My mother gathered us all together and told us we had to stick together. That we couldn't let people think we were afraid. That what she had done in making Dan go out and get the jacket was to let us know that she would not tolerate our becoming victims. I listened unconvinced. But I knew that in not going with Dan and John I'd missed something important. Dan was scared when he left the house. We were all scared. I knew I could never have faced up to that boy. How did Dan do it? I wanted to know everything.

15   "What happened? How did you do it? Did you have to fight? Did you beat him up?" I asked. Dan explained that when he went back to the playground the boy was still there, wearing John's jacket. He went up to him and demanded the jacket. The boy said no. Dan grabbed the jacket and began to take it off the boy. Dan was still crying, but the boy knew it was not from fear of him. A moment of resistance, but Dan's determination prevailed. The boy grew scared and Dan wrestled the jacket free. He even managed a threatening "You better never bother my brother again" as the boy fled.

16   Dan's description of the confrontation left me with more questions. I was trying to understand why Dan was able to get the jacket. If he could get it later, why didn't he take it back the first time? How come the boy didn't

fight? What scared him off? Even at four years old I knew I needed to know these things. I needed some clues on which I could build a theory of how to act. Dan's story couldn't help me much. It took many years of playing and hanging on the streets of the South Bronx before I began to put together the pieces of the theory. The only real lesson I learned from the jacket episode was if someone takes something from you, don't tell your mother you lost it, otherwise you might be in danger of getting your face punched in by some boy on the streets of New York City. This was a valuable bit of understanding for a four-year-old in the Bronx.

CANADA, *FistStickKnifeGun*

Exercise 5

Work with Words

Use context clues, word part clues, and if necessary the dictionary to write the definitions of the italicized words in the following sentences based on or related to Reading 2.

1. Daniel looked shocked. What did he have to do with this? And we all recognized the *edge* in my mother's voice. (par. 7)

   edge _____

2. But I also knew that look in my mother's eye. A look that *signified* a line not be crossed. (par. 10)

   signified _____

3. Mother gave him her *ultimatum*. "You go out there and get your brother's jacket or when you get back I'm going to give you a beating that will be ten times as bad as what that little thief could do to you." (par. 12)

   ultimatum _____

4. I waited a long ten minutes and then, to my surprise, John and Dan *triumphantly* strolled into the apartment. Dan had John's jacket in his hand. (par. 13)

   triumphantly _____

5. A moment of resistance, but Dan's determination *prevailed*. The boy grew scared and Dan wrestled the jacket free.

   prevailed _____

Exercise 6

Check Your Inferences

Write brief answers to the following questions about Reading 2. Use the clues you identified in the story to support your answers.

1. Why did the author's mother tell her boys that she didn't want people to think they were afraid?

_____

_____

_____

2. Why did the boy let Dan get the jacket back without a fight?

_____

_____

_____

3. Why do you think Dan was crying if it was not from fear of the boy?

_____

_____

_____

4. Why did the author infer at that time that if someone takes something from you it is better not to tell your mother that you lost it?

_____

_____

_____

_____

| Exercise 7 |

Make Connections: Collaborative Activity

Write short answers to the following questions based on Reading 2, your experience, and your observations. Then, to extend the exercise, discuss your answers with your class group. Working together, prepare a report for your class as a whole or a written summary for your instructor.

1. What do you think it was like for the boys' mother to be raising them alone as a single parent? How do you think she felt?

_____

_____

2. Do you think their mother did the right thing under the circumstances?

_____

_____

3. Do you think the author, now, as an adult, thinks his mother did the right thing under the circumstances?

_____

_____

LANGUAGE TIP

The Language of Imagery and Connotation

Imagery

Good writers and good speakers often use language that makes their ideas stronger by affecting our senses—that is, by making us see pictures in our minds or imagine how something feels or smells. For example, in "Codes of Conduct" Canada writes,

"My mother *exploded*. 'You let somebody take your brother's jacket and you did nothing?'"

The word "exploded" gives us a visual picture of how upset the mother was when the boys said they did nothing about the stolen coat. We know she didn't actually "blow up"; she was just very angry at the boys' lack of action.

Sometimes, also, writers do not make their point directly. The reader has to picture the images to figure out exactly what is being said. For example, what do you think teenagers in a gang mean when they say:

"I would rather be *judged by twelve* than *carried by six*."

What are the clues and visual images (pictures formed in your mind) in the sentence?

"Judged by twelve" means face a trial (there are twelve people on a jury)
"Carried by six" refers to being in a coffin. Six people (pallbearers) carry the coffin.

The entire statement means that I would rather be arrested for a crime than be killed.

Connotation

Words also convey positive and negative feelings, or emotions, in addition to their dictionary definition. If you look up the word "work" in the dictionary, you will find it defined as "physical or mental effort or activity," "labor," and "employment or job." This word does not have positive or negative feelings attached to it. But if you add the word "busy" in front of the word "work," the term has a negative feel. "Busy work" conveys work that is not meaningful, work that is just done to appear busy, to fill time. But "rewarding work" has a positive connotation, or feeling. As you read, be aware of the *connotations*, or feelings, of words. They will help you infer the writer's meaning, too.

Exercise 8   ## Understand the Language of Imagery ~picture~

In the following sentences, some examples of language that use imagery have been italicized. Explain (1) what visual images are formed when we read these words, and (2) what the words actually mean in the sentence.

1. The "man's world" outside the home was viewed as a *harsh and heartless jungle* in which men need to be strong, ambitious, and aggressive. (Thio, *Sociology*)

   visual image: _"harsh or heartless" jungle heartless_

   meaning: _The hard work needed_

2. For four days, he lived and studied on the subway at night, getting off to go to school during the day. This would *throw most kids for a loop.* (Shanker, "A Real Role Model")

   visual image: _____

   meaning: _____

3. "An eye for an eye. A tooth for a tooth." *(The Bible)*

   visual image: _hit back_

   meaning: _acting equal_

4. "We had the biggest yard, a basketball hoop, and it was just a *magnet for all the kids in the area,*" he remembers. (Alter, "What Works")

   visual image: _House with a big mass_

   meaning: _____

5. My mother gathered us all together and told us we had *to stick together.* (Canada, "Codes of Conduct")

   visual image: _____

   meaning: _take care each other_

6. But I also knew that look in my mother's eye. A look that signified *a line not to be crossed.* (Canada, "Codes of Conduct")

   visual image: _Don't cross that line_

   meaning: _Don't make me mad_

7. In Vietnamese culture, families are seen as *shelter from the storm.* Adolescents don't rebel, but rather *are nested* in extended families that they will be with forever. (Pipher, *Reviving Ophelia*)

   shelter from the storm

   visual image: _cover the head_

   meaning: _They support them_

are nested

visual image: _the bird_

meaning: _place to lives_

| Exercise 9 |

Recognize the Connotations of Words

Read the following paragraph about work and decide whether each of the uses of the word "work" has a positive or negative connotation. Write a plus (+) if the connotation is positive and a minus (−) if the connotation is negative.

"Work" is a word we all use freely. It has many different connotations. We might do a "good day's work." We have people in our organization who are "workaholics" and "workhorses." We "work a problem through." We "work out" on a dance floor or athletic field. (Roth, "The True Nature of Work")

_____ 1. good day's work

_____ 2. workaholic

_____ 3. workhorse

_____ 4. work a problem through

_____ 5. work out

Recognizing Facts and Opinions

You have already learned how to separate your own personal opinions from what a writer is saying. But what if the writer expresses his or her personal opinions? You need to be able to recognize these, too. One way to do this is to evaluate the evidence. Is the author's opinion based on facts?

fact Information that most people accept as true and that usually can be verified

A **fact** is information that most people would accept as true and that usually can be verified. Recognized experts in a field would be able to determine whether a stated fact is true or not. For example, if someone says, "One dollar equals 98 cents," you would immediately recognize this as an incorrect statement. The correct statement of fact is, "One dollar equals 100 cents."

opinion Someone's interpretation of facts

An **opinion** is someone's interpretation of facts. For example, if a grandfather says, "Five dollars is a lot of allowance for a young person," his grandchild may disagree. They may have different understandings of what five dollars will buy today and different expectations about what an allowance should be used for. You may or may not agree with an opinion that is stated. As another example, if your brother says, "Brand Q shampoo is the best shampoo to buy," you may or may not agree with him; you do not simply accept his opinion as fact. You will probably make your own decision—based on your own experience, the ingredients printed on the label, price, or friends' recommendations—about which shampoo to buy.

| Exercise 10 | ## Recognize Fact and Opinion

Read the following excerpt about raising Latino children, and determine which statements are facts and which are opinions. For the statements that follow, write "F" before statements of fact and "O" before statements of opinion.

demographics
Population statistics

As a parent, it is critical that you realize the changing demographics of this country. The face of America will not be white Anglo-Saxon for long. It will soon be mostly Hispanic and with it comes a great destiny for our children. Marvelous and extraordinary things await our children. Blessed with a legacy of achievement and a rich heritage from their ancestors as well as an array of talents and capabilities, our children have much to build on, as they will one day become the largest ethnic group in America. . . .

According to demographers, in 1997, Hispanics comprised almost 30 million people, or 11 percent of the U.S. population, while non-Hispanic whites comprised 73 percent. By the year 2000, Hispanics will comprise 15 percent of the population, or 39 million. By the year 2010, Hispanics will surpass the African-American population, with a population projected to be 41 million compared to a projected black population of 37.5 million. . . . By the year 2050, the Hispanic population is projected to almost triple in size to 87.4 million, comprising about one-fourth of the population of 392 million. Because of Hispanics' high fertility and immigration rates and because non-Hispanic whites are projected to continue to decline in population, Hispanics are projected to one day become the largest group in America. (Rodriguez, *Raising Nuestros Niños*)

projected   Predicted (based on current statistics)

_O_ 1. As a parent, it is critical that you realize the changing demographics of this country.

_O_ 2. Marvelous and extraordinary things await our children.

_O_ 3. [America] will soon be mostly Hispanic and with it comes a great destiny for our children.

_F_ 4. According to demographers, in 1997, Hispanics comprised almost 30 million people, or 11 percent of the U.S. population.

_F_ 5. Because of Hispanics' high fertility and immigration rates, and because non-Hispanic whites are projected to continue to decline in population, Hispanics are projected to one day become the largest group in America.

| **Exercise 11** | ## Make Connections: Collaborative Activity |

Write short answers to the following questions about the excerpt in Exercise 10 based on your reading, your experience, and your observations. Then, to extend the exercise, discuss your answers with your class group. Working together, prepare a report for your class as a whole or a written summary for your instructor.

1. Why does Rodriguez write to Latino parents, "As a parent, it is critical that you realize the changing demographics of this country"? Why does she think the demographics of the country are so important? Do you think that the demographics will make a difference for what our children's lives are like? Explain.

   _____

   _____

   _____

2. Do you think that the idea that "marvelous and extraordinary" things await our children is more true of Latino children than it is for children of other ethnic groups? Explain your answer.

   _____

   _____

   _____

| **READING 3** | # *Boys Today Are Falling Behind*   William Pollack |

In recent years, we have heard a lot about how girls tend to do well in school until they start middle school, and then they start performing poorly in math and science. In response to this information, schools across the country are trying to address the problems of educating our girls. Some people feel that, while girls do face discouragement in our classrooms, we should not forget that boys also have many problems in our educational institutions. Some argue they have many more problems than girls. The following reading, from Pollack's book, Real Boys, *examines some of these questions. As you read, consider which statements are facts and which are opinions.*

1   While it may seem as if we live in a "man's world," at least in relation to power and wealth in adult society we do not live in a "boy's world." Boys on the whole are not faring well in our schools, especially in our public schools. It is in the classroom that we see some of the most destructive effects of society's misunderstanding of boys. Thrust into competition with their peers,

vulnerable
Unprotected, easily
hurt

some boys invest so much energy into keeping up their emotional guard and disguising their deepest and most vulnerable feelings, they often have little or no energy left to apply themselves to their schoolwork. No doubt boys still show up as small minorities at the top of a few academic lists, playing starring roles as some teachers' best students. But, most often, boys form the majority of the bottom of the class. Over the last decade we've been forced to confront some staggering statistics. From elementary grades through high school, boys receive lower grades than girls. Eighth-grade boys are held back 50 percent more often than girls. By high school, boys account for two thirds of the students in special education classes. Fewer boys than girls now attend and graduate from college. Fifty-nine percent of all master's degree candidates are now women, and the percentage of men in graduate-level professional education is shrinking each year.

gender gap
Difference in
expectations and/or
success of men and
women

2   So, there is a gender gap in academic performance, and boys are falling to the bottom of the heap. The problem stems as much from boys' lack of confidence in their ability to perform at school as from their actual inability to perform.

3   When eighth-grade students are asked about their futures, girls are now twice as likely as boys to say they want to pursue a career in management, the professions, or business. Boys experience more difficulty adjusting to school, are up to ten times more likely to suffer from "hyper-activity" than girls, and account for 71 percent of all school suspensions. In recent years, girls have been making great strides in math and science. In the same period, boys have been severely lagging behind in reading and writing.

Boys' Self-Esteem—And Bragging

4   The fact is that *boys' self-esteem as learners is far more fragile than that of most girls.* A recent North Carolina study of students in grades six to eight concluded that "Boys have a much lower image of themselves as students than girls do." Conducted by Dr. William Purkey, this study contradicts the myth that adolescent boys are more likely than girls to see themselves as smart enough to succeed in society. Boys tend to brag, according to Purkey, as a "shield to hide deep-seated lack of confidence." It is the mask at work once again, a façade of confidence and bravado that boys erect to hide what they perceive as a shameful sense of vulnerability. Girls, on the other hand, brag less and do better in school. It is probably no surprise that a recent U.S. Department of Education study found that among high school seniors fewer boys than girls expect to pursue graduate studies, work toward a law degree, or go to medical school.

5   What we really need for boys is the same upswing in self-esteem as learners that we have begun to achieve for girls—to recognize the specialized academic needs of boys and girls in order to turn us into a more gender-savvy society.

6   Overwhelmingly, recent research indicates that girls not only out-perform boys academically but also feel far more confident and capable. Indeed the boys in my study reported, over and over again, how it was not "cool" to be too smart in class, for it could lead to being labeled a nerd, dork, wimp, or fag. As one boy put it, "I'm not stupid enough to sit in the front row and act like some sort of a teacher's pet. If I did, I'd end up with a head full of spitballs and then get my butt kicked in." Just as girls in co-educational environments have been forced to suppress their voices of certainty and truth, boys feel pressured to hide their yearnings for genuine relationships and their thirst for knowledge. To garner acceptance among their peers and protect themselves from being shamed, boys often focus on maintaining their masks and on doing whatever they can to avoid seeming interested in things creative or intellectual. To distance themselves from the things that the stereotype identifies as "feminine," many boys sit through classes without contributing and tease other boys who speak up and participate. Others pull pranks during class, start fights, skip classes, or even drop out of school entirely.

Schools and the Need for Gender Understanding

7   Regrettably, instead of working with boys to convince them it is desirable and even "cool" to perform well at school, teachers, too, are often fooled by the mask and believe the stereotype; and this helps to make the lack of achievement self-fulfilling. If a teacher believes that boys who are not doing well are simply uninterested, incapable, or delinquent, and signals this, it helps to make it so. Indeed when boys feel pain at school, they sometimes put on the mask and then "act out." Teachers, rather than exploring the emotional reasons behind a boy's misconduct, may instead apply behavioral control techniques that are intended somehow to better "civilize" boys.

8   Sal, a third-grader, arrived home with a note from his teacher. "Sal had to be disciplined today for his disruptive behavior," the teacher had written. "Usually he is a very cooperative student, and I hope this behavior does not repeat itself."

9   Sal's mother, Audrey, asked her son what he had done.

10   "I was talking out of turn in class," he said.

11   "That's it?" she asked. "And how did your teacher discipline you?"

12   "She made me stay in during recess. She made me write an essay about why talking in class is disruptive and inconsiderate." Sal hung his head.

13   "I was appalled," recalls Audrey. "If the teacher had spent one minute with my child, trying to figure out why he was behaving badly, this whole thing could have been avoided." The teacher had known Sal to be "a very cooperative student." It seems that, the night before, Sal had learned that a favorite uncle had been killed in a car crash. "I told my son that I understood that he was having a really hard day because of his uncle, but that,

even so, it's wrong to disrupt class. He was very relieved that I wasn't mad," Audrey said. "The episode made me think about how boys get treated in school. I think the teacher assumed that Sal was just 'being a boy.' And so, although what he really needed was a little understanding and extra attention, instead she humiliated him. It reminded me to think about how Sal must be feeling when something like this happens, because he often won't talk about what's bothering him unless we prompt him to."

POLLACK, *Real Boys*

Exercise 12

Work with Words

Use context clues, word part clues, and if necessary the dictionary to choose the best definitions of the italicized words in the following sentences from Reading 3.

1. Boys on the whole are not *faring* well in our schools, especially in our public schools. It is in the classroom that we see some of the most destructive effects of society's misunderstanding of boys. (par. 1)

   faring
   a. doing
   b. attending
   c. fighting

2. *Thrust* into competition with their peers, some boys *invest* so much energy into keeping up their emotional guard and disguising their deepest and most vulnerable feelings, they often have little or no energy left to apply themselves to their schoolwork. (par. 1)

   thrust
   a. invited
   b. crushed
   c. thrown

   invest
   a. use money to make more money
   b. use, devote time
   c. withhold

3. In recent years, girls have been making great *strides* in math and science. In the same period, boys have been severely lagging behind in reading and writing. (par. 3)

   strides
   a. failures
   b. stumbles
   c. steps forward

4. A recent North Carolina study of students in grades six to eight concluded that "boys have a much lower image of themselves as students than girls do." Conducted by Dr. William Purkey, this study *contradicts* the myth that adolescent boys are more likely than girls to see themselves as smart enough to succeed in society. (par. 4)

contradicts
a. agrees with
b. repeats
c. disagrees with

5. Boys tend to brag, according to Purkey, as a "shield to hide deep-seated lack of confidence." It is the mask at work once again, a *façade* of confidence and bravado that boys erect to hide what they perceive as a shameful sense of vulnerability. (par. 4)

façade
a. genuine quality
b. artificial front
c. extravagant parade

6. To *garner* acceptance among their peers and protect themselves from being shamed, boys often focus on maintaining their masks and on doing whatever they can to avoid seeming interested in things creative or intellectual. (par. 6)

garner
a. reject
b. maintain
c. gain

| Exercise 13 | **Recognize the Connotations of Words** |

Read the following sentences from Reading 3, noticing the italicized words. Each of these words has certain connotations. Choose the best descriptions of the definitions and connotations of these words as they are used in the sentences.

1. Over the last decade we've been forced to confront some *staggering* statistics. From elementary grades through high school, boys receive lower grades than girls. (par. 1)

staggering
a. uncertain; negative connotation
b. exaggerated; negative connotation
c. overwhelming; negative connotation

2. When eighth-grade students are asked about their futures, girls are now twice as likely as boys to say they want to *pursue* a career in management, the professions or business. (par. 3)

pursue
a. capture aggressively; negative connotation
b. strive to attain; positive connotation
c. avoid; negative connotation

3. In recent years, girls have been making great *strides* in math and science. In the same period, boys have been severely *lagging behind* in reading and writing. (par. 3)

strides
a. resistance; negative connotation
b. difficult choices; negative connotation
c. steps forward; positive connotation

lagging behind
a. failing to keep up; negative connotation
b. decreasing gradually; positive connotation
c. lingering or delaying; negative connotation

4. Indeed the boys in my study reported, over and over again, how it was not "*cool*" to be too smart in class, for it could lead to being labeled a nerd, dork, wimp, or fag. (par. 6)

cool
a. appearing enthusiastic; positive connotation
b. appearing unconcerned; positive connotation
c. appearing unconcerned; negative connotation

5. If a teacher believes that boys who are not doing well are simply un-interested, incapable, or *delinquent*, and signals this, it helps to make it so. (par. 7)

delinquent
a. a debt that is past due; negative connotation
b. guilty of an offense; negative connotation
c. incapable; negative connotation

| Exercise 14 |

Check Your Understanding: Recognize Facts and Opinions

Read the following sentences from or based on Reading 3, and write "F" before statements of fact and "O" before statements of opinion. On the line that follows, briefly explain your answer.

_____ 1. It is in the classroom that we see some of the most destructive effects of society's misunderstanding of boys.

_____

_____

_____ 2. Most often, boys form the majority of the bottom of the class.

_____

_____ 3. From elementary grades through high school, boys receive lower grades than girls.

_____

_____ 4. Boys experience more difficulty adjusting to school, are up to ten times more likely to suffer from "hyper-activity" than girls, and account for 71 percent of all school suspensions.

_____

_____ 5. Our schools must become more responsive to and understanding of the problems that boys face in the education process.

_____

| **Exercise 15** | ## Make Connections |

Write short answers to the following questions based on Reading 3, your experience, and your observations.

1. Think about your experiences in school. Who, as you recall, had more difficulty doing well as a group? Girls or boys? Explain your answer. What kinds of difficulties did they have, and why do you think that was so?

_____

_____

2. What experiences have you had while growing up that would lead you to think that you had it easier or harder because you were a boy or a girl?

_____

_____

Drawing Conclusions

conclusion A judgment or decision that you reach after careful thought

Drawing conclusions is "adding up" all you know about a topic and making some decisions about it. A **conclusion** is a judgment or decision that you reach after careful thought. William Pollack, in his book *Real Boys*, provides dozens of examples of boys who have had problems in their lives, but instead of learning how to deal with those problems, have worn a "mask" and pretended to be tough guys. After studying hundreds of boys in his research, Pollack has come to certain conclusions about the way we raise our boys in this society and the problems that arise from the expectations that we have of them. In the following excerpt, he explains some of his conclusions.

Although it's not always easy to tell, many adolescent boys—just like adolescent girls—suffer from a crisis of self-confidence and identity. There is, however, a major difference between the plight of boys and that of girls. Even when their voices are stifled in public, girls generally feel comfortable speaking in private to one another about their pain and insecurities. By contrast, though boys may exhibit bravado and braggadocio, they find it more difficult to express their genuine selves even in private, with friends and family. Their voices, as loud and forceful as they may sound, may not reveal what is really in their hearts and souls. Instead, most boys—whether in public or private—tend to act confident and contented, and even brag about their abilities. While we may joke about how adult males won't ask for directions when they're lost, it is no laughing matter that so many of our boys feel they can't reach out for the emotional compass they so desperately need.

braggadocio
Empty bragging

   What can we do to change all this? How can we help boys adjust to today's world and social environment and learn new ways of seeing and relating to other people? What can we do to draw boys out, to get boys to trust us, to let us join them inside their worlds, and help them be and become more fully the people they really are?

   . . . there is much we can do to support and connect with our boys. We can become aware of the boy stereotypes even the best of us carry in our minds, and consciously work to eliminate them from society, from our thinking and our language. We can learn to recognize the words that boys use when something is troubling them but they feel they can't talk about it—the "I'm fine," that actually means things are really not fine. We can learn how to get our sons to talk, without demanding or pressuring them to, by finding the safe spaces that will allow them to open up and express themselves: We can better anticipate the situations that might cause feelings of vulnerability and fear—the first day of school, the big test, the first date, the gym class, the school trip, the illness of a friend, the breakup of a romance, the move to a new place, the doctor's appointment, the onset of puberty—and find ways that will prepare a boy for them in advance, and allow him to talk about them after the fact. Above all, we can begin to teach connection as the basis of a new male model. (Pollack, *Real Boys*)

As an active reader, you need to recognize what conclusions the author has drawn, and how the author reached those conclusions. Once you have done that, you will consider whether or not you agree. Are the author's information and arguments convincing? Do they correspond with what you know about the subject? Do you recognize the problems that the author is discussing in your own experience, family, or community? What solutions is the author presenting? Do you think the author's solutions would work? By asking these questions and going through these thought processes, you can critically evaluate the information and ideas presented and arrive at your own conclusions.

Now let's go through these steps to evaluate the excerpt from William Pollack. First, you need to ask yourself the following:

- What is the conclusion that the author has drawn about the source or cause of many of boys' problems?

  Boys are ashamed of appearing weak or of showing their feelings, so they hide them from their friends and families as well as from the rest of the world.

- Are Pollack's information and arguments convincing? Do they correspond to the information and experience you have?

  He gives statistics on boys' performance in school, based on research.

  His arguments also seem convincing because I know boys who wear "tough guy" masks. And he gives lots of examples to back up his idea.

- What solutions are being presented by Pollack?

  He is suggesting that it is important that we understand how vulnerable boys are and that we learn to communicate with them, to get them to express how they feel. He is also suggesting that we try to change the stereotype of what it means to be a boy in our society.

- Do you think Pollack's solutions would work?

  It seems like a good idea to encourage boys to express how they really feel. I agree with Pollack that we need to change the stereotypes that people have about boys, but it might take a long time to change the people's ideas about how boys are supposed to act. In the meantime, I think boys may have to continue to look "tough" in certain places so that they won't become victims.

By going through the process of asking these questions, you, as a critical thinker, will reach your *own* conclusions. Drawing your own conclusions is a skill that you will use for your whole life when you read, when you think, when you talk, and before you act. You go through this process all the time.

A goal of this textbook has been to help you set this process in motion when you read. Here are the steps:

1. Figure out the main idea of a passage (stated or unstated).
2. Recognize the major and minor supporting details that a writer uses to support his or her conclusion.
3. Understand the pattern of organization the author uses so that you can recognize how the author frames his or her argument.
4. Make reasonable inferences regarding the author's assumptions about information that may not be stated directly.
5. Distinguish between facts and opinions.
6. Recognize the author's conclusions.
7. Evaluate those conclusions, deciding if you agree with them and whether or not they might be useful in your own circumstances.
8. Draw your own conclusions based on your reading, your observations, and your experience.

Exercise 16

Draw Conclusions

Choose a reading from the "Additional Readings" section of this text. "The Handicap of Definition," p. 472; "Persuasive Techniques in Contemporary Advertising," p. 482; "Exposure to Chemicals and Human Fertility," p. 498; and "Survival of the Fittest? The *Survivor* Story," p. 502, would all be good choices. Read carefully, and then answer the following questions about the reading.

Title of the reading ⎯⎯⎯⎯⎯⎯⎯⎯⎯⎯⎯⎯⎯⎯⎯⎯⎯

1. What conclusions does the author draw in this reading?

⎯⎯⎯⎯⎯⎯⎯⎯⎯⎯⎯⎯⎯⎯⎯⎯⎯⎯⎯⎯⎯⎯⎯⎯⎯⎯

⎯⎯⎯⎯⎯⎯⎯⎯⎯⎯⎯⎯⎯⎯⎯⎯⎯⎯⎯⎯⎯⎯⎯⎯⎯⎯

⎯⎯⎯⎯⎯⎯⎯⎯⎯⎯⎯⎯⎯⎯⎯⎯⎯⎯⎯⎯⎯⎯⎯⎯⎯⎯

2. What supporting details does the author use to demonstrate the correctness of his or her conclusion? Are the information and arguments presented convincing to you? Explain.

⎯⎯⎯⎯⎯⎯⎯⎯⎯⎯⎯⎯⎯⎯⎯⎯⎯⎯⎯⎯⎯⎯⎯⎯⎯⎯

⎯⎯⎯⎯⎯⎯⎯⎯⎯⎯⎯⎯⎯⎯⎯⎯⎯⎯⎯⎯⎯⎯⎯⎯⎯⎯

⎯⎯⎯⎯⎯⎯⎯⎯⎯⎯⎯⎯⎯⎯⎯⎯⎯⎯⎯⎯⎯⎯⎯⎯⎯⎯

⎯⎯⎯⎯⎯⎯⎯⎯⎯⎯⎯⎯⎯⎯⎯⎯⎯⎯⎯⎯⎯⎯⎯⎯⎯⎯

3. Does the author present solutions to a problem? What are the author's solutions?

_____

_____

_____

4. Based on your reading, your observations, and your experience, do you think that the author's solutions will work?

_____

_____

_____

5. What conclusions would you draw and/or what solutions would you propose? Explain.

_____

_____

_____

READING 4

A Minefield: Teenagers and Racism on the U.S.–Mexico Border

Enrique Dávalos

The following reading was written for this edition of Joining a Community of Readers. *In it, Mexican historian and border resident, Enrique Dávalos, explores the events of the summer of 2000 in San Diego, when a group of high school boys attacked Mexican workers who lived in a makeshift encampment made of cardboard boxes, crates, and scraps in the canyons near a well-to-do suburb. As you read, consider which parts of Dávalos's essay are facts and which parts are opinions. Also, what conclusions might you draw about the events that occurred and possible actions that should be taken?*

initiative A system in California by which citizens can get a "proposition" on the ballot with a certain number of signatures of registered voters. If it is approved in an election, it becomes law.

1 For several years, the political climate in southern California has been increasingly influenced by anti-immigrant attitudes. Mexicans and people of Mexican descent have frequently felt as if they are under attack in a state that once belonged to Mexico. Politicians have taken advantage of anti-immigrant feelings and have stirred up the antagonisms when it suited them to do so. (The same politicians, on other occasions, court the vote of the growing Latino population.) A variety of recent initiatives, turned into

laws, were designed to deny public health services and even school enrollment to migrants and their children. Once famed for its orange groves and
mild weather, California now has a cultural landscape that resembles a
minefield, planted with land mines of hatred and racial intolerance, and we
are beginning to reap the harvest.

2   In the beginning of the millennium, in San Diego County, during the
summer of 2000, a group of teenagers violently attacked a few elderly Mexican migrant workers. These children, boys between 14 and 17 years old,
lived in an upper-middle-class neighborhood and attended one of the most
prestigious high schools in San Diego. They became "hate" criminals and almost murderers. We have to learn from this experience to deactivate the
mines before more racial hatred explodes, destroying our kids.

3   Let's see what the group of teenagers did when they attacked the camp
of migrants on July 5, 2000. According to the reports of the local newspaper,
The *San Diego Union Tribune*, a group of eight adolescents drove a van to
several migrant encampments near their neighborhood and conducted three
raids over a period of two hours. It was "a very brutal, violent, cowardly attack," the San Diego police chief said. Some of the workers were hospitalized,
and the teenagers even tried to hide the body of a man that they believed
they had killed. All the victims were elders ranging in age from 64 to 69. They
were beaten with pipes and rocks and shot with pellet guns. Some migrants
confronted the attackers with machetes. The youths shouted racial slurs during the beating, and, according to authorities, they asked them to show proof
they were legal residents. Those who did not show documents were beaten.

4   Chief of police David Bejarano said that the attackers "wanted them
[the workers] to go back to Mexico." Some spray-painted graffiti messages
appeared in the camp, including "We're still here! KKK," "Jesus loves U," and
epithet   An abusive   some racial epithets. A red and yellow swastika was also painted. Police are
term   not sure, however, whether the attackers were responsible for the graffiti
because other young men had been seen around the encampment.

5   After the police captured the teenagers, prosecutors said the boys ad-
derogatory   mitted that they thought it was "cool to shoot beaners," a common deroga-
Insulting   tory term used against Mexicans. One of the adolescents added that he was
tired of listening to people speaking Spanish around him.

6   According to journalist Jeff McDonald, the students responsible for the
attack lived in a suburb of San Diego, Rancho Peñasquitos, which is full of
SUVs (sports utility vehicles), "soccer moms," playgrounds, and parks. Two-
thirds of the families are Caucasian and 31 percent are Asian. "Nearly three-
fourths of the residents report household incomes between $60,000 and
$150,000, far higher than the San Diego-wide average," said McDonald.
Most of the assailants attended Mt. Carmel High School, one of the county's
highest performing schools academically. In contrast, their migrant victims
lived in improvised camps near the Evergreen Nursery, where they worked.
They earned a minimal wage with no benefits. They could not afford hous-

ing in this country, and our laws don't require employers to provide homes for their workers. Some of the migrant workers had homes in Tijuana, Mexico, where they went on the weekends. Even in their precarious situation, they belonged to the neighborhood. "I have lived in Rancho Peñasquitos for 12 years," writes Kate Martin, and "I have grown up in the presence of these men in our community. These men are a familiar part of the community—the crowd every morning under the State Route 56 overpass, the occasional face in line with me at VONS [the local grocery store], the tireless man at the door asking for work."

7   The attack against the migrants caused confusion and stupefaction in the adult community, although it was not a big surprise to students of local high schools. The parents of the young attackers were shocked, their lawyers said. "It saddens me that these boys may have a such degree of hate in them," wrote a Rancho Peñasquitos neighbor (Ivonne Chau). However, some students affirmed, after the arrest, that they had "heard about students teasing migrant workers and stealing their bicycles," and that "at least one Latino student had been the victim of a race-motivated beating." Another student told reporters, "I wasn't very surprised; I can see them doing that." In fact, racial tension was not something unknown in Mt. Carmel High School. In the previous spring (2000), students and teachers organized several meetings to discuss ways to stop racial and ethnic insults on campus.

8   The students arrested had different personalities and belonged to different kinds of families. According to Jeff McDonald, some of them lived in broken families, but others were from more stable families. Some of them were known to pick fights and threaten other students at school. One of them already had a juvenile record and another was attending an alternative high school for students with discipline problems. However, one of the arrested students played football and the guitar. Some neighbors declared that one of the group was "the nicest guy, never violent—kind of shy. He was just like any other teenager, really." In the same way, another neighbor said about another of the teenagers involved in the attack that he was "very friendly. Even now, when he's riding his bike he says hello." Considering the variety of personal situations, it is difficult to explain the attack based only on the psychology, the "natural rebelliousness" of adolescents, or on the specific family problems of these young people. It is frightening to accept, but the attack has broader social and cultural roots.

9   For example, the legal process against the arrested students has brought to light and magnified the racial tension that already existed in San Diego. The teenagers were charged with robbery, assault, and a hate crime. The prosecutor asked that they be tried as adults, which would mean a more severe sentence if they are convicted. However, the parents of the arrested boys, while emphasizing that they were sorry about what their boys had done, also insisted, "Our children are not adults." The issue is controversial, especially after most Californians voted for a new law (Proposition 21, which

passed in the fall of 1999) that allows the prosecuting attorney to decide if criminal minors should be tried as adults. Lawyers and parents of Rancho Peñasquitos' students are challenging this law. Earlier it was applied against some African-American and Latino youths with no media attention. "Why is the law unconstitutional when it is used against whites?" asked a student from a local community college with a mostly African-American and Latino population. The irony is that people in Rancho Peñasquitos mostly voted for Proposition 21, never thinking that it might be used against their own children. "It is ironic," wrote Ronda Trapp, "that now that these kids from 'good' families, who go to 'good' schools in a 'good' community, have been charged as adults, others who likely voted for Prop. 21, now argue that it is unconstitutional and morally wrong." At the moment (September 13, 2000), a San Diego judge approved that the eight teenagers be tried as adults, but their parents were ready to appeal.

10   Several people and organizations in San Diego condemned the attack and pointed out that it is just the tip of the iceberg. Sonia Perez, from the National Council of La Raza, mentioned that a national study had found an increase in the number of hate crimes committed against Latinos nationwide. In San Diego, one of these attacks was perpetrated in 1994 by four Marines, members of an elite, SWAT-type military police, said Claudia Smith of California Rural Legal Assistance. She added that Latinos in San Diego are harassed every day: "It would be rare to talk to a group of migrant farm workers and not have them tell you of experiences when bottles were thrown at them from passing vehicles, epithets hurled at them."

11   It is disturbing that this wave of racism is poisoning the youth. The Anti-Defamation League has reported that in San Diego the assailants in about half of the hate crimes against Latinos are 20 years old or younger. "The reality is, we're seeing younger and younger kids who feel this is an okay thing to do, to beat someone because of their difference," said Jack McDevitt, director of the Center for Criminal Justice Policy Research at Northeastern University in Boston. Racial discrimination is illegal and assault is illegal, but it is not illegal to joke or be sarcastic about racial differences. How do children perceive racial attitudes and comments from their parents in neighborhoods like Rancho Peñasquitos? What do they learn from attitudes of disgust and indifference toward people who are different? "It is easy to ignore those dark faces, to mutter an exasperated groan each morning while driving under the Route 56 overpass, to close a door on pleading hands, to turn away, to ignore great poverty," wrote Kate Martin, resident of Rancho Peñasquitos. Children are very sensitive. Adults may joke and feel contempt for Mexican migrants, but they should realize that what they feel and think is what their children will put into actions, and the attack in Rancho Peñasquitos is a warning.

12   Finding a solution is not easy. How do we create a culture where our children and all members of our communities are safe? How do we clean up the landscape that has been planted with mines of hatred and social in-

tolerance? It is never easy to remove land mines or to deactivate them. They are usually hidden, difficult to find, and dangerous to handle.

13   Children are children, and they should not be tried as adults; however, the perpetrators of the hate crimes committed in Rancho Peñasquitos deserve a severe punishment. Will an experience in prison change the racist perceptions of the teenagers about Mexicans and other minorities? Probably not. Perhaps it would be more useful, as Jacqueline Giles said, that "the perpetrators and their parents should be required to learn Spanish, study Mexican history and culture and perform enough hard, manual labor to bring them to understand that the men whom they held in contempt and brutalized are real people deserving of respect." Perhaps after that experience, they will be able to understand why one of the Mexican workers assailed, Mr. Alfredo Ayala, 64, said that even though his attackers did not show any mercy, he held no animosity toward them. He only felt sorry for their families.

Sources

Chau, Ivonne. "Letters," *San Diego Union Tribune,* July 21, 2000, p. B9.

Giles, Jacqueline. "Will Prison Teach Teens Tolerance?" *San Diego Union Tribune*, July 21, 2000, p. B7.

Martin, Kate. "Fight Racism by Fighting Indifference," *San Diego Union Tribune,* July 27, 2000, p. B11.

McDonald, Jeff. "Some Suspects in Camp Attack Had Troubled Pasts," *San Diego Union Tribune,* July 22, 2000, p. B1.

"Mt. Carmel High Has a Way to Go Despite Its Many Triumphs," *San Diego Union Tribune,* July 18, p. B3.

Nguyen, Dong-Phuong. "Local Attack Mirrors Rise in Reported U.S. Hate Crime," *San Diego Union Tribune*, July 21, 2000, p. B3.

Roth, Alex. "Teen Admitted Role in Attack, Affidavit Says," *San Diego Union Tribune,* July 26, 2000, p. B4.

Roth, Alex, Joe Hughes, Kim Peterson, and Leonel Sanchez. "Police Arrest Seven Teens in Attacks at Migrant Camp," *San Diego Union Tribune*, July 18, 2000, p. B1.

Trapp, Ronda. "Letters," *San Diego Union Tribune*, July 24, 2000, p. B7.

DÁVALOS, "A Minefield"

| **Exercise 17** | ## Understand the Language of Imagery |

In the following sentences from Reading 4, some examples of language that use imagery have been italicized. Explain (1) what visual images are formed when we read these words, and (2) what the words actually refer to or mean in the sentence.

1. Once famed for its orange groves and mild weather, California now has *a cultural landscape that resembles a minefield, planted with land mines of hatred and racial intolerance, and now we are beginning to reap the harvest.* (par. 1)

   visual image: _____

   meaning: _____

   _____

2. We have to learn from this experience to *deactivate* the mines before the racial hatred *explodes,* destroying our kids. (par. 2)

   visual image: _____

   _____

   meaning: _____

   _____

3. How do we clean up *the landscape that has been planted* with mines of hatred and social intolerance? (par. 12)

   visual image: _____

   meaning: _____

4. It is frightening to accept, but the attack has broader social and *cultural roots.* (par. 8)

   visual image: _____

   _____

   meaning: _____

5. For example, the legal process against the arrested students has *brought to light and magnified* the racial tension that already existed in San Diego. (par. 9)

   visual image: _____

   meaning: _____

6. Several people and organizations in San Diego have condemned the attack and pointed out that it is just the *tip of the iceberg.* (par. 10)

   visual image: _____

   _____

   meaning: _____

7. It is disturbing that this *wave* of racism is poisoning the youth. (par. 11)

visual image: _____

meaning: _____

Exercise 18   # Check Your Understanding: Recognize Fact and Opinion

Examine each of the following sentences from or based on Reading 4, and write "F" before statements of fact and "O" before statements of opinion. On the line that follows, briefly explain your answer.

_____ 1. Mexicans and people of Mexican descent have frequently felt as if they are under attack in a state that once belonged to Mexico.

_____

_____ 2. A variety of recent initiatives, turned into laws, were designed to deny public health services and even school enrollment to migrants and their children.

_____

_____

_____ 3. In the beginning of the millennium, in San Diego County, during the summer of 2000, a group of teenagers violently attacked a few elderly Mexican migrant workers.

_____

_____ 4. The household incomes in Rancho Peñasquitos are higher than they are in most other areas of San Diego.

_____

_____ 5. The prosecutor asked that they be tried as adults, which would mean a more severe sentence if they are convicted.

_____

_____ 6. There is evidence that there has been an increase in the number of hate crimes in California recently.

_____

_____ 7. Children are children, and they should not be tried as adults.

_____

_____ 8. The perpetrators of this hate crime deserve a severe punishment.

_____

| Exercise 19 | Identify Inferences |

Choose the best way to complete the following statements about Reading 4.

1. In paragraph 1, we can reasonably infer that the author believes that
   a. the anti-immigrant feelings in California are setting the stage for problems for the young people as well as for the society as a whole.
   b. Mexicans and people of Mexican descent should not feel as though they are being attacked.
   c. politicians are clearly not to blame for the anti-immigrant attitudes in California.

2. We could reasonably infer that the migrant workers lived in encampments
   a. because they preferred to live outdoors.
   b. because it was illegal to rent apartments to them in Rancho Peñasquitos.
   c. because they could not afford housing in Rancho Peñasquitos.

3. In paragraph 8, we can reasonably infer that the author believes that
   a. the attackers were poor and viciously attacked the workers because they were rich.
   b. the boys come from different backgrounds so it's difficult to give a single simple reason for why they were involved in the attack.
   c. the natural rebelliousness of teenage boys explains the attack.

4. From paragraph 11, we can reasonably infer that the author believes that
   a. the adolescents are carrying out racist attacks because their parents make comments about the immigrants that show contempt for them.
   b. the adolescents are carrying out racist attacks even though their parents have tolerant attitudes for the most part.
   c. there is no explanation for why these boys carried out their attack against the immigrants.

5. Jacqueline Giles (par. 13) suggests that "the perpetrators and their parents should be required to learn Spanish, study Mexican history and culture and perform enough hard, manual labor to bring them to understand that the men whom they held in contempt and brutalized are real people deserving of respect." We can reasonably infer that Giles believes that
   a. learning the language of another people teaches you to understand their situation.
   b. understanding another culture's language, history, and work experience leads to tolerance and respect.
   c. the schools have failed these adolescent boys.

Exercise 20

Make Connections: Draw Conclusions

Write short answers to the following questions about Reading 4 based on your reading, your experience, and your observations.

1. What conclusions does Dávalos draw about how the incident should be understood?

   _____

   _____

   _____

   _____

2. What conclusions or solutions does Dávalos give for handling the court case and punishing the boys who committed this hate crime?

   _____

   _____

   _____

   _____

   _____

3. How do you think the case of the boys should be handled? Should they be tried as adults? If the boys are convicted, what type of sentence should they receive? Explain.

   _____

   _____

   _____

   _____

4. Do you think these boys were wearing the "tough guy" mask that William Pollack describes in other readings selected for this chapter? Explain.

   _____

   _____

   _____

5. Do you think the actions of these boys come from their personal problems or from problems in society? Explain.

_____

_____

_____

_____

| Exercise 21 | ## Make Connections: Collaborative Activity |

Discuss your answers to Questions 4 and 5 in Exercise 20 with your class group. Working together, prepare a written summary to turn into your instructor.

Chapter Review

To aid your review of the reading skills in Chapter 9, study the Put It Together chart.

Put It Together: *Inferences, Fact versus Opinion, and Conclusions*	
Skills and Concepts	**Explanation**
Inference (see pages 420–422)	Read "between the lines" to understand what a speaker or writer is saying indirectly.
Fact versus opinion (see pages 435–436)	Distinguish facts—information that most people accept as true or that can be verified—from opinions, which are interpretations of facts.
Drawing conclusions (see pages 443–446)	Evaluate the facts and opinions presented in a reading and, together with your own knowledge and experience, make decisions about what you agree with and what you do not.

To reinforce your thinking before taking the Mastery Tests, complete as many of the following activities as your instructor assigns.

Reviewing Skills

Answer the following skills-review questions individually or in a group.

1. Why is it important to be able to make reasonable inferences about a reading?

_____

_____

_____

2. Why is it important to be able to distinguish between facts and opinions? What are some examples of when you need this skill?

_____

_____

_____

Writing

Find a newspaper or magazine article about achievements or problems of adolescents. Write a brief summary of the article. Then use your skill at recognizing inferences to conclude your summary with what the author thinks are the causes of the way adolescents behave.

Collaborating

Bring your newspaper or magazine articles about adolescents to class to share with your class group. Discuss what the articles have in common. Then complete the accompanying chart. How do the readings in the chapter help you to draw conclusions about adolescents?

Types of Adolescents (girls, boys, kids with problems, achievers)	*Achievements or Problems*	*Causes*

Extending Your Thinking

Visit a high school, juvenile detention center, community club, or activity for young people. Develop a list of questions you would like to ask based on the readings in this chapter. Interview a counselor, a law officer, a club leader, or a coach about juvenile behavior. Bring the information you learn back to class to share with your fellow students and instructor.

Visiting the Web

The following Web sites provide more information as well as counseling on various aspects of (1) society's expectations of adolescent boys and girls, (2) the difficulties that young people have during adolescence, and (3) the difficulties that men and women continue to struggle with regarding their roles in life.

1. *Male Sex Roles*

   http://www.counsel.ufl.edu/CounselNet/cnetmale.html
   This Web page offers counseling to young men. The last twenty to thirty years has brought significant changes in male and female sex roles. The changes have caused many men to reevaluate "old" or "traditional" notions of manhood and masculinity. While many men welcome these changes, the redefinition of roles has caused confusion and problems for some. This page examines some of the ways men have been affected by changing sex-role definitions.

2. *The Peace Page*

   http://web.missouri.edu/~lvs9fa/peace.html
   This Web page is dedicated to reducing racism of all kinds—not just the black/white racism that you are used to hearing about, but prejudice against different religions, homosexuality, and different cultures.

3. *Bodytalk*

   http://www.bodytalkmagazine.com/
   "Bodytalk" started out as a radio talk-back program in Melbourne, Australia. The woman who started it, Kerryn Marlow, says, "I was sick of reading about 'figure flaws' and being told 'the waif look is in'! Don't get me wrong—I can appreciate an attractive person. But I won't be made to feel bad about myself just because I have cellulite and enjoy the odd hunk of mudcake."

Name _____ Date _____

When Money Is Everything, Except Hers
Dirk Johnson

In the following newspaper article, Dirk Johnson shows what it is like for a young person to grow up poor in the middle of a prosperous neighborhood. Johnson points out that adolescence can seem so much worse for kids who are not like their peers—especially when those peers taunt and isolate them. As you read, pay attention not only to how Johnson uses inferences to tell Wendy's story but also to how his imagery paints a clear picture of her life. Do you think the solutions offered by the counselor at the end of the reading adequately address the problem at hand?

1   Dixon, Ill. Watching classmates strut past in designer clothes, Wendy Williams sat silently on the yellow school bus, wearing a cheap belt and rummage-sale slacks. One boy stopped and yanked his thumb, demanding her seat. "Move it, trailer girl," he sneered.

2   It has never been easy to live on the wrong side of the tracks. But in the economically robust 1990s, with sprawling new houses and three-car garages sprouting like cornstalks on the Midwestern prairie, the sting that comes with scarcity gets rubbed with an extra bit of salt. Seen through the eyes of a 13-year-old girl growing up at Chateau Estates, a fancy name for a tin-plain trailer park, the rosy talk about the nation's prosperity carries a certain mocking echo.

3   The everyday discussion in the halls of Reagan Middle School in this city about 100 miles west of Chicago touches on computer toys that can cost $1,000, family vacations to Six Flags or Disney World and stylish clothes that bear a Nike emblem or Tommy Hilfiger's coveted label. Unlike young people a generation ago, those today must typically pay fees to play for the school sports teams or band. It costs $45 to play in the youth summer soccer league. It takes money to go skating on weekends at the White Pines roller rink, to play laser tag or rock-climb at the Plum Hollow Recreation Center, to mount a steed at the Horseback Riding Club, to gaze at Leonardo DiCaprio and Kate Winslet at the Plaza Cinemas, to go shopping for clothes at the Cherryvale Mall.

4   To be without money, in so many ways, is to be left out. "I told this girl: 'That's a really awesome shirt. Where did you get it?'" said Wendy, explaining that she knew it was out of her price range, but that she wanted to join the small talk. "And she looked at me and laughed and said, 'Why would you want to know?'" A lanky, soft-spoken girl with large brown eyes, Wendy pursed her lips to hide a slight overbite that got her the nickname Rabbit, a humiliation she once begged her mother and father to avoid by sending her to an orthodontist.

5   For struggling parents, keenly aware that adolescents agonize over the social pecking order, the styles of the moment and the face in the mirror, there is no small sense of failure in telling a child that she cannot have what her classmates take for granted. "Do you know what it's like?" asked Wendy's mother, Veronica Williams, "to have your daughter come home and say, 'Mom, the kids say my clothes are tacky,' and then walk off with her head hanging low."

6   This is not the desperate poverty of Chicago housing projects, where the plight of empty pockets is worsened by the threat of gangs and gunfires. Wendy lives in relative safety in a home with both parents. Her father, Wendell Provow, earns $9 an hour as a welder. Her mother works part-time as a cook for Head Start, the federal education program. Unlike students in some urban pockets, isolated from affluence, Wendy receives the same education as a girl from a $300,000 house in the Idle Oaks subdivision. The flip side of that coin is the public spectacle of economic struggle. This is a place small enough where people know the personal stories, or, at least, repeat them as if they did.

7   Even in this down-to-earth town, where a poor boy nicknamed Dutch grew up to become president, young people seem increasingly enchanted with buying, having, spending and status. R. Woodrow (Woody) Wasson, the principal at Reagan Middle School, makes it a point to sit down with every child and ask them about their hopes and dreams. "They want to be doctors, lawyers, veterinarians and, of course, professional athletes," said Mr. Wasson, whose family roots here go back to the 19th century. "I don't remember the last time I heard somebody say they wanted to be a police officer or a firefighter. They want to do something that will make a lot of money and have a lot of prestige."

8   He said a teacher in a nearby town has been trying to recruit high school students for vocational studies to become tool-and-die artisans, a trade that can pay $70,000 a year. "The teacher can't fill the slots," Mr. Wasson said. "Nobody's interested in that kind of work."

9   It is not surprising that children grow up believing that money is so important, given the relentless way they are targeted by marketers. "In the past, you just put an ad in the magazine," said Michael Wood, the director of research for Teen-Age Research Unlimited, a marketing consultant in suburban Chicago. "Now savvy marketers know you must hit them at all angles—Web sites, cable TV shows, school functions, sporting events." He noted the growth of cross-promotions, like the deal in which actors on the television show "Dawson's Creek," which is popular among adolescents, wear clothes by J. Crew and appear in its catalogue.

10   But young people get cues in their everyday lives. Some spending habits that would once have been seen as ostentatious—extravagant parties for small children, new cars for teenagers—have become familiar trappings

for middle-class comfort. The stock market, although it is sputtering now, has made millionaires of many people in Main Street towns. Building developers have recently won approval to build a gated community, which will be called Timber Edge.

11   "Wendy goes to school around these rich kids," her mother said, "and wonders why she can't have things like they do." A bright girl with a flair for art, writing, and numbers, Wendy stays up late most nights, reading books. *The Miracle Worker* was a recent favorite. But when a teacher asked her to join an elevated class for algebra, she politely declined. "I get picked on for my clothes and living in the trailer park," said Wendy, who never brings anyone home from school. "I don't want to get picked on for being a nerd, too."

12   Her mother, who watched three other daughters drop out of school and have babies as teenagers, has told Wendy time and again: "Don't lose your self-esteem."

13   One time a boy at school was teasing Wendy about her clothes—"they don't even match," he laughed—and her humble house in the trailer park. She listened for a while. He kept insulting her. So she lifted a leg—clothed as it was in discount jeans from the Farm & Fleet store—and kicked him in the shins. He told the authorities. She got the detention. It became clear to Wendy that the insults were not going to stop. It also became clear that shin-kicking, however deserved, was not going to be the solution.

14   She went to a guidance counselor, Cynthia Kowa Basler, a dynamic woman who keeps close tabs on the children, especially girls who fret about their weight and suddenly stop eating lunch. "I am large," she tells the girls, "and I have self-esteem."

15   Wendy, who knew that Mrs. Basler held sessions with students to increase their self-confidence, went to the counselor. "I feel a little down," Wendy told her. The counselor gathered eight students, including other girls like Wendy, who felt embarrassed about their economic station.

16   In this school named for Ronald Reagan, the students were told to study the words of Eleanor Roosevelt. One of her famous quotations was posted above the counselor's desk: "No one can make you feel inferior without your consent." As a group, the students looked up the definition of inferior and consent. And then they read the words out loud.

17   "Again," the counselor instructed.

18   "Louder," the counselor insisted. Again and again, they read the inspirational words.

19   In role-playing exercises, the children practiced responses to taunts, which sometimes called for nothing more than a shrug. "Mrs. Basler told us to live up to our goals—show those kids," Wendy said. "She told us that things can be a lot different when you're grown up. Maybe things will be the other way around then." Wendy smiled at the notion.

20   Life still has plenty of bumps. When Wendy gets off the school bus—the trailer park is the first stop, so everyone can see where she lives—she still looks at her shoes. She still pulls her shirt out to hide a belt that does not quite make the grade. And she still purses her lips to hide an overbite. But her mother has noticed her smiling more these days. And Wendy has even said she might consider taking an advanced course in math, her favorite subject. "I want to go to college," Wendy said the other day. "I want to become a teacher."

21   One recent day, she popped in to the counselor's office, just to say hello, then walked back down the halls, her arms folded around her schoolbooks. Mrs. Basler stood at the doorway and watched her skip away, a student with so much promise, and so many obstacles. For the girl from Chateau Estates, it is a long way from the seventh grade to college. "She's going to make it," the counselor said, with a clenched fist and a voice full of hope.

JOHNSON, "When Money Is Everything, Except Hers"

Use context clues, word part clues, and if necessary the dictionary to write the definitions of the italicized words in the following sentences from the reading.

1. Seen through the eyes of a 13-year-old girl growing up at Chateau Estates, a fancy name for a tin-plain trailer park, the rosy talk about the nation's prosperity carries a certain *mocking* echo. (par.2)

   mocking _____

2. The everyday discussion in the halls of Reagan Middle School in this city about 100 miles west of Chicago touches on computer toys that can cost $1,000, family vacations to Six Flags or Disney World and stylish clothes that bear a Nike emblem or Tommy Hilfiger's *coveted* label. (par.3)

   coveted _____

3. For struggling parents, keenly aware that adolescents agonize over the social *pecking order*, the styles of the moment and the face in the mirror, there is no small sense of failure in telling a child that she cannot have what her classmates take for granted. (par. 5)

   pecking order _____

4. Unlike students in some urban pockets, isolated from *affluence,* Wendy receives the same education as a girl from a $300,000 house in the Idle Oaks subdivision. (par. 6)

   affluence _____

5. "In the past, you just put an ad in the magazine," said Michael Wood, the director of research for Teen-Age Research Unlimited, a marketing consultant in suburban Chicago. "Now savvy *marketers* know you must hit them at all angles—Web sites, cable TV shows, school functions, sporting events." (par. 9)

   marketers _____

6. Some spending habits that would once have been seen as *ostentatious*—extravagant parties for small children, new cars for teenagers—have become familiar trappings for middle-class comfort. (par. 10)

   ostentatious _____

7. A bright girl with a *flair* for art, writing and numbers, Wendy stays up late most nights, reading books. (par. 11)

   flair _____

8. One of her famous quotations was posted above the counselor's desk: "No one can make you feel *inferior* without your consent." (par. 16)

   inferior _____

For the following groups of sentences, choose the reasonable inferences that you can make from the information and clues presented. There may be more than one. Circle the letter in front of the statements that you decide are reasonable inferences from the passage.

9. This is not the desperate poverty of Chicago housing projects, where the plight of empty pockets is worsened by the threat of gangs and gunfires.
   a. Most poor people are violent.
   b. In housing projects, violence frequently makes the experience of poverty much worse.
   c. Wendy's poverty does not affect her safety.

10. But when a teacher asked her to join an elevated class for algebra, she politely declined. "I get picked on for my clothes and living in the trailer park," said Wendy, who never brings anyone home from school. "I don't want to get picked on for being a nerd, too."
    a. You are considered a "nerd" if you take advanced classes.
    b. Only "nerds" take advanced classes.
    c. Wendy thinks that only "nerds" take advanced classes.

11. She went to a guidance counselor, Cynthia Kowa Basler, a dynamic woman who keeps close tabs on the children, especially girls who

fret about their weight and suddenly stop eating lunch. "I am large," she tells the girls, "and I have self-esteem."

a. Girls who stop eating frequently have self-esteem problems.

b. Cynthia Basler frets about her weight.

c. Cynthia Basler does not worry about her weight.

In the following sentences, some examples of language that use imagery have been italicized. Explain (1) what visual images are formed when we read these words, and (2) what the words actually mean in the sentence.

12. But in the economically robust 1990s, with *sprawling new houses and three-car garages sprouting like cornstalks* on the Midwestern prairie, *the sting* that comes with scarcity gets *rubbed with an extra bit of salt*.

sprouting like cornstalks on the prairie

visual image: _____

meaning: _____

the sting rubbed with an extra bit of salt

visual image: _____

meaning: _____

13. One boy stopped and yanked his thumb, demanding her seat. "Move it, *trailer girl*," he sneered.

trailer girl

visual image: _____

meaning: _____

14. Life still has *plenty of bumps.*

plenty of bumps

visual image: _____

meaning: _____

Read the following statements taken from the reading and write "F" before statements of fact and "O" before statements of opinion.

_____ 15. It has never been easy to live on the wrong side of the tracks.

_____ 16. Unlike students in some urban pockets, isolated from affluence, Wendy receives the same education as a girl from a $300,000 house in the Idle Oaks subdivision.

_____ 17. Wendy should stop feeling sorry for herself and just get on with her life.

Name _____ Date _____

Write short answers to the following questions based on your reading, your experience, and your observations.

18. What was your experience growing up? Was your family well-off? Middle-class? Poor? How much does money matter to adolescents? Why?

_____

_____

_____

_____

19. What do you think of Johnson's statement that "young people seem increasingly enchanted with buying, having, spending and status"? Do you agree or disagree with him? Why?

_____

_____

_____

_____

20. What conclusions can you draw about our society based on young people's relationship to consumerism (buying) and material goods?

_____

_____

_____

_____

Worshipping the Gods of Thinness Mary Pipher

The following reading from Mary Pipher's critically acclaimed book, Reviving Ophelia, *explores our society's obsession with thinness and the effect it has on adolescent girls. As you read, consider whether or not her statements are facts or opinions. What can you infer from her statements? And do you agree with her conclusions?*

1   Beauty is the defining characteristic for American women. It's the necessary and often sufficient condition for social success. It is important for women of all ages, but the pressure to be beautiful is most intense in early adolescence. Girls worry about their clothes, makeup, skin and hair. But most of all they worry about their weight. Peers place an enormous value on thinness.

2   This emphasis on appearance was present when I was a girl. Our high school had a "gauntlet" that we girls walked through every morning. It consisted of all the boys lined up by their cars along the sidewalk that led into the front doors. We walked past them to catcalls and remarks about our breasts and legs. I wore a girdle made of thick rubber to flatten my stomach on days I dressed in straight skirts.

3   But appearance is even more important today. Three things account for the increased pressure to be thin in the 1990s. We have moved from communities of primary relationships in which people know each other to cities full of secondary relationships. In a community of primary relationships, appearance is only one of many dimensions that define people. Everyone knows everyone else in different ways over time. In a city of strangers, appearance is the only dimension available for the rapid assessment of others. Thus it becomes incredibly important in defining value.

4   Secondly, the omnipresent media consistently portrays desirable women as thin. Thirdly, even as real women grow heavier, models and beautiful women are portrayed as thinner. In the last two decades we have developed a national cult of thinness. What is considered beautiful has become slimmer and slimmer. For example, in 1950 the White Rock mineral water girl was 5 feet 4 inches tall and weighed 140 pounds. Today she is 5 feet 10 inches and weighs 110 pounds.

5   Girls compare their own bodies to our cultural ideals and find them wanting. Dieting and dissatisfaction with bodies have become normal reactions to puberty. Girls developed eating disorders when our culture developed a standard of beauty that they couldn't obtain by being healthy. When unnatural thinness became attractive, girls did unnatural things to be thin.

6   In all the years I've been a therapist, I've yet to meet one girl who likes her body. Girls as skinny as chopsticks complain that their thighs are flabby or their stomachs puff out. And not only do girls dislike their bodies, they often loathe their fat. They have been culturally conditioned to hate their

bodies, which are after all themselves. When I speak to classes, I ask any woman in the audience who feels good about her body to come up afterward. I want to hear about her success experience. I have yet to have a woman come up.

7   Unfortunately girls are not irrational to worry about their bodies. Looks do matter. Girls who are chubby or plain miss much of the American dream. The social desirability research in psychology documents our prejudices against the unattractive, particularly the obese, who are the social lepers of our culture. A recent study found that 11 percent of Americans would abort a fetus if they were told it had a tendency to obesity. By age five, children select pictures of thin people when asked to identify good-looking others. Elementary school children have more negative attitudes toward the obese than toward bullies, the handicapped or children of different races. Teachers underestimate the intelligence of the obese and overestimate the intelligence of the slender.

8   Girls are terrified of being fat, as well they should be. Being fat means being left out, scorned and vilified. Girls hear the remarks made about heavy girls in the halls of the schools. No one feels thin enough. Because of guilt and shame about their bodies, young women are constantly on the defensive. Young women with eating disorders are not all that different from their peers. It's a matter of degree. Almost all adolescent girls feel fat, worry about their weight, diet and feel guilty when they eat. In fact, girls with eating disorders are often the girls who have bought the cultural messages about women and attractiveness hook, line and scales. To conform they are willing to make themselves sick.

9   Particularly in the 1980s and 1990s, there's been an explosion of girls with eating disorders. When I speak at high schools, girls surround me with confessions about their eating disorders. When I speak at colleges, I ask if any of the students have friends with eating disorders. Everyone's hand goes up. Studies report that on any given day in America, half our teenage girls are dieting and that one in five young women has an eating disorder. Eating disorders are not currently the media-featured problem they were in the 1980s, but incidence rates are not going down. Eight million women have eating disorders in America.

PIPHER, *REVIVING OPHELIA*

Use context clues, word part clues, and if necessary the dictionary to write the definitions of the italicized words in the following sentences from the reading.

1. Our high school had a *"gauntlet"* that we girls walked through every morning. (par. 2)

gauntlet _____

_____

_____

2. Three things *account for* the increased pressure to be thin in the 1990s. (par. 3)

   account for _____

3. We have moved from communities of *primary relationships* in which people know each other to cities full of *secondary relationships*. In a community of primary relationships, appearance is only one of many dimensions that define people. Everyone knows everyone else in different ways over time. In a city of strangers, appearance is the only dimension available for the rapid assessment of others. (par. 3)

   primary relationships _____

   secondary relationships _____

4. In a city of strangers, appearance is the only dimension available for the rapid *assessment* of others. (par. 3)

   assessment _____

5. Secondly, the *omnipresent* media consistently portrays desirable women as thin. (par. 4)

   omnipresent _____

6. In the last two decades we have developed a national *cult* of thinness. (par. 4)

   cult _____

7. They have been *culturally conditioned* to hate their bodies, which are after all themselves. (par. 6)

   culturally conditioned _____

8. Unfortunately girls are not *irrational* to worry about their bodies. Looks do matter. (par. 7)

   irrational _____

9. Being fat means being left out, scorned and *vilified*. (par. 8)

   vilified _____

10. Eating disorders are not currently the media-featured problem they were in the 1980s, but *incidence* rates are not going down. (par. 9)

incidence _____

In the following sentences, some examples of language that use imagery have been italicized. Explain (1) what visual images are formed when we read these words, and (2) what the words actually mean in the sentences.

11. Girls *as skinny as chopsticks* complain that their thighs are flabby or their stomachs puff out. (par. 6)

    visual image: _____

    meaning: _____

12. The social desirability research in psychology documents our prejudices against the unattractive, particularly the obese, who are the *social lepers* of our culture. (par. 7)

    visual image: _____

    meaning: _____

13. In fact, the girls with eating disorders are often the girls who have bought the cultural messages about women and attractiveness *hook, line, and scales*. (par. 8)

    visual image: _____

    meaning: _____

For the following groups of sentences, choose the reasonable inferences that you can make from the information and clues presented. There may be more than one. Circle the letter in front of the statements that you decide are reasonable inferences from the passage.

14. Girls as skinny as chopsticks complain that their thighs are flabby or their stomachs puff out.
    a. Girls have a good sense of how thin they really are.
    b. Girls think they are fat even when they are not.
    c. Girls understand that it is unhealthy to try to meet the skinny standard of beauty.

15. Teachers underestimate the intelligence of the obese and overestimate the intelligence of the slender.
    a. Teachers may be partly to blame for the way girls feel about their bodies.
    b. Teachers are good at estimating the intelligence of their students accurately.
    c. Teachers are as likely to have prejudices against the obese as much as anyone else in the society.

Examine each of the following sentences from or based on the reading, and write "F" before statements of fact and "O" before statements of opinion. On the lines that follow, briefly explain your answer.

_____ 16. Beauty should not be necessary for social success.

_____

_____

_____ 17. The media consistently portray desirable women as thin.

_____

_____

_____ 18. In 1950 the White Rock mineral water girl was 5 feet 4 inches tall and weighed 140 pounds. Today she is 5 feet 10 inches tall and weighs 110 pounds.

_____

_____

Write short answers to the following questions based on your reading, your experience, and your observations.

19. What conclusions can you draw about the influences on adolescent girls that lead them to eating disorders because of their desire to be thin?

_____

_____

_____

_____

20. What steps would you propose be taken to make it possible for adolescent girls to feel good about their appearance? Explain your answer.

_____

_____

_____

_____

Additional Readings and Exercises

READING 1

The Handicap of Definition   William Raspberry

The following reading discusses the way many assume that black people have special talents and abilities in sports and music. Unfortunately, the idea of what is "black" and what is "white" can have some negative consequences for young people. As you read, think about whether or not there are preset expectations that people have about you or a group of people you know.

1   I know all about bad schools, mean politicians, economic deprivation and racism. Still, it occurs to me that one of the heaviest burdens black Americans—and black children in particular—have to bear is the handicap of definition: the question of what it means to be black. Let me explain quickly what I mean. If a basketball fan says that the Boston Celtics' Larry Bird plays "black," the fan intends it—and Bird probably accepts it—as a compliment. Tell pop singer Tom Jones he moves "black" and he might grin in appreciation. Say to Teena Marie or the Average White Band that they sound "black" and they'll thank you. But name one pursuit, aside from athletics, entertainment or sexual performance, in which a white practitioner will feel complimented to be told he does it "black." Tell a white broadcaster he talks "black" and he'll sign up for diction lessons. Tell a white reporter he writes "black" and he'll take a writing course. Tell a white lawyer he reasons "black" and he might sue you for slander.

2   What we have here is a tragically limited definition of blackness, and it isn't only white people who buy it. Think of all the ways black children can put one another down with charges of "whiteness." For many of these children, hard study and hard work are "white." Trying to please a teacher might be criticized as acting "white." Speaking correct English is "white." Scrimping today in the interest of tomorrow's goals is "white." Educational toys and games are "white."

3   An incredible array of habits and attitudes that are conducive to success in business, in academia, in the nonentertainment professions are likely to be thought of as somehow "white." Even economic success, unless it involves such "black" undertakings as numbers banking, is defined as "white." And the results are devastating. I wouldn't deny that blacks often are better entertainers and athletes. My point is the harm that comes from too narrow a definition of what is black. One reason black youngsters tend to do better at basketball, for instance, is that they assume they can learn to do it well, and so they practice constantly to prove themselves right.

4   Wouldn't it be wonderful if we could infect black children with the notion that excellence in math is "black" rather than white, or possibly Chinese? Wouldn't it be of enormous value if we could create the myth that

academia Related to colleges and universities

traits
Characteristics

morality, strong families, determination, courage and love of learning are traits brought by slaves from Mother Africa and therefore quintessentially black? There is no doubt in my mind that most black youngsters could develop their mathematical reasoning, their elocution and their attitudes the way they develop their jump shots and their dance steps: by the combination of sustained, enthusiastic practice and the unquestioned belief that they can do it.

5   In one sense, what I am talking about is the importance of developing positive ethnic traditions. Maybe Jews have an innate talent for communication; maybe the Chinese are born with a gift for mathematical reasoning; maybe blacks are naturally blessed with athletic grace. I doubt it. What is at work, I suspect, is an assumption, inculcated early in their lives, that this is a thing our people do well. Unfortunately, many of the things about which blacks make this assumption are things that do not contribute to their career success—except for that handful of the truly gifted who can make it as

concede   Give up

entertainers and athletes. And many of the things we concede to whites are the things that are essential to economic security. So it is with a number of assumptions black youngsters make about what it is to be a "man": physical aggressiveness, sexual prowess, the refusal to submit to authority. The prisons are full of people who, by this perverted definition, are unmistakably men.

6   But the real problem is not so much that the things defined as "black" are negative. The problem is that the definition is much too narrow. Somehow, we have to make our children understand that they are intelligent, competent people, capable of doing whatever they put their minds to and making it in the American mainstream, not just in a black subculture. What we seem to be doing, instead, is raising up yet another generation of young blacks who will be failures—by definition.

RASPBERRY, "The Handicap of Definition"

Exercise 1   ## Work with Words

Use context clues, word part clues, and if necessary the dictionary to choose the definitions of the words that are italicized in the following sentences from Reading 1.

1. Tell a white broadcaster he talks "black" and he'll sign up for *diction* lessons. (par. 1)

   diction
   a. clarity in speech
   b. precision in writing
   c. critical thinking

2. Tell a white lawyer he reasons "black" and he might sue you for *slander*. (par. 1)

slander
a. telling the truth
b. making a damaging report
c. relying on a witness

3. An incredible array of habits and attitudes that *are conducive to* success in business, in academia, in the nonentertainment professions are likely to be thought of as somehow "white." (par. 3)

are conducive to
a. lead to
b. guarantee
c. are not important for

4. What is at work, I suspect, is an assumption, *inculcated* early in their lives, that this is a thing our people do well. Unfortunately, many of the things about which blacks make this assumption are things that do not contribute to their career success—except for that handful of the truly gifted who can make it as entertainers and athletes. (par. 5)

inculcated
a. hinted at
b. released
c. taught forcefully

5. The prisons are full of people who, by this *perverted* definition, are unmistakably men. (par. 5)

perverted
a. exaggerated
b. distorted
c. insincere

| Exercise 2 |

Check Your Understanding

Choose the best way to complete the following statements about Reading 1.

1. The main idea of paragraph 1 is that
   a. "black" accomplishments are to be expected in music and sports.
   b. white professionals always like it when they are told they do it "black."
   c. if you tell a lawyer he reasons "black," he might sue you.

2. The author believes that
   a. it is unfortunate that many young black people think of habits and attitudes that lead to success as "white."

      b. Chinese are born with a gift for mathematical reasoning.

      c. Jews have an innate talent for communication.

3. The author believes that
   a. blacks are naturally blessed with athletic grace.
   b. black young people do well in athletics because they believe they can and they practice hard.
   c. the definition of black—i.e., what black people are good at doing—is correct.

4. When he writes that it is important to develop "positive ethnic traditions," the author means that
   a. athletics and music are positive traditions.
   b. athletics and music are not positive traditions.
   c. being good at the things that are essential to economic security should also be a tradition of the black community.

5. This reading is probably mostly written for
   a. the black community.
   b. children of all ages.
   c. teachers.

6. The main idea—or thesis—of the reading is that
   a. there are many ways black children can put one another down with charges of "whiteness."
   b. everyone should be able to make it in the American mainstream.
   c. the assumptions of what it is to be black are too narrow, and limit the success of black young people.

7. The author thinks that
   a. black children are doing fine.
   b. black children hold themselves back unnecessarily.
   c. white children are holding black children back.

Exercise 3   ## Make Connections

Write short answers to the following questions based on your reading, your experience, and your observations.

1. Raspberry writes that black youngsters think that being a man is proven by physical aggressiveness, sexual prowess, and the refusal to submit to authority. And he writes, "The prisons are full of people who, by this perverted definition, are unmistakably men." Do you think that he agrees with this list of qualities as being important to being a man? Explain your answer.

    _____

    _____

_____

_____

2. What is Raspberry's idea of being "successful"? What do you think being "successful" means?

_____

_____

_____

_____

3. What characteristics do you think people need to have to be successful in our society?

_____

_____

_____

_____

READING 2

Nonverbal Communication: Speaking without Words

Deena R. Levine and Mara B. Edelman

The following reading explores how people communicate without the use of words. As you read, think of the different ways that you have of expressing an attitude or a feeling using your face or your body rather than language.

"He didn't look at me once. I know he's guilty. Never trust a person who doesn't look you in the eye."   —American Police Officer

1 Language studies traditionally emphasized verbal and written communication. Since about the 1960s, however, researchers seriously began to consider what takes place without words in conversations. In some instances, more nonverbal than verbal communication occurs. For example, if you ask an obviously depressed person, "What's wrong?" and he answers, "Nothing, I'm fine," you probably won't believe him. Or when an angry person says, "Let's forget this subject. I don't want to talk about it anymore!" she hasn't stopped communicating. Her silence and withdrawal continue to convey emotional meaning.

2   One study done in the United States showed that 93 percent of a message was transmitted by the speaker's tone of voice and facial expressions. Only 7 percent of the person's attitude was conveyed by words.[1] Apparently, we express our emotions and attitudes more nonverbally than verbally.

Cultural Differences in Nonverbal Communication

3   Nonverbal communication expresses meaning or feeling without words. Universal emotions, such as happiness, fear, and sadness, are expressed in a similar nonverbal way throughout the world. There are, however, nonverbal differences across cultures that may be a source of confusion for foreigners. Let's look at the way people express sadness. In many cultures, such as the Arab and Iranian cultures, people express grief openly. They mourn out loud, while people from other cultures (e.g., China and Japan) are more subdued. In Asian cultures, the general belief is that it is unacceptable to show emotion openly (whether sadness, happiness, or pain).

4   Let's take another example of how cultures differ in their non-verbal expression of emotion. Feelings of friendship exist everywhere in the world, but their expression varies. It is acceptable in some countries for men to embrace and for women to hold hands; in other countries, these displays of affection are discouraged or prohibited. . . .

5   We are often not aware of how gestures, facial expressions, eye contact, and the use of conversational distance affect communication. To interpret another culture's style of communication, it is necessary to study the "silent language" of that culture.[2]

Facial Expressiveness

6   Facial expressions carry meaning that is determined by situations and relationships. For instance, in American culture the smile is typically an expression of pleasure. Yet it also has other functions. A woman's smile at a police officer does not carry the same meaning as the smile she gives to a young child. A smile may show affections, convey politeness, or disguise true feelings. It also is a source of confusion across cultures. For example, many people in Russia consider smiling at strangers in public to be unusual and even suspicious behavior. Yet many Americans smile freely at strangers in public places (although this is less common in big cities). Some Russians believe that Americans smile in the wrong places; some Americans believe that Russians don't smile enough. In Southeast Asian cultures, a smile is frequently used to cover emotional pain or embarrassment. Vietnamese people may tell the sad story of how they had to leave their country but end the story with a smile.

Eye Contact

7   Eye contact is important because insufficient or excessive eye contact can create communication barriers. In relationships, it serves to show intimacy, attention, and influence. As with facial expressions, there are no specific rules governing eye behavior in the United States, except that it is considered rude to stare, especially at strangers. In parts of the United States, however, such as on the West Coast and in the South, it is quite common to glance at strangers when passing them. For example, it is usual for two strangers walking toward each other to make eye contact, smile, and perhaps even say "Hi," before immediately looking away. This type of contact doesn't mean much; it is simply a way of acknowledging another person's presence. In general, Americans make less eye contact with strangers in big cities than in small towns. People would be less likely to make eye contact in bus stations, for example, than in more comfortable settings such as a university student center.

8   Patterns of eye contact are different across cultures. Some Americans feel uncomfortable with the gaze that is sometimes associated with Arab or Indian communication patterns. For Americans, this style of eye contact is too intense. Yet too little eye contact may also be viewed negatively, because it may convey a lack of interest, inattention, or even mistrust. The relationship between the lack of eye contact and mistrust in the American culture is stated directly in the expression, "Never trust a person who doesn't look you in the eyes." In contrast, in many other parts of the world (especially in Asian countries), a person's lack of eye contact toward an authority figure signifies respect and deference.

Conversational Distances

9   Unconsciously, we all keep a comfortable distance around us when we interact with other people. This distance has had several names over the years, including "personal space," "interpersonal distance," "comfort zone," and "body bubble." This space between us and another person forms invisible walls that define how comfortable we feel at various distances from other people.

10   The amount of space changes depending on the nature of the relationship. For example, we are usually more comfortable standing closer to family members than to strangers. Personality also determines the size of the area with which we are comfortable when talking to people. Introverts often prefer to interact with others at a greater distance than do extroverts. Cultural styles are important too. A Japanese employer and employee usually stand farther apart while talking than their American counterparts. Latin Americans and Arabs tend to stand closer than Americans do when talking.

11   For Americans, the usual distance in social conversation ranges from about an arm's length to four feet. Less space in the American culture may

be associated with either greater intimacy or aggressive behavior.[3] The common practice of saying, "Excuse me," for the slightest accidental touching of another person reveals how uncomfortable Americans are if people get too close. Thus, a person whose "space" has been intruded upon by another may feel threatened and react defensively. In cultures where close physical contact is acceptable and even desirable, Americans may be perceived as cold and distant.

12   Culture does not always determine the message of nonverbal communication. The individual's personality, the context, and the relationship also influence its meaning. However, like verbal language, nonverbal language is linked to a person's cultural background. People are generally comfortable with others who have "body language" similar to their own. One research study demonstrated that when British graduate students imitated some Arab patterns of nonverbal behavior (making increased eye contact, smiling, and directly facing their Arab partners), the Arabs felt that these students were more likeable and trustworthy than most of the other British students.[4]

13   When one person's nonverbal language matches that of another, there is increased comfort. In nonverbal communication across cultures there are similarities and differences. Whether we choose to emphasize the former or the latter, the "silent language" is much louder than it first appears.

Notes

1. Albert Mehrabian and Morton Wiener, "Decoding of Inconsistent Communications," *Journal of Personality and Social Psychology, 6* (1964): 109–114; Albert Mehrabian and Susan R. Ferris, "Inference of Attitudes from Non-verbal Communication in Two Channels," *Journal of Consulting Psychology*, *31* (1967): 248–252.

2. Edward T. Hall, *The Silent Language* (Greenwich, Conn.: A Fawcett Premier Book, 1959).

3. Edward T. Hall, *The Hidden Dimension* (Garden City, N.Y.: Doubleday & Company, 1966), pp. 126–127.

4. Peter Collett, "Training Englishmen in the Nonverbal Behavior of Arabs," *International Journal of Psychology, 6* (1971), 209–215.

LEVINE AND EDELMAN, *Beyond Language*

| Exercise 1 | ## Work with Words |

Use context clues, word part clues, and if necessary the dictionary to write the definitions of the italicized words in the following sentences from Reading 2.

1. One study done in the United States showed that 93 percent of a message was transmitted by the speaker's tone of voice and facial expressions. Only 7 percent of the person's attitude was *conveyed* by words. (par. 2)

   conveyed _____

2. *Nonverbal communication* expresses meaning or feeling without words. (par. 3)

   nonverbal communication _____

3. For example, it is usual for two strangers walking toward each other to make eye contact, smile, and perhaps even say "Hi," before immediately looking away. This type of contact doesn't mean much; it is simply a way of *acknowledging* another person's presence. (par. 7)

   acknowledging _____

4. The common practice of saying, "Excuse me," for the slightest accidental touching of another person reveals how uncomfortable Americans are if people get too close. Thus, a person whose "space" has been *intruded upon* by another may feel threatened and react defensively. (par. 11)

   intruded upon _____

5. One research study demonstrated that when British graduate students imitated some Arab patterns of nonverbal behavior (making increased eye contact, smiling, and directly facing their Arab partners), the Arabs felt that these students were more likeable and *trustworthy* than most of the other British students. (par. 12)

   trustworthy _____

Exercise 2 | Check Your Understanding

Write brief answers to the following questions.

1. What do we express more nonverbally than verbally?

   _____

2. Give one example of how people express friendship in some countries, but not in others.

   _____

3. What surprises Russians in the United States?

   _____

4. What is the typically "American" reaction to too little eye contact?

_____

5. What does "personal space" refer to?

_____

_____

6. What are some of the influences on our idea of how much distance it is comfortable to maintain with another person?

_____

_____

7. Write the main idea—or thesis—of this reading in your own words.

_____

_____

| Exercise 3 |

Make Connections

Write short answers to the following questions based on your reading, your experience, and your observations.

1. How do you feel if someone looks at you without ever taking his or her eyes away during a conversation?

_____

_____

2. What would you do if someone stood too close to you?

_____

_____

3. Why is it important for business people to understand nonverbal communication in other cultures? Give examples.

_____

_____

4. What might people from the United States think if they are talking to a child about his behavior, and the child looks down and smiles? In what cultures might the child's reaction be appropriate?

_____

_____

Persuasive Techniques in Contemporary Advertising   Richard Campbell

The following reading from a textbook about mass communications presents the various strategies that advertisers use to get us to buy their products. As you read, think about the kinds of items that you buy and whether or not you have seen those items advertised. Consider what kinds of advertising seem to influence you or the people you know.

1   Ad agencies and product companies often argue that the main purpose of advertising is to inform consumers straightforwardly of available products. In fact, many types of advertisements, like classified ads in newspapers, are devoted primarily to delivering price information. Most consumer ads, however, merely tell stories about products without revealing much about prices. Since national advertisers generally choose to buy a one-page magazine ad or a thirty-second television spot to deliver their pitch, consumers get little information about how a product was made or how it compares with similar brands. In managing space and time constraints, advertising agencies engage in a variety of persuasive techniques. . . .

Conventional Persuasive Strategies

2   One of the most frequently used advertising approaches is the *famous-person testimonial,* whereby a product is endorsed by a well-known person, such as former senator and presidential candidate Bob Dole touting the benefits of the drug Viagra. Another technique, the *plain-folks pitch*, associates a product with simplicity. Over the years, Volkswagen ("Think Small"), General Electric ("We bring good things to life"), and Microsoft ("Where do you want to go today?") have each used slogans that stress how new technologies fit into the lives of ordinary people. By contrast, the *snob-appeal* approach attempts to persuade consumers that using a product will maintain or elevate their social station. Advertisers selling jewelry, perfume, clothing, and luxury automobiles often use snob appeal. For example, Infiniti cars, associated with elegance, are frequently advertised against a backdrop of high-society parties; ads for Mitsubishi sedans use phrases like "a new level of luxury," "superb road manners," "full-size refinement," and "an upscale attitude."

3   Another approach, the *bandwagon effect*, points out in exaggerated claims that everyone is using a particular product. Brands that refer to themselves as "America's favorite" or "the best" imply that consumers will be left out—or that they are not hip—if they ignore these products. A different technique, the *hidden-fear appeal*, plays on consumers' sense of insecurity. De-

odorant, mouthwash, and dandruff-shampoo ads frequently promote anxiety, pointing out that only a specific product could possibly relieve embarrassing personal-hygiene problems. . . .

The Association Principle

4   Historically, American car advertisements have displayed automobiles in natural settings: on winding back roads that cut through rugged mountain passes or across shimmering wheat fields. These ads rarely contain images of cars on congested city streets or in other urban settings where most driving really occurs. Instead, the car—an example of advanced technology—merges effortlessly with the natural world.

5   This type of advertising exemplifies the *association principle*, a persuasive technique used in many consumer ads. Employing this principle, an ad associates a product with some cultural value or image that has a positive connotation but may have little connection to the actual product. For example, Chevrolet's slogan in the 1980s—"the heartbeat of America"—associated the car with nationalism. In trying "to convince us that there's an innate relationship between a brand name and an attitude,"[1] agencies and advertisers associate products with happy families, success at school or work, natural scenery, and humor. (Some ad agencies contend, however, that viewers do not always remember products associated with funny or quirky associations.) Over the years, the most controversial use of the association principle has been the linkage of products to stereotyped caricatures of women. In numerous instances, women have been portrayed either as sex objects or as clueless housewives who, during many a daytime TV commercial, needed the powerful offscreen voice of a male narrator to instruct them in their own kitchens.

6   Another strong association used in advertising is nature. In one of the most striking and enduring magazine ad campaigns, Kool cigarettes have been associated with cool mountain waterfalls and tranquil beaches, neither of which has a logical connection to cigarettes. These settings, however, conjure up positive images and link the product to nature. Philip Morris's Marlboro brand also used the association principle to completely transform the product's initial image. In the 1920s, Marlboro began as a fashionable "woman's" cigarette. Back then, the company's ads equated smoking with emancipation and a sense of freedom, attempting to appeal to women who had just won the right to vote. Marlboro, though, did poorly as a women's product, and new campaigns in the 1950s and 1960s transformed the brand into a man's cigarette. In these campaigns, powerful images of active, rugged men were the central characters. Often, Marlboro associated its product with the image of a lone cowboy roping a calf, building a fence, or riding through a pristine natural landscape. Ironically, over the years two of the Marlboro Man models died of lung cancer associated with

© 2002 by Addison-Wesley Educational Publishers Inc.

pristine Clean and beautiful

smoking. Yet in 1993 *Financial World* magazine called Marlboro the world's "most valuable brand name," having an estimated worth of $39 billion.

7   As a response to corporate merger mania and public skepticism toward large impersonal companies, the *disassociation corollary* has emerged as a recent trend in advertising. The nation's largest winery, Gallo, pioneered the idea in the 1980s by establishing a dummy corporation, Bartles & Jaymes, to sell jug wine and wine coolers, thus avoiding the Gallo corporate image in ads and on its bottles. The Gallo ads featured Frank and Ed, two low-key, grandfatherly types as "co-owners" and ad spokesmen. . . .

8   In the 1990s, the disassociation strategy was used by Miller Brewing Company's Red Dog beer, sold under the quaint Plank Road Brewery logo, and by R. J. Reynolds's Moonlight Tobacco Company, which sells local brand cigarettes such as City and North Star. In addition, General Motors, still reeling from the failed Oldsmobile campaign and a declining corporate reputation, "disassociate[d] itself from its innovative offspring, the Saturn." GM ads have packaged the Saturn as "a small-town enterprise, run by folks not terribly unlike Frank and Ed," who provide caring, personal service.[2] As an advertising strategy, disassociation links new brands in a product line to eccentric or simple regional places rather than to the image conjured up by giant conglomerates.

The Stories

9   Even though the stories ads tell are usually compressed into thirty seconds or onto a single page, they still include the traditional elements of narrative. For instance, Marlboro ads often tell the mini-story of a lone and tough cowboy and his horse, dwarfed by towering pines and snow-covered mountains. The ads ask us to imagine his adventure, as he returns home after an autumn cattle drive, perhaps. The cowboy's ability to survive amid the forces of nature is a tribute to rugged individualism, probably America's most powerful cultural value. The conflict is generated by the audience's implicit understanding of what is not in the ads—a fast-paced technology-driven urban world where most smoking actually takes place. This implied conflict between the natural world and the manufactured world is apparently resolved by invoking the image of Marlboro. Although Marlboros are an addictive, manufactured product and advertisers are mandated by the FTC and the Surgeon General to warn us about the lethal dangers of cigarettes, the ads attempt to downplay those facts. Instead, they offer an alternative story about the wonders of nature. The natural is substituted for the manufactured, and the "spirit of Marlboro" becomes the soothing negotiator between these competing worlds.

10   In an increasingly technology-dependent environment, modern societies have come to value products that claim affiliation with the *real* and the *natural*. Coke sells itself as "the real thing," and the cosmetics industry

rugged individualism The idea that the individual can be strong and independent

downplay Make something appear unimportant

synthetic Artificial, not genuine

offers synthetic products that make us look "natural." These twin adjectives, which saturate American ads, almost always describe processed goods.

11   Most advertisers do not expect consumers to accept without question the stories they tell or the associations they make in their ads; they do not "make the mistake of asking for belief."[3] Instead, ads are most effective when they create attitudes and reinforce values. Then they operate like popular fiction, encouraging us to suspend our disbelief. Although most of us realize that ads create a fictional world, we often get caught up in their stories and myths. Indeed, ads often work because the stories offer comfort about our deepest desires and conflicts—between men and women, nature and technology, tradition and change, the real and the artificial. Most contemporary consumer advertising does not provide much useful information about products. Instead, it tries to reassure us that through the use of familiar brand names everyday tensions and problems can be managed.

Notes

1. Leslie Savan, "Op Ad: Sneakers and Nothingness," *Village Voice*, April 2, 1991, p. 43.

2. Mary Kuntz and Joseph Weber, "The New Hucksterism," *Business Week,* July 1, 1999, p. 79.

3. Michael Schudson, *Advertising, the Uneasy Persuasion* (New York: Basic Books, 1984), p. 210. See also Arthur Marquette, *Brands, Trademarks, and Good Will* (New York, McGraw-Hill, 1967).

CAMPBELL, *Media and Culture*

Exercise 1

Work with Words

Use context clues, word part clues, and if necessary the dictionary to write the definitions of the italicized words in the following sentences from Reading 3.

1. Since national advertisers generally choose to buy a one-page magazine ad or a thirty-second TV spot to deliver their pitch, consumers get little information about how a product was made or how it compares with similar brands. In managing space and time *constraints*, advertising agencies engage in a variety of persuasive techniques. (par. 1)

   constraints _____

2. One of the most frequently used advertising approaches is the famous-person *testimonial*, whereby a product is endorsed by a

well-known person, such as former senator and presidential candidate Bob Dole touting the benefits of the drug Viagra. (par. 2)

testimonial _____

3. This type of advertising exemplifies the *association principle*, a persuasive technique used in many consumer ads. Employing this principle, an ad associates a product with some cultural value or image
that has a positive connotation but may have little connection to the
actual product. (par. 5)

association principle _____

_____

4. As an advertising strategy, *disassociation* links new brands in a product line to eccentric or simple regional places rather than to the
image conjured up by giant conglomerates. (par. 8)

disassociation _____

_____

5. Although Marlboros are an addictive, manufactured product and
advertisers are *mandated* by the FTC and the Surgeon General to
warn us about the lethal dangers of cigarettes, the ads attempt to
downplay those facts. (par. 9)

mandated _____

| Exercise 2 |

Check Your Understanding

Choose the best way to complete the following statements about Reading 3.

1. The *plain-folks pitch*
   a. associates a product with simplicity.
   b. makes the consumer feel plain.
   c. makes the consumer feel that using the product will raise her status.

2. The bandwagon effect is an advertising strategy that tries to convince a consumer to buy a product because
   a. it solves a problem she has.
   b. it is the least expensive.
   c. everybody else buys it.

3. Advertisements of Kool cigarettes that show cool mountain waterfalls would be an example of
   a. the famous-person testimonial.
   b. the association principle.
   c. the hidden-fear appeal.

4. Advertisements that show a well-known politician or actor endorsing a product are using the advertising strategy of
   a. the plain-folks pitch.
   b. the bandwagon effect.
   c. the famous-person testimonial.

5. The Marlboro ads are directed at
   a. men who find the Marlboro man's rugged individualism appealing.
   b. women who find the Marlboro man's rugged individualism appealing.
   c. women who wish to be independent.

6. The main idea, or thesis, of the reading is that
   a. disassociation is a strategy for advertising that links new brands in a product line to simple regional places rather than to the image of large corporations.
   b. smoking is dangerous to your health.
   c. most contemporary consumer advertising does not provide much useful information; rather, it uses a number of strategies to sell products.

7. The author probably thinks that
   a. advertising should be illegal.
   b. advertisers frequently provide useful information.
   c. advertisers manipulate our feelings.

8. The author included the information about two of the models for the Marlboro man dying of lung cancer to show that
   a. you really can look like a strong man if you smoke Marlboros.
   b. the sad fact behind smoking is that many people get lung cancer.
   c. there is no relationship between smoking and cancer.

| Exercise 3 |

Make Connections

Write short answers to the following questions based on your reading, your experience, and your observations.

1. Give an example of an advertisement that uses each of the following persuasive strategies.

   a. Famous-person testimonial: _____

   b. Snob-appeal: _____

   c. Bandwagon effect: _____

   d. Hidden-fear appeal: _____

2. What kinds of advertisements influence you or people you know the most? Explain your answer.

_____

_____

_____

_____

How to Land the Job You Want

Davidyne Mayleas

Hunting for a job can be stressful and bewildering. In the following reading, think about Mayleas's suggestions for a job search. As you read, consider how these strategies might work for someone on the job market and how you might use them in the future. Also, consider how the advances in technology and the use of the Internet would affect your job search techniques.

1 Louis Albert, 39, lost his job as an electrical engineer when his firm made extensive cutbacks. He spent two months answering classified ads and visiting employment agencies—with zero results. Albert might still be hunting if a friend, a specialist in the employment field, had not shown him how to be his own job counselor. Albert learned how to research unlisted openings, write a forceful résumé, perform smoothly in an interview, even transform a turndown into a job.

2   Although there seemed to be a shortage of engineering jobs, Albert realized that he still persuaded potential employers to see him. This taught him something—that his naturally outgoing personality might be as great an asset as his engineering degree. When the production head of a small electronics company told him that they did not have an immediate opening, Albert told his interviewer, "You people make a fine product. I think you could use additional sales representation—someone like me who understands and talks electrical engineer's language, and who enjoys selling." The interviewer decided to send Albert to a senior vice president. Albert got a job in sales.

3   You too can be your own counselor if you put the same vigorous effort into *getting* a job as you would into *keeping* one. Follow these three basic rules, developed by placement experts:

4 **Find the Hidden Job Market.** Classified ads and agency listings reveal only a small percentage of available jobs. Some of the openings that occur through promotions, retirements and reorganization never reach the personnel department. There are three ways to get in touch with this hidden market:

5   *Write a strong résumé with a well-directed cover letter, and mail it to the appropriate department manager in the company where you'd like to work.* Don't worry whether there's a current opening. Many managers fill vacancies by reviewing the résumés already in their files. Dennis Mollura, press-relations manager in the public-relations department of American Telephone and Telegraph, says, "In my own case, the company called me months after I sent in my résumé."

6   *Get in touch with people who work in or know the companies that interest you.* Jobs are so often filled through personal referral that Charles R. Lops, executive employment manager of the J.C. Penney Co., says, "Probably our best source for outside people comes from recommendations made by Penney associates themselves."

7   *Drop in on the company.* Lillian Reveille, employment manager of Equitable Life Assurance Society of the United States, reports: "A large percentage of the applicants we see are 'walk-ins'—and we do employ many of these people."

8   **Locate Hidden Openings.** This step requires energy and determination to make telephone calls, see people, do research, and to keep moving despite turndowns.

9   *Contact anyone who may know of openings,* including relatives, friends, teachers, bank officers, insurance agents—anyone you know in your own or an adjacent field. When the teachers' union and employment agencies produced no teaching openings, Eric Olson, an unemployed high-school math instructor, reviewed his talent and decided that where an analytical math mind was useful, there he'd find a job. He called his insurance agent, who set up an interview with the actuarial department of one of the companies he represented. They hired Olson.

10   *It's a good idea to contact not only professional or trade associations in your field, but also your local chamber of commerce and people involved in community activities.* After Laura Bailey lost her job as retirement counselor in a bank's personnel department, she found a position in customer relations in another bank. Her contact: a member of the senior-citizens club that Mrs. Bailey ran on a volunteer basis.

11   *Use local or business-school libraries.* Almost every field has its own directory of companies, which provides names, addresses, products and/or services, and lists officers and other executives. Write to the company president or to the executive to whom you'd report. The vice president of personnel at Warner-Lambert Co. says, "When a résumé of someone we could use—now or in the near future—shows up 'cold' in my in-basket, that's luck for both of us."

12   *Consult telephone directories.* Sometimes the telephone company will send you free the telephone directories of various cities. Also, good-sized public libraries often have many city directories. Fred Lewis, a cabinet

maker, checked the telephone directories of nine different cities where he knew furniture was manufactured. At the end of five weeks he had a sizable telephone bill, some travel expenses—and ten interviews which resulted in three job offers.

13   **After You Find the Opening, Get the Job.** The applicants who actually get hired are those who polish these six job-getting skills to perfection:

14   *Compose a better résumé.* A résumé is a self-advertisement, designed to get you an interview. Start by putting yourself in an employer's place. Take stock of your job history and personal achievement. Make an inventory of your skills and accomplishments that might be useful from the employer's standpoint. Choose the most important and describe them in words that stress accomplishments. Avoid such phrases as "my duties included. . . ." Use action words like planned, sold, trained, managed.

15   *Ask a knowledgeable business friend to review your résumé.* Does it stress accomplishment rather than duties? Does it tell an employer what you can do for him? Can it be shortened? (One or two pages should suffice.) Generally, it's not wise to mention salary requirements.

16   *Write a convincing cover letter.* While the résumé may be a copy, the cover letter must be personal. Sy Mann, director of research for Aceto Chemical Co., says: "When I see a mimeographed letter that states, 'Dear Sir, I'm sincerely interested in working for your company,' I wonder, 'How many other companies got this valentine?'" Use the name and title of the person who can give you the interview, and be absolutely certain of accuracy here. Using a wrong title or misspelling a prospective employer's name may route your correspondence directly to an automatic turndown.

17   *Prepare specifically for each interview.* Research the company thoroughly; know its history and competition. Try to grasp the problems of the job you're applying for. For example, a line in an industry journal that a food company was "developing a new geriatric food" convinced one man that he should emphasize his marketing experience with vitamins rather than with frozen foods.

18   You'll increase your edge by anticipating questions the interviewer might raise. Why do you want to work for us? What can you offer us that someone else cannot? Why did you leave your last position? What are your salary requirements?

19   An employer holds an interview to get a clearer picture of your work history and accomplishments, and to look for characteristics he considers valuable. These vary with jobs. Does the position require emphasis on attention to detail or on creativity? Perseverance or aggressiveness? Prior to the interview decide what traits are most in demand. And always send a thank-you note immediately after the interview.

20   *Follow up.* They said you would hear in a week; now it's two. Call them. Don't wait and hope. Hope and act.

21   *Supply additional information*. That's the way Karen Halloway got her job as fashion director with a department store. "After my interview I sensed that the merchandise manager felt I was short on retail experience. So I wrote to him describing the 25 fashion shows I'd staged yearly for the pattern company I'd worked for."

22   *Don't take no for an answer*. Hank Newell called to find out why he had been turned down. The credit manager felt he had insufficient collection experience. Hank thanked him for his time and frankness. The next day, Hank called back saying, "My collection experience is limited, but I don't think I fully emphasized my training in credit checking." They explored this area and found Hank still not qualified. But the credit manager was so impressed with how well Hank took criticism that when Hank asked him if he could suggest other employers, he did, even going so far as to call one. Probing for leads when an interview or follow-up turns negative is a prime technique for getting personal referrals.

23   The challenge of finding a job, approached in an active, organized, realistic way, can be a valuable personal adventure. You can meet new people, develop new ideas about yourself and your career goals, and improve your skills in dealing with individuals. These in turn can contribute to your long-term job security.

MAYLEAS, "How to Land the Job You Want"

| Exercise 1 |

Work with Words

Use context clues, word part clues, and if necessary the dictionary to choose the definitions of the italicized words in the following sentences from Reading 4.

1. Albert learned how to research unlisted openings, write a forceful résumé, perform smoothly in an interview, even transform a *turndown* into a job. (par. 1)

   turndown
   a. change
   b. rejection
   c. recent interview

2. Contact anyone who may know of openings, including relatives, friends, teachers, bank officers, insurance agents—anyone you know in your own or an *adjacent* field. (par. 9)

   adjacent
   a. behind
   b. in front
   c. similar

3. Using a wrong title or misspelling a *prospective* employer's name may route your correspondence directly to an automatic turndown. (par. 16)

   prospective
   a. likely
   b. unlikely
   c. admirable

4. Does the position require emphasis on attention to detail or on creativity? Perseverance or aggressiveness? *Prior to* the interview decide what traits are most in demand. (par. 19)

   prior to
   a. after
   b. during
   c. before

5. The credit manager felt he had insufficient collection experience. Hank thanked him for his time and *frankness.* (par. 22)

   frankness
   a. honesty
   b. consideration
   c. help

Exercise 2

Check Your Understanding

Choose the best way to complete the following statements about Reading 4.

1. The main idea of paragraphs 1–3 is that
   a. it is impossible to get a job in the current market.
   b. if you put as much effort into getting a job as you do in keeping one, you can be your own job counselor.
   c. learning how to interview well will help you get a job because the interview is the single most important factor in finding employment.

2. The "hidden job market" refers to
   a. a placement service.
   b. a mysterious listing service that you have to subscribe to.
   c. job openings that are not listed in classified ads or agency listings.

3. One way to find the hidden job market is to
   a. get in touch with people who work in or know the companies that interest you.
   b. find out the secret password so that you can access the information as well as your competition.
   c. refuse to take no for an answer.

4. One way to locate hidden openings in the job market is to
   a. listen to radio spots.
   b. supply companies with additional information about yourself.
   c. use local or business-school libraries.

5. A résumé is
   a. a self-advertisement with your job history and personal achievements.
   b. a summary of everything you have done in life up until now.
   c. a part of the job application process that you don't need to worry about.

6. A convincing cover letter must
   a. use the correct name and title of the person in the company.
   b. be a standard form letter that you send with your résumé.
   c. be a handwritten note that says thank you.

7. A technique for getting a job offer after you're invited to an interview is to
   a. act grateful.
   b. prepare specifically for each interview.
   c. be informal.

8. The statement that best sums up the reading is,
   a. trying to find a job is horrible and depressing.
   b. don't try to find a job on your own; always go to a job placement service.
   c. finding a job on your own is possible if you are active and well organized.

Exercise 3

Make Connections

Write short answers to the following questions based on your reading, your experience, and your observations.

1. How do most people you know find jobs? Give some examples. (You can include your own experiences as well.)

   _____

   _____

   _____

   _____

   _____

2. How can you use the Internet to improve your success at finding a job?

_____

_____

Toxic Metals, Dioxins, and PCBs

Curtis O. Byer and Louis Shainberg

The following passage from a health textbook describes the toxic materials that pollute our environment. Some of these chemicals can be found in our houses, others in our communities. Some of them make people sick. There is a good chance that some even affect our ability to have children. Notice that the authors of this textbook selection have defined important words in the margins for you. Be sure you understand these words.

compounds
Combinations of metal

1 Various metallic elements or their compounds have been found to be hazardous to our health. These metals include mercury and lead.

Mercury

2 Mercury is a by-product of coal and industrial wastes. As mercury is produced, it is released into the air and water, and travels into sewers and surface waters. Mercury is also a by-product of natural sources produced from vapors from the earth's crust and from ocean bottom sediments. Consumption of any foods containing mercury, such as fish living in contaminated waters, can be hazardous.

3 Methyl mercury is an extremely toxic form of mercury. Methyl mercury remains in the body for months, and can affect the central nervous system, kidneys, liver, and brain tissues. It is known to be responsible for birth defects. In the late 1950s, 649 Japanese people died and 1,385 suffered mercury poisoning after methyl mercury was released into bay waters.

Lead

4 We are exposed to lead every day in our water, food, and air. Seventy-seven percent of the United States population has unsafe levels of lead in their blood, according to a 1986 EPA study. This lead comes from many sources, most of them unnatural.

5 A number of measures have been taken to eliminate lead from our environment. In 1973, all new cars were required to use only unleaded gasoline. In 1986, that law was amended to make the requirement more rigid, reducing the amount of lead in unleaded gasoline from 2.5 grams per gal-

lon to 0.1 gram per gallon. In 1976, a measure was enacted requiring paint manufacturers to reduce the amount of lead in their products. Another requirement enacted to control the use of lead was a 1987 ruling requiring public water installations and private buildings to use plastic pipes instead of the old lead pipes.

6   There are measures that individuals can take to protect themselves. If you are occupying an old building at work, school, or at home, run the water for two to three minutes in order to clean out most of the lead. Also, look into the safest and most effective way to remove leaded paint and apply new, unleaded paints instead.

7   Since the bodies of young children easily absorb lead, their ingestion of lead products can be fatal. About 200 children in America die yearly from lead poisoning, and another 12,000 to 16,000 children are treated for it each year. Survivors of lead poisoning often suffer from palsy, blindness, partial paralysis, and mental retardation. Studies show that lead in the blood can lower intelligence in children; even low levels of lead contamination can cause hearing loss and elevated blood pressure.

Dioxins

dioxin   Family of over 75 toxic chemicals

herbicide   A chemical that kills plants

exposed to   Open to, having experience with

8   Dioxins are a group of seventy-five chemicals, some of which are formed during the manufacture of the herbicide 2,4,5-T. One by-product of 2,4,5-T production, usually referred to as TCCD, is a highly toxic dioxin. TCCD can cause liver cancer, birth defects, and death of laboratory animals when administered at very low levels. Workers exposed to TCCD in industrial accidents may suffer from headaches, hair and weight loss, liver disorders, irritability, insomnia, nerve damage in the arms and legs, loss of sex drive, and disfiguring acne.

9   Major cases of dioxin contamination have been found in Times Beach, Missouri. In 1971 in this St. Louis suburb, dioxin-contaminated oil was sprayed on dirt roads to control dust. The resulting contamination was so severe that in 1983, the EPA bought the town for a cost of $36.7 million and relocated all of its 2,200 people. Other dioxin contamination has been found in fish taken from the Great Lakes and from rivers flowing into these lakes.

10   Although some federal agencies have established maximum exposure levels for dioxins, these levels are not universally accepted as representing hazardous levels. Researchers do not agree on the level of dioxins or exposure time that is hazardous to humans.

polychlorinated biphenyls (PCBs)
Mixtures of at least 70 widely used compounds containing chlorine that can be biologically magnified in the food chain with unknown effects

PCBs

11   Polychlorinated biphenyls (PCBs) are mixtures of almost seventy different, but related chlorinated hydrogen compounds that were manufactured in the United States before 1979. PCBs were widely used in consumer products such as plastics, paints, rubber, waxes, and adhesives. They have also been used as insulation and cooling fluids in electrical transformers. In 1968,

PCB-contaminated food was accidentally eaten in Japan. Victims suffered from liver damage, kidney damage, reproductive disorders, and skin lesions; there was also an unusually high incidence of stomach and liver cancer.

12   PCBs enter the body through food, the skin, and the lungs, and accumulate in the fatty tissues. PCBs are very resistant to biological and chemical breakdown. As a result, the PCBs that have been dumped in landfills, sewers, and along roadsides have found their way into the food chain.

BYER AND SHAINBERG, *Living Well: Health in Your Hands*

| Exercise 1 |

Work with Words

Use context clues, word part clues, and if necessary the dictionary to choose the definitions of the italicized words in the following sentences from Reading 5.

1. Mercury is also a by-product of natural sources produced from vapors from the earth's crust and from ocean bottom *sediments*. (par. 2)

   sediments
   a. matter that rises to the top of a liquid
   b. matter that settles to the bottom of a liquid
   c. matter that floats around a liquid

2. In 1973, all new cars were required to use only unleaded gasoline. In 1986, that law was *amended* to make the requirement more rigid, reducing the amount of lead in unleaded gasoline from 2.5 grams per gallon to 0.1 gram per gallon. (par. 5)

   amended
   a. improved
   b. canceled
   c. ignored

3. TCCD can cause liver cancer, birth defects, and death of laboratory animals when *administered* at very low levels. (par. 8)

   administered
   a. dispensed
   b. performed
   c. managed

4. PCBs enter the body through food, the skin, and the lungs, and *accumulate* in the fatty tissues. (par. 12)

   accumulate
   a. disperse
   b. damage
   c. collect

5. PCBs are very *resistant* to biological and chemical breakdown. (par. 12)
   a. having to do with fighting back
   b. having to do with being flexible
   c. having to do with giving up easily

| Exercise 2 |

Check Your Understanding

Choose the best way to complete the following statements about Reading 5.

1. The main idea of the reading is that
   a metallic compounds, dioxins, and PCBs are harmless if left alone.
   b. metallic compounds, dioxins, and PCBs bring health benefits.
   c. metallic compounds, dioxins, and PCBs are hazardous to our health, and we should eliminate them from our environment.

2. Mercury is
   a. a by-product of coal and industrial wastes.
   b. a by-product of gasoline.
   c. a by-product of herbicides, similar to dioxins.

3. We are exposed to lead
   a. once in a while.
   b. almost never.
   c. every day.

4. People can protect themselves from lead poisoning by
   a. using gloves when painting.
   b. running the water for two to three minutes before using it if they live or work in an old building.
   c. eating a little lead every day to build up a tolerance to it.

5. A herbicide is
   a. a chemical that kills plants.
   b. a chemical that kills insects.
   c. a PCB.

6. Major cases of dioxin contamination have been found in
   a. Lake Tahoe, California.
   b. Times Beach, Missouri.
   c. Kansas City, Missouri.

7. Researchers
   a. agree on the level of dioxins or exposure time that is hazardous to humans.
   b. have not studied the toxicity level of dioxins.
   c. do not agree on the level of dioxins or exposure time that is hazardous to humans.

8. Which of the following is *not* true of PCBs?
   a. They are mixtures of different but related chlorinated hydrogen compounds.
   b. They have been used as insulation and cooling fluids in electrical transformers.
   c. They have never found their way into the food chain.

Exercise 3

Make Connections

Write short answers to the following questions based on your reading, your experience, and your observations.

1. Did you ever think of things in your home as toxic? What cleaning and gardening supplies should be checked? Where else will you look for toxins in your home?

   _____

   _____

   _____

   _____

2. Do you know of any places in your neighborhood that might use toxic chemicals? What are they? How do you think these chemicals are handled?

   _____

   _____

   _____

   _____

READING 6

Exposure to Chemicals and Human Fertility
Ruth Markowitz Heifetz, M.D.

The following reading discusses the effects of chemicals in our environment, such as DDT, on human fertility. As you read the following article, consider the information carefully. Why is it important for employees to know as much as possible about the chemicals in their workplace?

1 Over 30 years ago, Rachel Carson wrote a book called *Silent Spring.* She warned that DDT and other pesticides were killing birds and other creatures and that the health of human beings was also being threatened. At that

time, the government and the chemical producers said that DDT was perfectly safe to use on food, in homes, and on public beaches without any type of warning. Carson illustrated that the DDT had made the eggshells of birds so fragile that offspring could not survive, causing a decline of certain bird populations.

fragile Delicate

2   As a result of Carson's book and the pressure of many citizens, DDT was banned in the United States, although it was and continues to be produced in this country and shipped to countries around the world. Years after the elimination of the use of DDT many of the birds, like pelicans, have begun to increase in numbers.

3   Since the publication of *Silent Spring* many chemicals, especially certain pesticides, solvents, and lead, have been identified as causing problems such as miscarriages, birth defects and infertility (inability to have children). One dramatic example of a workplace chemical that caused a number of men to become sterile (unable to father children) was the pesticide DBCP that was produced in a chemical plant in Lathrop, California for a number of years, until its use was banned in 1977. An extremely common substance that has a variety of similar negative effects is lead, which is still used in paints, construction, the auto industry and until recently as a component of most gasoline.

defect[s] Something wrong

4   An increasing amount of evidence suggests that many of the chemicals of modern industrial society can cause dangerous changes in the processes that create new life, by interfering with the chemical messages (hormones) that influence the normal growth and development of many of the body's organs, including the sex organs, the brain, the nervous system and the immune system. A number of studies, from many countries including the United States, France, and Denmark, described the decrease in sperm counts around the world. One of the reports based on a review of the world's medical literature calculates that there has been a 50 percent decrease in the sperm counts during the past 40 years. Not all reports confirm these findings, but at the present time the multiple findings on decreased sperm counts and the data on increased infertility have convinced most scientists that we have a serious problem that requires careful attention.

confirm Agree with

5   In the past, most of the studies on the impact of chemicals on human reproduction were focused on women during pregnancy. Now we realize that these toxic exposures to men and women may be just as important before they plan to have children, because the cells that are in their bodies, sperm forming tissues (men) and eggs (women), can be affected. Also, during the early weeks of pregnancy before the mother realizes that she is pregnant, she can be seriously affected by certain chemicals.

6   It is important to know about the chemicals you are working with. You have the *right to know* this information. You should always carefully read the ingredients, directions, and caution statements of any products you use at home. At work, your employer has the responsibility under the Federal

Hazard Communication regulation (1) to provide you with information on all the hazardous chemicals you are working with and, (2) to provide you with training concerning their safe use (ventilation, protective equipment you may need to wear, like a respirator). There are specific protective regulations concerning chemicals like lead, where employers must test for the chemical and provide alternative sites for you to work if you are exposed and pregnant or planning to have a child (man or woman). Know your rights and protect yourself and your future ability to have healthy children.

alternative sites
Other locations

HEIFETZ, "Exposure to Chemicals and Human Fertility"

| Exercise 1 |

Work with Words

Use context clues, word part clues, and if necessary the dictionary to define the italicized words in the following sentences from Reading 6.

1. Carson illustrated that the DDT had made the eggshells of birds so *fragile* that offspring could not survive, causing a *decline* of certain bird populations. (par. 1)

   fragile _____

   decline _____

2. As a result of Carson's book and the pressure of many citizens, DDT was *banned* in the United States, although it was and continues to be produced in this country and shipped to countries around the world. (par. 2)

   banned _____

3. An extremely common substance that has a variety of similar negative effects is lead, which is still used in paints, construction, the auto industry and until recently as a *component* of most gasoline. (par. 3)

   component _____

4. An increasing amount of evidence suggests that many of the chemicals of modern industrial society can cause dangerous changes in the processes that create new life, by interfering with the chemical messages *(hormones)* that influence the normal growth and development of many of the body's organs, including the sex organs, the brain, the nervous system and the immune system. (par. 4)

   hormones _____

| Exercise 2 | **Check Your Understanding** |

Choose the best way to complete the following statements about Reading 6.

1. The warning that Rachel Carson voiced in her book *Silent Spring* was that
   a. DDT and other pesticides posed a danger not only to birds and other creatures, but to human beings as well.
   b. DDT posed no threat at all to humans, but was killing birds in record numbers.
   c. DDT was healthy for birds, and other creatures, but not for humans.

2. Carson's book helped lead to
   a. the skyrocketing of DDT prices.
   b. the banning of DDT in the United States.
   c. increased use of DDT in the United States.

3. Many chemicals, such as pesticides, solvents, and lead, can cause physical problems such as
   a. uncontrollable emotions.
   b. excessive fertility.
   c. miscarriages, birth defects and infertility.

4. Sterility means
   a. inability to bear children.
   b. ability to bear children.
   c. any disability.

5. The countries cited by Heifetz as having conducted studies on sperm counts are
   a. Japan, China, and Taiwan.
   b. United States, France, and Denmark.
   c. Poland, Hungary, and Greece.

6. It is important, according to the reading, that people understand the effects of toxic exposures
   a. as soon as they have children.
   b. while they're pregnant.
   c. before they plan to have children.

7. You
   a. have the right to know information about the chemicals you are working with.
   b. should inquire about the chemicals you are working with because it is your responsibility to take the initiative to find out these things.
   c. may or may not have the right to know information about the chemicals you are working with—it depends on where you work.

8. The regulation your employer must abide by is called
   a. the Federal Hazard Communication regulation.
   b. the Local Hazard Communication regulation.
   c. the State Communication regulation.

Exercise 3   ## Make Connections

Write short answers to the following questions based on your reading, your experience, and your observations.

1. Do you know what chemicals are used in your workplace or in workplaces you are familiar with? What are they?

   _____

   _____

   _____

   _____

2. What do you think could happen to the human population in the future if infertility continues to increase? What can we as individuals do to help solve this problem?

   _____

   _____

   _____

   _____

READING 7

Survival of the Fittest? The Survivor Story

Kelly Mayhew

Several million Americans tuned in to watch the TV show Survivor *in the summer of the year 2000, and in 2001 it was followed by* Survivor, The Australian Outback. *What was it about these programs that got people so involved? As you read the following essay, think about how people are motivated to think of themselves. Does our society value individuals over community? What do you think?*

1 Take a healthy helping of *Gilligan's Island*, throw in two tablespoons each of Trader Vic's, *Lord of the Flies*, and Disney's Jungle Cruise, and add a dash of *Swiss Family Robinson* and *Robinson Crusoe*. Finally, swirl in a cup each of *The Jerry Springer Show* and *Who Wants To Be a Millionaire?* and half a cup of *Blind Date*. Mix just enough to blend and bake for 2 minutes at a

very high temperature. Result? CBS's 2000 summer series, *Survivor*. Billed as "reality TV," *Survivor* took audiences by storm, inspiring *Survivor* parties, and endless conversations. There were also spin-offs, attempting to achieve the same kind of popularity as *Survivor* had. Along with *Big Brother*, there have been and will be a bunch of other shows of this type coming our way, not to mention more *Survivor* episodes in different locales and with new groups of people. Why was this show so popular? What kept people glued to their television screens week after week, wondering, with a weird kind of pleasure, who would be kicked off next? The answer is that *Survivor* and the similar shows go to the very heart of the ways Americans view individuals and their role in communities, and how we define winners and losers in our society. *Survivor* was unique because it chose to explore these issues in a seemingly "natural" setting, thus making its audience buy into the illusion, or dream, that the contestants were reduced to their most basic states. We were led to think that the "best" and strongest *individual* would win the million dollar prize. That we would want to see such a picture says a lot about us as Americans.

2   *Survivor* began as a mid-summer fill-in by a network hungry for ratings in the rerun-dominated summer viewing period. The creators of the show put fourteen "castaways" onto a supposedly deserted island in the middle of Micronesia, deprived them of outside contact, gave them very little food, and made them form two teams to compete against each other. As the show progressed night after night (for a total of thirty-nine), people were judged incompetent by their team members in a phony "Tribal Council," and kicked off the island. The last one left—the "survivor"—won a million dollars. Many people saw the exotic location as a way to experience—if not directly, at least vicariously through the contestants' actions every night— what it would be like to live "savagely," close to nature and the elements, like our prehistoric forebears. The winner, we were led to believe, would really prove himself or herself to be the strongest, the smartest, and the most "outdoorsy." So, night after night, we watched as people tried to fish, dealt with the unpredictable weather by staying warm or cool, fought off biting insects, and so on—all demonstrating what humans have to deal with when they are stripped of social niceties and conveniences. "Ah ha," we were supposed to think, "so this is what 'survival of the fittest' looks like!"

3   Yet there was nothing natural about the show at all. From the ridiculous *Gilligan's Island*–inspired decor of the "Tribal Council," to the fake Polynesian team names (like "Pagong"), *Survivor* was mere illusion, a television simulation, or imitation, of the "natural world." B.B., Sue, Rudy, Jervase, Ramona, Kelly, Colleen, Rich, Sean, and the rest had their lives engineered for however long they lasted in the game. The show's creators designed all sorts of humiliating "challenges" to keep things spicy: the contestants had to spend hours standing on boards in the water; or they had to keep their hand on a giant "immunity idol" (a cross between a totem pole and a tiki

torch); or they had to eat insects; or they had to remember personal details about each other; or they had to recite lists of all the things that were dangerous about "their" island. In truth, if the contestants really had had to "survive," most of them would have starved to death, drowned, or caught some bacterial infection—slow, but more importantly, boring, deaths indeed. It's no fun to watch someone suffer over a long period of time. It's much more fun to watch them possibly embarrass themselves, then lose their chance to wear the "immunity idol" that would prevent them from being eliminated from the competition during the next "Tribal Council" meeting.

4   *Survivor* played on people's desire to believe that the most capable individual would win the game. We all like to believe that we are winners, that we can "do it alone," not take anyone's help, and make it big. And to do all of this in nature, where one's true character and abilities could emerge, was a stroke of genius on the part of the creators of *Survivor.* Yet the creators didn't stop there. They kept reminding the audience that they were pulling all the strings—like "a law of nature" or "a law of God"—which added an even more unpredictable element to the show. Supposedly anyone who could make it through the obstacle course of the unfriendly environment and the ridiculous games would be chosen the "fittest" contestant of them all. While it seemed like many of the contestants came on the show because they were adventure or nature enthusiasts who thought it would be fun and profitable to test their abilities in such a setting, the person who won the million-dollar prize, Rich, was not an outdoorsman at all. He was a gay, pudgy (before his post-show tummy-tuck) corporate trainer. The folks who thought their rock-climbing or tree-loving attributes would help them to win were gotten rid of left and right. The people who could psychologically manipulate others or stay aloof from their colleagues by not getting personally involved with anyone were the last ones on the show. "Natural" ability, therefore, had nothing to do with who was "fittest."

5   Underhandedness, scheming, emotional distance, and dishonesty, however, had a lot to do with who would win. All of these behaviors are learned behaviors, products of an individualistic society such as exists in the United States. In a *real* natural landscape, back-stabbing your fellow travelers would lead to failure and perhaps death. If there were no Banana Republic–clad hosts running around in luxury yachts monitoring your every move—indeed, if there were no cameras, no microphones, and no 35-million-person audience tuning in to see what you do next—you would need the help of your human companions. If only one of you knew how to find water, or make a fire, or fish, then you would have to work cooperatively. To survive, you would need each other—as every subsistence-level human society has known. While individual skills might gain special respect in such a community, people would have to work together so that everyone could eat, have shelter, and be protected from the ravages of nature. Indi-

vidual attributes alone would get you nowhere. In a *real* survival experience, the winner would be plural, not singular. It would be the community, not the individual.

6   Thus, we can learn a great deal from watching *Survivor*. The show lets us see how the concepts of winning and losing and individualism function in our society. The individual winner, the so-called "fittest" person, is the one who can see that it is all "just a game." It is an illustrative game, however, because it reminds us that our beliefs about each other, about what it takes to get ahead in this world, are just that—beliefs. What would have happened if the show had valued cooperation instead of competition? Would people have still tuned in every night to watch people get along with each other? If not, perhaps we need to change the rules of *our* games to make room for such a possibility.

MAYHEW, "Survival of the Fittest?"

<table>
<tr><td>

Exercise 1

</td><td>

Work with Words

</td></tr>
</table>

Use context clues, word part clues, and if necessary the dictionary to define the italicized words in the following sentences from Reading 7.

1. There were also *spin-offs*, attempting to achieve the same kind of popularity as *Survivor* had. Along with *Big Brother*, there have been and will be a bunch of other shows of this type coming our way. (par. 1)

   spin-offs _____

2. Many people saw the exotic location as a way to experience—not directly, but at least *vicariously* through the contestants' actions every night—what it would be like to live "savagely," close to nature and the elements, like our prehistoric *forebears*. (par. 2)

   vicariously _____

   forebears _____

3. The people who could psychologically *manipulate* others or stay *aloof* from their colleagues by not getting personally involved with anyone were the last ones on the show. (par. 4)

   manipulate _____

   aloof _____

<table>
<tr><td>

Exercise 2

</td><td>

Check Your Understanding

</td></tr>
</table>

Choose the best way to complete the following statements about Reading 7.

1. According to the author, *Survivor* was appealing to audiences because
   a. it showed naked men and women.
   b. it explored issues related to individuals and communities.
   c. it explored issues related to nature.

2. *Survivor* was billed as
   a. "reality TV."
   b. a documentary.
   c. a major TV movie.

3. The contestants had to form teams and live
   a. on tough city streets.
   b. on a boat in the middle of the ocean.
   c. on a seemingly deserted island.

4. The prize that went to the winner of the show was
   a. a hundred dollars.
   b. a hundred thousand dollars.
   c. a million dollars.

5. The "Tribal Council" was where
   a. contestants judged each other to see who would be eliminated from the show.
   b. contestants handed out jobs for the day.
   c. contestants got together to talk about their problems with each other.

6. According to the author, being a nature enthusiast
   a. determined the winner of the show.
   b. had nothing to do with winning because scheming and underhandedness won the day.
   c. saved peoples' lives on the show because it was essential to understand nature to be successful on the island.

7. In the author's opinion, surviving in a harsh environment
   a. depends on cooperation and not individualism.
   b. depends on individualism and not cooperation.
   c. depends on neither individualism, nor cooperation, but on realism.

8. The main idea of the reading was that
   a. we can learn a lot from *Survivor* because it shows us how to win a lot of money.
   b. we can learn a lot from *Survivor* because it shows us how our beliefs about individualism and community and "winners" or "losers" can be damaging to our society.
   c. we can learn a lot from *Survivor* because it gives us a realistic picture of how to live in a natural environment, but is also relevant to our daily lives.

| Exercise 3 | **Making Connections** |

Write short answers to the following questions based on your reading, your experience, and your observations.

1. Did you watch *Survivor* or one of the other shows like it? Why did you watch it? Did you like it? Why or why not?

_____

_____

_____

_____

2. What do you think is more important: acting as an individual or acting for the benefit of the community? Why?

_____

_____

_____

_____

| READING 8 |

What Everyone Should Know about Aasiya

Roberta Alexander

The following reading discusses attitudes that many Americans have to certain groups of people in our society. In it, the author shares her experiences in public places with her daughter-in-law, who is different and who attracts a lot of attention. As you read, think about how you would feel if you were her daughter-in-law.

1   A trip to the supermarket is never a normal event with my daughter-in-law, Aasiya. People stare at us. Actually, they stare mostly at her, but also at me. Sometimes the stares reflect their fear and apprehension, as though some harm could come to them by being near us. Sometimes the stares seem to reflect surprise, or astonishment at seeing someone who is different from anyone they have ever seen before. Sometimes the stares reflect what seems to be pity, revealing thoughts of "Oh, that poor woman." Mostly their stares convey a sense of complete disbelief, as if they were wondering how it is possible for them to see such a woman in a supermarket in suburban America. Just today, when Aasiya and I were in the supermarket aisle between the spices, the flour, and sugar, a woman came around the corner and was so startled when she saw Aasiya that she jumped back and gasped.

2   When I am with Aasiya in public, I try to act normal and friendly because I know that everyone is looking at us. I smile more than usual. I want
everybody to understand that I am not weird, that I am just a normal, pretty
well-educated African-American grandmother living in the suburbs. But, in
spite of all my efforts, when I go to the supermarket with my daughter-in-
law, we *are* weird. We probably even provide people something to talk
about when they get home to their families.

3   Aasiya is pretty and she is not unlike any other bright 22-year-old
woman who has recently immigrated to the United States. She has black
hair, long, and beautiful. She has huge, soft eyes. Her mouth is big and her
smile is wide and friendly. She loves to laugh and she loves to act silly. She
has had very little traditional schooling as we know it, but she speaks, reads
and writes five languages. She is comfortable around all my highly educated
women friends. She easily becomes the life of the party. Aasiya likes to ride
the swings in the park, she wants to go to Disneyland, and she loves to eat
Hershey's chocolate bars. As the months go by, she is becoming increasingly anxious to visit her mother and family in India.

4   But Aasiya *is* different. When she goes out in public or when she is
around any man who is not an immediate member of her family, she wears
a veil. Not just an ordinary scarf around her head like many Muslim women
do, but a veil—a *nikab*—that covers her entire face, even her eyes. In fact,
Aasiya's *nikab* has three levels of covering. She can wear it having a slit for
her eyes. She can wear it with a kind of gauze covering over the slit for her
eyes. Or, she can put another piece of material over the gauze covering,
which makes it absolutely impossible to see her eyes. Aasiya can see out,
though not very well. She also wears a *ubaya*, a kind of black robe which
completely covers her regular clothes, and comes down almost to her feet.
So, if you were to see her on the street, you would not know what she
looked like. You would only know that she is completely covered in black,
including her eyes. If you ever saw the movie *Star Wars*, you might think
that she looks like a miniature Darth Vader with the veil replacing his plastic
mask. If you ever saw Aasiya in her *nikab* and *ubaya,* you would never
know that she is beautiful, and funny, and friendly, and sensitive, and ever
so intelligent.

5   People's verbal responses to Aasiya are always interesting, and almost
always offensive. People have told her, "You're in America now," and, "Why
don't you go back where you come from?" and, "How can she see where
she's going?" and, "What kind of an outfit is that?" and, "Look! She's wearing a mask." Children also stare. Aasiya asked me the other day if I can tell
when she is smiling by just looking at her eyes while she has her veil on.
She wants the children to know that she is smiling at them. Unfortunately,
you can't tell when she's smiling.

6   I first met Aasiya two years ago at the Los Angeles International Airport.
I had been waiting at the spot where people come walking out after clear-

ing immigration and customs. I had seen Mexican soccer teams, Central American immigrants, Japanese tourists, and people returning from vacations in Singapore. Finally, I saw my son, who was dressed, in my mind, like Laurence of Arabia, and Aasiya, who was completely covered. She said, "Hi, Mom" and gave me a warm hug. It wasn't until an hour later that I was able to see what she looked like. When we arrived home, Aasiya, in her very limited English, managed to keep up a conversation with all of us, and she even had us laughing about all the things that had happened to her during her first airplane trip. When she volunteered to help cut up the chicken for dinner, she sat on the floor, put the knife against the corner of the wall, holding it down with her foot, and proceeded to cut the chicken pushing the chicken pieces past the knife. We were all shocked, but we didn't say anything because we didn't want her to feel uncomfortable. When we sat down to eat, Aasiya ate everything with her fingers. Rice, salad, chicken, vegetables, everything. Then, when she was finished eating, she licked each finger individually to clean it off. Again, I was shocked, but my kids kind of liked this fascinating woman with her interesting habits. No one said anything, nor did we communicate our surprise and discomfort to her.

7   Now, Aasiya is more used to American customs. She doesn't prepare food on the floor, but she is still much more comfortable eating with her hands as people do in India and much of the world. She also has continued to wear her veil and practice her religion.

8   Islam is not much different from other major religions that are familiar to us. It comes from the same tradition as Judaism and Christianity. Muslims believe in one God, and they follow basic rules of morality, which perhaps can best be summed up by the commandment, "Do unto others, as you would have others do unto you." Live a moral life on earth and you will be rewarded by going to heaven. Personally, I don't find any of these beliefs offensive, and although my son converted to Islam and married a Muslim woman, I have accepted his decision, and I love his wife.

9   Unfortunately, I don't think most Americans share my views. I think that Muslims are the new group in this country that are easy to fear, to blame, and to hate. Much of this fear, blame, and hate comes from our ignorance. As a group, they are like anyone else. Period. So often though, the bad guy in the movies looks like an Arab (the way we think Muslims look), the "suspects" for most terrorist acts are Muslims, and by extension, we Americans tend to not trust Muslims. We tend to see them as the enemy, almost the same way that Communists were the enemy during the Cold War. Almost the same way that many people thought African-Americans, or Jews, or immigrants were the enemy for much of this century.

10   At the supermarket, people view my daughter-in-law with suspicion. They think she is strange, threatening, mysterious, oppressed, and probably timid. She could be the wife of a "terrorist." Understandably, we fear what we cannot know, and I believe we also fear what we cannot see. However,

most peoples' assumptions about Aasiya could not be farther from the truth. She is confident and smart and she can stand up for herself. She is not subjugated by her husband. She makes her own decisions about how she will dress when she goes out on the street. (The other women in her family do not wear the extreme veil that Aasiya wears.) Nobody tells her what to do. I wish everyone in this country could see her when she gets on the back of the grocery cart and pushes off, racing around the parking lot with her *ubaya* flowing behind her. That image reminds us that there is a completely normal, young, playful woman under all of that black.

11   I grew up in the 50s, and I got used to being stared at when I was a child. People stared at us because my father was black and my mother was white. It was illegal for interracial couples to marry in California at that time, and it was very unusual to see interracial couples at all. That has changed, but not the mentality that led to the law and to people staring at us. Hopefully we will learn to know and accept the latest group of people who are objects of intolerance. I don't like being stared at in the supermarket, but I am blessed with a beautiful daughter-in-law. For me, she is no longer mysterious. I have learned from her, laughed with her, taught her, and we have both grown as human beings together. I wish everyone could be so lucky.

ALEXANDER, "What Everyone Should Know about Aasiya"

| Exercise 1 |

Work with Words

Use context clues, word part clues, and if necessary the dictionary to write the definitions of the words that are italicized in the following sentences from Reading 8.

1. Sometimes the stares reflect their fear and *apprehension,* as though some harm could come to them by being near us. (par. 1)

   apprehension _____

2. Mostly their stares convey a sense of complete *disbelief,* as if they were wondering how it is possible for them to see such a woman in a supermarket in suburban America. (par. 1)

   disbelief _____

3. When she goes out in public or when she is around any man who is not an immediate member of her family, she wears a veil. Not just an ordinary scarf around her head like many Muslim women do, but a veil—a *nikab*—that covers her entire face, even her eyes. (par. 4)

   nikab _____

4. She also wears a *ubaya,* a kind of black robe which completely covers her regular clothes, and comes down almost to her feet. (par. 4)

ubaya _____

5. She is confident and smart and she can stand up for herself. She is not *subjugated* by her husband. She makes her own decisions about how she will dress when she goes out on the street. (The other women in her family do not wear the extreme veil that Aasiya wears.) Nobody tells her what to do. (par. 10)

subjugated _____

| Exercise 2 |

Check Your Understanding

Choose the best answers to the following multiple-choice questions.

1. What is the main idea for paragraph 1?
   a. people think Aasiya is strange and different and perhaps threatening when they see her.
   b. people are startled when they see Aasiya in the supermarket.
   c. people pity Aasiya.

2. The author believes that Aasiya is similar to other bright, young immigrant women because
   a. Aasiya dresses differently from most Americans.
   b. Aasiya likes to swing in the park, she wants to go to Disneyland, and she misses her family.
   c. Aasiya is beautiful.

3. The emphasis of this article is that Aasiya is different because
   a. she speaks other languages.
   b. she comes from another country.
   c. she wears the *nikab* and the *ubaya.*

4. The author writes that when she is with Aasiya in public, she tries to act normal and friendly. This is so because
   a. she always acts normal and friendly.
   b. she tries extra hard because she wants people to just accept Aasiya and herself, and not to treat them differently.
   c. she knows that she is not really a normal person in any case, so when she and Aasiya go out in public, they are quite a spectacle.

5. The main idea of paragraph 8 is that
   a. Muslims believe in one God, and they follow basic rules of morality.
   b. Muslims believe that if you live a moral life on earth you will be rewarded by going to heaven.
   c. Islam is not much different from other major Western religions that are familiar to us.

6. The main idea of paragraph 9 is that
   a. because of ignorance, people tend to consider Muslims as the enemy.
   b. Communists were the enemy during the Cold War.
   c. the bad guys in the movies frequently look Arab.

7. The author believes that if
   a. everyone had a Muslim daughter-in-law, everything would be better in this world.
   b. people could only know Aasiya, many of their prejudices and fears toward Muslims would disappear.
   c. we are ever to solve our problems, we must stop staring at people in the supermarket.

Exercise 3

Make Connections

1. Have you ever gotten to know someone who was very different from you? Explain who the person was and how knowing that person affected you. Did you come to trust him/her? Explain.

_____

_____

_____

_____

2. How do you think Aasiya feels when she is in public? What would you do in her position? What do you think she should do, assuming that she is not going to change her beliefs or the way she dresses?

_____

_____

_____

_____

3. How do you hope people think about you when they see you for the first time? Explain, considering Aasiya's experiences when people see her.

_____

_____

_____

_____

Bibliography

Adler, Mortimer J., and Charles Van Doren. *How to Read a Book.* New York: Simon & Schuster, 1972.

Agee, Warren K., Phillip H. Ault, and Edwin Emery. *Introduction to Mass Communications*, 12th ed. New York: Addison Wesley Longman, 1997, p. 294.

Alter, Jonathan. "Everyday Heroes," *Newsweek*, May 29, 1995.

Althen, Gary. *American Ways: A Guide for Foreigners in the United States.* Yarmouth, ME: Intercultural Press, 1988.

The American Heritage Dictionary, Second College Edition. Boston: Houghton Mifflin, 1991, entries: *advocate, alter, array, benefit, bit, cadaver, conceptualize, critical, dexterity, deprive, deprived, dizzy, incorporate, load, loaded, myriad, pit, prep, prohibit, proliferate, prototype, short-term, simulation, stream, synthesis, target, track, trauma, virtual, ware, yield,* and *zoom.*

The American Heritage Talking Dictionary. Cambridge, MA: The Learning Company Properties Inc., 1998, entries: *array, copy, gist, imprint, precision,* and *solitary.*

Anderson, Craig A. "Impact of Media Violence on Kids." Congressional Testimony, March 21, 2000. Federal Document Clearing House, Inc., 2000; Infonautics Corp., 2000.

Appelbaum, Richard P., and William J. Chambliss. *Sociology: A Brief Introduction.* New York: Addison-Wesley Educational Publishers, 1997, pp. 302–305.

Black, Deborah. "The Single-Parent Family." In Elizabeth Penfield, *Short Takes: Model Essays for Composition,* 5th ed. New York: HarperCollins College Publishers, 1996, pp. 188–90.

Blakeslee, Sandra. "Experts Learn More on Why Memory Changes and How." *San Diego Union*, September 22, 2000 (adapted).

"Building a Better Brain." *Life,* July 1994.

Byer, Curtis O., and Louis W. Shainberg. *Living Well: Health in Your Hands.* New York: HarperCollins, 1995.

Campbell, Richard. *Media and Culture.* New York: St. Martin's Press, 1998, p. 317.

Campbell, Richard, with Christopher R. Martin and Bettina Fabos. "Persuasive Techniques in Contemporary Advertising." In *Media and Culture: An Introduction to Mass Communication,* 2d ed. Boston: Bedford/St. Martin's, 2000, pp. 359–364.

Canada, Geoffrey. *FistStickKnifeGun.* Boston: Beacon Press, 1995.

Cavan, Ruth Shonle. "Family." In *The New Best Book of Knowledge.* Danbury, CT: Grolier, 1982.

Chenoweth, Karen, and Cathy Free. "Homeless Children Come to School." *American Educator* (Fall 1990).

"China." *Encyclopedia Britannica*, 15th ed. Chicago: Encyclopedia Britannica, 1984, p. 296.

Choueke, Esmond. "She Gives from the Heart." *AMI Specials: The Many Faces of Oprah.* Boca Raton, FL: American Media Specials Inc., 2000, Vol. 1, no. 7 (April 25, 2000): 58.

Clinton, Hillary Rodham. *It Takes a Village and Other Lessons Children Teach Us.* New York: Simon & Schuster, 1996, pp. 11–13.

Cohen, Daniel. *Re: Thinking: How to Succeed by Learning How to Think.* New York: M. Evans and Company, 1982.

Curran, Delores. "What Good Families Are Doing Right." *McCall's,* March 1983, pp. 458–459.

Dávalos, Enrique. "Aztec Education on the Eve of the Spanish Conquest" (written for this edition of *Joining a Community of Readers*).

Dávalos, Enrique. "A Minefield: Teenagers and Racism on the U.S.–Mexican Border" (written for this edition of *Joining a Community of Readers*).

Eshleman, J. Ross, Barbara G. Cashion, and Lawrence A. Basirico. *Sociology,* 5th ed. New York: HarperCollins, 1993.

Franco, Aline. "Trouble on the Air" (written for this edition of *Joining a Community of Readers*).

Frankel, Max. "Universal E-Mail: Worthy of a 'New Frontier' Commitment." Reprinted in Rise B. Axelrod and Charles R. Cooper, *The St. Martin's Guide to Writing,* 5th ed. New York: St. Martin's Press, 1997, pp. 249–50.

Gardner, David Pierpont. "If We Stand, They Will Deliver." *New Perspectives Quarterly* (1990).

Garraty, John. *The American Nation,* 8th ed. New York: HarperCollins, 1996.

Glazer, Nona. "Family." In *The World Book Encyclopedia.* Chicago: World Book, 1993.

Golden, Daniel. "Building a Better Brain." *Life,* July 1994, 63–70.

Goodwin, Doris Kearns. "From Father, with Love." International Creative Management, Inc., 1986.

Gordon, Christine. "RU Ready to Dump Your Glasses?" *Time,* October 11, 1999, 58–63.

Gray, Paul. "Teach Your Children Well." *Time,* 142 (Fall 1993): 68.

Hamburg, David A. "The American Family Transformed." *Society* 30, no. 2 (January–February 1993): 21–24.

Hamill, Pete. "Crack and the Box." *Esquire* 113 (May 1990): 63.

Harris, Louis. "2001: The World Our Students Will Enter." In William Vesterman and Josh Ozersky, *Reading for the Twenty-First Century.* Boston: Allyn and Bacon, 1994.

Heifetz, Ruth Markowitz, M.D. "Exposure to Chemicals and Human Fertility." Reprinted by permission of Dr. Ruth Markowitz Heifetz, M.D., M.P.H., senior lecturer, Department of Family and Preventive Medicine, School of Medicine, University of California, San Diego.

Hsu, Lee-Nah. "Drug Use and the Family." *World Health* 46, no. 6 (November–December 1993): 21–24.

Hubler, Shawn. "Fledgling Teacher Gets Tough Lessons, Unexpected Rewards." *Los Angeles Times,* June 16, 1996.

Insel, Paul M., Walton T. Roth, L. McKay Rollins, and Ray A. Petersen. *Core Concepts in Health,* 8th ed. Mountain View, CA: Mayfield Publishing Company, 1998.

Jewler, A. Jerome, and John N. Gardner. *Your College Experience.* Belmont, CA: Wadsworth, 1993.

Johnson, Dirk. "When Money Is Everything, Except Hers." *The New York Times,* late edition (East Coast), October 14, 1998, A-1, © 1999 by the New York Times Company.

Jordan, Michael. *I Can't Accept Not Trying.* San Francisco: Harper-Collins, 1994.

Joseph, Elizabeth. "My Husband's Nine Wives." *The New York Times,* May 23, 1991.

Kantrowitz, Barbara. "Finding a Niche in e-ducation." In *How to Use the Internet to Choose or Change Careers.* Newsweek, Inc. and Kaplan, Inc., 2000, p. 68.

Kean, Patricia. "Blowing Up the Tracks." *Washington Monthly* 25 (January 1993).

Kozol, Jonathan. *Illiterate America.* New York: Bantam Doubleday Dell, 1996.

Laidman, Jenn. "Violence, Video Games May Be a Volatile Mix." *Washington Times*, May 4, 1999, E4.

Lamanna, Mary Ann, and Agnes Riedmann. *Marriages and Families.* Belmont, CA: Wadsworth, 1994.

Langone, John. *How Things Work.* Washington, DC: National Geographic Society, 1998, pp. 94, 15.

Lehnert, Wendy G. *Light on the Internet: Essentials of the Internet and the World Wide Web.* Reading, MA: Addison Wesley Longman, 1999, pp. 12, 31, 7, and sentences from various pages in the book for vocabulary examples.

Lehnert, Wendy G. *Internet 101: A Beginner's Guide to the Internet and the World Wide Web.* Reading, MA: Addison Wesley Longman, 1998, pp. 5, 24–26, and sentences from various pages in the book for vocabulary examples.

Levin, Diane. "Marketing Violence to Children." Testimony to U.S. Senate Commerce, Science, and Transportation Committee Hearing, May 4, 1999. Federal Document Clearing House, Inc., 1999, via Infonautics Corp., 1999.

Levine, Deena R., and Mara B. Adelman. *Beyond Language: Cross Cultural Communication,* 2d ed. Englewood Cliffs, NJ: Regents/Prentice Hall, 1993, pp. 101–110, 208, 209, 210.

Lindsay, Richard. "Television and Popular Culture" (written for this edition of *Joining a Community of Readers*).

"Live and Kicking: Black in the USA." *The Voice*, February 22, 1999, 14.

Livingston, Shawna, "Get Rick Quick" (written for this edition of *Joining a Community of Readers*).

Lucky, Robert W. "Music on Hold," *IEEE Spectrum* 37, no. 7 (July 2000): 25.

Malcolm X with Alex Haley. *The Autobiography of Malcolm X.* New York: Random House, 1964.

Martin, James Kirby, et al. *America and Its Peoples: A Mosaic in the Making,* 3d ed. New York: Addison-Wesley Educational Publishers, 1997.

Mayhew, Kelly. "Diana: The People's Princess" (written for this edition of *Joining a Community of Readers*).

Mayhew, Kelly. "Survival of the Fittest? The *Survivor* Story" (written for this edition of *Joining a Community of Readers*).

Mayhew, Kelly, and Elena Marie Peifer. "Someday My Prince Will Come" (written for this edition of *Joining a Community of Readers*).

Mayleas, David. "How To Land the Job You Want," *Empire,* May 23, 1976.

Miller, Jim. "Sports and Television: Isolation or Community" (written for this edition of *Joining a Community of Readers*).

Mings, Turley. *The Study of Economics: Principles, Concepts, and Applications,* 5th ed. Guilford, CT: Dushkin Publishing Group, 1995.

Miranda, David. "I Hated Myself." In Kay Philip, Andrea Estepa, and Al Desetta, eds., *Things Get Hectic: Teens Write About the Violence That Surrounds Them.* New York: Touchstone Press, 1998, p. 133.

Mohr, Nicholasa. In foreword to *Latinas: Women of Achievement*, ed. Diane Telgen and Jim Kamp. Detroit: Visible Ink, 1996.

Moltenbrey, Karen. "Real-Time Racing." *Computer Graphics World* 23, no. 7 (July 2000): 84.

Montgomery, Lori. "Short of Funds, the Nation's Capital Is Falling Apart." *San Diego Union-Tribune,* March 16, 1996.

Mujica, Barbara. "Bilingualism's Goal." *The New York Times*, February 26, 1984, E17.

Newton, David. *Teen Violence: Out of Control.* Springfield, NJ: Enslow Publishers, 1995.

"Parents in Brawl at Kids' Soccer Game." *San Diego Union-Tribune,* September 11, 2000.

Peifer, Elena Marie. "Teen Girl Magazines: The Good, the Bad, and the Beautiful" (written for this edition of *Joining a Community of Readers*).

Peifer, Marley. "Video Games: The Reality of the Digital World" (written for this edition of *Joining a Community of Readers*).

Pipher, Mary. *Reviving Ophelia: Saving the Selves of Adolescent Girls.* New York: Ballantine Books, 1994, pp. 86, 183–185.

Pollack, William. *Real Boys: Rescuing Our Sons from the Myths of Boyhood.* New York: An Owl Book, Henry Holt and Company, 1998, pp. xxv–xxvi, 3–6, 15–17.

Raspberry, William. "The Handicap of Definition," *Washington Post*, 1982. Copyright © 1982, Washington Post Writers Group.

"Reading, Writing, and . . . Buying." *Consumer Reports*, 63 (September 1998): 382–385.

Rodriguez, Gloria G. *Raising Nuestros Ninos.* New York: Fireside Books, 1999, pp. 4, 5.

Roth, William F., Jr. "The True Nature of Work." *Work and Rewards* Westport, CT: Greenwood Publishing, 1989.

Ruggiero, Vincent Ryan. *The Art of Thinking: A Guide to Critical and Creative Thought,* 5th ed. New York: Addison-Wesley Educational Publishers, 1998, pp. 41–43.

Samovar, Larry. *Oral Communication: Speaking Across Cultures.* Madison, WI: Brown and Benchmark, 1995 (adapted).

Scarr, Sandra, Deborah Phillips, and Kathleen McCartney. "Working Mothers and Their Families." In Arlene S. Skolnick and Jerome H. Skolnick, *Family in Transition,* 8th ed. New York: HarperCollins, 1994, p. 412.

Scott, Cathy. "Rap Goes from Urban Streets to Main Street." *Christian Science Monitor*, February 26, 1999.

Shanker, Albert. "A Real Role Model." *On Campus*, September 1996.

Sherry, Mary. "In Praise of the F Word." *Newsweek*, May 6, 1991.

Skolnick, Arlene, and Jerome Skolnick. *Family in Transition,* 8th ed. New York: HarperCollins, 1994.

Skolnick, Jerome, and Elliott Currie. *Crisis in American Institutions.* Boston: Allyn and Bacon, 2000 (adapted).

Smith, Kerri S. *Caring for Your Aging Parents*, rev. ed. San Luis Obispo, CA: Impact Publishers, Inc., 1994, p. 33.

Sorid, Daniel, and Samuel K. Moore. "The Virtual Surgeon." *IEEE Spectrum* 37, no. 7 (July 2000): 26–31 (adapted).

Stoughton, Craig. "Media Violence and What's Being Done About It" (written for this edition of *Joining a Community of Readers*).

Stoughton, Craig. "The Oprah Hour, the Oprah World" (written for this edition of *Joining a Community of Readers*).

"Think Eth-Nickelodeon: Talking to a Diverse Audience." In *Selling to Kids*, December 9, 1999 (Phillips Publishing, Inc. via Comtex, 1999).

Thio, Alex. *Sociology*, 4th ed. New York: HarperCollins, 1996.

Thio, Alex, *Sociology*, 5th ed. New York: Addison-Wesley Educational Publishers, 1998, p. 373.

Thompson, William E., and Joseph V. Hickey. *Society in Focus: An Introduction to Sociology*, 3d ed. New York: Addison-Wesley Longman, 1999, pp. 374, 392–393, 394–395, 406, 409.

Trescott, Jacqueline. "For Blacks, 50 Years on the TV Fringes; There's Been Progress—but Too Little Has Changed." *Washington Post*, April 25, 1999, G01 (adapted).

"Voice Security." *PC Tips*, Smart Computing Learning Series, Vol. 6, no. 8. Lincoln, NE: Sandhills Publishing Company, 2000, pp. 60–61.

Waitley, Denis. *The Psychology of Winning*. New York: Berkeley Books, 1979.

Walther, Daniel R. "Some Reflections on Reading." In *Toolkit for College Success*. Belmont, CA: Wadsworth Publishing, 1994.

"Who Wants To Be a Billionaire?" In *AMI Specials: The Many Faces of Oprah*. Boca Raton, FL: American Media Specials Inc., 2000, Vol. 1, no. 7 (April 25, 2000): 36–37.

Wolf, Robin. *Marriages and Family in a Diverse Society*. New York: HarperCollins, 1996.

Credits

From: Agee, Ault and Emery, *Introduction to Mass Communication*. Copyright ©1997. Reprinted by permission of Addison-Wesley Educational Publishers Inc.

Aline Franco Flores, "Trouble on the Air." (written for this edition of *Joining a Community of Readers*). Reprinted by permission of the author.

Pete Hamill, "Crack and the Box." First published in *Esquire*, May 1990. Reprinted by permission of International Creative Management, Inc. Copyright ©1990 by Pete Hamill.

Jim Miller, "Sports and Television: Isolation or Community?" (written for this edition of *Joining a Community of Readers*). Reprinted by permission of the author.

"Fighting Over Sneakers." Copyright ©August 1997 by Bedford Press. From *Media and Culture* by Richard Campbell. Reprinted with permission of Bedford/St. Martin's.

Shawna Livingston, "Get Rich Quick." Copyright © Shawna A. Livingston. Reprinted by permission.

"My Husband's Nine Wives," by Elizabeth Joseph in the *The New York Times*, May 23, 1991 (Op-Ed). Copyright ©1991 by The New York Times Company.

Martin, James Kirby, et al. *America and Its People: A Mosaic in the Making*, 3rd Edition. Reprinted by permission of Addison-Wesley Educational Publishers Inc.

Wolf, Robin, from *Marriages and Family in a Diverse Society*. HarperCollins, 1996.

Appelbaum, Richard P., and William J. Chambliss, from *Sociology: A Brief Introduction*, 1997. Reprinted with permission of Addison-Wesley Educational Publishers Inc.

Hillary Rodham Clinton. From: *It Takes a Village and Other Lessons Children Teach Us*. New York: Simon & Schuster, 1996.

Deborah Black, "The Single-Parent Family." in Elizabeth Penfield, *Short Takes: Model Essays for Composition*, 5th ed. New York: HarperCollins, 1996.

Delores Curran, "What Good Families Are Doing Right," *McCall's*, March 1983.

"From Father, with Love," Doris Kearns Goodwin. International Creative Management, Inc., 1986

From: *Real Boys: Rescuing Our Sons From The Myths Of Boyhood* by William Pollack, copyright ©1998 by William Pollack. Used by permission of Random House, Inc.

Geoffrey Canada. From *FistStickKnifeGun*. Boston: Beacon Press, 1995.

Dávalos, Enrique, "A Minefield: Teen-Agers and Racism on US-Mexican Border" (written for this edition of *Joining a Community of Readers*). Reprinted with permission of the author.

Dirk Johnson, "When Money Is Everything, Except Hers," *The New York Times*, October 14, 1990. Copyright © 2000, The New York Times Company. Reprinted by permission.

"Worshipping the God of Thinness," from *Reviving Ophelia* by Mary Pipher, Ph.D., copyright ©1994 by Mary Pipher, Ph.D. Used by permission of Putnam Berkley, a division of Penguin Putnam, Inc.

William Raspberry, "The Handicap of Definition," *Washington Post*, 1982. ©1982, The Washington Post Writers Group. Reprinted with permission.

Levine, Deena, R., and Mara B. Adelman. From: *Beyond Language: Cross Cultural Communion*, 2nd Edition. Regents/Prentice-Hall, Englewood Cliffs, NJ

"Persuasive Techniques in Contemporary Advertising." Copyright August 1997 by Bedford/St. Martin's. From: *Media and Culture* bu Richard Campbell. Reprinted by permission of Bedford/St. Martin's.

Davidyne Mayleas, "How to Land the Job You Want," *Empire*, May 23, 1976.

Kelly Mayhew, "Survial of the Fittest? The *Survivor* Story" (written for this edition of *Joining a Community of Readers*). Reprinted by permission of the author.

Heifetz, Ruth Markowitz, M.D., "Exposure to Chemicals and Human Fertility." Reprinted by permission of Dr. Ruth Markowitz Heifetz, M.D., M.P.H., senior lecturer, Department of Family and Preventive Medicine, School of Medicine, University of California, San Diego.

Photo Credits

Page 1:	F. Martinez/PhotoEdit
Page 64:	Mark Harmel/FPG International LLC
Page 121:	AP/Wide World Photos
Page 170:	Bob Mahoney/The Image Works
Page 177:	The Everett Collection
Page 211:	Patrik Giardino/CORBIS
Page 261:	Reuters NewMedia Inc./CORBIS
Page 319:	Tony Freeman/Photo Edit
Page 333:	Bettmann/CORBIS
Page 369:	Stever Niedorf/Imagebank
Page 416:	Jean-Claude Lejeune/Stock, Boston

Index